THE MYSTERIOUS WORLD
An Atlas of the Unexplained

Francis Hitching

THE MYSTERIOUS WORLD
An Atlas of the Unexplained

Holt, Rinehart and Winston

New York

First published in the United States of America in 1979 by
Holt, Rinehart and Winston, 383 Madison Avenue, New York, New York 10017.

First published in Great Britain in 1978 as *The World Atlas of Mysteries.*

Library of Congress Cataloging in Publication Data

Hitching, Francis.
        The mysterious world.

        Originally published in 1978 under title: The world
atlas of mysteries.
        Bibliography: p.
        Includes index.
        1. Curiosities and wonders.   I. Title.
AG243.H46   1979   001.9'4   78-14162
ISBN Hardbound: 0-03-044036-X
ISBN Paperback: 0-03-044031-9

First American Edition

Printed in the United States of America

10 9 8 7 6 5 4 3 2 1

Contents

General introduction

So overwhelming have been the scientific advances of the 20th Century that it takes some effort of will to stand back and remember that quite soon the 21st Century will be upon us, and with it a science surpassing everything we know now. Already, physicists can observe and predict the behaviour of matter down to 10^{-15} of a centimetre, a figure so vanishingly small that minute particles lose their identity and are seen simultaneously as waves of energy. At the other end of the scale, astrophysicists have located invisible galaxies so vast that they probably contain 10 million planetary systems like our own; not that we are ever likely to contact them, for they are 10,000 million light years away. Confronted with such awesome examples of information made possible by modern scientific technology, we can be forgiven for imagining that there is not much left to discover and that unsolved mysteries will soon be things of the past.

But we would be wrong. In many scientific disciplines, the more that is discovered, the farther the horizon of knowledge seems to recede. In others, the underlying assumptions have become so shaky that they will soon be discarded and replaced. All contain mysterious and uncomfortable facts which cannot be explained by conventional reasoning and which tend to be pushed aside as someone else's problem.

Understandably, text-books do not usually describe the doubts and debates held at the highest levels of each brand of science, and one of the aims of this Atlas is to redress the balance somewhat by demonstrating the impermanence of scientific theory. Models of science and prehistory succeed each other with surprising rapidity; after reading, for instance, of the about-face made by geologists concerning the shifting continents on which we live, or how physicists decided at last to believe in balls of lightning (even though they do not understand them), it would be a rash person who predicted confidently that future geology and future physics will not be able to encompass, say, lost worlds and levitation.

If a puzzle remains unexplained long enough, the chances are that a radically new solution is needed, even though there may not yet be a scientific theory to incorporate it. Almost by definition, a mystery is an awkward fact or event that cannot be explained in an orthodox way. Research on the Atlas showed time and again that after conscientiously examining the whole spectrum of possible solutions, it was the unorthodox that made best sense of the unexplained. By a process of elimination, the book became an atlas of alternative thinking, a reference point for anybody uneasy about established views.

As for the general direction which 21st-century science may take, one can only suppose that it will be more inclusive and less rigidly specialized than today's. There are a number of examples in the Atlas of how innovative thinking on a subject has been rejected by the scientists or historians in the disciplines concerned simply because the suggestion was made by an outsider. This exclusiveness works against the growth of scientific knowledge because a scientist's polite reluctance to tread on another's territory gives him an excuse for not examining difficult phenomena; if a storm of small frogs comes raining from the sky, a biologist will say that it is a meteorological problem and a meteorologist that the problem is biological.

In the past such natural wonders were readily accepted as facts of life and it is a continuing theme of this Atlas that when, today, countless people see UFOs, experience ESP or find themselves spontaneously healed, these events have a reality of their own and deserve a place in the overall scheme of things. Whether they are the result of unknown energies coming from other dimensions, or marvels produced in our minds, they are important and they may have been better understood in early times. From the legend of Atlantis through the genius of the megalith and pyramid builders to the philosophical and mathematical literature of Classical times burned in the fire at the library of Alexandria, there are tantalizing hints of a body of lost knowledge that had come to terms with phenomena which are now scientifically unacceptable. It would come as no surprise if the principles of future science turned out to be the result of re-discovery as much as discovery.

The Atlas is arranged so that each section and each entry is complete as it stands. Many subjects are related to one another, and those with the perseverance to read from the beginning will find a chronological development that starts before man was recognizably human and stretches towards a future that can hardly yet be glimpsed.

Francis Hitching, London 1978

Acknowledgements

Publication of a book as wide-ranging as this Atlas would be impossible without the patient assistance of many people who offered their time and their critical judgment on what was being drafted, who tracked down elusive references and offered alternative solutions, and who above all gave invaluable encouragement by constantly arguing for a balanced approach towards subject-matter that by its nature is invariably surrounded by heated debate. Prime among these have been my editor, Kyle Cathie; and Peter James, associate editor of the *Journal* of the Society for Inter-Disciplinary Studies, whose research effort has been prodigious, particularly in the interpretation of ancient history. He has known about the Atlas almost since its conception, and through long hours of discussion has helped crucially in formulating the approach to many of the contentious issues that are covered. Much original research was also offered by Patrick Smith, especially in the areas which seem to defy contemporary science. Other help has come from Robert Rickard, who was generous in opening his files and his library containing the results of many years spent cataloguing natural phenomena; Philip Attwood at the British Museum; Laura Grumitt who found many obscure books, and Anne Conybeare who helped to finalize the text.

The vital visual contribution, after the book had been designed by Peter Holroyd at Pan Books, came from Kenneth Smith, who single-handedly created nearly all the maps and line drawings in a style that is uniquely his own and who made it possible to call this book an Atlas. Picture research from often difficult sources was by Anne-Marie Ehrlich.

Britain's library system worked wonders. Brian Moore at Hartlepool and District Library made a special contribution in offering an unusual variety of references. Public libraries as a rule went out of their way to help, and even in libraries run primarily for the benefit of members of private learned societies it was rare to find anything but courteous co-operation. I want to thank especially: the Franciscan Friars of the Atonement Catholic Central Library; the Geological Museum, London; Lambeth Central Library; the Royal Geographical Society; the Rudolph Steiner Library; the School of Oriental and African Studies; the Society of Antiquaries; the Society of Egyptian Archaeology; the Theosophical Society; the Zoological Library at the Natural History Museum, London.

Finally there are all the scholars in their various disciplines, too many to mention here without being invidious, whose published writings and personal communication are the bedrock of this Atlas; for those interested in a particular subject, their work should be read in full and references are given at the end of the Atlas. To all of them, for their continuing contribution to knowledge and debate, this book is gratefully dedicated.

Section one
The unstable universe

For more than a century, geophysics has been unduly racked with dogmatic debate, at the heart of which is the question of whether the Universe, and in particular the planetary system around our Sun, has evolved smoothly and gradually. If this is so, then by measuring all the forces and shapes in the world today, whether this is gravity or magnetism (physics) or the structure and composition of the Earth's surface (geology), scientists ought to be able to extrapolate all their figures backwards in time and work out exactly how the world and its inhabitants came to be as we see them now. This is called uniformitarianism. It is the established view and its watchword is that 'the present is the key to the past'.

Catastrophism, the opposite view, suggests that global disasters of cosmic proportions have also had a hand in our destiny; and in the early part of the 19th Century, the main disaster was supposed to have been the biblical Deluge. It was almost unthinkable to question the literal truth of the Bible and 'scientific' evidence that the Deluge, or even a number of deluges, had happened as a matter of actual fact was said to be available in the millions of marine fossils found in rock strata on dry land.

It was as much for political as scientific reasons that the new theory of uniformitarianism grew up to challenge this doctrine. If the Bible told the truth, there was no way of peaceably challenging the monarchy in Britain, for sovereignty was supposed to descend from God to the King; but if the Bible could be shown to be inaccurate, particularly in respect to the key event of the Deluge, then the whole philosophical foundation on which the monarchy based its power would be shattered. That, at any rate, was the reasoning of a group of Whig lawyers and MPs, one of whom, Charles Lyell, published in 1830 his *Principles of Geology*. In its 100-page introduction he argued brilliantly that the story of the Deluge was mythological and that the gradual forces of erosion

and the effects of volcanic uplift, taking place over many millions of years, could easily explain the geological features of the Earth. He had instant success, and was elected secretary and then president of the Geological Society. Darwin later acknowledged a debt to him for providing the necessary time-scale on which a process of 'natural selection' could operate and when Darwin's theories triumphed the acceptance of uniformitarianism was assured.

Lyell was only partly right and even uniformitarians now agree that, for instance, continental drift is an essential factor in shaping the Earth's surface. But the most damaging effect of his victory was that, because of its political and religious overtones, geologists had to accept *either* uniformitarianism *or* catastrophism, not a mixture of both. In this section we trace a number of cases where progress has been much regarded by the scientific pendulum swinging too far in Lyell's direction. It is now becoming increasingly clear that all manner of catastrophes have happened to Earth – drastic changes in climate, seismic upheavals, fluctuations and reversals of the Earth's magnetic field, massive extinctions; huge meteorites have struck us (page 182) and we may even have nearly collided once with Venus. In 1977, the scientific journal *Nature* reported on a catastrophic environmental change in the distant past that quickly laid down massive salt deposits in the Mediterranean, a fact which, said the paper, does 'much to throw doubts on Lyell's substantive uniformitarianism'.

Scientists generally, as one of them admits in his discussion of why dinosaurs so mysteriously disappeared, still have a lingering aversion to catastrophes. They make the world a less comfortable and predictable place, and the scientist's job much harder. But the pendulum is swinging back and we can be sure that 21st-century science will pay much more attention to them than has been the case for the last 100 years.

Death of the dinosaurs

Slip back in time sixty-five million years, and you would find a comfortably familiar look about much of the surface of the Earth. A mild, even tropical climate enabled broad-leaved trees to grow vigorously far north of what is now the Arctic circle. As today, there were forested hillsides and mountains; desert sands and oases; fertile, grassy plains; and along thousands of miles of what is now land leading up to the sea-shore, swamps and marshes much like the Everglades of Florida, populated by easily recognizable reptiles such as crocodiles and turtles. Inland, you might even catch a glimpse of some of man's most distant ancestors: small, tree-climbing, shrew-like animals that were the most advanced form of mammal at the time.

This balmy planet was dominated by creatures neither reptile nor mammal – the dinosaurs. For 150 million years (compared with a mere 50,000 years of modern man), while continents edged gradually apart and hills were compressed upwards to form mountains, the dinosaurs had evolved into a staggering array of different forms that filled virtually every ecological niche and inhabited all Earth except Antarctica. The most advanced of them seemed poised for an evolutionary leap that might have changed the course of history; *Saurornithoides*, christened from its appearance a 'bird-like reptile', had a large brain, wide-set eyes that gave it stereoscopic vision, and manipulating fingers with opposable thumbs that made it quite capable of catching and eating small mammals – shrews, for instance. According to Adrian J. Desmond, one of the world's leading authorities on the subject, such creatures were separated from other dinosaurs 'by a gulf comparable to that dividing men from cows . . . who knows what peaks the sophisticated "bird-mimics" would have attained had they survived.'

But they did not survive. Something catastrophic happened, and it completely wiped out all species of dinosaur, large and small, on land and in the sea, and in different climates right across the globe. Geologists think they know when it happened – 63 million years ago. How long the process took is still open to doubt – perhaps a few hundred thousand years, but more likely a much shorter time, and possibly only a few days. Compared to the eons in which the dinosaurs had mastered the Earth, it happened in an eye-blink. The devastation struck at almost all forms of life, simultaneously annihilating many mammals, reptiles, shellfish, and plants. The cause of any extinctions is something of a mystery; this was the greatest extinction the world has ever seen.

Changing opinions

In order to guess at the nature of this cataclysm, it is necessary to know something of the creatures it affected, and here, as in many disciplines, scientists have recently been changing their minds. The classical (and popular) idea of dinosaurs was one of hulking, dull-witted, cold-blooded reptiles, an 'over-evolved' species too massive for their own good. Robert T. Bakker of Yale University summed up this traditional picture in 1968: 'Generally, palaeontologists have assumed that in the everyday details of life, dinosaurs were merely overgrown alligators or lizards. Crocodilians and lizards spend much of their time in inactivity, sunning themselves on a convenient rock or log, and, compared to modern mammals, most modern reptiles are slow and sluggish. Hence the usual reconstruction of a dinosaur such as *Brontosaurus* is as a mountain of scaly flesh which moved around only slowly and infrequently.'

When people first focused their attention on the dinosaurs in the 18th Century, it was assumed

Development of life on Earth, from the time of dinosaurs to the emergence of man.

first men	first hominids	primate boom	primitive apes and monkeys	primitive horses, cattle, deer and pigs	first primates – (prosimians) expansion of mammals

	End of Ice Ages	Ice Ages		Africa joined to Eurasia	Gulf of Aden begins to form	Separation of Australia from Antarctica	Separation of Greenland from Euras

epoch	RECENT	PLEISTOCENE	PLIOCENE	MIOCENE	OLIGOCENE	EOCENE	PALAEOCENE
period	QUATERNARY				TERTIARY		
era				CENOZOIC			
years ago	11,000	2–3 (millions)	12	25	38	55	6

from their reconstructed skeletons that they were simply gigantic reptiles, and that like their supposed descendants still alive on Earth, they must have been cold-blooded. Right through the 19th and the first half of the 20th Century this remained the view, although as ever more accurate skeletal reconstructions showed the vast scale and variety of dinosaurs, the view became increasingly absurd. Then, in the 1960s, a number of calculations began to swing opinion the other way.

Mostly, these mathematics were about the energy needed to keep a particular life-form alive. Warm-blooded creatures eat relatively vast amounts of food, 80–90 per cent of which is converted into the energy needed to maintain a constant body temperature, and the remainder used up by the muscles that enable us to move about and breathe. A man-sized lizard, were it warm-blooded, would eat about 40 times as much food as a cold-blooded one.

Cold-blooded creatures, on the other hand, spend most of their time in inactivity. A lizard gains most of its body heat by lying collapsed on the ground basking in the sun; for 90 per cent of its life it is motionless, and only occasionally does it make a rapid lunge in order to swallow an insect, or run and hide. But the larger the lizard, the more difficult it is for the sun to provide enough heat. In 1946, three scientists showed that if a dinosaur with cold blood dropped just one degree in temperature below the level needed to keep it on the move – in other words, if the dinosaur became just cold enough to doze into a state of hibernation – then it would have to lie in hot sun for three whole days to get its temperature back to normal. What was more, the sun would probably have to be so hot that in the process of warming up, the

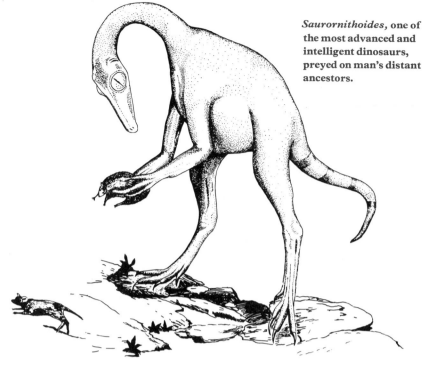

Saurornithoides, one of the most advanced and intelligent dinosaurs, preyed on man's distant ancestors.

dinosaur would probably be blistered to death (as happened with three unfortunate alligators on which one of the scientists experimented).

Equally, it was calculated that the body temperature needed to keep the larger dinosaurs on the move, or even upright, was far more than could be provided by the sun. The eight-ton bulk of *Tyrannosaurus* would have had to make an enormous effort just to stay on its feet. According to Adrian Desmond: 'Unlike the lizard, which runs for short spurts before flopping on to its belly to recuperate, *Tyrannosaurus* did not sprawl with its belly just off the ground but walked with its legs tucked under the body and belly raised high into the air. It was not built for flopping on to the ground. Usually, it was forced to remain balanced on its feet.' With the gigantic *Brontosaurus,* colossal

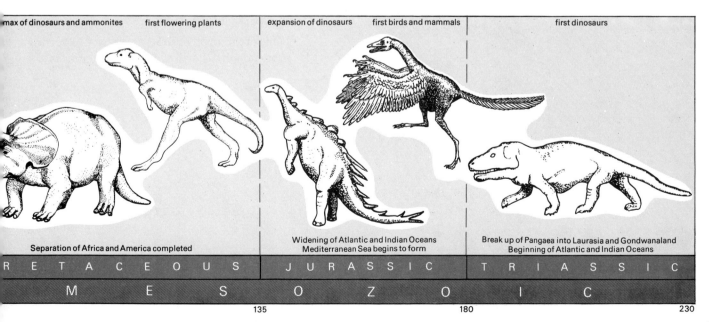

| max of dinosaurs and ammonites | first flowering plants | expansion of dinosaurs | first birds and mammals | first dinosaurs |

| Separation of Africa and America completed | Widening of Atlantic and Indian Oceans
Mediterranean Sea begins to form | Break up of Pangaea into Laurasia and Gondwanaland
Beginning of Atlantic and Indian Oceans |

C R E T A C E O U S | J U R A S S I C | T R I A S S I C

M E S O Z O I C

135   180   230

muscular effort was needed just to stop its 50-ton frame collapsing.

So gradually it has come to be accepted that dinosaurs of all kinds must have had warm blood; and with this acceptance has come the general recognition that some at least were much more intelligent and highly evolved than had been traditionally thought. Warm blood would provide the energy needed for those dinosaurs with impressive teeth, fangs and claws to become fighters and killers in the way that they had long been depicted in sci-fi movies.

Pterosaurs developed large brains, and breathing systems at least as efficient as those of modern birds; they flew (some flapping, some gliding) as well as, possibly better than birds; they were also covered in thick fur (proving unequivocally that they were warm-blooded) and had wing-spans of up to 15 metres. *Archaeopteryx*, the smallest of the dinosaurs, anticipated birds by developing feathers as a means of temperature control.

What is more, dinosaurs were unique – neither reptiles nor mammals, but in a class of their own. They ruled their world in all their variety; and then they suddenly died out, leaving enough mammals and reptiles behind for life to have evolved as we see it today. Just what caused this massive and selective extinction is hotly argued by fossil experts. Twice before in the Earth's history something similar had happened.

Around 500 million years ago, two-thirds of the marine shell creatures known as *trilobites* were destroyed; and around 230 million years ago, just before continents began to split apart from the main land-mass of Pangaea (page 15), they disappeared altogether in a devastating extinction during which nearly half the creatures known from the fossil record disappeared for ever. Of the many orthodox explanations, the most recently favoured has been an upset of the ecology by changes in sea-levels.

But the end of the dinosaurs is special both for its suddenness and its violence. Dale Russell, of the National Museum of Natural Sciences in Ottawa, has written: 'Nearly half of the species of flowering plants, and many varieties of small egg-laying and pouched mammals disappeared, as did all of the diverse groups of dinosaurs and other large reptiles . . . The famous chalk cliffs of Dover are an accumulation of minute limey platelets shed by tiny floating single-celled plants, contemporaries of the dinosaurs, many of them sharing their fate. Numerous other marine organisms, such as floating single-celled animals, the bizarre shellfish, the squid-like creatures and octopoid forms with coiled shells, marine turtles, lizards and giant long-necked reptiles were severely decimated or disappeared, either as a result of starvation or from the causes that depleted the oceanic plants.'

Supernova explosion

Of the many suggested ways in which these extinctions may have been triggered (see panel opposite), Dale Russell's own explanation is perhaps the closest to being accepted. He believes that the normally stable environment of those times was upset by a colossal stellar explosion called a supernova, in which a star larger than our Sun suddenly runs out of its nuclear fuel and begins to collapse, emitting atomic elements and colossal amounts of lethal radiation. Such explosions have been seen and recorded at least eight times on Earth, the first being by a Chinese astronomer in 1006 AD who wrote that 'a star appeared to the south of the Ti lunar mansion, east of Ku-Lou and west of Chi-Kuan. At one time it resembled the half-moon, shown with pointed rays, and was so bright that objects could be seen by its light . . .'

None of these recent supernovae have happened near enough to Earth to have had a significant

Some dinosaurs are known to have been warm-blooded. In the snow-covered regions of what is now southern Africa, they developed furry coats and manes.

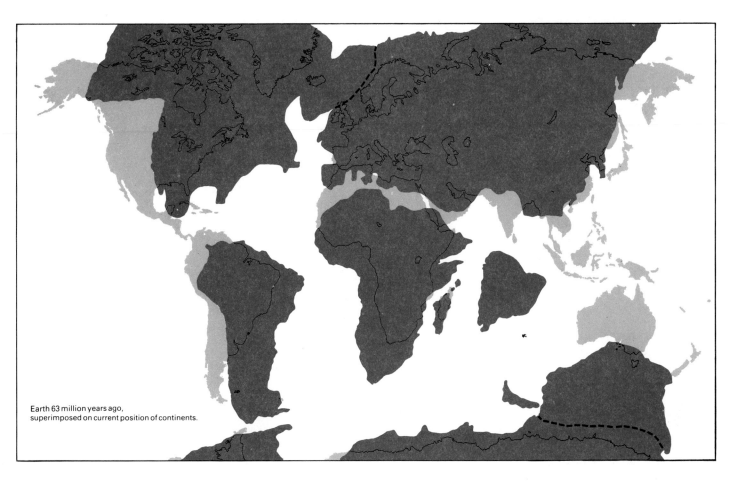

Earth 63 million years ago,
superimposed on current position of continents.

effect in spite of their spectacular brightness. But statistically, it is probable that at least one supernova will occur within 100 light years away from us every 50 million years – and as close as this, its force would be enough to disrupt our protective upper atmosphere, shower the Earth with cosmic rays, and bring about a marked and prolonged drop in temperature.

Exactly this seems to have happened at the death of the dinosaurs. Dinosaurs and large flowering plants, highly evolved and vulnerable because of their size, would be initially devastated by radiation, while smaller plant-forms and more primitive creatures would remain unaffected. At the same time the sudden cold would exterminate the remainder of the dinosaurs (most of them uninsulated by fur or feathers), and marine life that had grown accustomed to warm water.

Mammals and reptiles capable of hibernating through the cold – the shrews, the lizards, turtles and crocodiles – did so, and survived. According to this scenario, it was a catastrophe that brought an era to an end; as Adrian Desmond has put it: 'The geologist's lingering aversion to cataclysms notwithstanding, it is becoming difficult to disagree with the idea that the dinosaurs departed with the most spectacular bang since Creation.'

Ten ways the dinosaurs may have died

1 Racial senescence and over-specialization The idea that races of creatures, like individuals, reach old age and die; the dinosaurs 'over-evolved'; developing bodies too massive and cumbersome for their environment, their metabolisms or their tiny brains, they simply died of awkwardness.
Certainly not true of all dinosaurs, and why was the extinction so sudden?

2 Rise of the mammals Mammals, in competition with dinosaurs, eventually defeated them. *Most unlikely, as mammals were in fact dominated and suppressed by dinosaurs; it was only after dinosaurs died out that mammals began to develop.*

3 Egg-stealing by mammals Mammals, although still small, destroyed the dinosaurs by eating their eggs. *Far-fetched, and does not explain the other simultaneous extinctions.*

4 The laramide revolution A geological phenomenon that gave rise to our modern system of mountain ranges, affecting plants and climate; the dinosaurs died as they could not adapt to this new environment. *But the dinosaurs in fact enjoyed the new environment; they expanded alongside flowering plants, and thrived on the new flora.*

5 Pathogenic fungi These may have developed alongside flowering plants, and destroyed the dinosaurs by parasitism. *No evidence whatsoever.*

6 Chemical aggression by plants Flowering plants developed potent alkaloids to deter creatures trying to eat them; dinosaurs, however, were unable to detect the poisons, and eating large quantities, died. *But why did dinosaurs flourish on the new fauna for several million years before dying?*

7 Epidemic Dinosaurs were wiped out by an unknown disease. *But could an epidemic simultaneously destroy all the myriad species of dinosaur, as well as ammonites, plankton, and many mammals?*

8 A change in the oxygen concentration Flowering plants increased the amount of oxygen in the air, and the dinosaurs were unable to cope with it. *Fails to explain why several species of flowering plants disappeared at the same time.*

9 Geomagnetic reversals (page 17) Frequent reversals had a harmful effect on dinosaurs at this time. *But the reversals may have been merely symptomatic of a more general catastrophe.*

10 Collision with a large meteorite (page 182) Accompanied by modification of the climate and terrestrial magnetism. *Apart from a supernova, probably the best bet so far.*

Continents on the move

Scientists on the whole do not like the idea of big bangs interrupting the relentless evolution of the Earth and its inhabitants. Since Darwin's time they have worked out their ideas according to the theory of uniformitarianism – 'the present is the key to the past.' This says that all the forces and processes which we can measure on Earth today – e.g. gravity, or heat from the Sun – are much the same now as they have always been; they thus enable geologists and others to work out how the world has come to look as it does. The opponents of this theory, a minority, are known as catastrophists. They believe that, on the contrary, our past has been punctuated by cosmic and terrestrial disasters; to assume that the universe is stable, and that the Earth has evolved serenely and gradually is complacent, arrogant and simplistic.

The intellectual dog-fight between the two sides has been going on now for more than a century, and never more fiercely than in the debate over how the great land and sea masses came to be laid out on the face of the globe. For according to text-book uniformitarianism, 'a large rotating planet with a powerful gravitational field should mould itself into a smooth, featureless spheroid which, given the chemistry of the earth, should be covered by a layer of water about 2.4 kilometres deep.' But as any visitor from outer space could tell at once, our Earth isn't like that. There is no symmetry. Not only does 29 per cent of the surface emerge through the water, but it does so in a mysteriously non-uniform way. Some 80 per cent of the total land area is crushed inside the northern hemisphere, the tips of the continents tapering v-shaped towards great expanses of ocean in the south.

What is also noticeable from a cursory glance at any atlas is the marked similarity between many coastlines – the west coast of Africa with the east coast of South America, for instance. This superficial resemblance has long been noted (Francis Bacon, in 1620, was one of the first to do so), but never as more than an academic curiosity, about as interesting as the fact that Italy is shaped like a boot. The vastness of the Pacific was usually explained as the effect of the Moon separating from Earth (now known to be untrue), and the coastline matches as coincidences. Certainly no respectable uniformitarian geologist ever dared suggest seriously that the continents were one day joined together; apart from anything else, they seemed far too heavy to be capable of movement – even the smallest, Australia, weighs about 500 million million million kilogrammes.

A theory run wild

Still, there have always been enough unexplained

Alfred Wegener, explorer, meteorologist and adventurer, whose radical theories on drifting continents infuriated geologists of his time.

geological anomalies for a few scientists to persist with the idea that the map of the world had once been very different, and in 1915 a young German meteorologist named Alfred Wegener produced for the first time a coherent picture of what it might have looked like, with all the continents merged into a single land-mass. He was derided for his efforts. Geology, said one professor, could no longer be regarded as science if it was 'possible for such a theory as this to run wild'. Another protested: 'If we are to believe Wegener's hypothesis we must forget everything which has been learned in the last 70 years and start all over again.'

One of the reasons for their hostility was something that has become increasingly apparent as the various scientific disciplines grow ever more specialized: Wegener was not a single-minded, narrowly-trained, fellow geologist. His lifestyle was that of an academic adventurer. His hobby was ballooning. He died shortly after his fiftieth birthday in 1930 exploring a remote and bitterly inhospitable area of Greenland. In presenting his revolutionary theory of continental drift, he drew on evidence not only from physical geology, but from geodesy, geophysics, palaeontology, zoology and palaeoclimatology. He belonged, as the eminent British physicist Sir Edward Bullard put it, 'to the wrong trade union'.

Unanswered questions

With hindsight, we can see that he picked on all the major inconsistencies of contemporary geological thinking. Why did mountains occur in ranges – the Himalayas, the Alps, the Rockies, the Appalachians – when the rest of the Earth's surface was relatively flat? Why did the characteristics of these mountains – the Appalachians are geologically identical to the

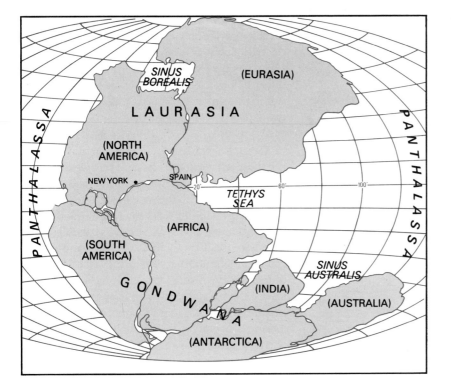

The giant continental land-mass called Pangaea 200 million years ago, before it split apart.

The predicted map of the world 50 million years from now.

the kangaroo family be found only in Australia and the Americas? How was it possible for tropical ferns to have grown in Europe and as far north as Greenland, when simultaneously glaciers were covering equatorial Africa and South America? How could there be fossil palm trees in Spitzbergen and coal in Antarctica, unless these places were once warm?

His own answer was that once, in a time known geologically as the late Palaeozoic era, all continents were joined together in a land-mass that covered half the globe. He named his supercontinent Pangaea – 'all earth' – and except in detail, the map he drew became suddenly, in the 1960s, scientific orthodoxy.

Abrupt change

The cause of this abrupt change in attitude was the unwelcome discovery by physicists (as opposed to geologists) that measurements of magnetic 'stripes' on the ocean beds seemed to show conclusively that great areas of the planet were moving slowly about. Gradually, a picture emerged of the Earth's surface being divided into about a dozen great plates, the division between them marked by a serpentine ocean ridge and trench system some 40,000 kilometres long, and by the winding belts of volcanic activity that continue from the ocean on to the land (map page 56). It is the relentless and unthinkable pressure of these constantly moving plates, on which the continents rest, that causes volcanoes to erupt, mountain ranges to be forced upwards to ever-increasing heights, and new expanses of ocean to be formed.

The energy to keep this whole shifting enormity

range that runs through Scotland and Norway – span an entire ocean? Why were fossils from the ocean depths found on their very peaks? Why did geological evidence show the land-mass now known as Switzerland to have once been ten or twelve times wider than it is today?

In zoology and climatology there were similar unsolved puzzles. Why did the diminutive lemur monkey live only in two widely separated areas: one, Africa's east coast and nearby Madagascar; two, the other side of the Indian Ocean in Sri Lanka, India, and South-east Asia? Why could

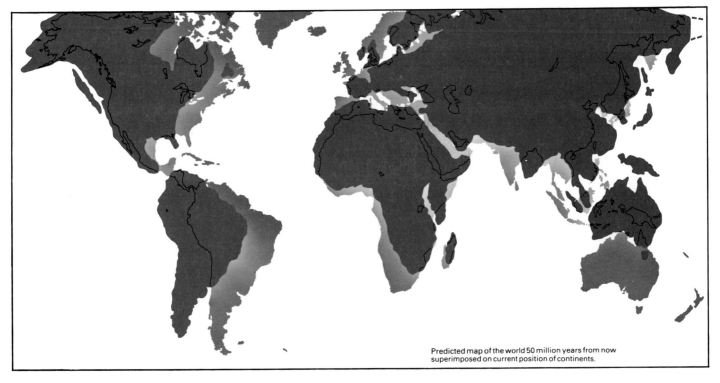

Predicted map of the world 50 million years from now superimposed on current position of continents.

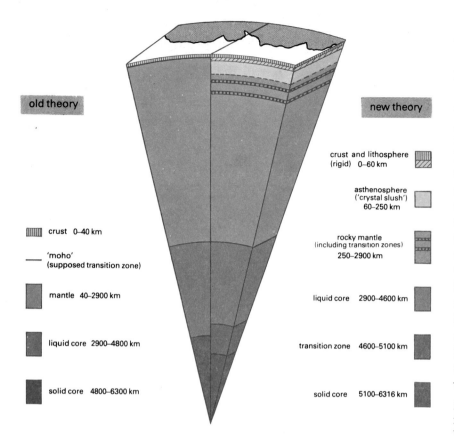

old theory

new theory

crust and lithosphere
(rigid) 0–60 km

asthenosphere
('crystal slush')
60–250 km

rocky mantle
(including transition zones)
250–2900 km

liquid core   2900–4600 km

transition zone   4600–5100 km

solid core   5100–6316 km

crust 0–40 km

'moho'
(supposed transition zone)

mantle 40–2900 km

liquid core 2900–4800 km

solid core 4800–6300 km

Section through Earth's interior (not to scale). The Earth's crust can be compared with the thickness of an apple's skin.

been toying with the notion that one of the uniformitarian constants, gravity, has in fact decreased with time. If so, it means that the Earth has gradually become larger, and in so doing has cracked apart along the lines of the dozen lithospheric plates. If this is proved, geologists will once again have to revise their ideas.

However, for the time being continental drift is the accepted wisdom. The land that we live on shifts perceptibly sideways – on average about two metres – within the span of a single lifetime. Computer matching has shown that the edges of the continental shelf – a shallow extension of the sea-shore that has not always been covered by water – fit one another elegantly (if not indisputably), rather like a giant jigsaw. A crater on the moon, on the side we never see, has been honoured with Wegener's name; and within a decade lasers on the moon will have measured just how much, if at all, continents continue to move.

on the move is thought to derive from the Earth's internal heat, convected upwards and outwards like thick soup in a giant boiling saucepan. Theories about the Earth's interior have also changed. The crust is now thought to be no more than five kilometres thick in some places, on top of a layer of more substantial rock known as the lithosphere, 30–300 kilometres deep. It is this lithosphere which is on the move, divided into plates and carried on top of a hot crystal slush called the asthenosphere, a semi-molten underground 'sea' transmitting heat from the inferno at the Earth's core.

There is perhaps something suspiciously unanimous about the way that geologists have so enthusiastically adopted a theory they previously ridiculed. Indeed, some physicists have lately

Whether or not this dramatic turnaround by the geologists represents a victory for catastrophism is open to some doubt. Dietz and Holden, two US scientists who have been in the forefront of this new science of plate tectonics, admit reluctantly that there must have been one great 'catastrophic event' that caused Pangaea to split apart in the first place some 200 million years ago. However, from then onwards the process is supposed to have continued remorselessly, undisturbed by further cataclysms or cosmic upheavals. And it is now thought that the pace of continental drift is slowing down, since the Earth is known to be cooling and the thickness of the lithosphere increasing. Maybe, to those few geologists who still believe that land formations are stationary, this will bring some comfort, for it means that one day they will be proved right – in the fullness of time, continents will undoubtedly come to a standstill. But they will have to wait awhile. On current calculations, it is going to take another 200 million years.

Continuously, the Earth's crust moves downwards into the molten mantle, while at the same time new land is formed under the sea.

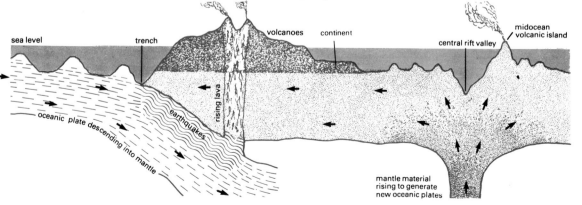

sea level   trench   volcanoes   continent   midocean volcanic island

central rift valley

oceanic plate descending into mantle

earthquakes

rising lava

mantle material rising to generate new oceanic plates

Magnetism and life

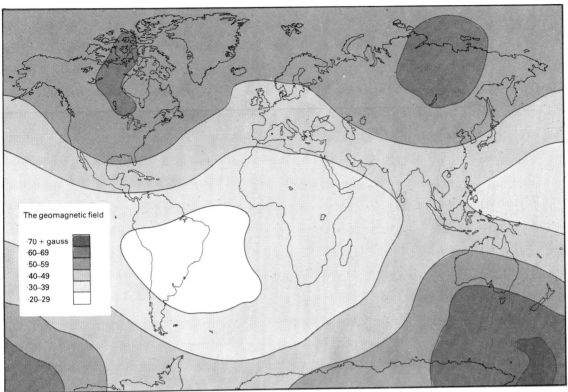

NASA measurements have shown the Earth's magnetic field is weakest near Rio de Janeiro, strongest near the poles.

The geomagnetic field

- ·70 + gauss
- ·60–69
- ·50–59
- ·40–49
- ·30–39
- ·20–29

Accustomed as we are to seeing a compass needle point unwaveringly at the magnetic north pole, it came as an astonishment to geologists in the 1950s to discover that on many occasions in the Earth's history the opposite seemed to have been the case – the poles were reversed, so that north became south, and vice versa. It would be like waking up one morning on board ship and finding the compass pointing in the opposite direction – a mystery in the true sense of being inexplicable in scientific terms. 'The idea that the Earth's magnetic field reverses at first seems so preposterous,' wrote three geologists who were about to undertake a major investigation, 'that one immediately suspects a violation of some basic laws of physics, and most investigators working on reversals have sometimes wondered if the reversals are really compatible with the physical theory of magnetism.'

In fact, so far as the Earth is concerned, the theory itself is sketchy. It is assumed that our planet is magnetized because, like a dynamo, it spins, and that electricity is generated somewhere within its core; but there is no proof, and nobody really knows. As the trio of scientists went on to admit: 'After centuries of research the Earth's magnetic field remains one of the best described and least understood of all planetary phenomena.'

However, the Earth's magnetism certainly exists, and its subtle gradients can be measured. It is as if there was a giant bar magnet at the core, generating what has always been regarded as a remarkably steady field of force. By the time this force has worked its way through the Earth's surface (if that is what happens), it is relatively feeble. The unit of measurement in magnetism is called a gauss, and a child's typical horseshoe magnet would have a strength of about 1000 gauss. The Earth's field, now plotted completely for the first time by NASA space probes, varies from around 0.7 gauss near the poles, to around 0.3 gauss at its weakest point near Rio de Janeiro.

Magnetic discoveries

Nevertheless, its mysterious properties have long been known to man. As early as the 11th Century AD the Chinese were using a form of magnetic compass made of 'lodestone', a mineral which is naturally magnetized. Early astronomers everywhere recognized the direction of north by the star that hung over the pole. By the 13th Century – long before Newton discovered the much more easily sensed force of gravity – a remarkable French engineer named Petrus Peregrinus had even laid down correctly the main properties of magnetism: that it has two poles where the magnetic force is concentrated, and that like poles repel while unlike poles attract.

What nobody realized was that this force, far from being stable, was the opposite – dramatically so. From the beginning of the 20th Century onwards, repeated observations have shown that not once, but many times, the field has reversed itself and fluctuated in strength; today, it is 50 per cent weaker than 2500 years ago, and within a few centuries, at the present

17

Dowsers are said to have special sensitivity to small changes in the Earth's magnetic field.

These findings are still controversial. But what is now certain is that reversals have happened repeatedly and for varying periods ever since the world was formed into a solid. Nobody knows for sure why they happen, how often, or how long the process takes. However, the chart below shows the *minimum* number of reversals that everyone agrees to have occurred within the last 3 million years – the whole history of Man and his forebears – and as the geomagnetism correspondent of *Nature* sees it, these could be 'but the tip of the iceberg'. A reversal may have occurred about 330,000 BC, a date curiously coincidental with the first trace of modern man, (page 34). There is evidence of further reversals some 111,000 and 30,000 years ago. Recently, Swedish geologists found definite evidence of reversals and drastic fluctuations in the Earth's field about 10,000 BC – in other words, at the very end of the last Ice Age.

rate, it will have disappeared altogether, with perhaps catastrophic effects on life.

One of the first indications that this might be so came at the turn of the century, when an Italian, Giuseppe Folgheraiter, tried to discover the orientation of the Earth's magnetic field at various times in history by studying what is known as 'remanent' magnetism in ancient Etruscan vases. When clay, or brick, is baked and then cooled (or when the same process happens in rocks through volcanic activity), the direction of the pole gets locked in – a permanent footprint on time. What he expected to find was a series of minor variations – the kind of small adjustment that a navigator has to make when calculating the difference between true north and magnetic north. What he actually found amazed him: in the 8th Century BC, at least in Italy and Greece, the poles had flipped into reverse.

Magnetic upheavals
Folgheraiter's tests were confirmed by P. L. Mercanton from Geneva in 1907, who also found that in 1000 BC the field had been normal. The work of these two was reviewed in 1949, because the idea of a reversal so recently in history was mistrusted, and yet more evidence from rocks in Sweden put the date of a reversal around 860 BC – shortly before the days that saw the rise of the Assyrian Empire and the first flowering of Greek and Roman civilization.

Extinction patterns
Such an event is far more than a geological curiosity – more, even, than the descriptions 'major geomagnetic disturbance' or 'great geophysical event' which are often applied to them. For during the last two decades it has become steadily clearer that as far as living beings are concerned, a reversal can be catastrophic.

It was while drilling cores of rock from the ocean bed in search of evidence for continental drift that the crucial importance of magnetism in the history of the Earth began to emerge. Geologists found to their surprise that magnetic reversals coincided with massive waves of extinctions. For instance, out of eight extinctions of various species of marine life in the Pacific, six occurred during, or very close to, polarity reversals. This finding is now generally accepted. The imperceptibly shifting force of magnetism has an evolutionary effect quite out of proportion to its strength.

Why this should be so raises questions beyond the bounds of current scientific knowledge. Richard Uffen, of New York State University, believes that during reversals the intensity of the magnetic field would be so reduced that the Earth would no longer be protected by the Van Allen belts in outer space. Living things would then be at the mercy of the solar wind and cosmic rays,

Many times in the Earth's history the magnetic pole has switched from north to south, with catastrophic effects on life.

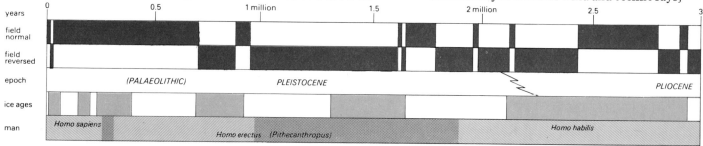

which would cause mutations and extinctions. But several scientists have said in reply that, because most of these harmful rays are absorbed by the atmosphere or fail to penetrate to the depths of the sea, the increase in radiation would be only about 10 per cent – not enough to be significant.

Alternatively, the link between reversals and volcanic activity has been suggested as a cause – if the Sun was obscured by volcanic ash for long periods, life would be affected. But again, although this might be a partial answer, volcanoes do not invariably erupt all over the world during a reversal. Another suggestion, which may also have a bearing without being a complete solution, is that a reversal might trigger off a drastic climatic change, such as an ice age, and would thus indirectly affect evolution.

But lately there has been an even more controversial speculation: can weak magnetic fields affect life directly? And the answer seems to be – contrary to all orthodox theory – that they can, and do.

Sensitivity experiments

It is perhaps not surprising that the question has not been asked earlier. Human beings do not normally notice magnetism – after all, if you place your finger inside a child's horseshoe magnet, you apparently feel nothing, nor is there any obvious effect. Moreover, the Earth's own field is, as we have seen, relatively so feeble that even if it vanished altogether, such a tiny alteration in our environment ought to be swamped and randomized by the general molecular activity in our body.

It now seems that somehow, mysteriously, this is not the case. All types of living things, from the most primitive to the most sophisticated, seem to have a built-in magnetic detection system. We are all able, unconsciously, to sense minute changes in the level of a magnetic field – and this finding is leading us to the verge of a biological revolution.

Evidence has come from a variety of sources. The approach of thunderstorms causes the Earth's field to reduce suddenly; psychiatric admissions to hospitals increase, as do suicide rates. Animals can detect the imminence of an earthquake by sensing the magnetic changes built up by pressure in the underground rocks. Experimentally, people have been placed for ten days in a laboratory in a null magnetic field (to simulate life on other planets); after a while,

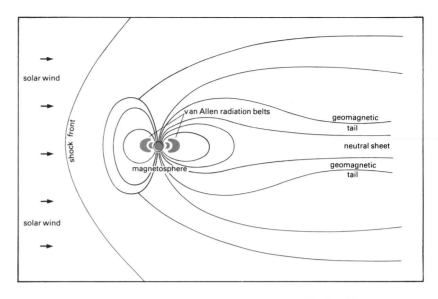

they could not tell whether an electric light bulb was flickering or not.

Insects and birds orient themselves magnetically: cockroaches, bees, crickets and many flies always land, in calm weather, in a certain direction; the orientation of the bee-dance on a honeycomb can be altered by changing the strength of the magnetic field; homing pigeons become confused and unable to find their way if tiny magnets are attached to them. Mice placed in a very weak field reproduce less, lie in unusual positions, go bald, become more docile, and die early.

Unknown mechanisms

The magnetic field changes being talked about in these experiments are stunningly small – too low, at the moment, for most scientists to be able to accept them. Yet humans as well as animals seem susceptible. The US physicist Zaboj Harvalik has shown that 90 per cent of us can distinguish a variation of 1/100,000th of the Earth's field, and one man – a German water diviner – was able to recognize a change of *one billionth* of a gauss. This is phenomenal. Nobody has the least idea of the mechanism in the body that allows this to happen; but since it does, it may well have contributed importantly to the massive mysterious waves of extinctions that have punctuated the Earth's history.

It is also a reminder that however familiar and secure our environment seems, we should not take it for granted. For at least 2500 years, the strength of the Earth's magnetic field has been dropping inexorably, and at the present rate it will have vanished altogether about 200 years from now. Is this the sign of the next major pole reversal? And will it once again change the course of evolution?

The Earth's magnetosphere stretches far into space, deflecting the cosmic rays which threaten life on the planet.

Spontaneous human combustion

On the bitterly cold morning of 5 December 1966, Don E. Gosnell set off on his normal working-day routine, reading gas meters in the county town of Coudersport, Pennsylvania. His first call was to one of the best-loved characters in the district: Dr John Irving Bentley, for more than half a century the local family physician, now at the age of 92 retired and semi-invalided, but still able to look after himself and move around his house with the help of a walking-aid.

The front door of 403 North Main Street was shut but not locked. Don Gosnell let himself in, and shouted a greeting along the corridor to the old man's living room. Mildly surprised to get no reply, he went downstairs to the meter in the basement. A curious smell which first struck him when he entered the house grew stronger – 'somewhat sweet, like starting up a new oil-burning central heating system.' It seemed to come from a light-blue smoke that hung in the

air. On the floor was a neat cone of fine dark ash; it was about 35 centimetres high – perhaps enough to fill a bucket. Idly, he scattered it with his foot. The floor underneath was unmarked. Had he glanced up at the ceiling then, he would have seen a hole through which the ash had fallen – an irregular area approximately one and a half by half a metre, charred round the edges, burned clear through the floorboards above. Instead, he read the gas meter, went upstairs again, and into the doctor's room to see if he needed anything. The smoke was a little denser. Dr Bentley wasn't there. Don Gosnell put his head into the adjoining bathroom. What he saw appalled him.

Tilted over the blackened hole in the floor was the doctor's walking-aid. Alongside it was the sole, macabre remain of Dr Bentley: the lower part of his right leg, browned by the heat, the shoe still intact. Trying not to vomit, Don Gosnell turned and fled out of the house, down the road, and into the gas company's office; 'as white as a sheet', his colleagues later described him. Breathless, he used just four words to express his horror:

'Dr Bentley burnt up . . .'

He had been a rare first witness of an extraordinary and gruesome phenomenon: spontaneous human combustion, in which a person's body is reduced, sometimes within minutes, to a heap of cinders. It happens seldom, and unpredictably (although it has recently been suggested that a pattern of magnetic disturbances seem to occur at the same time). No case is exactly like another, but some of the usual features, according to one authority, are: the speed and intensity of the process, often associated with an oily smoke; a mystifying kind of fuel, which cannot be extinguished by water; the way that it is selectively directed, for example leaving the extremities of the body unharmed, and sometimes not even damaging the clothes encasing the body.

Consuming heat

Compared with the global catastrophies of mass extinctions and colliding continents, it is a peculiarly personal cataclysm. It has never been observed in animals. Medically, it is hardly ever discussed, because its paradoxes make it theoretically impossible. For its central contradiction is this: there is no known way in which burning human tissue can generate the colossal temperatures needed to effect almost total consumption of the body; and if such temperatures were produced, they would certainly not confine their effect to the body alone, leaving highly combustible materials

The remains of Dr John Irving Bentley, found in his bathroom by a meter reader. The floor was burned through, but little else was damaged.

nearby almost untouched. On the few occasions when the subject is professionally argued, the term 'preternatural combustibility' is preferred (the idea of the fire happening spontaneously being yet another theoretical impossibility), and here it is reluctantly agreed that over the centuries there have been some rare cases of this. Dr Gavin Thurston, a London coroner, wrote in a 1961 issue of the *Medico-Legal Journal* that 'there are undisputed instances where the body has burned in its own substance, without external fuel, and in which there has been a remarkable absence of damage to surrounding inflammable objects.'

However, the mystery of how this happens is completely unsolved, and the phenomenon can readily be seen as another example of us not understanding just how volatile may be the environment in which we live. The case of Dr John Bentley was a particularly well-observed one, and it left the coroner, John Dec, a series of unanswerable questions. The rational solution was that the old man, a pipe-smoker, had set his robe on fire while he sat in the living-room and had staggered to the bathroom with it alight; here he took it off and flung it into the bathtub. But why was the robe relatively undamaged (and spotted with innumerable marks where his pipe ash had on previous occasions failed to ignite it)? How could a smouldering cloth generate enough heat to cremate a human body beyond recognition? With the house tightly shut up, where was the oxygen supply to feed a fire as powerful as this? Why was there no stench of burning flesh when Don Gosnell entered – only the 'somewhat sweet' blue smoke? If the fire had started in the living-room, why was there no trace of this? Why was the paint on the bathtub, only inches away from the charred floor, blackened but not blistered?

Disintegration

Above all, why was there so little left of the body? John Dec says that all he found was the one lower leg, a knee joint on a post in the basement, and the ashes; others remember seeing an unrecognizable skull, and the ovoid mass beneath the fallen walking-aid in the photograph may be this. But John Dec's experience as a coroner included a car crash, followed by a fire, in which the heat had been so intense that nobody had been able to go near the car to rescue the three trapped occupants, who were incinerated beyond recognition. Even in such a holocaust, their skeletal remains – rib cage, limbs, skull, teeth – were intact. So, baffled, John Dec wrote down on Dr Bentley's Certificate of Death that the immediate cause had been 'asphyxiation and 90 per cent burning of body', admitting afterwards

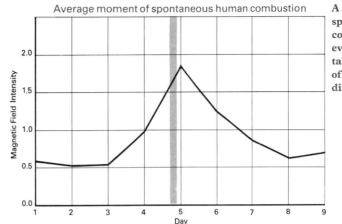

Average moment of spontaneous human combustion

A sample of six cases of spontaneous human combustion shows the event is most likely to take place during a time of strong magnetic disturbance.

to the writer Larry E. Arnold that 98 per cent or 99 per cent would have been nearer the mark, and that the whole incident was 'the oddest thing you ever saw'.

Cremation

This almost total disintegration of the body into powdery ash is a major unsolved problem. In an earlier case of human combustion, the remains of Mrs Mary Reeser were found one July morning in 1951 by a neighbour in St Petersburg, Florida. She had died in her armchair, which was also destroyed, along with a standard lamp, in the fire. In a blackened circle little more than a metre in diameter, all that could be seen were a few coiled springs, and the metal framework of the lamp. Mary Reeser having been fairly weighty, some 80 kilos in total, had been incinerated into four kilos of ash. As with Dr Bentley, one foot remained, encased in a black satin slipper. A small piece of backbone was recognizable. The skull had shrunk to the size of an orange.

It was particularly this last effect that caught the eye of Dr Wilton M. Krogman, Professor of Physical Anthropology at the University of Pennsylvania's School of Medicine, and an internationally reputed forensic scientist. In many years of experiments and observations at crematoria, he has put on record that this never happens to skulls exposed to normal radiation of intense heat – they either become swollen, or break into pieces. And even after 12 hours continuously in a heat of 3000°F, he says bones have never been known to disappear altogether: they shatter into small calcined fragments that can still be identified as bones.

So something beyond the effects of normal fire is evidently happening; and looking at the historical accounts of spontaneous human combustion, it is clear that although broadly similar, there are elements unique to each case – almost capriciously so, as if the phenomenon was wilfully defying classification and analysis. In the 17th and early 18th Centuries, the theory

was that it was caused by heavy drinking.
'Two noblemen', said one report, 'died after a
drinking bout of suffocation by the flames which
issued with great violence from their stomachs.'
But it soon became recognized by many writers to
be more mysterious and widespread than this.
Zola, Marryat, Melville, de Quincey, and
Dickens all mentioned it in their books, the latter
being particularly impressed by the well-known
case in 1763 of the Contessa Cornelia di Bandi,
whose death was discovered by her maid after
pulling back the bedroom curtains one morning:

'She saw her corpse on the floor in the most
dreadful condition. At the distance of four feet
from the bed there was a heap of ashes. Her legs,
with the stockings on, remained untouched, and
the head, half-burned, lay between them.
Nearly all the rest of the body was reduced to
ashes. The air in the room was charged with
floating soot. A small oil lamp on the floor was
covered with ashes, but had no oil in it; and in
two candlesticks, which stood upright upon a
table, the cotton wick of both the candles was
left, and the tallow of both had disappeared.'

In this case, the alarm had been given by

neighbours who saw a yellowish smoke coming
from the room, its smell apparently terrifying the
Contessa's lap-dog. This colour is unusual.
More often, a bluish flame is reported, as with
the Paris house-painter in 1851 who bet he could
eat a lighted candle: 'Scarcely had he placed it in
his mouth when he uttered a slight cry, and a
bluish fame was seen upon his lips ... In half an
hour the head and upper portion of the chest were
entirely carbonized. The fire did not cease until
bones, skin and muscles were all consumed, and
nothing remained but a small heap of ashes.'

So it was with Professor James Hamilton of the
Mathematics Department at Nashville
University in 1835, who seems to have been one
of the rare people to have extinguished a
spontaneous fire. Feeling a sharp stinging pain in
his left leg, he looked down and saw a bright flame
about 10 centimetres long spurting up like a
powerful cigarette lighter. Slapping it had no
effect, but pressing his hand hard over it to cut off
the oxygen gradually extinguished it.

Official 'accidents'

Just how many indisputable cases there have
been in the last century is uncertain.
Ivan Sanderson, the English traveller and
biologist who founded the Society for the
Investigation of the Unexplained in New Jersey
in 1967, compiled a list of some two dozen from
various sources; he stressed that this was
incomplete – indeed, probably only the tip of the
iceberg, since so many cases would go
unrecognized by coroners and fire departments
prepared to identify them as 'accidental deaths',
and leave the matter at that. They include the
case of Mrs Mary Carpenter, in a boat on the
Norfolk Broads in the summer of 1938, who
suddenly burst into flames and was reduced to
ashes in front of her husband and children.
They and the boat were unharmed. Charles Fort,
the American writer who spent a lifetime
collecting the world's odd and inexplicable
happenings, noted several more cases, including
that of Mrs Euphemia Johnson, a 68-year-old
widow living in the London suburb of
Sydenham. Her calcined bones were found lying
in a heap within her undamaged clothes on a
summer morning in 1922.

However, it is evidently an uncommon event, and
one into which there has been very little serious
research. A link with geomagnetic variations has
been suggested by the American, Livingston
Gearhart, in an article for *Pursuit*, the journal of
the Society for the Investigation of the
Unexplained. He took as his base the data
collected each day by the US National Oceanic
and Atmospheric Administration in Boulder,

Six cases of human
combustion correlated
with magnetic activity
on Earth
(after Livingston
Gearhart).

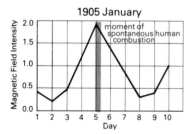

1905 January

Elizabeth Clark, found dying
of burns in an unscorched room.
She could not explain.

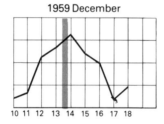

1959 December

Billy Peterson, third degree
burns of body and internal
burns; clothing not singed.

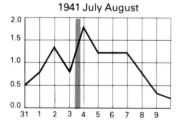

1941 July August

Lois Irene Chapman 'found
sitting dead on burning davenport'.
Little damage to surroundings.

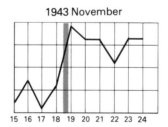

1943 November

Madge Knight, severely burned
in bed with unscorched sheets.
(Died 6 December).

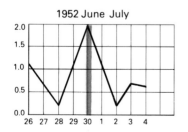

1952 June July

Unidentifiable man 'burned
beyond recognition' in a
car that did not burn.

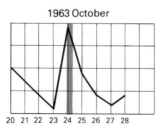

1963 October

Olga Worth, burned to death
in a car that did not burn.

Colorado; observatories all over the world send in readings of the Earth's magnetic field strength in their area, and these are then combined to provide a global average for that particular day. The scale goes in decimal points from 0 (quiet) to 2 (magnetic storm). In six cases where he was able to establish the time of a spontaneous human combustion, he found each one coincided with a sharp increase of magnetic intensity over the previous couple of days.

This may be a valuable first step towards understanding the phenomenon. Weak magnetic fields can indeed have unpredictable and not always benign effects on living things (page 18); and the biological mechanism by which magnetic changes work in the body is not understood at all. So perhaps the sudden strange fire generated during spontaneous human combustion is some kind of molecular or chemical disintegration, triggered by a magnetic change, and giving off a certain amount of localized heat while the process takes place.

But this in no way explains why it happens so seldom; nor, perhaps, why the localized fires, once started, do not spread. Many writers, seeking a solution, have drawn a parallel with the way that it appears suddenly, as if from another dimension, like poltergeist behaviour. Certainly, many of the cases have irrational elements that would be very hard to contain within the orthodox framework of science, or even the usual concepts of space and time.

History of a spontaneous human exaggeration

In March 1955, a *Fate* magazine article on unexplained fire deaths listed two for April 1938: George Turner, a lorry-driver in Upton-by-Chester in northern Britain found burned to a cinder in his cabin with a can of petrol unignited beside him; and Willem ten Bruik at the wheel of his Volkswagen near Nijmegen in Holland. A third fire disaster in 1938 was 'discovered' by the *Sunday Star-Ledger* of Newark, New Jersey, in 1966 – John Greeley, at the helm of the *Ulrich* off the coast of Cornwall; amazingly, the 'triple finger of fire' happened on the same day, 7 April. Since then the story has appeared many times, most recently in Michael Harrison's *Fire From Heaven*, where he also notes the coincidence of a perfect isosceles triangle connecting the events. Alas for truth, diligent local enquiries have established that there is no record in Cheshire of the death of George Turner, lorry-driver; the Volkswagen factory was not started until May 1938; and no ship named *Ulrich* has ever been on Lloyds Register.

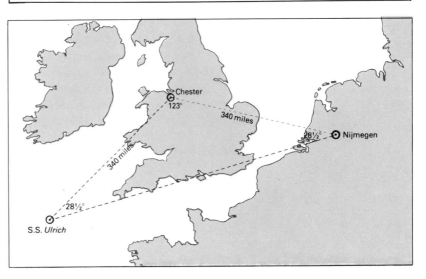

Balls of fire

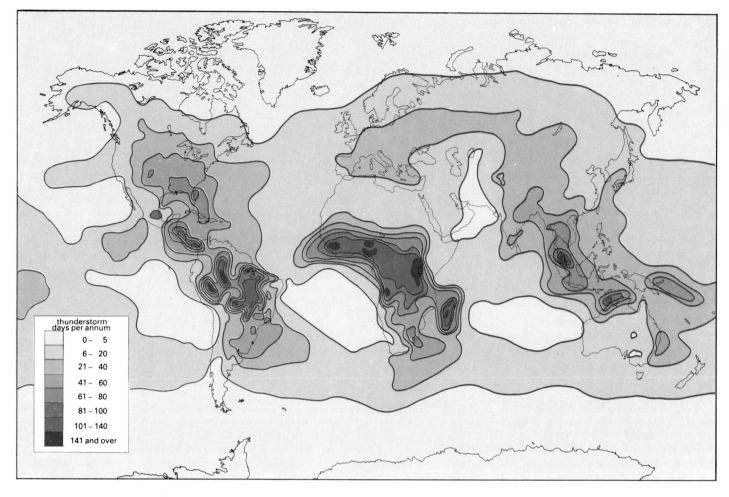

thunderstorm
days per annum

	0 – 5
	6 – 20
	21 – 40
	41 – 60
	61 – 80
	81 – 100
	101 – 140
	141 and over

**Distribution of number
of thunderstorm days
has been plotted by the
World Meteorological
Organization in Geneva.**

Around 5 a.m. on a cold March morning in
1963, a solitary passenger and air hostess
were dozing in their seats on Eastern
Airlines Flight 539 from New York to
Washington, on opposite sides of the cabin aisle.
Their seat belts were firmly fastened, the captain
having warned of thunderstorms and turbulence
– rightly so, since they were both jerked suddenly
wide awake by a brilliant crack of lightning that
seemed to strike and envelop the whole
aeroplane. Even seasoned fliers, who know that
such an incident rarely causes severe damage, can
nevertheless be unnerved by the sudden surprise
of such an explosion; but what happened next
was still more scary – ghostly, even. Out of the
door leading to the pilot's cabin came a glowing,
symmetrical sphere about 20 centimetres in
diameter, blue-white in colour, and hovering
about knee-height above the carpeted floor.
As the two passengers watched, it moved steadily
down the aisle, passed between them, and
disappeared towards the lavatory at the far end of
the plane. A UFO? A spectral vision?
Spots before the eyes? The air hostess said
afterwards that although she had been terrified,
she was convinced the eerie globe was something
to do with the thunderstorm. The passenger said
firmly: 'I had no alcohol on this flight.'
In fact, what they both saw was a particularly

remarkable example of a phenomenon known as
ball lightning, in which a self-contained bright
light, usually spherical but sometimes pear-
shaped, fuzzy at the edges and in a variety of
colours, hovers, bounces, or moves erratically
about before disappearing – often with a loud
bang and a smell of ozone, sulphur or nitrogen
oxide. The average speed works out at around
two metres per second, and the duration may
range from several seconds to several minutes.
There is no accepted scientific explanation for
these balls of fire. Indeed, as with most
phenomena for which there is no agreed theory,
many scientists have refused to believe in them at
all, trying to rationalize them away as
hallucinations or the result of hysteria.
What made this event more interesting than
most was not just that it took place, impossibly
it would seem, in the sealed confines of an
all-metal aeroplane, but because the passenger
was exceptionally well qualified to observe it,
being Professor R. C. Jennison of the Electronics
Laboratories at the University of Kent, Canterbury.
Thus he was able to make careful observations of
its dimensions and velocity, and also noted that it
gave off little heat and was probably not magnetic
in nature, since a pen-knife and tobacco tin in
his jacket pocket were not affected. In due course
his account of the incident was accepted for

publication by the learned scientific journal *Nature*, and since then the subject of ball lightning has become an increasingly respectable, if no less baffling, subject for scientific investigation.

Unique properties

What makes ball lightning so odd is that nothing else in physics behaves in the same way. Dr Neil Charman, of the Manchester Institute of Science and Technology, summarizing the properties of a 'typical' ball for the *New Scientist*, said that local air currents did not affect it, it often spun, and although not apparently giving off much heat when in motion, it nevertheless released heat when it disappeared. 'Some lightning balls display an affinity for metal objects and may move along conductors such as wires or metal fences. Others appear within buildings, passing through closed doors and windows with curious ease. Again, chimneys, fireplaces and ovens seem to be favoured haunts for these exotic objects. It is remarkable that several reports exist of the appearance of a ball within an all-metal aircraft. In at least one case, the ball was apparently seen to enter and leave the aircraft without causing any damage; since the aircraft in question was a tanker loaded with aviation fuel, the relief of the pilot can be imagined.'

Among the many uncertainties about the nature of lightning balls is the question of just how often they happen. The standard reference book on the subject contains almost 600 well-observed accounts, in which the size of the ball ranges from one centimetre to more than one metre. A survey of 4000 NASA personnel indicated that they might occur much more commonly than had been thought – 'the occurrence may be nearly as frequent as that of ordinary cloud-to-ground strokes.' This seems unlikely. In 1975, three scientists at Wyoming University examined 100,000 photographs of lightning strokes, and uncovered only six that had unusual, ball-like qualities. Even so, there are around 13 million lightning strokes on Earth every day, which suggests a global annual total for ball lightning approaching 300,000.

Degrees of danger

Scientific opinion now is coming round to the opinion that fireballs are relatively benign. A characteristic event took place in August 1975, from which some energy calculations could be made. A young housewife was in the kitchen of her home in the Midlands town of Smethwick when a sphere of light appeared over the cooker; it was about 10 centimetres across, and surrounded by a flame-coloured halo; its colour was bright blue to purple. The ball moved straight towards her, staying about a metre above the ground, too quickly for her to get out of the way: 'The ball seemed to hit me below the belt, as it were, and I automatically brushed it from me and it just disappeared. Where I brushed it away there was a redness and swelling on my left hand. It seemed as if my gold wedding ring was burning into my finger.' The ball went off with a bang, and scorched a small hole in her skirt, but she was otherwise unaffected. However, the effects of fireballs when they hit highly-inflammable fuel stores can certainly be lethal; the research department of Amoco Oil has collected several examples of trucks, barges, and even large tankers exploding after contact with a lightning ball.

As for how and why they occur, there are as many theories as there are physics departments investigating the phenomenon. It is not known whether the energy source comes from within the ball, or whether an external form of energy somehow compresses the ball and sustains it during its life. Nor is it known if the energy is electric, electromagnetic, nuclear, or from some other source; even minute fragments of meteoritic anti-matter from the upper atmosphere have been suggested.

While remaining for the time being a puzzle, the existence of ball lightning may help to explain at least two other phenomena. In spontaneous human combustion, it is possible to imagine the process being started by a fireball. Perhaps a large one, colliding with a human being, might affect the body in much the same way as a microwave oven would, cooking the tissue inside and leaving the outer covering untouched; after this, a so far unknown physiological process of disintegration would set in, rather as it does in some cases when forked lightning strikes people. Secondly, fireballs are more and more often being given as an explanation for some pilot sightings of UFOs – trying to solve one mystery, you might say, by invoking another.

Rare photograph by M. R. Lyons of object believed to be ball lightning.

The Venus effect

The world we live in is not a stable place. Continents shift under our feet; the magnetic field around us, switching unpredictably, alters the course of evolution; from time to time, some unknown factor in the environment causes individual people to disintegrate without warning, their remains forming a small pile of greasy ash; thunderbolts of ball lightning hover and strike at random over the Earth's surface. And although all these phenomena took a long time to become respectable scientific subjects, and nobody understands them properly, each is now being minutely examined with the aim of bringing it within the framework of knowledge.

So it does not seem altogether irrational to consider the idea that the solar system itself might be equally subject to sudden change – that the disposition of the Sun and its planets, including Earth, has not always been exactly as we see it today. In 1950, just this suggestion was made. Immanuel Velikovsky's newly-published book *Worlds In Collision* proposed that Venus was (in the astronomical time-scale) a very recent addition to our universe; spun off from Jupiter, it had settled into its present orbit less than 4000 years ago – the kind of theory, an outsider might think, that would either be ignored as being too lunatic for serious consideration, or alternatively put on the list of bizarre possibilities which future research would one day prove or disprove. Unpleasantly, something else happened. The book was certainly not ignored; but neither was it seriously examined or debated. Instead, it (and its immediate successors *Earth in Upheaval* and *Ages in Chaos*) created a blind academic furore on a scale perhaps unprecedented since the raging 19th-century arguments over the literal truth of the Bible versus the evolutionary findings of *The Origin of Species*. Velikovsky himself anticipated this in the Preface to his book: 'Harmony or stability in the celestial and terrestrial spheres is the point of departure of the present-day concept of the world as expressed in the celestial mechanics of Newton and the theory of evolution of Darwin. If these two men of science are sacrosanct, this book is a heresy.'

Outrageous theory

He was not overstating the case. His single, fundamental hypothesis – that the orbit of Venus had approached closely to Earth within historic times, causing catastrophic effects on life here – was as outrageous as those of Galileo and Copernicus in the Middle Ages. What was unpleasant was the scientific community's immediate reaction – or rather, over-reaction. Professor Harlow Shapley, director of Harvard College Observatory, said bluntly: 'If Dr Velikovsky is right, the rest of us are crazy.'

Dean B. McLaughlin, Professor of Astronomy at the University of Michigan, wrote to Velikovsky's publishers protesting furiously against the 'promulgation of such *lies* – yes, *lies*, as are contained in wholesale lots in *Worlds In Collision*'.

Yet neither man had gone so far as to read the book, as indeed they made a point of saying. Instead of doing so, they joined with others in an academic pressure group that succeeded in persuading the publishers to drop it; taken up by another publisher, it became a best-seller. The attempt to suppress the book's ideas rebounded. To the frustration of the hierarchy, Velikovsky became a phenomenon in his own right.

Biblical truths

By any standards, he was always an extraordinary man. Born in Vitebsk, Russia, on 10 June 1895, he learned several languages as a child, travelled widely for his studies, which included law and ancient history, before graduating in medicine in 1921. A distinguished European and Israeli academic and medical career, particularly in psychoanalysis, brought him to America in 1939. Here, during researches into early Israelite history, he became convinced that certain sections of the Old Testament of the Bible were literally true; they described the catastrophic events caused by Earth's near-collision with another heavenly body. Either the Earth's rotation stopped briefly, or its axis tilted, causing floods and disasters. Joshua was reporting the accurate truth when he said: 'The Sun stood still in the midst of Heaven and did not go down about a whole day.'

Immanuel Velikovsky, whose theories on the origin of Venus strike at the foundation of many sciences.

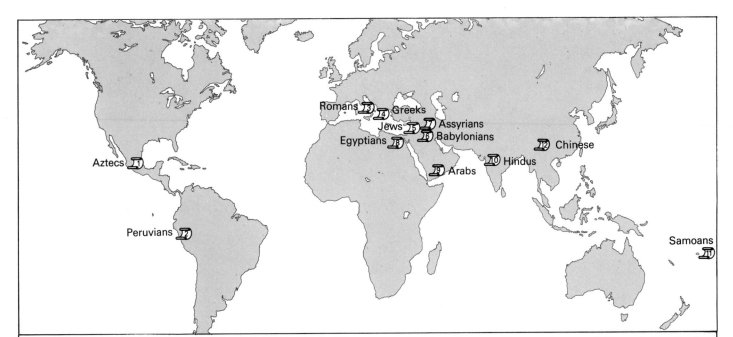

1 Venus was called 'the star that smoked' and Quetzalcoatl ('Feathered Serpent') – 'the sun refused to show itself and during four days the world was deprived of light. Then a great star appeared; it was given the name Quetzalcoatl . . . a great number of people . . . died of famine and pestilence.'

2 Venus was called Chaska – 'the wavy haired'.

3 Tradition said that 'in the well-known star Venus . . . there occurred so strange a prodigy that it changed its colour, size, form and course; which never happened before nor since', during the time of Moses.

4 Myths tell how Phaethon ('Blazing Star') nearly destroyed the world with fire, and then was transformed into the planet Venus. Afterwards the world was flooded.

5 The *Talmud*: 'Fire is hanging down from the planet Venus.' *Midrash*: 'The brilliant light of Venus blazes from one end of the cosmos to the other.'

6 The Sumerians addressed Venus as the 'Wild Cow', 'Supreme One, who are Inanna of heaven and earth, who rains flaming fire over the land . . . You have filled the land with venom, like a dragon.' The Chaldaeans: 'Queen of heaven', 'bright torch of heaven', 'a stupendous prodigy in the sky'.

7 Venus (Ishtar) was called 'the fearful dragon', 'who is clothed in fire and bears aloft a crown of fearful splendour'.

8 The Arabs called Venus Zebbaj – 'one with hair', and offered human sacrifices to it.

9 Venus was known as Sekhmet, the lion-faced goddess of destruction, 'a circling star which scatters its flame in fire . . . a flame of fire in her tempest'. Myths told how Sekhmet had once tried to destroy the human race.

10 The *Vedas* say that Venus looked like 'fire and smoke'; 'As a bull thou hurlest thy fire upon earth and heaven.'

11 'The planet Venus became wild and horns grew out of her head.'

12 In the reign of the Emperor Yao a 'miracle is said to have happened that the sun during a span of ten days did not set, the forests were ignited' and 'the entire land was flooded'. In Yao's reign 'a brilliant star issued from the constellation Yin'.

For this to be proved, he had to find similar legends elsewhere, except that on the other side of the globe these would logically be about a time when the Sun failed to rise. And find them he did, in ancient documents from pre-Columbian America, China, India, Iran, Babylon, Iceland, Finland, Greece and Rome. Mexican manuscripts told how the Sun did not appear for a four-fold night. Other legends seemed to parallel the plagues and upheavals described in the Bible, and which Velikovsky saw as being natural events preceding the near-collision.

Out of all this came Velikovsky's vast reconstruction of history. Venus, he decided, was the cause of the cataclysm, for in ancient mythology Jupiter and Venus represented deities of paramount importance. Moreover, nearly all the ancients recounted stories of the birth of Venus, which was traditionally grouped in a trinity with the Sun and the Moon – a strange association if it was always as small and distant as it appears today.

He told his story of the times when Venus approached in a style that was excitingly – almost provocatively – unacademic, writing of 'hurricanes of global magnitude, of forests burning and swept away, of dust, stones, fire and ashes falling from the sky, of mountains melting like wax, of lava flowing from riven ground, of boiling seas, of bituminous rain, of shaking ground and destroyed cities, of humans seeking refuge in caverns and fissures of the rock in the mountains, of oceans upheaved and falling on the land, of tidal waves moving towards the poles and back . . .'

Such language is not the means by which scientists normally communicate with one another, and this boldness in pursuing and describing the living consequences of his theory was one reason why the scientific establishment scorned him. But also, his ideas struck at the foundations of a large number of sciences – notably astronomy, geology, and ancient history – in a time when each discipline was becoming increasingly specialized and resistant to innovation. 'The claim of universal efficacy or universal knowledge is the unmistakeable mark

The planet Venus was described throughout the ancient world as an intensely bright, comet-like body – myths told of its birth and the effects on the Earth.

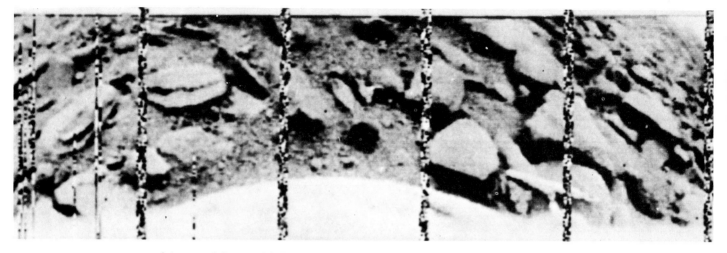

The rocky surface of Venus, photographed by the Russian space probe *Venera 9,* described as 'surprisingly young-looking'. How does such bright sunlight penetrate the thick cloud cover?

of the quack,' wrote McLaughlin. 'No man today can hope to correct the mistakes in any more than a small sub-field of science. And yet Velikovsky claims to be able to dispute the basic principle of several sciences! These are indeed delusions of grandeur!'

Neither of these criticisms can nowadays be seen as just. Velikovsky's books are amply annotated, so that anyone can check his references (unlike Darwin's *The Origin of Species*, he has wryly noted); and if in describing the consequences of catastrophe he erred on the side of the dramatic, this at least demonstrates the courage of his conclusions. For there is no doubt concerning the fundamental challenge he was throwing out. In 1950, the theory of uniformitarianism was in full flood, holding that all geological features on Earth must be explained as being the result of a gradual process moulding the landscape as we see it today. Velikovsky said this must be modified by his theory of catastrophism: random, rare, violent events had had profound effects on our evolution, and would do so again.

Catastrophic events
Since 1950, scientists have reluctantly become much more receptive to this. A catastrophe of some sort split the giant continent of Pangaea (page 15); magnetic polarity reversals (page 17) can be regarded as catastrophic; some of the Earth's biggest craters, such as the Diablo Canyon in America, are now thought to have been caused by huge meteors (page 182); the possibility of an axis tilt, brought about by near-collision with a large cosmic body, and causing great cracks in the Earth's surface, is discussed calmly.

Yet at the same time Velikovsky is still largely ignored or derided. His most adamant critics, such as Professor Carl Sagan of Cornell University, conclude that 'where Velikovsky is original, he is very likely wrong; and where he is right, the idea has been pre-empted by earlier workers.' This is in spite of an extraordinary

number of predictions, outrageous when they were made, which space explorations have proved true. Dr William T. Plummer of Massachusetts University wrote in *Science*: 'Some of the least expected discoveries made by planetary astronomers in recent years were correctly predicted by Velikovsky. He argued that Jupiter should be a likely source of radio waves, that the Earth should have a magnetosphere, that the surface of Venus should be hot, that Venus might exhibit an anomalous rotation, and that Venus should be surrounded by a blanket of petroleum hydrocarbons. All except the last of these predictions have been verified, most of them by accident.'

Why, then, are Velikovsky's theories still not considered worthy of serious consideration? Partly, perhaps, because of what Arthur Koestler, another inter-disciplinarian, has described as 'the inertia of professionals with a vested interest in tradition and in the monopoly of learning'. Partly, too, because so many of his predictions are vague or tentative ('Venus is hot', 'Venus may have an anomalous rotation'); and because some of his most crucial predictions have not yet been proved true – indeed may even be incapable of proof. For instance, although most scientists say hydrocarbons have not been found in the atmosphere of Venus, Velikovsky continues to argue that a different interpretation of the evidence shows that they are in fact present. Who is to say if he is right – or wrong?

The arguments between the two sides (for Velikovsky now has an increasing number of high-powered supporters) is summarized on the next pages. What is notable are the drastic modifications which scientists have been forced to make to their theoretical models in order to accommodate the new discoveries of the space age. At the same time many of these discoveries were predicted by Velikovsky as far back as 1950, all deriving from a unified theory, which in its main points has yet to be refuted.

Velikovsky's predictions

Possible sequence of orbits leading to present situation of planets (after C. H. Ransom and L. H. Hoffee).

'*Some of these predictions were said to be impossible when you made them. All of them were predicted long before proof that they were correct came to hand. Conversely I do not know of any specific prediction you made that has since been proven to be false.*' – the late H. H. Hess, chairman, Space Science Board, National Academy of Science, in a letter to Velikovsky for public record, 1963.

The birth of Venus

Venus is a young planet, split off from Jupiter not many thousands of years ago. It approached close to Earth in the 15th Century BC, and appeared to be threatening Earth about every 52 years afterwards, until during the 9/8th Century BC it almost collided with Mars. Mars then threatened Earth a number of times with close approaches. Gradually the orbits adjusted themselves until, in the 7th Century BC they reached their present equilibrium.

Objection *Nonsense. All the planets were formed and fixed in their present position billions of years ago, about the same time as Earth. The odds against multiple planetary near-collisions are 10^{23} to 1.* (C. Sagan) *The mathematical laws of celestial mechanics make the changed orbits of Venus and Mars dynamically impossible.* (I. Asimov and others)

Response Professor Robert W. Bass, one of the world's leading astrophysicists, has demonstrated convincingly that the changes in the solar system suggested by Velikovsky are compatible with traditional celestial mechanics: Carl Sagan, opposing this, has compounded a statistical fallacy, and also ignores the effects of the law of gravity when planets approach each other. The Ransom/Hoffee orbits (see illustration) are one possible way for the planets to have reached their present positions. And you cannot mathematically predict stability in the planetary system for more than 300 years.

Heat of Venus

Prediction Velikovsky said there was no theoretical problem about the surprise discovery by astronomers in 1926 that the cloud cover on the night side of Venus had the same temperature (about 25°C) as the sunlit side. The cause of the temperature was that Venus itself was hot (indeed, being a young planet, very hot). It had generated heat during its explosive rupture from Jupiter, and during its close encounters with Earth and Mars; it had not yet cooled down, and because of its origin, might have an anomalous rotation. It would have a massive atmosphere, and sunlight would hardly penetrate the cloud cover.

First objection (in the 1950s, following publication of *Worlds In Collision*) *Wrong. The*

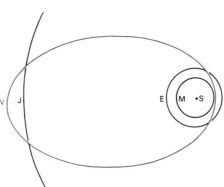

The 'proto-planet' Venus on a comet-like orbit after its explusion from Jupiter.

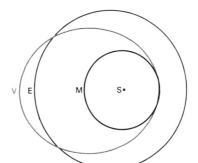

The orbit of Venus after its encounters with the Earth in the 15th Century BC, until the 9th/8th Century BC.

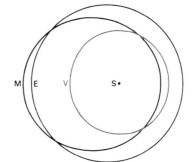

Venus has settled into an orbit inside that of the Earth; 9th/8th Century BC. Now the orbit of Mars has been disturbed.

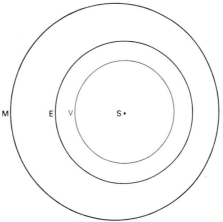

Present 'stable' configuration of the planets.

	S	Sun
E	Orbit of the Earth	
V	" "	Venus
M	" "	Mars
J	" "	Jupiter

only heat on Venus comes from the Sun. The night side of the cloud cover remains the same as the day side probably because Venus rotates more quickly than we had thought; there is no reason to suggest it rotates in a different direction from the other planets. Its atmosphere is if anything lighter than the Earth's, and the history of the two planets 'should be very similar'. (H. Urey and others)

Second objection (in the 1960s, after space probes had confirmed all Velikovsky's predictions above: Venus was indeed very hot – around 400–500°C – rotated backwards, and had a massive atmosphere, as was dramatically proved when it crushed *Venera 3*.) *OK, it's hot. We knew that all along. A scientist called Rupert Wildt said it was hot in 1940. It is caused by a 'greenhouse effect' – carbon dioxide in the atmosphere of Venus traps the sunlight like glass. You can see the sunlight in the Russian space photographs.* (C. Sagan and others)

Response Wildt's views were widely ignored at the time. In any case, the temperatures generated by his theories were no more than 93–135°C (subsequently modified to 77°C) at the tropical midday surface, and gave an average surface temperature for the entire planet of −23°C. Subsequent attempts to explain Venus's extreme heat by an 'enhanced' greenhouse effect (C. Sagan) or a 'runaway' greenhouse effect (S. I. Raspool and C. de Bergh) depend on a significant amount of water vapour in the atmosphere, for which there is no evidence. As for the photographs, the Russians have not revealed if *Venera 9* was carrying its own lighting, nor even the wavelengths at which the images were made; the shadows from the rocks look too sharp to be caused by sunlight diffused to about one per cent by cloud.

Hydrocarbons on Venus

Prediction As described in the Bible and elsewhere, the comet-like appearance of Venus, and falls from the sky of fire, dust, manna, and pestilence, means that the atmosphere of Venus 'must be rich in petroleum gases. If and as long as Venus is too hot for the liquefaction of petroleum, the hydrocarbons will circulate in gaseous form.'

Objection *Venus is not a comet, it's a planet. A comet is a heavenly body of unknown origin with an eccentric orbit, a long gaseous tail, and a relatively small mass [e.g. smaller than the mass of the Moon]. Infra-red reflection analysis of the upper atmosphere of Venus shows no evidence of hydrocarbons, and is entirely consistent with a cloud layer made of very small or slender ice particles.* (W. T. Plummer)

Response Venus was always described as comet-like in ancient literature, which is why Velikovsky adopted the word; in any case, the

Mayan hieroglyph of 'burning water' (i.e. petroleum), often associated with the planet Venus.

upper limit of the mass of large comets is disputed – one estimate (Bobrovnikoff) puts it at 10^{24} grams, which approaches the 10^{27} grams of Venus. Although evidence of hydrocarbons has yet to be produced, Plummer's negative finding is not conclusive, and his suggestion of ice crystals is not nowadays generally accepted; the lower atmosphere of Venus, separated from the upper atmosphere by a cloud layer 15 kilometres thick, has so far proved too inaccessible to be fully analysed, and may well contain vaporized hydrocarbons (Velikovsky and others).

The solar system

Prediction Space is not a vacuum. The forces of electromagnetism have played as important a part in the formation of the solar system as gravity. The Sun carries a powerful electric charge. Jupiter will be found to emit radio noises. The Earth itself has a powerful magnetosphere that extends at least as far as the Moon.

First objection (in the 1950s) *Velikovsky was compared to flat-earthers and accused of inventing 'electromagnetic forces capable of doing precisely what he wants them to do. There is no scientific evidence whatever for the powers of these forces.'* (M. Gardner). *His electrical model of the Sun was said to require an 'impossible' charge of 10^{19} volts.* (D. Menzel)

Second objection (in the 1960s, after space probes had conclusively proved Velikovsky right about electromagnetic forces and the Earth's magnetosphere; after Jupiter's radio waves had been recorded and the Sun's electrical potential had been calculated, independently, at 10^{19} volts) *OK, so he was lucky with some of his guesses.*

Response They weren't guesses; they were deductive predictions based on a coherent, if unorthodox, theory of the solar system.

Effect on Moon and Mars

Prediction Space landings on the Moon and Mars will show various consequences of the catastrophes that occurred less than 3500 years ago. There will be found: hydrocarbons; magnetism in the Moon's rocks, caused by them having been heated during the event; excessive amounts of neon and argon; evidence from core samples that the Moon was heated during historic times.

Objection (after all these predictions except the last had come true) *While these surprising facts have now been established, they are not consequences of catastrophe. There are other ways in which they could have arisen. Nor are they recent. Various tests show the rocks on the Moon to have been formed more than four billion years ago.* (D. York and others)

Response Catastrophe is much the simplest and most consistent way of explaining these

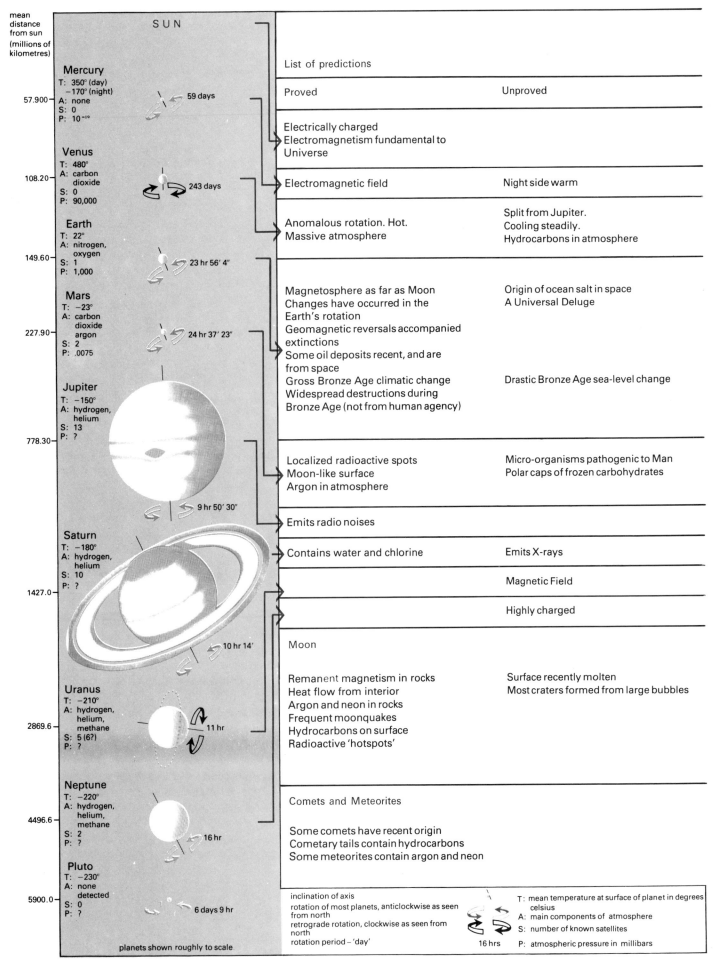

mean
distance
from sun
(millions of
kilometres)

SUN

Mercury
T: 350° (day)
   −170° (night)
A: none
S: 0
P: 10⁻¹⁰

57.900 — 59 days

Venus
T: 480°
A: carbon
   dioxide
S: 0
P: 90,000

108.20 — 243 days

Earth
T: 22°
A: nitrogen,
   oxygen
S: 1
P: 1,000

149.60 — 23 hr 56′ 4″

Mars
T: −23°
A: carbon
   dioxide
   argon
S: 2
P: .0075

227.90 — 24 hr 37′ 23″

Jupiter
T: −150°
A: hydrogen,
   helium
S: 13
P: ?

778.30 — 9 hr 50′ 30″

Saturn
T: −180°
A: hydrogen,
   helium
S: 10
P: ?

1427.0 — 10 hr 14′

Uranus
T: −210°
A: hydrogen,
   helium,
   methane
S: 5 (6?)
P: ?

2869.6 — 11 hr

Neptune
T: −220°
A: hydrogen,
   helium,
   methane
S: 2
P: ?

4496.6 — 16 hr

Pluto
T: −230°
A: none
   detected
S: 0
P: ?

5900.0 — 6 days 9 hr

planets shown roughly to scale

List of predictions

Proved	Unproved
Electrically charged Electromagnetism fundamental to Universe	
Electromagnetic field	Night side warm
Anomalous rotation. Hot. Massive atmosphere	Split from Jupiter. Cooling steadily. Hydrocarbons in atmosphere
Magnetosphere as far as Moon Changes have occurred in the Earth's rotation Geomagnetic reversals accompanied extinctions Some oil deposits recent, and are from space Gross Bronze Age climatic change Widespread destructions during Bronze Age (not from human agency)	Origin of ocean salt in space A Universal Deluge Drastic Bronze Age sea-level change
Localized radioactive spots Moon-like surface Argon in atmosphere	Micro-organisms pathogenic to Man Polar caps of frozen carbohydrates
Emits radio noises	
Contains water and chlorine	Emits X-rays
	Magnetic Field
	Highly charged

Moon

Remanent magnetism in rocks Heat flow from interior Argon and neon in rocks Frequent moonquakes Hydrocarbons on surface Radioactive 'hotspots'	Surface recently molten Most craters formed from large bubbles

Comets and Meteorites

Some comets have recent origin
Cometary tails contain hydrocarbons
Some meteorites contain argon and neon

inclination of axis
rotation of most planets, anticlockwise as seen
from north
retrograde rotation, clockwise as seen from
north
rotation period – 'day'

16 hrs

T: mean temperature at surface of planet in degrees
   celsius
A: main components of atmosphere
S: number of known satellites
P: atmospheric pressure in millibars

The surface of Mars, pitted with craters as predicted by Velikovsky.

(above right)
The rayed crater of Tycho on the moon, perhaps the result of an interplanetary lightning bolt.

(right)
Quetzalcoatl, the name given by ancient Mexicans to the planet Venus. Records describe its approach to Earth.

anomalies, so why not consider it? It isn't a question of when the rocks were formed, but when they were most recently heated – and there is as yet no satisfactory method of finding this out. The core sample test shows heating at around 8000 BC, and this date may have to be adjusted to make it more recent. At least five separate pieces of evidence from Moon rocks suggest recent heating (Velikovsky).

Effects on the Earth
Prediction The close approach of other celestial bodies has reversed the Earth's magnetic field many times, even as late as the 15th and 8th Centuries BC – as was shown by the work of G. Folgheraiter, who found evidence of a reversed field in Greek and Etruscan vases of the mid-8th Century BC.
Objection *Geomagnetic reversals are not caused by the approach of other large bodies. There is no evidence of geomagnetic reversals in recent times from archaeological material. [As stated in* Nature, *6 October 1972.] Folgheraiter was wrong in his conclusions – the pottery was simply fired upside-down, which is what E. Thellier deduced from Carthaginian pottery of the same date with*

apparent 'reversed magnetism' (editor of *Science News* and others).
Response Many scientists (including Harold Urey, one of Velikovsky's most bitter critics) now believe that geomagnetic reversals are caused by interaction with external bodies, such as comets or groups of large meteorites. In the very issue of *Nature* cited above, a reversal was reported from an Australian Aboriginal fireplace (Lake Mungo) around 30,000 BC; since then a reversal around 12,500 BC has been confirmed, and *Nature* reported a geomagnetic 'event' of roughly the 9th Century BC, which its discoverers linked with that claimed by Folgheraiter and Velikovsky (page 18).
Prediction Ancient civilizations were simultaneously overthrown by vast natural upheavals, which marked the ends of the Old, Middle and Late Bronze Age periods; this was exactly the conclusion reached independently in 1948 by the eminent French archaeologist Claude Schaeffer, who wrote: 'Our enquiry has demonstrated that these repeated crises . . . were not caused by the action of man.'
Objection *These were the result of extensive earthquakes, not cosmic catastrophes.*
Response Only if one ignores the testimony of all the ancients who thought global disasters were sky-borne. Even Carl Sagan has admitted: 'I find the concatenation of legends which Velikovsky has accumulated stunning . . . My own position is that if twenty percent of the legendary concordances which Velikovsky produces are real, there is something important to be explained.'

Section two
The emergence of man

Of all the learned disciplines, the disputatious world of those who study the beginnings of man is perhaps the most unsure of itself. After more than a century, the accepted dogma of Darwinism is still hopelessly inadequate as an explanation for a host of evolutionary oddities, and the missing link between ourselves and our ape-like forebears is as far as ever from being discovered. With each newly discovered skull, there are endless arguments as to whether it represents an 'ape-man', or a 'man-ape', or neither. Orthodox estimates of when our branch of the family tree first started growing range from 25 million to five million years ago. Nobody knows where modern man was cradled, nor how and why our brains took the qualitative leap that has made us unique among creatures on Earth.

The reasons for all this doubt and uncertainty boil down to two: the poverty of evidence, and the difficulty of dating what little evidence there is. Anthropologists are inclined to base large claims on tiny remains, and very often their deductions are wildly wrong. At the notorious 'monkey' trial in 1925, John Scopes, a high-school teacher in Dayton, Tennessee, was indicted for the crime of teaching Darwinian evolution in defiance of a State law that required the Biblical version to be taught. Although the prosecution was ridiculed and in the end humiliated, we can see now that the evidence for the Darwinian defence was surprisingly thin: two fossil skulls, some small pieces of thigh-bone, and a broken molar tooth – in fact, the total fossil evidence available at the time for human species earlier than *Homo sapiens*.

One skull and thigh-bone, of Java Man, has since been proved genuinely old (though how old is not certain, since its discoverer, Eugene Dubois, was so terrified of the pious wrath of his two elderly sisters that he kept the fossils hidden under floorboards for 30 years and muddled the records of the excavation). The second skull, of Piltdown Man, was a ludicrously obvious forgery. The molar tooth, from which an elaborate reconstruction of our supposed forebears Mr and Mrs Hesperopithecus was made (page 37), was unfortunately later found to have come from an extinct pig.

That was more than 50 years ago, and things don't seem to have changed much. In 1970 an age-blackened piece of lower jaw was discovered by Bryan Patterson of Harvard's Museum of Comparative Zoology, on Lothagam Hill in Kenya. For the following six years it was widely recognized as 'the oldest hominid fossil yet known apart from *Ramapithecus*' – an exciting discovery, indeed. In June 1977, *Current Anthropology* announced laconically that new measurements showed it could not after all have come from an early type of man; it was from a chimpanzee or gorilla instead.

Similar doubts surround the scientific dating methods now used. Radiocarbon dating is helpful back to around 50,000 BC (although it is always worth making an allowance of a couple of thousand years either side of the given date; recently, the shell of a living oyster gave a radiocarbon date of 600 BC). Then there is a huge hiatus back to around 400,000 BC. Before that, potassium argon dating is used. Many scientists are highly sceptical about its value. In one recent test, on volcanic lava in Hawaii, it was up to 2960 million years wrong.

Nevertheless there is a broad consensus among anthropologists that they are now able to say approximately how man emerged. The first part of this section of the Atlas is a summary of their latest thinking; the latter part is the alternative, Russian, view.

The missing links

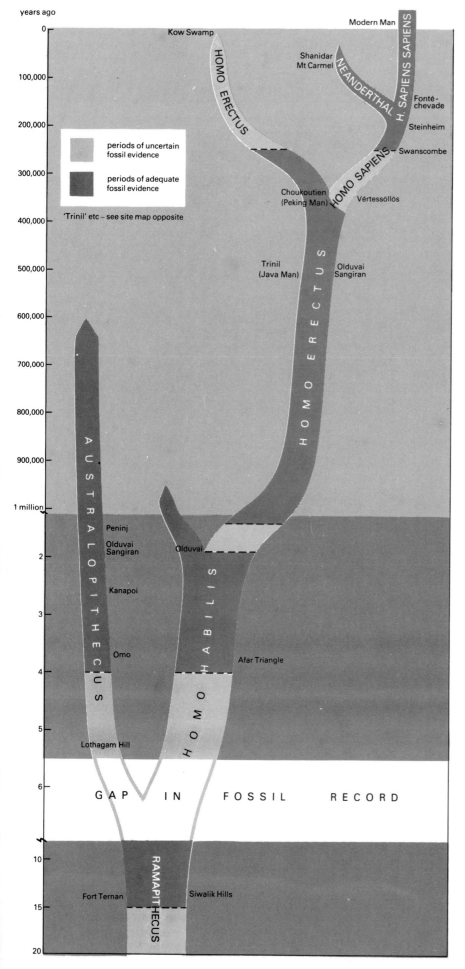

years ago

Modern Man

Kow Swamp

HOMO ERECTUS

Shanidar
Mt Carmel

NEANDERTHAL

H. SAPIENS SAPIENS

Fonté-
chevade

Steinheim

Swanscombe

HOMO SAPIENS

periods of uncertain
fossil evidence

periods of adequate
fossil evidence

'Trinil' etc – see site map opposite

Choukoutien
(Peking Man)

Vértessöllös

Trinil
(Java Man)

Olduvai
Sangiran

HOMO ERECTUS

AUSTRALOPITHECUS

Peninj

Olduvai
Sangiran

Olduvai

HOMO HABILIS

Kanapoi

Omo

Afar Triangle

Lothagam Hill

G A P   I N   F O S S I L   R E C O R D

RAMAPITHECUS

Fort Ternan

Siwalik Hills

0

100,000

200,000

300,000

400,000

500,000

600,000

700,000

800,000

900,000

1 million

2

3

4

5

6

10

15

20

When the dinosaurs were so mysteriously wiped out some 63 million years ago, there was little to suggest that the undistinguished mousy creatures that hopped from branch to branch of the lush, tropical forests would one day inherit the Earth. These tiny animals, none bigger than a man's hand, each with a long shrew-like snout, had taken to the trees in order to avoid being eaten by dinosaurs, or other mammals, or both. In doing so, they had evolved in such a way that their eyes moved a little forward towards the front of their heads, giving them stereoscopic vision and an understanding of perspective; it enabled them to jump more accurately between the branches, which they gripped between fingers and thumbs that grew stronger and more efficient with each generation.

Little else marked out these insignificant animals from the rest of the mammal world. Yet it seems to have been enough – it was destined to set them on an inevitable evolutionary path that led to monkeys, apes, and the human race. In their various forms they survived catastrophic changes of climate that destroyed less adaptable creatures. Their snouts grew ever shorter, diminishing their sense of smell; as if to compensate, their eyes moved further forward and their sight became gradually more acute. And in these ancestral monkeys (or pro-simians) there is also the first faint glimmering of the one thing which, above all, was eventually to mark out the human race from the rest: their brains, to start with only the size of a pea in a 5 mm skull, began to grow. In particular that part of the brain known as the cerebral cortex, which co-ordinates complex muscular behaviour and information from the five senses, slowly became larger and more important compared with the rest of the brain.

Uniqueness of man

Somewhere along the path, monkeys, apes and men parted company and went their separate ways. When this happened, and why, and how, has been the subject of a century of debate – and still, today, nobody knows. The one certain thing is that man is uniquely different from other primates. There are at least 312 listed physical traits that set us apart from our 'cousins' – among them our strange general hairlessness; the way that we stride along upright; our helpless infancy and prolonged childhood, making us dependent on society at large for our survival. But above all there is our domed, globular head, its thin skull containing a brain large out of all proportion to our apparent needs, which seems to have grown to its present size in a number of explosive, inexplicable, quantum jumps. At present it is around one-forty-fifth (1:45) of

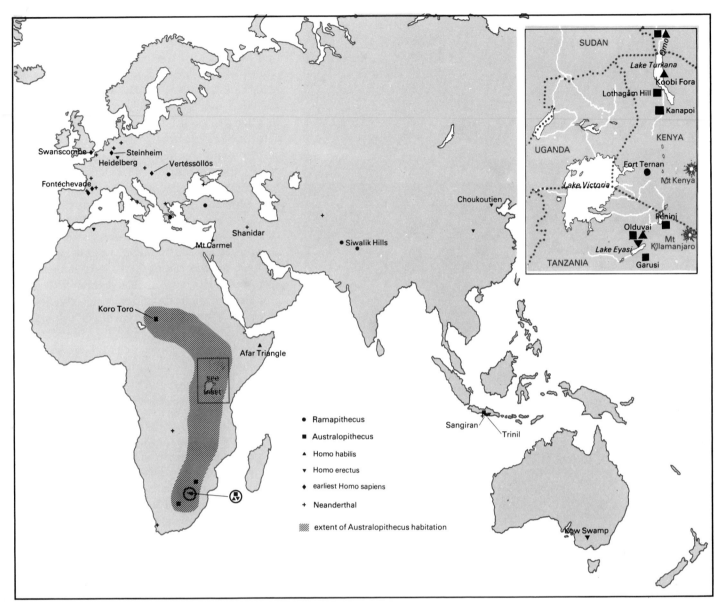

- ● Ramapithecus
- ■ Australopithecus
- ▲ Homo habilis
- ▼ Homo erectus
- ◆ earliest Homo sapiens
- + Neanderthal
- ▨ extent of Australopithecus habitation

Sites of early man, as
shown by significant
fossil finds.

our body weight. With a chimpanzee the
proportions are 1:75, and a gorilla 1:200. Our
brain is also larger in gross size than any other
mammal except the dolphin, the elephant and the
whale, and with these three species too the brain
is much smaller than man's as a proportion of
total body weight, being 1 : 100, 1 : 600 and
1 : 10,000. The effects of this phenomenal brain
size, together with the way it is structured, can
hardly be over-rated: it has enabled us, alone
among creatures on Earth, to control how we
live, to develop a sense of the aesthetic, and to
ponder on what happens to life after death.

Darwin's doubts

As well as being, perhaps, the greatest mystery,
our brain is also one of the most worrying
question-marks over the traditional Darwinian
theory of evolution by natural selection, as
Darwin himself recognized. His great friend
Alfred Russell Wallace, who had independently
and simultaneously come to the same conclusion
about the general principle of evolution, later

decided it did not apply to just one species: man.
In our case, he wrote, we had defied natural
selection, which proclaims that 'Nature never
over-endows a species beyond the demands of
everyday existence.' Yet here was an instrument
– the brain – which had been developed far in
advance of our needs. In no way could genius,
or even normal artistic, mathematical, and
musical abilities be explained on the basis of
natural selection and the struggle for existence.
Something else must be operating – in Wallace's
view, Divine will.

Loren Eiseley, one of the foremost
anthropologists in the United States, said that
when Darwin first read this account from his
friend, 'he wrote in anguish across the paper
"No!", and underlined the "No" three times
heavily in a rising fervour of objection.'
Later he wrote sorrowfully to Wallace: 'If you
had not told me you had made these remarks, I
should have thought they had been made by
someone else. I differ grievously from you and

Skull of a pro-simian,
man's earliest
ancestor.

35

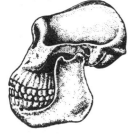

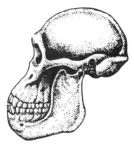

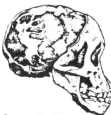

Louis Leakey, the great
anthropologist whose
ambition was to prove
that man's origins were
in Africa.

Australopithecus,
first discovered by
Raymond Dart in 1924.

The two types of
Australopithecus:
gracile (top) and
robust. They may be
different species or
different sexes.

I am very sorry for it. I hope you have not
murdered too completely your own and my
child.' In fact, although Wallace's objection is as
relevant and unanswerable today as it was then,
Darwinian theory has never been buried. It is
increasingly under attack for being unable to
explain all manner of minor but inexplicable
evolutionary anomalies – bristles on the side of
the head of the *Drosophila* fruit fly, or ear tufts
on certain squirrels, are often quoted as
examples – but natural selection is still regarded
as a good guiding principle through which the
existence of most living things can be explained.

Fossil scarcity
In the hunt for man's earliest ancestors, it has
meant concentrating primarily on three of our
distinctive characteristics: brain size, upright
walking, and flat teeth. The great problem has
been the lack of fossils from which to build up a
satisfactory picture – indeed, during the 70 years
after publication of the *Origin of Species* only two
skulls of early man were discovered and one of
these – Piltdown Man – turned out to be a fake.
Even today, for the whole of a crucial period of
nine million years, the only clue we have to the
emergence of man in east Africa is a single,
broken molar tooth. The reason for this is partly
the relatively small populations of early man, but
also because usually only certain kinds of death
create fossils – according to one authority, 'a man
may get caught in quicksand or fall down a
pothole; he may come too close to the undercut
bank of a river swollen in flood; he may get his
head taken off by a rival tribe, his brain eaten
and his skull thrown in the refuse heap. This is
how man, and the ancestors of men, became
fossils.'

Thanks largely to the work of the Leakey family

in the Great Rift valley that runs through
Ethiopa, Kenya and Tanzania, and lately other
international work in a fruitful geological strata
at the foot of the Himalayas in Pakistan, a better
record is at last emerging. Even so, the sparsity of
evidence tends to make the experts on early man
somewhat more diffident and tentative in their
conclusions than in many branches of science,
and the family tree that is being drawn up is
constantly being adjusted in the light of new
finds. It is hotly debated, for instance, as to
whether man's ancestors, at the time of the
dinosaurs and after, in fact ever lived in trees,
or instead were small, active animals which
already had legs longer than their arms, small
jaws without protruding teeth, and relatively
large skulls. However, attractive though the idea
may be philosophically and anatomically, there
are absolutely no fossil finds to back it up, and
in the absence of this evidence, the generally
accepted scenario for our arrival tries to link up
in a straight evolutionary line the various
skeletons (often heavily reconstructed) that have
been painstakingly found.

Men-apes and ape-men
To begin with, the tropical forests that
dominated the landscape during the era of the
shrew-like tree-creatures gave way to a cooler
climate, which in turn brought huge expanses of
open grassland: the savannah. Mammoths, horses,
bisons, wolves and tigers evolved and adapted to
this landscape. Also forced to come to terms with
the new environment were the tree-dwellers,
who slowly grew to the size of small monkeys.
Loren Eiseley imagined what happened: 'On the
edge of the forest, a strange, old-fashioned
animal still hesitated. His body was the body of a
tree-dweller, and though tough and knotty by
human standards, he was, in terms of that world
into which he gazed, a weakling. His teeth,
though strong for chewing on the tough fruits of
the forest, or for crunching an occasional unwary
bird caught with his prehensile hands, were not
the tearing sabres of the great cats. He had a
passion for lifting himself up to see about, in his
restless, roving curiosity. He would run a little
stiffly and uncertainly, perhaps, on his hind legs,
but only in those rare moments when he ventured
out upon the ground. All this was the legacy of his
climbing days.'

Early ancestors
No doubt something of this kind happened – but
the question is, when? The first fossil candidate,
probably too early, comes from a desert area 60
miles south of Cairo called Fayum, where the
world's oldest primate skull has been dug up and
dated at 26 to 28 million years old. It still has
a longish snout and large incisor teeth; named

Aegyptopithecus, it is much more an ancestral ape than an ancestral man.

The next fossil candidates are a group of jaws and teeth scattered over a wide area of Europe, Asia and Africa. More than 100 fragments of jaws and teeth have been collected, analysed and reconstructed, and almost everyone agrees that the shape of the lower skull which emerges marks a sharp move forward towards true man. The name given to these men-apes is *Ramapithecus* – 'currently many people's favourite for the first true human ancestor', according to Martin Pickford, a geologist who has taken part in many expeditions looking for pre-human fossils in Africa and Pakistan. The time covered by these remains is vast – the whole of the epoch known as the Miocene, which lasted from 25 million to 12 million years ago.

Scientists can only speculate just how these men-apes lived. Presumably at some point during this long period they stood on two legs and ran, or ambled, about. There is some evidence from Pakistan that, rather as baboons do today, they lived in open woodlands or bushlands, hunting in the empty grasslands and returning to the woods for shelter at night. Quite likely, they used primitive tools, perhaps in much the same way as chimpanzees have now been shown to do, stripping the bark off twigs and poking them into ant nests. From their probable brain size, they must have been about as intelligent as chimpanzees.

Fossil gap
For all that they mark an evolutionary advance most of us would be hard put, if we saw them alive, to recognize much of ourselves in them. It is as well, too, to remember the colossal time-scale: the most recent fossils we have of them are eight million years old, and after that comes a huge gap in the record until four million years ago. It is a particularly infuriating time to have the pieces of jigsaw go missing, for during it some very odd things may have been happening: when the fossils of this new period came to light at least two types of potential men seem to have lived alongside each other. The first type has been known since 1924, when Professor Raymond Dart found near Johannesburg the skull of a young child that had unquestionably man-like teeth, a more upright forehead, and a brain size estimated at 525 cc – larger than that of modern apes. He called it *Australopithecus* (meaning 'southern man-ape', and nothing to do with Australia,) and as more and more fossils accumulated, people were led to believe that here truly was our ancestor. Pelvic bones showed that the creature, although not fully upright, could jog trot along with quick, rather short steps, its

Illustrated London News **version of Mr and Mrs Hesperopithecus, wrongly reconstructed from the molar tooth of an extinct pig (see introduction page 33).**

knees and hips slightly bent. In Kenya, Mary Leakey later discovered a 300 square metre 'living floor', with areas set aside for splintering rocks and shattering bones – clear evidence, for the first time, of early tool-users.

New developments

But *Australopithecus* led everybody up a blind alley, it now seems. His brain size, calculated from other fossil discoveries, gradually diminished to an average below 450 cc, too small to be a dramatic development. Instead, the excitement came from the discovery, by Jonathan Leakey in 1960, of a contemporary, different hominid, which he dubbed *Homo habilis*. Here at last was the first of the mysterious quantum jumps to modern man with a brain size averaging 680 cc, half that of ours. How had he emerged? Did he descend from *Ramapithecus*? Again, nobody knows. Nor is there yet enough evidence to describe his style of life. But almost certainly for the first time we have a predecessor who strode along just as we do, two million or more years ago, even though he was only 1.3 metres tall, and whose jaw dimensions perhaps held a tongue used for speech.

But was he an ancestor of ours? There is yet another candidate – Java Man, found by a young

Dutch anatomist on a river bed as long ago as 1891, and for many years (apart from the Piltdown hoax) the only clue to what we once looked like. This species, *Homo erectus*, is unquestionably a real man, 1.65 to 1.75 metres tall, a brain size in the order of 800–900 cc, and thigh bones exactly like ours. Java Man himself was originally dated at 700,000 years old (most text books still assume that this was about the time that he emerged) and this was felt to be far too recent for him to qualify as the first of our ancestors. However, recent examples of his skulls in Europe and Africa have shown that he was around elsewhere at least two million years ago – a third contemporary species in the list of man's predecessors.

Link still missing

So the missing link is as far as ever from being discovered. *Homo erectus* is surely our immediate predecessor, but we still don't know where he came from, nor his relationship with the other men-apes. However, it was during his reign on Earth that, explosively and inexplicably, our brain size continued its crucial increase. From the first time we can observe him until now there have been about 80,000 generations. In that time our brains have become twice as large – 10 fresh cells a day, 90,000 each generation – while our bodies have remained much the same. To begin with, new ways of using this brain potential developed very slowly. *Homo erectus* probably discovered, and certainly used, fire. He was a cannibal. He managed to make crude hand-axes. Little else is known. But when he faded from the scene, mankind was at last anatomically poised for the final breakthrough: to become the unique thinking species of creature that we are today.

This cartoon of Darwin in *The Hornet* in 1871 labelled him 'a venerable orang-outang'.

Neanderthal inheritance

Neanderthal faces as reconstructed by the Russian Mikhail Gerassimov.

For around one quarter of a million years after man emerged from the misty forests of prehistory in a recognizably human shape, we have to guess what development went on from the evidence of scarcely half a dozen fossil specimens, none of them complete. However, such fragments as there are suggest that the mystifying and explosive increase in our brain size went smoothly ahead, and that there was a 'straight-line' evolution from *Homo erectus* (previous page) to *Homo sapiens*, our immediate predecessor.

But then something strange happened. Rather as if Nature was having two attempts to get it right, two separate types emerged: Neanderthal Man (*Homo sapiens neanderthalensis*), and us (*Homo sapiens sapiens*). By this stage in our evolution, there are at last numerous skulls and skeletons of both types from which to build up a picture of life at the time – but still, the mystery of our origins remains as baffling as ever. According to Ralph S. Solecki, Professor of Anthropology at Columbia University, New York, and the excavator of the key Neanderthal site of Shanidar in Northern Iraq: 'Although we know so much about him, Neanderthal Man still seems to hang in space on the tree of human evolution.' At the same time our own roots remain totally obscure. Shortly after 40,000 BC, we appeared from nowhere, so to speak, and within a few thousand years of our arrival (an instant in the time-scale of evolution) Neanderthal Man was wiped off the map.

Changing portraits

Perhaps the most intriguing development in the studies of this period is the way that Neanderthal Man has been upgraded. Instead of the brutish, club-wielding, thick-witted character beloved of cartoonists, he is now portrayed as representing a giant leap forward from the primitive *Homo erectus* before him. The first skull finds date from around 80,000 years ago, and their size, 1400–1450 cc, compares favourably with that of modern man, which ranges from 1200–1800 cc – indeed, later Neanderthals living in western Europe, achieved the remarkable evolutionary feat of having brains on average *larger* than modern man. At the same time, we may have been mistaken about his appearance. Although the heavy brow-ridge would have given him bulging, prominent eyebrows, not all Neanderthals had the steeply sloping forehead beloved by 19th-century anatomists, and certainly their faces would have looked no more out of the ordinary than those of many Australian aboriginals today. As one writer put it: 'You can, with equal facility, model on a Neanderthaloid skull the features of a chimpanzee or the lineaments of a philosopher.' And another: 'In the last century the fame of Neanderthal man has increased. He is pictured as a crouching, stooping, squat and brutal creature, with huge jaws and little or no forehead, and a low grade of intelligence. Flesh reconstructions of his face make him look like an ape. In this guise he has become the prototype of innumerable cartoons, in which a slant-browed man, clad in a skin, hits a woman over the head and drags her unconscious body into a cave. This, the popular image of Neanderthal man, will probably be with us for decades to come, because it is picturesque, exciting, and flattering to ourselves. But it is wrong, and so are most of the elements in the total Neanderthal concept.'

Their material achievements were substantial. By learning to wear clothes for the first time – the furry skins of animals, cleaned with stone scrapers to prevent them rotting – they were

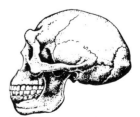

Reconstruction of Peking Man, now classed as *Homo erectus*.

able to extend significantly the area in which man lived, moving away northwards from the warmer latitudes to which they had previously been restricted, and remaining there in spite of the intense cold of the various waves of the Ice Age. Their stone tools became steadily more sophisticated, with local 'industries' that turned out axes, scrapers, cutters, and so on, in standardized patterns. They were the first people, so far as is known, to build their own dwellings: at the site of Molodova in the Ukraine, remains have been found of a structure made of large mammoth bones placed in a circle, having two entrances and containing 15 small fireplaces.

Resurrection

But above all what sets them apart from earlier hominids, and indeed from the rest of living things on Earth, was their struggle to understand the nature of death, and their belief in some kind of an after-life. Neanderthals were conscious of what death meant, and tried to do something to control it: ceremonial burials began to take place. The earliest grave so far found is in a cave at Le

Moustier in southern France (the site that gives the name *Mousterian* to Neanderthal culture as a whole), and from the care taken at the ceremony it is clear that burial must have had great ritual significance. A 15 or 16 year-old boy had been lowered into a trench and placed on his right side in a sleeping position, with his knees slightly drawn up. A pile of flints formed a pillow under his head, and an excellently made stone axe was near his hand. Charred cattle bones around the remains were presumably the remnants of a burial feast, or perhaps food provided for him on his journey beyond.

At other sites there is an even stronger sense of continuity between those times and ours. A cave in the mountains of Uzbek in central Asia was found to contain the skeleton of a young boy in a grave, the top end of which was surrounded by six pairs of ibex horns stuck in the ground; an ibex cult still survives in the area, some 50,000 years later. At Shanidar in northern Iraq, Ralph Solecki uncovered two graves in which wild flowers had been strewn by mourners, just as the flower-loving Kurds do there today, following a tradition of their country dating back 60,000 years. He wrote: 'It seems logical to us today that pretty things like flowers would have been placed with the cherished dead, and it comes as no great revelation. But to find flowers with Neanderthals, the first flower people, is another matter.'

Caring for the sick

There is some evidence at Shanidar, too, that Neanderthals experienced the first stirrings of a humane society. A skeleton was found of a man (nicknamed 'Nandy') around 40 years old, who had been an arthritic cripple. One of his arms had not developed properly, and had been amputated below the elbow; this severely handicapped individual had been cared for well enough to attain manhood. His teeth are unusually worn, perhaps to compensate for the lack of one arm – but also, it has been suggested, because the community may have given him, sitting by the hearth-side, some useful function to perform. Even the cannibalism that Neanderthals are known to have practised is arguably a mark of intelligence; selecting only the skull and eating only the brains requires a certain amount of intelligence and perception, for they were identifying what they imagined to be the source of the soul of their ancestors or their enemies. It was a symbolic act, hardly different in intent (though grotesquely so in practice) from the Christian who partakes of a wafer and wine.

However, compared with what was to happen next, these achievements were slow and limited. For onto the stage of Europe and the Near East

The world's first flower burial, from Shanidar in northern Iraq (after Ralph Solecki).

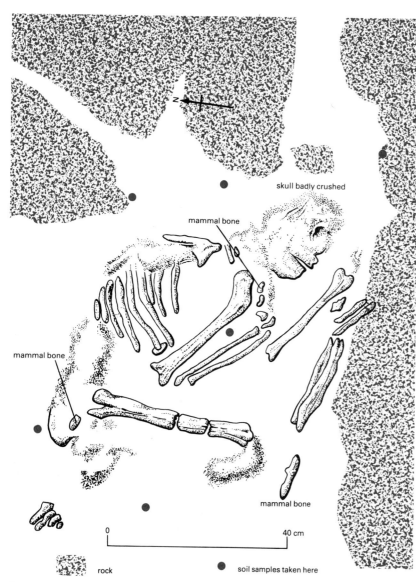

skull badly crushed

mammal bone

mammal bone

mammal bone

0   40 cm

rock   ● soil samples taken here

Reindeer, Le Gabillou

Hare, Le Gabillou

Black stag, Lascaux

Ibex, Lascaux

• sites of Cro-Magnon cave paintings

France

Le Gabillou

Lascaux

Rouffignac

Dordogne

Cougnac

Garonne

Loire

Rhône

Altamira

Les Trois Frères

Ebro

Douro

Tagus

Portugal

Spain

Drawing of sorcerer
(centre below)

Jumping cow and horses, Lascaux

Black bull, Lascaux

Mammoth, Rouffignac

Sorcerer, Les Trois Frères

Bison, Lascaux

41

strode a race of tall strangers, in appearance much like modern Europeans, who must have seemed almost god-like to more lowly creatures, with their athletic speed, their sophisticated hunting tools, their language, and the abruptness of their arrival. Dubbed Cro-Magnon Man (from a site in the Dordogne in southern France where the first skeleton was discovered), they marked the final arrival of *Homo sapiens sapiens*, unmistakably fellow humans, even men we might look up to, since their average height at around six feet was a little more than today, and their brain size strikingly larger. Their physique was that of the mythical Greek ideal of manhood, or the archetypal Aryan hero. And true to heroic myth, they conquered.

Helpless infancy

But where did Cro-Magnon Man come from? Ever since the first fossil find in 1868, experts have argued whether he was an invader from some unknown region, or whether he evolved from the womb of Neanderthals. Lately, the anthropologist Desmond Collins has put forward an elegant theory to support the second view. He supposes that as Neanderthal brains steadily increased in size, childbirth became difficult; 'infant mortality normally running in non-literate hunters at about fifty per cent would rise steeply to ninety per cent or more.'

The survivors, he suggests, would be a newly-evolved breed of people with a different skull shape, the brow ridge of the Neanderthals disappearing and being replaced by a more bulbous forehead containing the 'intelligence' brain cells of the cerebral cortex. His theory would also explain the mystery of why we have such a curiously prolonged infancy compared with other mammals – in order to emerge from the womb at all, we have learned to do so at a helplessly early stage.

However, most scientists prefer the idea of an invading race of people, if only because of the suddenness with which the Cro-Magnon takeover seems to have happened, and the dramatic introduction of a sense of the aesthetic – art for art's sake. Neanderthals raised their techniques of tool-working to an adequate level and then lost any further creative urge, simply producing their instruments like automata over thousand of years. François Bordes, of the University of Bordeaux, retrieved no less than 19,000 of their stone tools of the type known as 'Quina' and came to the conclusion: 'They made beautiful things stupidly. Digging Quina layers can be quite boring. For the first week you are impressed with the tools, but after that you see scrapers and more scrapers *and* still more scrapers until you are sick of them!' Cro-Magnon flint tools, on the other hand, are things of rare beauty,

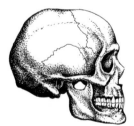

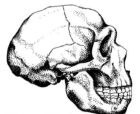

Skulls of *Homo sapiens sapiens* (above) and classic Neanderthal compared. Difference in brain-case structure is pronounced.

delicately flaked in individual shapes that go far beyond what was needed for practical purposes alone.

Cave art

Above all there is their cave art, the phenomenon that brought such wonder to the little Spanish girl who first spotted it on the ceiling of a cave in Altamira in 1879 and cried out to her father '*Toros, toros!*' – 'look, bulls!'. For many years it was thought inconceivable that such marvellous paintings and engravings, whose continuing discovery culminated at Lascaux in 1940, could be the work of stone age man – but the portrayal of several extinct species of animals proved it must indeed be so. We know now that they were executed over a period of some twenty thousand years, beginning around 30,000 BC, and unquestionably they represent 'man's mastery of higher culture' as Desmond Collins puts it. For him, Neanderthals had already shown a potential for art in their ability to cut stone and bone, and their knowledge of pigments capable of being used for painting. But nobody has yet discovered a Neanderthal work of art, so again most experts think that Cro-Magnon cave painting is evidence of invasion by a new type of people, whose art embodied a sense of religious magic. Some paintings are in the innermost cramped recesses of the caves; they could only have been created there with the utmost difficulty, and viewed afterwards by one person at a time.

Musical instruments

In other ways, Cro-Magnon life developed in a way that would make it comfortably familiar to armchair anthropologists today watching scenes of contemporary tribal life in TV documentaries. People played music on bone flutes and whistles. They wore beads round their necks, and tailored skin suits like modern Eskimos. They hunted deer, mammoths, bears, and many other animals. They lived, towards the end, in large tented huts housing ten or more people. They fished, swam, and almost certainly used boats. At the height of their reign they were supremely well adapted to the fierce conditions of the Ice Age in Europe – stronger, taller, and longer-lived than their descendants in the warm climate that followed.

Whether they came from Neanderthals or not, they were certainly different. As the distribution map shows, much earlier fossil bones than the original Cro-Magnon discovery have now been found in places scattered widely over the continents, the earliest 38,000 years old in Java. So perhaps their evolution happened spontaneously in many parts around this time. On the other hand, the writer Stan Gooch has the idea that the cradle of Cro-Magnon Man was on the plains of northern India, in the region of the

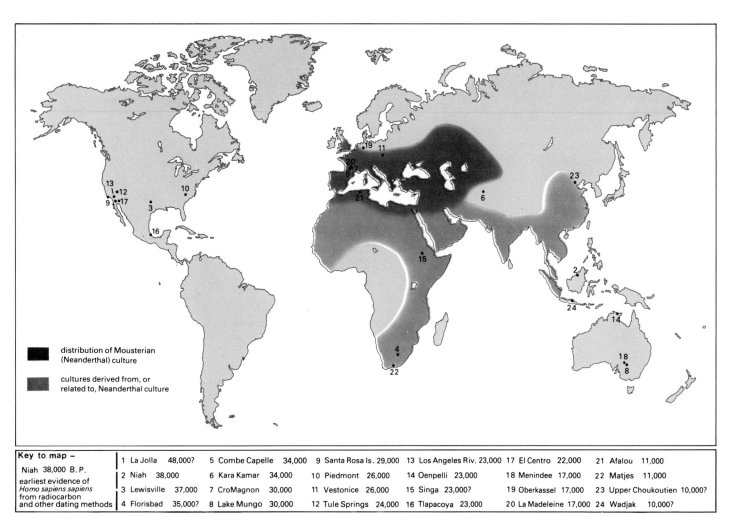

Key to map –						
Niah 38,000 B.P. earliest evidence of *Homo sapiens sapiens* from radiocarbon and other dating methods	1 La Jolla 48,000?	5 Combe Capelle 34,000	9 Santa Rosa Is. 29,000	13 Los Angeles Riv. 23,000	17 El Centro 22,000	21 Afalou 11,000
	2 Niah 38,000	6 Kara Kamar 34,000	10 Piedmont 26,000	14 Oenpelli 23,000	18 Menindee 17,000	22 Matjes 11,000
	3 Lewisville 37,000	7 CroMagnon 30,000	11 Vestonice 26,000	15 Singa 23,000?	19 Oberkassel 17,000	23 Upper Choukoutien 10,000?
	4 Florisbad 35,000?	8 Lake Mungo 30,000	12 Tule Springs 24,000	16 Tlapacoya 23,000	20 La Madeleine 17,000	24 Wadjak 10,000?

Key to map:
- distribution of Mousterian (Neanderthal) culture
- cultures derived from, or related to, Neanderthal culture

Indus, Brahmaputra and Ganges rivers, from a stock of people who had been isolated there for millions of years for a combination of geographical and climatological reasons. To white Europeans, it is an idea with a number of attractions: the arrival of invaders from this area would solve the problem of where the basis of their mysterious Indo-European language derived; how they came to have pale skins (page 44); and account for the widespread tradition that their origins lie in the East. But there is no fossil evidence whatsoever to make his theory more than a speculation.

Inter-marriage

Today, the human race may be built from the genes of both Neanderthal and Cro-Magnon Man. Near Mount Carmel in Palestine, skeletons have been found that combine the characteristics of both sorts of people, indicating that around 35,000 BC the two met, mixed, and married; and it is thought that the same happened widely elsewhere. In which case, what characteristics have we inherited? Just as the explosive increase in brain size was one of the first main indications of the uniqueness of man, from now on the way the brain is organized provides the main clue. In Neanderthal Man that part called the *cerebellum* is more prominent; it lies at the back of the head, and seems to deal mostly with our unconscious, instinctive reactions. During our evolution it has steadily been pushed back and down until today it is largely buried by the *cerebrum*, including the high frontal lobes that are a feature of Cro-Magnon Man, and us; it is here that we seem to be able to sort out unlikely combinations of ideas (the basis of intelligence).

When the two dominant strands of instinct and intelligence were mated, perhaps something was lost as well as gained. Many people believe that telepathy was commonplace to Neanderthals, as it has been until recently among Australian aboriginals and some North American Indians; it has even been suggested that the Neanderthal jaw was not capable of speech, in which case telepathy would have been essential. At the same time Cro-Magnon Man, for all his intelligence, did not fare too well in the warmer weather that marked the end of the Ice Age, and which brought the invention and spread of farming. As the open plains on which he had hunted became wooded, entire species of the animals on which he fed became extinct. So too, in archaeological terms, did Cro-Magnon Man. By 10,000 BC, all traces of him had gone; as suddenly and mysteriously as he appeared, he vanished.

Distribution map of important sites of man's immediate ancestors. The birthplace of modern man is still a mystery.

The racial question

Hottentots (left) and Eskimos (below) show physical evidence of Darwinian adaptation to local conditions.

Not long after writing had been invented, and the ancient civilizations of Sumer and Egypt began to develop, the budding Egyptian government set up an immigration post on its southern border to control the northward movement of Negroes – the first known racist act in the history of mankind. Indeed, the Egyptians made no secret of their dislike of outsiders. On many wall-paintings and friezes of buildings at the time there are depicted other 'vile' foreigners (as they were usually described): Pygmies from even further south, white-skinned, blue-eyed, red-haired Berbers from Libya to the north-west, Semites, Puntites, and so on, all of them having in common the unfortunate fact that they simply weren't Egyptian.

Evidently, the feeling that there is a basic difference between 'us' and 'them' has been around for a long while, and the attempt to classify the differences on a hereditary basis goes back at least to Biblical times. In the book of Genesis, the Hebrews recognized the unity of the human species (all descendants of Adam), but split this up into three broad groupings, the descendants of Noah's sons Shem, Ham and Japheth, each group supposedly recognizable by a similarity of language. Greeks and Romans, seemingly without having any racial bias in the matter, were puzzled about the obvious variations in skin colour from one person to another, and observed that in general people became darker the further south they lived. But it was the end of the 18th Century before the inappropriate labelling of people just by colour became scientifically respectable: Johannes Friedrich Blumenbach, a pioneer anthropologist, divided the world's population into White, Yellow, Black, Red and Brown (a classification, almost unbelievably, which is sometimes still used today).

How many races?

The paradox that every investigator has had to face is that while it is perfectly obvious that groups of people differ generally in their looks – Europeans from Aboriginals, Eskimos from Hottentots – the border-line between them is gradual and indistinct; moreover the differences between individuals in any one group are often so great as to make a generalization very difficult – within a single family, one grown male may be twice the size of another. In fact, no other animal species varies as much in shape, size and colour except the dog, which man himself has domesticated. So it is scarcely surprising that no two experts agree on just how many races there are (or were); in the various text-books the figure is put at anything from two to more than 200. Whatever the number finally arrived at, all classifications are an attempt to answer questions that have mystified people since the beginning of recorded history, and no doubt before: why don't we all look much the same? When did we start looking different? Since Darwin, the first has been the easier to resolve, for his theories of survival and adaptation can clearly be seen at work in the many faces of man. People differ in looks enormously in various parts of the world, and this is very largely due to the way that they have evolved as a result of the climate: the slender, lanky Watusi tribes of the Sudan have

become like that because their large skin area, relative to their bulk, makes it easier for them to get rid of excess heat; Hottentot women in the African bush, when well-fed, accumulate large amounts of fat in their buttocks, a storehouse of food for times of need in the same way as a camel acquires a hump. The narrow, slanted eyes of orientals are the result of descent from Mongoloid people who formed an extra layer of fat to keep out the cold of the Ice Ages in the northern hemisphere. An extreme example can be seen in Eskimos, whose faces developed, according to the anthropologist William W. Howells, during the last glacial advance (beginning around 25,000 BC) 'under intense natural selection among peoples trapped north of a ring of mountain glaciers and subjected to fierce cold, which would have weeded out the less adapted, in the most classic Darwinian fashion, through pneumonia and sinus infections. If the picture is correct, this face type is the latest human adaptation.'

Our diversity is a measure of our success; since the dinosaurs, no other creature has been able to adapt so readily to extremes of heat, cold, drought and deluge. Well into the present century, the Akaluf Indians of southern Chile went about unclothed in sleet, snow and high winds; central Australian aboriginals even today sleep naked in the freezing temperatures of a desert night.

Darwinian defects

However, there are still a number of puzzles left unsolved by the Darwinian approach, notably the puzzle of why some skins are darker than others. If our skin pigments had evolved in such a way that we obtained maximum benefit from the heat of the sun – an obvious target for natural selection, one might think – then pale-skinned people in cool northern latitudes ought to be much darker, so that they would absorb warmth more readily; and vice versa in the hot regions, where pale skins would more efficiently reflect the sun's rays.

As the opposite is what happens, more ingenious evolutionary theories have had to be formulated. One is that because ultra-violet light from the sun causes skin cancer, perhaps only those races shielded by their dark skins from these harmful rays were able, in the long run, to survive in sunny climates. The same rays also produce vitamin D in the body, and this has given rise to another theory: too much or too little vitamin D can be fatal, and it may be that the skin's pigmentation acts as a regulator, allowing us to receive the critical amount needed for good health.

But even if both these solutions play a part in deciding our colour, they are unlikely to be a complete answer, for some of the darkest-skinned tribes in the world see scarcely any sunlight, living in shady equatorial forests.

World distribution of sunshine hours (after Carleton Coon).

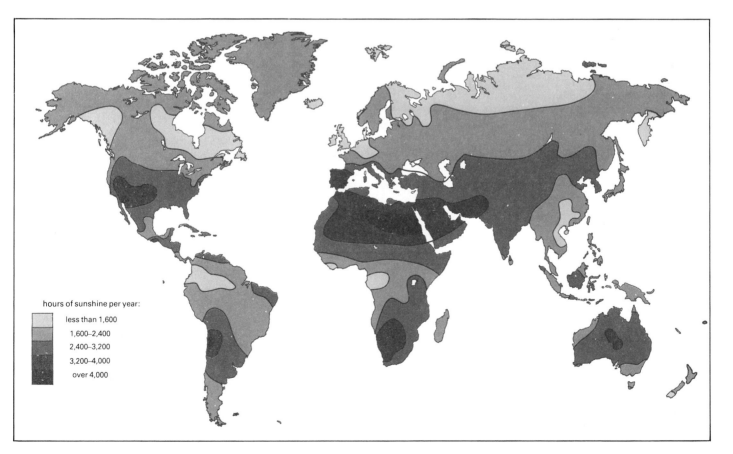

hours of sunshine per year:

- less than 1,600
- 1,600–2,400
- 2,400–3,200
- 3,200–4,000
- over 4,000

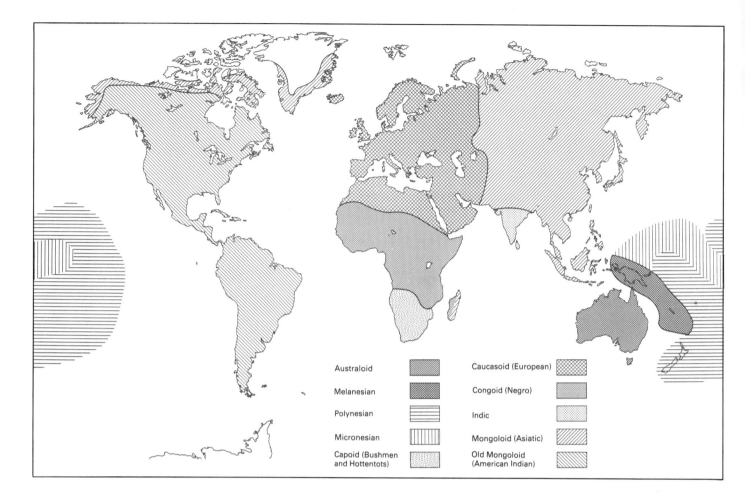

Australoid
Melanesian
Polynesian
Micronesian
Capoid (Bushmen and Hottentots)

Caucasoid (European)
Congoid (Negro)
Indic
Mongoloid (Asiatic)
Old Mongoloid (American Indian)

Did their colour develop as a camouflage? Or did they evolve in the burning desert sun before moving into the forest? Other physical characteristics of African people have been scrutinized without conclusion. Howells again: 'As for woolly hair, it is easy to see it (still without proof) as an excellent non-matting insulation against solar heat. Thick Negro lips? Every suggestion yet made has a zany sound. They may only be a side effect of some properties of heavily pigmented skin (ability to produce thick scar tissue, for example), even as blond hair is doubtless a side effect of general pigmentation of men that has occurred in northern Europe.'

Taboo subject

One reason why these puzzles still remain unsolved may be that the subject of race is nowadays such a sensitive issue that questions like this sound offensive, even though they are part of the central mystery surrounding the emergence of man. Academically, enquiry has almost ceased since the furore surrounding the publication in 1962 of Professor Carleton S. Coon's masterwork *The Origin of Races*, a monumental research that involved collecting and analysing, as he put it, 'every scrap of existing information about every single fossil-man bone and tooth in the world.' From this he distinguished five basic races that had existed

from extremely early times up until the Age of Discovery began with the development of modern transportation (a convenient starting point being Columbus's voyage to America in 1492); he identified them as Caucasoid, Mongoloid, Congoid, Capoid and Australoid.

So far so good, and few would quarrel with his classification except perhaps to add a sub-division here and there. What became immediately controversial, and has remained so, was his idea that racial differences existed as much as 500,000 years ago, and that the various races evolved into *Homo sapiens* 'not once but five times, as each sub-species, living in its own territory, passed a critical threshold from a more brutal to a more *sapient* state'. Moreover, the dates he gave for crossing the threshold were *c*. 250,000 BC for Caucasoids and 40–50,000 BC for Congoids. By inference, the white race had enjoyed at least 200,000 years longer as thinking, modern people than the black race.

Racial tensions

By any standards, it was a provocative thought, especially so in the United States in 1962, because of the tension surrounding the recent de-segregation decisions of the Supreme Court. Predictably, his work was taken up and misused by various racist groups trying to assert an

Pre-1492 distribution of races (i.e. before the Age of Discovery encouraged inter-marriage).

Spread of modern man according to theory of genetic drift.

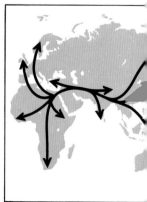

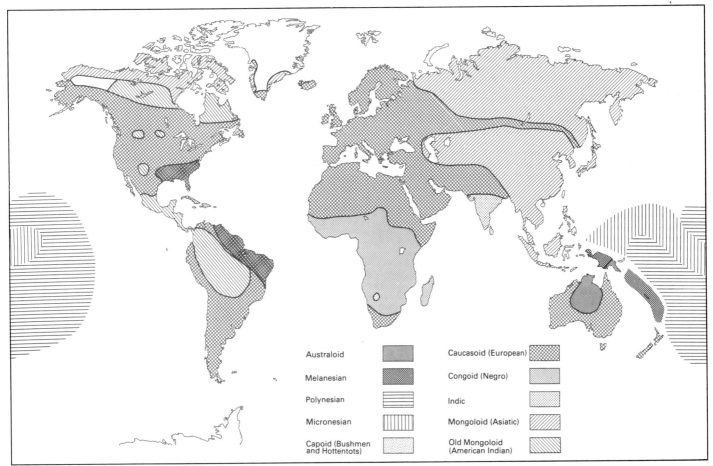

Australoid		Caucasoid (European)	
Melanesian		Congoid (Negro)	
Polynesian		Indic	
Micronesian		Mongoloid (Asiatic)	
Capoid (Bushmen and Hottentots)		Old Mongoloid (American Indian)	

Current distribution of races (compiled from various sources).

inherent superiority by white people over black people, and as a result, according to the editor of the journal *Biological Anthropology*, 'the whole issue of human racial differences and similarities was quietly dropped.' Perhaps to help soothe the wounds that resulted from his finding, Carleton Coon was one of the signatories of a major UNESCO declaration on race two years later which begins: 'All men living today belong to a single species, *Homo sapiens*, and are derived from a common stock. There are differences of opinion regarding how and when different human groups diverged from this common stock.' It ends by stating roundly that there is no justification, whether on grounds of intelligence, culture, or physique, for the concept of 'inferior' and 'superior' races.

Genetic drift

Since the subject is now more or less taboo, it is difficult to establish just how near the truth Coon came. Many geneticists feel that the leap forward to *Homo sapiens sapiens* is so huge that the chance of it having happened more than once, in one place, is 'vanishingly small'. For them, the event happened somewhere in southern Asia, perhaps 50,000 years ago, and the new genetic strain of mankind dispersed gradually through the rest of the world. On the other hand, recent fossil finds show that at least two modern races, Australoids

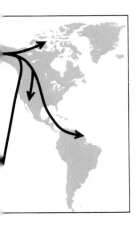

and Mongoloids, seem to have been distinct as long as two million years ago (ironically for Coon, long before the European race was recognizable, although the finds support his theory in general).

On balance, the probability is that something extraordinary indeed happened to mankind in some undiscovered Eden around 50,000 BC, and that this powerful mutation spread wherever its carriers migrated and bred. Certainly, since 1492 the racial map has become ever more complicated, and the races ever less distinct. US Negroes and US Caucasoids have about twenty-one per cent of their genes in common, and some surveys have shown that seventy per cent of US Negroes report having at least one white ancestor. A current distribution map of people predominantly of the five ancient racial types shows enormous changes from the time of emerging man, and the process is still going on.

Edward Babun, an anthropologist who agrees with Coon's five-times-emerging theory, has perhaps put the matter in perspective by saying that, today, he can distinguish no less than 36 races, 'some very old, some quite young, but all equally real'. Pure races do not exist, and may not have done for half a million years; but human races, in all their continually changing diversity, are a fact of nature.

Hominid survival

In 1925, Major General Mikail Stephanovich Topilsky was pursuing White Army forces as they retreated through the Pamir Mountains of southern Russia, when his troops found naked footprints in the snow leading off a cliff-face too steep to be climbed by man. Nearby were human-like faeces containing remains of dried berries. There was a rustling disturbance in a cave, and they opened fire with machine-guns on what they imagined to be a fleeing band of soldiers.

Out of the cave staggered a wild, hairy man-like creature uttering inarticulate sounds of pain. He dropped dead at their feet – a relic hominid so rare that it is still the only specimen this century to have become available for study at first-hand.

Topilsky's careful record of what he saw shows him baffled by what sort of creature his troops had inadvertently shot: 'At first glance I thought the body was that of an ape: it was covered with hair all over. But I knew there were no apes in the Pamirs. Also, the body itself looked very much like that of a man.' A doctor, however, swore 'it was not a human being', although 'we didn't find any important anatomical differences between it and a man. The genitalia were like man's. The arms were of normal length, the hands were slightly wider and the feet much wider and shorter than man's.'

In fact, apart from being naked and almost completely covered with thick hair (the exceptions being the knees, feet, hands and face), it was unquestionably human. 'The eyes were dark, and the teeth were large and even and shaped like human teeth. The forehead was slanting and the eyebrows were very powerful. The protruding jawbones made the face resemble the Mongol type of face. The nose was flat . . . the lower jaws were very massive.'

So man-like was the old creature, lying there with dead, open eyes and bared teeth, that the troops, unable to take it with them, buried it

under a cache of stones. And thus the old man went to join what many Russians believe to be his forebears, the Neanderthals, in much the same way as he would have been buried some 40,000 years before.

No modern anthropology student, reading that description, would have much difficulty in relating it to what is now known of Neanderthal physiology; the skull description could come from a text-book. Only the thick covering of hair might raise an eyebrow – but as Neanderthal reconstructions are made on the basis of bones only, it is impossible to say for sure whether their skins were hairy or not.

However, orthodox theory has long been (page 39) that Neanderthals were wiped out on the arrival of Cro-Magnon Man, our immediate ancestors. It was not until the 1950s that anybody of true academic standing came forward to suggest that this view was rubbish: Professor Boris Porshnev, director of the Modern History Department of Moscow Academy, an inter-disciplinarian scholar of world renown.

In his opinion, the idea that all Neanderthals died out or were instantly assimilated (within 3000 years) was 'totally *a priori* and biologically absurd'. He regarded the many authenticated sightings, from classical and historical times right up to the present, of the kind of wild men called Almas in Mongolia, as Neanderthal descendants who had degenerated into a pitiful parody of their previous life-style.

The trouble was, that as with the Yeti or Bigfoot (page 202), there was precious little first-hand evidence. Though sightings had been made by a small number of reputable scientists since the beginning of the century, the official attitude was to ignore, or ridicule, such stories, and many valuable opportunities must have been lost for the study of what may be a steadily dwindling population of relic hominids.

Partly as a result of Porshnev's persistence, the

from left to right:

1 Hairy wild man from 18th-century Peking anatomical dictionary.

2/3 Pottery in Classical times frequently portrayed satyrs (or Neanderthals?).

4/5/6 A Greek statue, a Chinese dictionary illustration, and a 7th-century Carthaginian bowl all have realistic depictions of satyrs/ hominids.

7 An engraving of a wild woman from Bontius's *Historia Naturalis* of 1658.

climate in the 1960s changed radically, and the person who was to become his successor, Dr Jeanne Kofman, was able to set up a proper base in the Caucasus from which she built up an 'identikit' picture of the Almas drawn from interviews with some 300 peasants and tea-pickers. She rejected about thirty per cent as unreliable, but from the rest a convincing portrait emerged, the more so because it was drawn from consistent reports gathered from people of different backgrounds and separated geographically.

In March 1966 she announced her first findings to the Geographical Society in Moscow. The face of an Alma was remarkably similar to that of the creature shot by Major General Topilsky's soldiers: 'the brow low, narrow and backward-sloping, the nose small and flat as if pushed back, the receding chin round and heavy, and the cheek bones high and Mongolian in character.'

Porshnev was delighted by her findings, which he regarded as finally refuting the 'antiquated views expressed by contemporary anthropology', and described graphically the scene of her lecture: 'She drew a sketch of the skull of modern man on the blackboard. And there, beside it, the skull of fossil Neanderthal man. Next to it she drew, with the chalk transforming words into lines, the combined result of scores of records about the skull of the Almas. Before our eyes the outcome seemed plain. The third sketch was identical with the second.'

Further evidence was forthcoming. Jeanne Kofman's team discovered two lairs in tall, ordinarily impenetrable weeds – a heaped-up larder consisting of two pumpkins, eight potatoes, a half-chewed corn-cob, two-thirds of a sunflower centre, blackberries, and the remains of three apples. Mixed up in this hoard were four round pellets of horse dung, apparently part of the Almas' diet because of its salt content. Nearby was a maize field where a total of 30 witnesses had seen an Alma girl, in human terms

around 16 years old, over a period of time; apparently, she had been searching for the sweetest corn-cobs, for she had left tooth imprints on the ones she had discarded. Comparison with human teeth showed that she had a much wider jaw; from the footprints she left on the soil she had flat, naked, inward-turning feet, as if she were bow-legged.

The descriptions of these creatures inhabiting the thinly-populated steppes, deserts and mountains stretching from China to the Caucasus leaves little doubt that they are about the same kind of hominid. Boris Porshnev and his colleagues have also convincingly linked the Almas to the wild men reported throughout western Europe during the Middle Ages, and the *satyrs* of Greek tradition; all of them have similar features, such as reddish-brown hair on all parts of the body except the face, hands, knees and feet. As one authority puts it: 'It would strain credulity to attribute all these close correspondences to chance, or to traditions commonly borrowed from some source or other.'

But are they Neanderthals? Apart from the obvious similarity of the facial features, how does the picture fit? After the recent rehabilitation of Neanderthal achievements, the easy answer would seem to be: not too well, and it has been seriously suggested that these creatures may be relics of an even earlier man, *Australopithecus* (page 36). Compared with the present-day scavenging, secretive, troglodyte existence of Almas, the archaeological record shows Neanderthals to have been industrious tool-makers who scraped skins for clothing, built simple dwellings, buried their dead with great care and ritual, and used fire.

Boris Porshnev, before he died, met this objection head-on. Just as species could evolve, he said, so they could also regress if circumstances were unfavourable. He supposed that the reason Almas no longer made Neanderthal-type stone tools was because the

References to wild
hairy people come
from a wide number of
good sources, and
extend throughout
written history, as the
panel below shows.

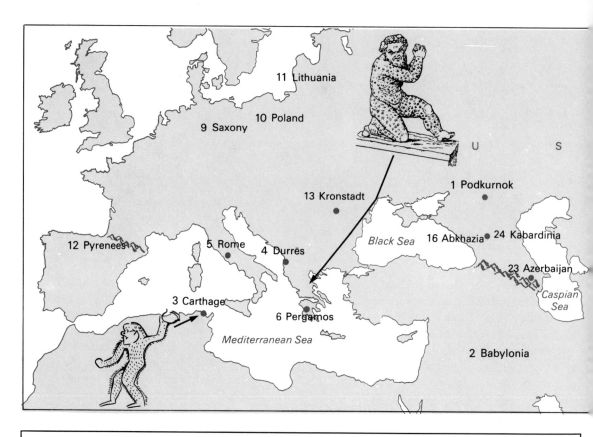

1 Discovery of Neanderthaloid skull dating from the Bronze Age.

2 The *Epic of Gilgamesh* (7th Century BC) describes the wild man of the steppes Enkidu: 'Shaggy with hair in his whole body ... with the wild beasts he drinks at the watering-place ... strength he has ...'

3 A 7th-century Carthaginian (or Phoenician) bowl shows four hairy hominids.

4 In 86 BC a sleeping *satyr* was captured and brought before the Roman general Sulla. It was brutish in appearance and its 'speech' was 'something between the neighing of a horse and the bleating of a goat'.

5 The philosopher Lucretius (died *c.*55 BC) wrote a surprisingly accurate description of the appearance and habits of *pre-sapiens sapiens* man.

6 The Greek geographer Pausanias (2nd century AD) described the grave of the famous *satyr* Silenus here, and concluded that *satyrs* were mortal.

7 The 10th-century Arab Makdisi wrote of the *Nasnas*, a name still used to describe 'wild men': 'One species of *Nasnas* is found in the Pamirs, and in desert regions between Kashmir, Tibet and China. They are beast-like men, covered, except on the face, with hair.'

8 The 12th-century Nizami al-Arudi wrote of the *Nasnas* of the plains of Turkestan: which, 'after mankind, is the highest of the animals, in as much as in several respects it resembles man: first in its erect stature, secondly in the breadth of its nails, and third in the hair on its head.'

9 The 13th-century philosopher Albertus Magnus reported the capture of two hairy forest-dwellers that resembled men.

10 A 17th-century Russian manuscript describes the capture of a 'bear-man' that was shaggy and speechless.

11 In 1661 soldiers captured a 'bear-man', and sent him to Warsaw. The Queen of Poland taught him a few simple tasks.

12 In 1774 shepherds spotted an extremely agile wild man, with hair like a bear.

13 A wild boy that had been captured in the woods was studied by the anthropologist Michael Wagner in 1784. He had very primitive features, a sloping forehead, prominent eyebrows, a very hairy body and an awkward gait. He was kept for some years but never learnt to speak or perform complex tasks.

14 An 18th-century *Anatomical Dictionary* shows a hairy 'man-animal' in a serious catalogue of Tibetan fauna.

15 A 19th-century edition also shows the wild man, and says he 'lives in the mountains, his origin is close to that of the bear, his body resembles that of man and he has enormous strength.'

16 The Abkhazians tell of the *abnauayu*, one of which was captured and tamed by villagers, and named 'Zana'. She was covered with reddish hair, with a flat nose and powerful jaws, a robust physique and an 'animal-like' expression. She never learnt to speak, but left several children by human fathers. Porshnev exhumed the body of

one of her daughters and found it had Neanderthaloid features.

17 An expedition of the Russian Geographical Society (1905–7) came across a hair-covered, long-armed 'wild man'.

18 From 1910 the zoologist Khakhlov collected stories of 'wild men' from the Kazakhs – who once captured one, a male with sloping forehead, prominent eyebrows, massive jaws, small nose, pointed ears and thick reddish hair on its body.

19 The Topilsky case (see text).

20 In 1925 the geologist Zdorik recorded the story told him by Tadjiks of the capture and escape of a *Dev* ('Unclean Spirit') – he was a small thickset man covered with brown hair. In 1934 Zdorik himself saw a sleeping *Dev*.

21 The Mongolian scientist Rinchen collected many eye-witness accounts from the Gobi Desert about the *Almas*, who are covered with reddish-brown hair, have sloping foreheads, large jaws and prominent eyebrows. In 1927 a caravan found a group of *Almas* warming themselves by a dying camp-fire.

22 Porshnev collected numerous eye-witness accounts from the 1930s to 50s.

23 Locals tell of the *Kaptars*, creatures just like *Almas*. In 1959 Y. Merezhinsky, Professor of Ethnography and Anthropology at Kiev University, saw an albino *Kaptar* himself and verified their existence.

24 Base of Kofman since 1962 (see text).

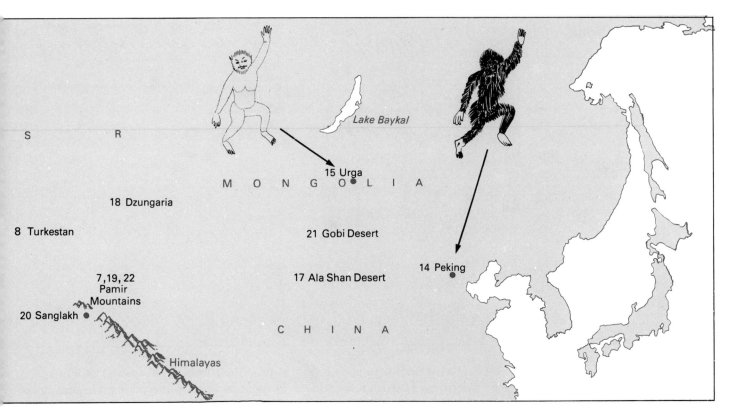

Cro-Magnon invaders had seized their flint-mines; forced into conditions and environments they found negative, their culture slipped back. He found a parallel with the Vikings of Greenland, who, cut off from their supply of metals, almost lost their art of metal-working before finally dying out.

Professor John Napier, a universally respected authority on anatomy and primate biology, cautiously approves this: 'It is not impossible that pockets of Neanderthals living in geographically remote regions of eastern Europe, Siberia and Mongolia could have avoided the consequences of either physical extermination or racial absorption and still be surviving as relict populations in these regions today.'

Where Porshnev's views still outrage orthodoxy is his contempt for those who try to find traces of humanity in the multifarious early hominids, from *Australopithecus* on: 'What kind of man is it that has no art, is hairy, and cannot speak? They are merely man-like, a separate group from men.' One by one, he dismissed the 'achievements' of these creatures whom he termed *Troglodytidae*: their use of stone implements is paralleled by the modern ape's use of sharpened sticks; they became adapted to fire, rather than created it; walking came about because they were scavengers, which made them use their hands to carry and crush bones; their brains grew in size because their particular way of finding food involved several complex steps of thought – for instance, deciding where and when to scavenge.

But they were not *people*. For that, for the flowering of art and abstract thought, you need the power of speech; and even Neanderthals, he believes, could not speak, a view supported by researchers from Yale and the University of Connecticut who have concluded that they were capable only of 'inefficient and monkey-like sounds'.

So where did we, *Homo sapiens sapiens*, come from so suddenly? What catapulted us forward in our giant evolutionary leap? Alas, Professor Porshnev, for all his appealing thoughts on relic Neanderthals, is no wiser than anyone else on this, the greatest mystery of all.

But for those who like the idea of cloning by extra-terrestrials some 40–50,000 years ago, he is on record with a remark both provocative and sinister: the speed of our evolution, he says, 'indicates a mechanism of selection somewhat akin to artificial selection.'

The vanished mammoths

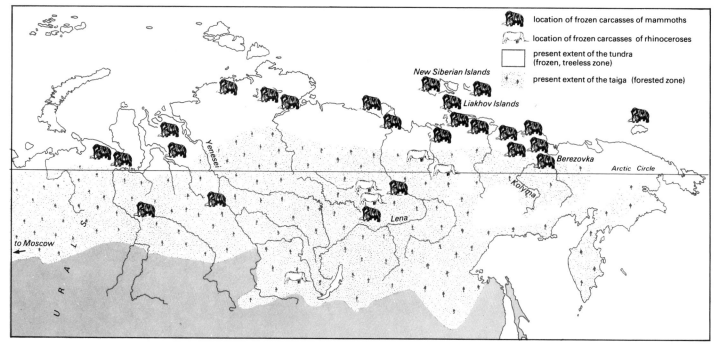

location of frozen carcasses of mammoths

location of frozen carcasses of rhinoceroses

present extent of the tundra
(frozen, treeless zone)

present extent of the taiga (forested zone)

New Siberian Islands

Liakhov Islands

Berezovka

Arctic Circle

Yenesei

Kolyma

Lena

U R A L S

to Moscow

Frozen remains of mammoths have been found over a large part of Siberia. The climate when they lived is still not known.

Early 18th-century portrayal of a Siberian mammoth.

Mammoth found frozen in ice in 1799 at the mouth of the Lena river, as depicted by an ivory trader named Boltunov.

As the Ice Age ended and the great glaciers shrunk back northwards, the new warmth was to the liking of mankind. Our population swelled, and over ever-larger areas of the globe, people settled down to practise farming – the first major step on the road to modern civilization. To large sections of the animal world, however, the changed conditions were less agreeable. The emerging dominance of man, and the growth of woodland where before there had been open plains, upset the delicate balance of the ecology. It proved too much for many species in the northern hemisphere, and another of the massive waves of extinctions that have punctuated the flow of life on Earth took place, reaching its height around 8000 BC; among those that died out were sabre-toothed cats, steppe bison, and certain kinds of sloth, tapir, armadillo, wolf, and mammoth.

Most of these extinctions are not especially mysterious to scientists. Although they argue about the precise nature of what triggered off the process, there are a number of plausible suggestions. But there is one unanswerable question which still sticks out uncomfortably as a half-buried secret: what happened to the woolly mammoths of Siberia? What extraordinary series of events can have taken place to leave the massive bulk of hardy, tough-skinned beasts as quick-frozen as a TV dinner?

These frozen mammoths have been discovered regularly. The most renowned is the specimen found at Berezovka in 1900, standing upright deep in the Arctic permafrost, its stomach containing undigested food, and on its tongue fresh buttercup flowers which for some unaccountable reason it had not had time to swallow. Frozen portions of some 50 other mammoths, and tens of thousands of their ivory tusks, have been recovered over the years: in the summer of 1977 the best specimen of all, a six-month old baby, was bulldozed to the surface in the Yakutsk Republic of the USSR, so perfectly preserved that the two 'fingers' on the end of its trunk were still intact – the first time this had been observed except in the cave paintings of Cro-Magnon Man. Their deaths leave a trail of question-marks. Did they die of natural causes? Did they all die at the same time? How did they become buried so deep in the permafrost? How have the carcasses lasted so long and so well?

The trouble with trying to discover the answers is that nobody is emphatically sure what the climate was like in Siberia when the great herds of mammoths roamed the plains there. This leads to two totally different scenarios for what happened to them at their death, one written for warm weather, and one for cold – and infuriatingly, neither quite adds up. It's as if you bought a double-sided jigsaw, one side showing a summer scene and the other winter; no matter which picture you complete, you always have some bits left over – some awkwardly shaped facts that belong to one side or the other, but not to both.

Take the warm-weather scenario first. In this, you have to regard Siberia as a climatic oddity, for from 100,000 BC to about 10,000 BC, the northern hemisphere was predominantly very cold; occasionally, the glaciers crept backwards to allow brief spells of milder weather, but on the whole all animal life living in these latitudes was

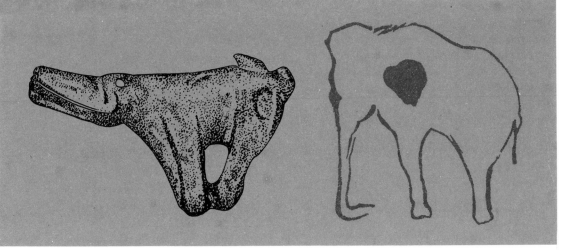

Depiction of mammoths such as these, painted on cave walls by Cro-Magnon Man, show that they were adapted to moderate climates.

adapted to severely low temperatures. However, the glaciers never formed in Siberia, except on the tops of mountains, and although it is unorthodox to say so, it's quite possible that for some reason Siberia was exceptional – while the rest of the northern hemisphere alongside shivered, it basked. Buttercups need springtime temperatures, and so do the rest of the broad-leaved plants found in the mammoths' stomachs. Musk ox, stag, elk and sabre-toothed cats, all warm-climate animals, lived alongside the mammals (as, it must be said, did many cold-climate species). Moreover, a single mammoth has to eat several hundred kilos of food per day, and there were at least 50,000 mammoths living in Siberia at any one time. It is difficult to imagine them thriving on the chill tundra of today, with its short summer and sparse foliage.

Such clues about the climate as we can get from the anatomy of the mammoths themselves can be interpreted either way. They stood about three metres high, somewhat smaller than modern elephants, covered with coarse hair sometimes more than half a metre in length, on top of a reddish-yellow woolly fleece. Underneath this was a solid, tough skin, and a layer of fat up to nine centimetres thick. They had broad, four-toed feet, suited to marshy countryside. None of this proves much. Certainly they *might* have enjoyed living in the cold; but equatorial animals such as tigers have thick fur, elephants in the tropics have the same sort of skin, and camels have just as large stores of fat. Moreover, their skin (like elephants) lacked sebaceous glands – an important feature of virtually all cold-climate animals' defence against the weather.

So suppose it was a mild spring day in 10,000 BC when the Berezovka mammoth idly munched its buttercups. What might happen next to strike it dead and then freeze it so quickly that all those years later the meat was still fresh enough to be eaten by sledge-dogs? For a quick killing, asphyxiation would seem the best bet.

It appeared to have fallen into a gulch (an odd thing to do when munching buttercups, but not impossible), so perhaps earth got into its windpipe during the fall; or perhaps the asphyxiation was all part of an amazing deep-freeze process that happened next. According to this part of the scenario – pure sci-fi, critics say – an almost unimaginable catastrophe happened: there was a sudden shift in the Earth's crust, or even a tilt in the Earth's axis as suggested by Velikovsky (page 26). Either way, the associated earthquakes and volcanoes caused global climatic disasters on a scale that the world has not seen since. Huge clouds of volcanic dust were thrown into the air, blocking out the sun for months on end, with ferocious snowstorms, winds, and tidal waves. In this maelstrom poisonous gases gathered high in the atmosphere and plummeted abruptly to the ground, bringing local drops of temperature of as much as 100°C. And this, the tale goes, is what happened to the mammoths. It explains how the Berezovka specimen was frozen quickly enough to prevent the contents

Six-month-old mammoth bulldozed to the surface of the permafrost in the Yakutsk Republic of the USSR in the summer of 1977. Two 'fingers' at the end of the trunk were the same as shown in cave paintings.

of its stomach putrefying; why it was found upright in a half-squatting position, one hip broken by the force of the violently shaking earth. It explains why other mammoths have been found literally torn to pieces; how great heaps of mammoth bones have been found piled together elsewhere, apparently crushed and mangled by some great force; and how all that ivory (Siberia has historically provided more than half the world's supply) came to be preserved, for just like flesh it needs to remain frozen to stop it deteriorating.

But now the bits of jigsaw left over, the awkward pieces that won't fit. When did such a cataclysm happen? Almost certainly not in the time proposed by Velikovsky (*c.* 1500 BC), for radiocarbon dates on various mammoth specimens range from 30,000 to 10,000 BC. So is it seriously proposed that there were *several* catastrophes? And the 'muck', or permafrost, in which the mammoths are found – why doesn't it contain great quantities of volcanic dust and debris?

The cold-weather scenario, a more prosaic one, accounts for this by saying that there is no mystery about the death of the mammoths. The climate in Siberia has always been much as it is today, with seasonal melting and freezing, and those mammoths that have been found preserved today died accidentally through being trapped in bogs, land slips or mud flows, through falling into a chasm, or by drowning in a river. They were frozen in a relatively short time, probably less than one year, and the 'muck' has gradually built up around them.

But this cautious, uniformitarian scenario leaves even more bits of jigsaw that won't fit. Slow freezing will not leave unburst cells in the stomach. Seasonal freezing and unfreezing will cause the skin to fall off and the flesh to rot. What about the huge number of frozen tusks, enough to have supplied the ivory for half the world's billiard balls? What turned Siberia into an icy waste and destroyed countless herds of robust animals, which had happily lived in the climate for two-and-a-half million years?

So there is no satisfactory solution. Because of the scientist's natural aversion to catastrophe, the cold-weather picture is the one generally favoured, for all its loose ends. But perhaps that is because the catastrophist view hasn't had as much attention as it deserves. Either way, there is a basket of question-marks, including the basic, infuriating, unanswerable one: how do you deep-freeze eight and a half tons of living flesh and bones?

Modern drawing of the most famous frozen mammoth, found at Berezovka in 1900. Although rumoured to have been eaten at a dinner of Soviet Academicians in Moscow, it is now known that this did not happen.

Section three Earth patterns

For reasons that can still barely be imagined, early peoples everywhere seem to have been driven by the urge to mark out their sacred places on the Earth's surface in a complex, geometrical way. Learned priesthoods of burgeoning societies the world over became preoccupied with the movement of the Sun, Moon, planets and stars, and built their temples and monuments to enshrine what they had learned. Even today, ruins of ancient sites contain fragmentary and mystifying clues that their architects may have had a knowledge of the universe in many ways deeper than our own, gained by methods that we would not now understand.

The archaeological evidence for this begins in western Europe, moves to Egypt and the near East, and emerges a little later in America. What is striking to any observer is an underlying similarity between monuments separated by such great distances, and so different in shape and size. The megalithic standing stones and stone circles of north-west Europe (e.g. Stonehenge) may at first glance seem to have no relationship with the strange and complex desert patterns of Nazca in Peru; yet both turn out, on closer examination, to have been remarkable examples of precise surveying methods, and in both there is an incomprehensible determination to lay out long straight lines on the face of the Earth. The megalith builders, too, had a passion for geometry and astronomy that was matched simultaneously by the way that the Egyptian priests constructed the Great Pyramid so that it could be used both as an observatory and a central experimental laboratory for arcane mathematical computations.

This way of looking at prehistory – that is to say, the idea that early civilizations and even pre-literate societies searched for and perhaps found a body of knowledge that is now lost to us – is anathema to most archaeologists. They call 'pyramidiots' those scholars who insist on the Great Pyramid being something more than just a big tomb; antiquarians who tramp the British countryside looking for leys (the alignment of ancient sacred sites) are dubbed 'the lunatic fringe'.

Yet a revolution is taking place in archaeology itself as radiocarbon dating establishes that early man was indeed capable of astonishing intellectual achievements, and was nothing like the ignorant savage that most text-books still portray. Many parts of this Atlas show how he could farm, design, build, compute, sail, navigate, and perhaps even fly long before the time with which he is usually credited.

This section concentrates on his ability to survey in detail large areas of the terrain in which he lived; it implies a deep understanding of Earth's place in the universe, and must have taken many generations of sustained effort, both physical and mental. Just as Neanderthal Man's burial ceremonies indicated our first hope for an after-life, and Cro-Magnon Man's cave paintings our first awareness of art, so the earth patterns marked out by early man represent our first attempt to understand the nature of cosmic forces.

Crystalline planet

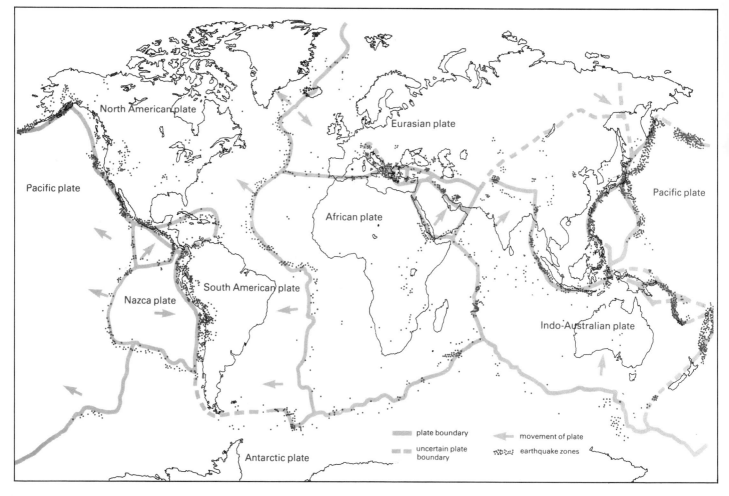

Boundaries of the
shifting continental
plates (see page 14) are
marked by violent
earthquake activity.

'Is the Earth a large
crystal?' – the Soviet
illustration as it
appeared in *Khimya
i Zhizn*.

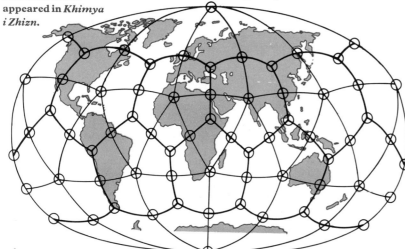

The belief that our Earth has a basic harmonic symmetry is very ancient. Socrates told his pupil Simmias: 'My dear boy, the real earth viewed from above is supposed to look like one of those balls made out of twelve pieces of skin sewn together.' Some 2000 years later, in the 1960s, three Russian scientists had the idea of re-examining the globe to see if any pattern should emerge linking significant places in history; it did. After several years' research in Moscow, they published their findings in *Khimiya i Zhizn*, the popular science journal of the USSR Academy of Sciences, entitled: 'Is the Earth a Large Crystal?'.

Drawing from their combined experience of history, engineering, and electronics, they decided that there was nothing in theory to have prevented a lattice-work pattern – a 'matrix of cosmic energy', as they put it – being built into the structure of the Earth at the time it was formed, whose shape could still be dimly perceived today. *Komsomol's Pravda*, the official Russian journal for the younger generation, followed up the idea with a suggestion that Earth had begun life as a crystal, and that only slowly did it mould itself into the spheroid it is today.

According to their hypothesis, the crystal can still be seen in twelve pentagonal slabs covering the surface of the globe – a dodecahedron. Overlaid on this are 20 equilateral triangles. The entire geometric structure, they claim, can be seen in its influence on the siting of ancient civilizations, on earth faults, magnetic anomalies, and many other otherwise unrelated locations, which are placed either at the intersections of the grid, or along its lines.

Is the idea crazy? In one sense, certainly. If the overwhelming evidence for continental drift (page 14) is to be accepted, the lithosphere, or outer surface of the Earth, has moved so much that it would surely have destroyed the symmetry of a crystal with the passing of time.

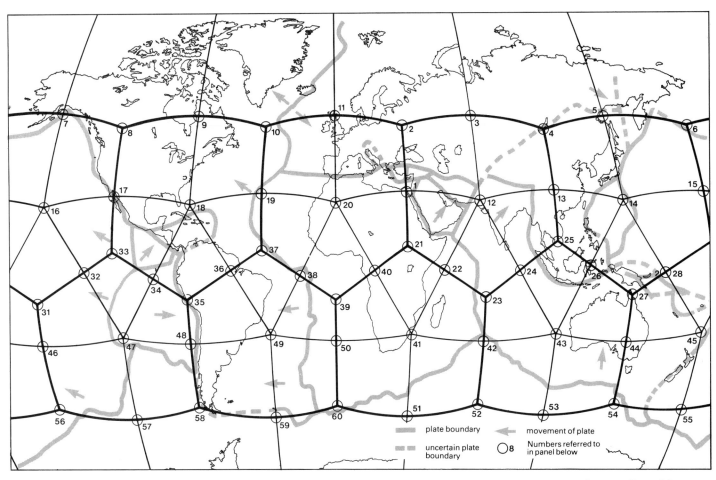

plate boundary — movement of plate

uncertain plate boundary — ○8 Numbers referred to in panel below

'Vile Vortices' – ten areas of violent magnetic and climatic disturbance spread symmetrically round the globe, according to the investigator Ivan T. Sanderson. They include the Bermuda Triangle (page 219), and are said to be places where phenomena are concentrated: 16, 18, 20, 12, 14, 47, 49, 41, 43, 45.

Volcanoes – the geometrical lines are said to follow the edges of the lithospheric plates, where volcanic activity takes place.

Magnetic anomalies – said to 'overlap with the vertices of the polygons'.

Meteorology – centres of cyclones and anti-cyclones lie at the nodes of the grid, giving birth to hurricanes, whose path then follows the ribs of the grid; so do many prevailing winds and water currents.

Earth faults – the mid-Atlantic underwater ridge lies between 10 and 37.

Solar radiation – maximum amounts of solar radiation (map page 45) are received at 1, 17, 41.

Atomic explosion – 1700 million years ago, a spontaneous atomic reaction based on U-235 occurred at 40.

Mineral ores – mineral deposits are concentrated along lines of grid that coincide with edges of continental plates; oil deposits are found at intersections (e.g. huge Tyumen oil find at 3).

Space photographs – photographic data collected by US and Russian satellites have recently made the map of the world more accurate, and confirm some of the oddities suggested by the grid: a 'fault-line' from Morocco to Pakistan is marked by the line from 20 to 12; Gemini spacecraft have shown circular geological structures 200–350 kilometres in diameter located at 17, 18 and 20.

Soil content – lack of certain elements in soil at 2 and 4 has led to freak evolution of plant life; at 4 (Lake Baikal) three-quarters of plants and animals are unique.

Bird migration – birds overwinter (page 86) at 12, 20, 41.

Ancient civilizations – people unconsciously sited their early centres at key intersections: Egyptians (1), Indus Valley (12), megalith builders (11), Peru (45), Easter Island (47), northern Mongolia (4).

(If drift is due to the world expanding, this objection would disappear.) Nor, when you superimpose the supposed grid on what are now confidently thought to be the dividing lines of the shifting continental plates, is there as good a match as the Russian scientists claim – the crystalline faults no longer show.

Another criticism is that the lines on the published Russian maps, and the circles that mark their intersections, are so thick as to make almost any approximation possible; doubtless hundreds of similar grids could be designed, with similar results.

But even so, the basis of the Russian research is certainly worth considering. As outlined throughout this section of the Atlas, people seem to have felt instinctively that some places on Earth are intangibly more important than others, and are very possibly connected with one another; it is encouraging that Russian scientists are investigating this very old idea. In common with these ancient traditions, the Russians believe the energy involved in the crystalline pattern is not constant, but ebbs and flows in rhythmic cycles, in accordance with its own internal mathematical harmony. The evidence that they claim to have discovered so far is summarized on the left.

Megalithic engineering

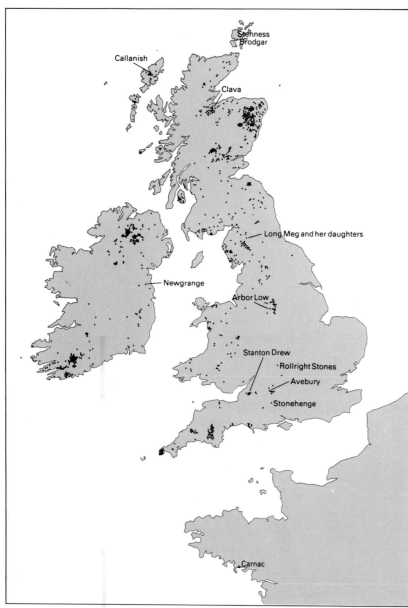

Distribution of stone circles in the British Isles and Brittany (after Aubrey Burl).

Dotted enigmatically along a 2500-kilometre swathe of Europe's Atlantic seaboard are some of man's oldest and most mysterious monuments: the gaunt standing stones, earthen mounds and burial chambers of a lost civilization that culminated in the building of Stonehenge. The earliest of them come from a time that is hauntingly remote, perhaps before anyone could read or write; until quite recently, archaeologists were prepared to dismiss the people who, carefully and laboriously, put these rough stones into their positions as illiterate barbarians and savages whose lives were too primitive to be of much importance in the main course of prehistory.

That attitude has changed dramatically. Detective work by a handful of people working independently from different standpoints has shown that these stones may not be just the oldest monuments in the world, but possibly the most remarkable. The people who put them there, without the help of writing as a memory aid or for instruction, were astronomers and mathematicians of extraordinarily high ability; obsession is hardly too strong a word to use for the painstaking way in which observation of the Sun, Moon, and other heavenly bodies became the focus of their religious life.

Baffling stones

Orthodox recognition of this ability has been a long time coming – perhaps not surprisingly, given the limitations of traditional archaeological techniques. For centuries, antiquarians and prehistorians have confessed themselves baffled by the thousands of stones, some standing singly, some arranged into what look like rough circles, apparently spaced at random in the middle of a field or on the side of a hill: Daniel Defoe summed up the attitude in the 18th Century: 'all that can be learn'd of them is, that *there they are*.' Excavation at many of the sites often yields little, for if you dig up a standing stone there is nothing beneath it but earth or bedrock. Inside the stone circles there is usually some evidence of cremation, and round the outside there is occasionally charcoal, hinting at ceremonies that involved the use of fire; but that, and some fragments of pottery, is hardly enough to answer all the puzzling questions that surround the stones.

Heavy labour

Why was so much energy devoted to hewing great blocks of stone and dragging them,

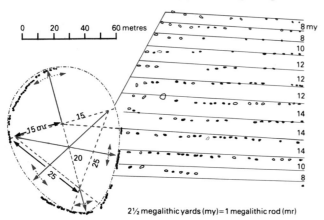

2½ megalithic yards (my) = 1 megalithic rod (mr)

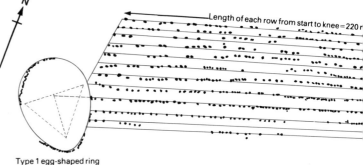

Type 1 egg-shaped ring
Perimeter = 304.4 my

sometimes many miles, to their appointed place?
The bluestones at Stonehenge came
200 kilometres from the Prescelly mountains in
Wales. And impressive though Stonehenge is,
many stones at other sites are even larger. The
Grand Menhir Brise at Locmariaquer in Brittany,
northern France, once stood 50 metres high and
weighed 340 tons; an earthquake or similar
disaster felled it, and it now lies broken in four
pieces, a mute reminder of the gigantic strength
and technique that was once needed to erect it.

Nearby at Carnac are more than 3000 stones
arranged in rows that stretch as far as the eye
can see to the horizon, and beyond – and
these are but a fraction of a formerly vast
geometrical pattern that has been mutilated
almost beyond recognition, like so many of the
ancient sites, by builders who have removed the
stones and incorporated them in the structure of
local houses.

Indeed, it is hard to resist the impression that
there is some special pagan sanctity about these
places that, throughout recorded history, has
generated emotions of fury and reverence far
beyond what would be expected from such
rough and inoffensive objects.

Modern witchcraft ceremonies are still held in
some circles. In France, girls used to slide down
the stones with bare bottoms in the expectation
that this would make them fertile. Nearly all the
sites have legends that the stones contain some
sort of magic power, and can move about, or heal
people. So nervous of this power was the early
Christian church that it ordered its missionaries
to absorb the stone sites, with the result that
even today many old churches can be seen within
the outlines of prehistoric mounds, or contain the
ancient stones in their walls. At the huge site of
Avebury in southern Britain, whose scale and
engineering greatly exceeds Stonehenge, the
Middle Ages saw the introduction of a ceremony
in which, every 25 years, one of the stones was
ritually dislodged and attacked, under the
auspices of the Church, in order to symbolize
the conquest of the Devil.

Megalithic secrets

So what secrets may the megalith builders have
understood? Why should their monuments
inspire irrational reactions so long after they
were built? One thing that has recently become
clear is that if the sites indeed had an occult
power, it was in some way derived from careful
astronomical observation. A new academic
discipline of 'astro-archaeology' has grown up
to study this. The British antiquarian
writer John Michell, in his history of how
astro-archaeology has promoted itself in status

Alignments of menhirs
at Carnac in Brittany.

Two of the three stone
circles in Brittany are
attached to the
amazing alignments
near Carnac
most of them
re-erected early this
century.
Statistical analysis has
established their
original geometry.
(after Alexander Thom).

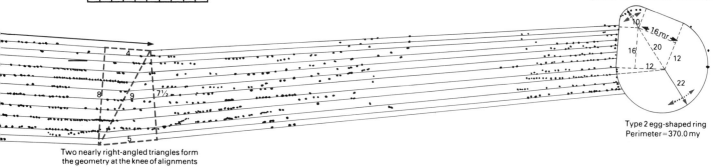

0   50   100 metres

Two nearly right-angled triangles form
the geometry at the knee of alignments

◄ Distance between centres of rings = 495 mr ►

Type 2 egg-shaped ring
Perimeter = 370.0 my

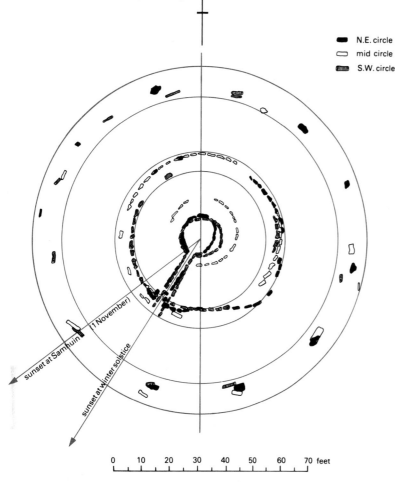

N

N.E. circle
mid circle
S.W. circle

1 November)
sunset at Samhuin
sunset at winter solstice

0 10 20 30 40 50 60 70 feet

In the 1920s Admiral Boyle Somerville's surveys proved that stone circles were carefully laid out. He superimposed three circles at Clava, Scotland, to prove his point.

Lengthy analysis by Alexander Thom showed that circles were often flattened or egg-shaped as in three examples below. The geometry of the middle 'egg' was used at Clava (above).

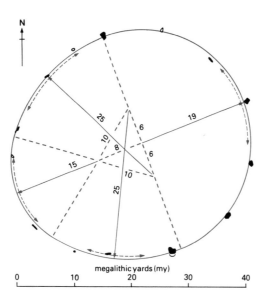

N

25 19
6
10 8
6
15 10
25

megalithic yards (my)

0 10 20 30 40

'from lunacy to heresy to interesting notion and finally to the gates of orthodoxy', has written that: 'The idea seems harmless enough, but it arouses passions; for behind the question of whether or not the megalith builders four thousand years ago practised scientific astronomy there are other, more serious issues; and these concern the history and the very nature of civilization . . . Resistance to astro-archaeological theory has been intensified by the understanding that, if ancient people of Neolithic culture are credited with an astronomical science far in advance of mediaeval, and even in some respects of modern, standards, current faith in the unique quality of our own scientific achievement is undermined. Yet evidence of a remarkably developed and widespread Stone Age science continues to accumulate.'

Of course, it has long been known, in a general way, that Stonehenge and other ancient temples were orientated towards the sunrise on certain significant days; the visionary antiquarian Rev. William Stukeley wrote in 1740 that the avenue leading from Stonehenge and containing what is now called the Heel Stone was aligned to the north-east 'where abouts the sun rises when the days are longest', and he ascribed the monument to the Druids of around 460 BC, this being the oldest priesthood known at the time. (One notable feature of archaeology has been frequent revision of estimates of the age of the stones, each new guess providing an ever-greater antiquity; it is now thought that the first version of Stonehenge was laid down around 2800 BC, and the version we see now around 1560 BC).

Ancient Sun-worship

It was not until the end of the 19th Century that archaeologists began to notice a consistent pattern of Sun-worship in many countries, and in 1901 they gained their most notable recruit, the great astronomer and scientist Sir Norman Lockyer, Fellow of the Royal Society, Director of the Solar Physics Laboratory, founder and for 50 years editor of the scientific journal *Nature*. Having already established the solar orientation of the Pyramids in Egypt, he now turned his attention to Britain and five years later published

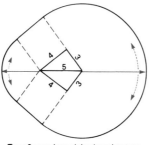

Type 2 egg-shaped ring based on two Pythagorean triangles with a common hypotenuse

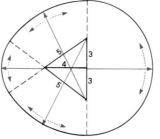

Type 1 egg-shaped ring based on two Pythagorean triangles placed back to back

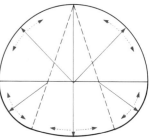

Flattened circle

Stonehenge and Other British Stone Monuments, in which he concluded that many of the country's stone circles, including those in Cornwall, on Dartmoor, at Stanton Drew in Somerset, and in Scotland, were aligned not just towards the Sun, but on many of the stars as well. Easy though it is nowadays to fault the book's inaccuracies, and Lockyer's tendency to believe that any number of minor and unimportant stars formed part of the megalithic alignments (statistically ruining his case), he opened, in John Michell's words, 'an entirely new view of prehistoric society that contradicted the most fundamental beliefs of contemporary archaeology.'

Among the few scholars willing to follow up his theories, the most notable was Admiral Boyle Somerville, not by training an archaeologist, but whose knowledge of surveying convinced him that Lockyer was, at the very least, on the right lines. As a result of some 90 surveys that he made, he concluded that 'in every instance orientation of one kind or another has been found.' Superimposing three circles at Clava, in Scotland, on top of one another, he made the revelationary discovery that, so nearly identical were they, a common unit of measurement must have been used.

Archaeologists in the 1920s, under the influence of the diffusionist theory, which stated that all civilized matters began in the Near East or Egypt and spread outwards from there, would have none of this. Sir Mortimer Wheeler, President of the Society of Antiquaries in London, wrote about the existence of ancient astronomy: 'The idea has led a generation of antiquaries to waste much time and ink upon the supposed astronomical properties of these circles.' And there matters might have stood had it not been for the efforts of a man who spent more than half his life putting together what has been described as 'a well constructed parcel-bomb' under the foundations of contemporary archaeology.

Lone achievement

Dr Alexander Thom, Emeritus Professor of Engineering Science at Oxford University from 1945 to 1961, became addicted to megalithic design methods when on a sailing trip in the north of Scotland during the 1930s; stepping ashore at the great stone circle of Callanish, he noted its alignment to due north – 'a very difficult thing for people to achieve in those times, because the Pole Star wasn't where it is now.' From that moment on, he spent the greater part of his spare time tramping the fields and mountains of Britain meticulously surveying the circles that he found. By the time his 'parcel-bomb', *Megalithic Sites in Britain*, was published

NEWGRANGE
Co. Meath

decorated stone

roof box

0   2   4   6   8   10 metres

▨ Passage of light at midwinter sunrise

The stone chamber and mound at Newgrange in Ireland has a 'light-box' allowing the sunrise to be glimpsed briefly on a midwinter day.

The dimensions and geometry of Stonehenge in megalithic measurements, as calculated by Alexander Thom.

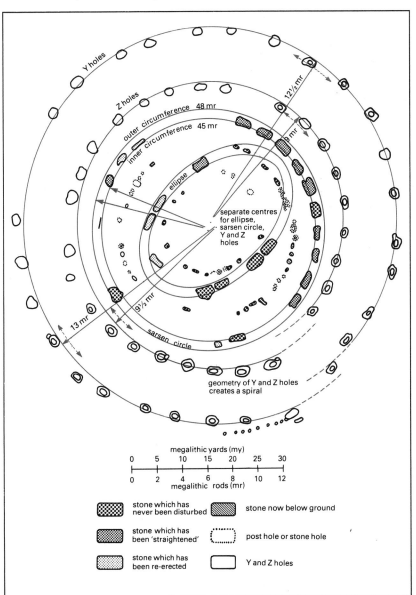

Y holes

Z holes

outer circumference 48 mr

inner circumference 45 mr

ellipse

separate centres for ellipse, sarsen circle, Y and Z holes

12½ mr

13 mr

9½ mr

sarsen circle

geometry of Y and Z holes creates a spiral

megalithic yards (my)
0   5   10   15   20   25   30

0   2   4   6   8   10   12
megalithic rods (mr)

▨ stone which has never been disturbed
▨ stone now below ground
▨ stone which has been 'straightened'
⬚ post hole or stone hole
▨ stone which has been re-erected
▢ Y and Z holes

in 1967 he had obtained results from no less than 600 sites on which to base his conclusions: *all* the circles, rough as they might look in a field, were designed geometrically and aligned astronomically to an astonishing degree of perfection.

Megalithic yard

A common unit of measurement had been used: the 'megalithic yard' of 2.72 feet. With this the builders had constructed not just circles, but elegant ellipses, egg-shapes, and flattened circles, all based on an internal geometry that showed use

Small irregularities on the distant horizon at Stonehenge were created artificially to mark the significant moments when the sun and moon rose and set (after Alexander Thom).

of certain right-angled triangles whose discovery had formerly been credited to the school of Pythagoras more than a thousand years later.

Indeed, like Pythagoras, there was evidence that some of the integral numbers used in the dimension of triangles – for instance, 5, 12, 13, or 8, 15, 17 – had a symbolic or magical significance. This in turn implied a knowledge of the value of π at least two millennia before it was first recorded in writing by the Hindu sage Arya-Bhata in the 6th Century AD.

With larger structures, such as Avebury, Carnac and Stonehenge, the 'megalithic rod' was used, a unit precisely two-and-a-half times the megalithic yard. At all three sites the geometrical harmony is astounding; in the middle of the extraordinary rows of stones at Carnac there is a 'knee' where the rows change direction; Alexander Thom regards the way this was achieved, with the use of two near-perfect Pythagorean triangles, as a pinnacle of geometric accomplishment – 'something that any engineer at any time in the world's history would have been proud to achieve.'

Ancient mathematicians

So the megalith builders were mathematicians on a grand scale, and operating their skills probably before anyone else in the world did so. That thought alone was upsetting enough to orthodox archaeologists, but Thom's parcel-bomb had still more explosive in it. They were also, in their own way, astronomers of equally fine ability. Using the local materials available – outlying stone markers, notches in hills, specially-constructed platforms – they turned their stone circles into observatories that measured not just relatively simple things, such as the midsummer and midwinter sunrises, but a host of sophisticated movements that required an observation accuracy of one part in 1000. They were even able to detect the Moon's 'minor standstill', a phenomenon caused by its elliptical orbit that has a cycle of 18.6 years; discovering

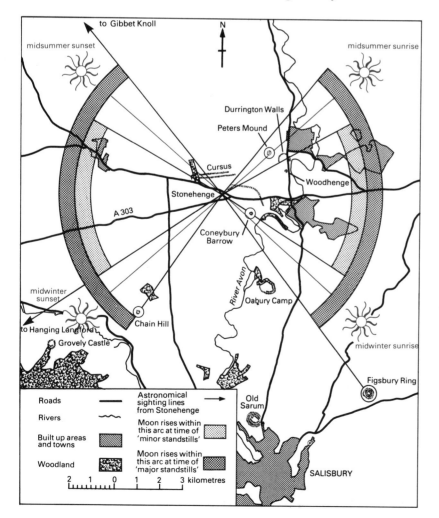

this tiny, 9′ irregularity in the Moon's orbit must have taken many generations of scientific study. Although Thom's is now the definitive study, other astronomers have made contributions.

In 1963 Gerald Hawkins, Professor of Astronomy at Boston University in America, claimed to have 'decoded' the way Stonehenge was used as an observatory, and in 1965 his book on the subject appeared. Its many inaccuracies, including the fundamental one that the map on which he based all his computer calculations was imprecise, made his ideas easily resistible in academic circles. However, work of greater scholarship by C. A. Newham (whose book is now sold alongside the official guide book at Stonehenge), has shown that Stonehenge was, as sightseers throughout the ages had always imagined, of central importance to the astronomer priests of the time. Standing in the centre of the great circle, they could tell from their view of the Sun or the Moon as it slipped over mark-points on the horizon, when it had reached the extreme limit of its orbit, and a new cycle was about to begin. Holes where experimental posts had been inserted over the years, in order to establish these exact horizon points, were discovered in the avenue. The proof of the intellectual capacity of these early people is now complete.

Archaeological upheaval

Professor Richard Atkinson of Cardiff University, Wales, who had earlier scorned Gerald Hawkins's work with a review of his book entitled 'Moonshine on Stonehenge', explained how disrupting all this was to archaeological thought, and why he personally had changed his mind. Thom's work, he wrote, upset 'the conceptual model of the prehistory of Europe, which has been current during the whole of the present century, and even now is only beginning to crumble at the edges . . . In terms of this model, it is almost inconceivable that mere barbarians on the remote north-west fringes of the continent should display a knowledge of mathematics and its applications hardly inferior, if at all, to that of Egypt at about the same date, or that of Mesopotamia considerably later.

'It is hardly surprising, therefore, that many prehistorians either ignore the implications of Thom's work, because they do not understand them, or resist them because it is more comfortable to do so. I have myself gone through the latter process; but I have come to the conclusion that to reject Thom's thesis because it does not conform to the model of prehistory on which I was brought up involves also the acceptance of improbabilities of an even higher order.'

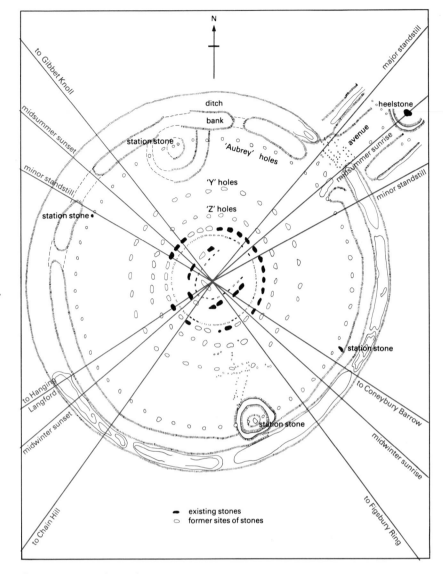

The six key astronomical directions centred on Stonehenge (after Alexander Thom).

Stone-age university

Acceptance of megalithic achievements in some ways presents even larger mysteries. How did the astronomer-priests gain this knowledge? How did they pass it on from generation to generation? As the British astronomer Sir Fred Hoyle put it, 'a veritable Newton or Einstein must have been at work,' and there would have to have been a university where students could be taught. In 1976, Dr Euan MacKie, of the Hunterian Museum in Glasgow, announced that he believed he had discovered this at a prehistoric site called Durrington Walls, near Stonehenge, where excavations had shown evidence of a diet much richer than usual, and the first evidence of woven cloth.

As to where the megalith builders originally came from, he points to the fact that the oldest radiocarbon dates for megalithic building, some as early as 4500 BC, are on the Atlantic seaboard, and get steadily younger as they move inland – exactly the opposite direction from the text-book diffusion originating in Egypt. Is it just possible that this is indirect evidence for the

The Grand Menhir
Brise at Locmariaquer
in Brittany once stood
17 metres tall and
could be used as a
distant foresight from
which moon eclipses
could be predicted.

existence of Atlantis (page 132), and that a
few survivors from an earlier, vanished culture
brought some of this knowledge with them?
Or did the skills emerge independently, perhaps
from the influence of a single, original genius?
Or did the early priesthoods which are presumed
to have existed on the eastern coastline of the
Mediterranean sail towards the Atlantic, as
Euan MacKie thinks, and settle in southern
Portugal?

In truth, nobody knows. At the same time, it is
baffling how astronomical knowledge could have
been passed on without writing – as Richard
Atkinson put it, you have to suppose that 'the
Astronomical ephemeris is not published, but is
transmitted by word of mouth from its compilers
to its users in the form of epic verse which
must be strictly memorized and reproduced.'

The Druid connection
Such feats of memory are not totally impossible.
When Julius Caesar arrived in Britain, some 1500
years after the final phase of Stonehenge, he
wrote that the Druid priesthood 'was taught to

repeat a great number of verses by heart, and
often spends twenty years on this institution; for
it is deemed unlawful to commit their statutes to
writing, for two reasons: to hide their mysteries
from the knowledge of the vulgar, and to exercise
the memory of their scholars.' So is it possible
that these Druids were the inheritors of the
ancient wisdom of the megalith builders, and the
oft-derided Druid connection with Stonehenge
may turn out to have a foundation in fact?

Today, that possibility looks more and more
likely. What is certain is that a period of
several thousand years, perhaps the longest
surviving cultural development the world has
known, culminated in a climax of observatory
building around 1850 BC; what powerful motive
impelled people in those times to expend so much
physical and intellectual effort is now only
dimly discernible; the speculation (page 82)
is that its roots lie in the earth energies
detectable by people who lived closer to the
rhythms of nature than we do now, and whose
strength was in some way connected with the
movement of the Sun, Moon, planets and stars.

Pyramid placing

If you took a satellite photograph of Egypt and tried to find a more perfect place to site the Great Pyramid of Cheops, you couldn't. It lies meticulously central between the two lines of longitude that marked the ancient boundary between Egypt and her neighbours. A quarter-circle arc taken from the centre of the pyramid precisely circumscribes the Nile Delta.

The square base was carefully placed so that its 230-metre long sides were aligned exactly N/S/E/W, the exactness marginally distorted today by the shifting continent on which it stands. How, at such an early stage of civilization, was such precision achieved? And why? Some 40 major pyramids were built along the Nile, but among them the Great Pyramid stands unique. Lavished within its geometry are marvels and mysteries which even today, nearly 5000 years later, we still cannot fully comprehend; assuredly, whoever laid out the design of the world's most renowned tomb was aiming for something more sublime than mere funerary pomp.

For a start there is its size, significantly larger than any pyramid that came before or after, as if it marked a summit of achievement after which there was no need to go further. Without a visit there, it is hard to gather an impression of its vastness. The two and a half million blocks of limestone, fitted together so tightly that the gaps between them are never more than a few millimetres, cover a ground area of more than 13 acres – enough to enclose in one place the huge cathedrals of Milan and Florence, St Paul's Basilica in Rome, and Westminster Abbey.

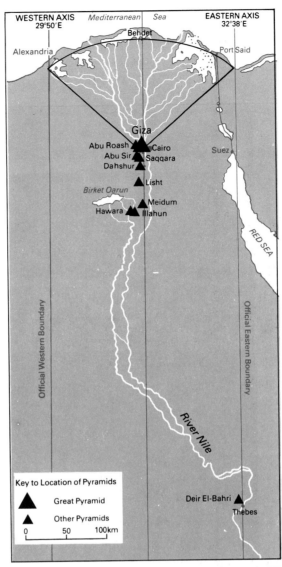

(left) The Great Pyramid of Cheops was precisely placed between the two vertical boundaries of ancient Egypt.

According to Charles Piazzi Smyth, whose extravagant 19th-century interpretations have since been discredited, the Great Pyramid also stood at the centre of the world.

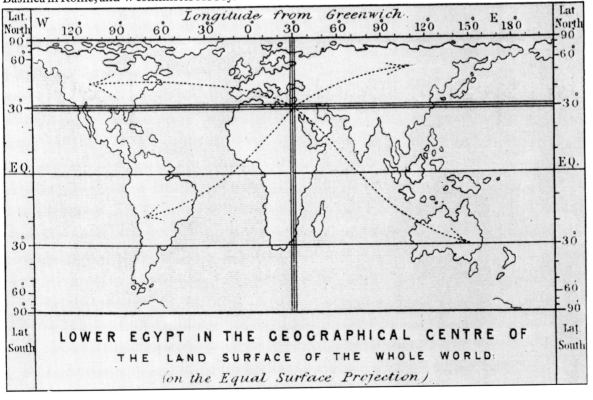

LOWER EGYPT IN THE GEOGRAPHICAL CENTRE OF THE LAND SURFACE OF THE WHOLE WORLD.
(on the Equal Surface Projection)

Dimensions of the Grand Gallery make it perfect for use as an astronomical observatory.

Napoleon's surveyors calculated that together with its two sister pyramids at Giza, there was enough stone to build a wall around France three metres high and one metre thick. How this immense structure was built at all, let alone how it was built so that it could incorporate complex mathematical formulae, is still not resolved. Of the building methods, no contemporary records or portrayals exist; the first written account comes from the Greek historian Herodotus, who visited Egypt in 440 BC, some 2000 years after it was built, and said that it took a work-force of 100,000 labourers 22 years to complete. Nowadays this is thought to be a considerable over-estimate, but as nobody knows the size of Egypt's population at the time, nor whether the stones were (1) dragged up earthen ramps or (2) lifted into place by means of engineering equipment, the question remains open. An elegant solution has been suggested as to how the builders overcame the first challenge – establishing a perfectly level foundation over such a huge area: they probably put earth banks around the circumference, and then flooded the inside with water. Humps and irregularities showing through the surface could gradually have been smoothed down as the water was drained away, with the result that the site is now level to an accuracy of one part in 10,000, at least as good as anything being built today.

Conflicting ideas

And what was the purpose of this vast constructional effort? At least since the 17th Century, when Sir Isaac Newton drew some mistaken mathematical conclusions from erroneous data that had been given him, Egyptologists have been polarized into two camps: the orthodox, who hold that a pyramid is a tomb and nothing else, its size determined largely by how rich and powerful the particular Pharaoh happened to be; and those they ridicule as 'pyramidiots', who believe the most important thing about a pyramid, and especially the Great Pyramid, is occult numerological/prophetical knowledge encapsulated in its dimensions.

Most modern Egyptologists belong in the first category; to them, the Great Pyramid is simply a fortress-tomb designed to be impenetrable, in which was secreted the body of the Pharaoh Khufu, known to the Greeks as Cheops. They point to the similar but lesser pyramids surrounding it, each with the same sort of hidden corridor leading directly to the apparent resting-place of a dead Pharaoh. The central belief of ancient Egyptian religion was that attainment of an after-life depended on the corpse remaining undisturbed. Hence many important Egyptians spent a life-time preparing for the moment when they died, building tombs designed to last for ever, and which contained a complex maze of secret passages and tunnels to defeat the attention of future grave-robbers intent upon the riches buried with them. Cheops, according to this view, must have lived at an especially wealthy time in Egyptian history, and was able to enforce the construction of a tomb of monstrous size and ingenuity; if the tradition recorded by Herodotus is to be trusted, given that it was 2000 years old when he heard it, Cheops was a tyrannical and hated king.

Lack of bodies

One trouble with interpreting pyramids in this straightforward way is that not a single body has ever been discovered in any of them. In most, including the Great Pyramid, there is an impressive sarcophagus, presumably designed to hold the Pharaoh's coffin; but invariably, the sarcophagi are empty. In some cases, they were even found closed and sealed, apparently untouched since the time they were first put there – and still empty. So what happened to the bodies? Were they (the usual explanation) taken away by grave-robbers? Although there is documentary evidence on papyrus that a wave of grave-robbing did indeed take place some time later, it seems unlikely. Thieves in the Valley of the Kings, a site of many later royal burials, usually and sensibly stole only the grave goods, taking care to leave the great majority of mummified bodies undisturbed.

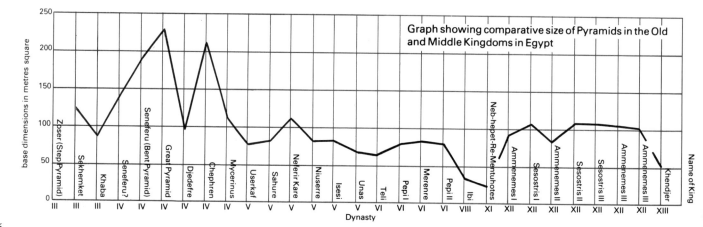

Graph showing comparative size of Pyramids in the Old and Middle Kingdoms in Egypt

A more likely idea is that priests, worried by the success of the grave-robbers, reverently opened up the secret chambers in the various pyramids, took away the bodies, and re-buried them in unpretentious tombs elsewhere. Or perhaps the chambers found so far are simply bluffs – false clues laid to persuade grave-robbers that others had been there before them – and the Pharaohs lie to this day in another part of their pyramid, awaiting discovery by archaeologists, themselves arguably the greatest grave-spoilers of all.

Finding the chamber

In the case of the Great Pyramid, the circumstances in which workmen first re-entered

The Great Pyramid of Cheops

Pyramidiocy: ten ideas best forgotten

1 Pyramid/Earth weight ratio The weight of the pyramid, being 5,923,400 tons, equals the weight of the Earth divided by one thousand billion (10^{15}).

Nobody knows how heavy the pyramid is, because there is no agreed figure for the number of blocks used to make it, nor the exact weight of each one. Estimates : 2.3–2.6 million blocks, 5.75–6.5 million tons. The Earth weighs about 6.6×10^{20} tons. The equation doesn't work.

2 Pyramid/Sun distance ratio The height of the pyramid multiplied by one thousand million (10^9) equals the distance between Earth and Sun.

The height of the pyramid cannot be measured precisely as approximately ten metres are missing from the top.

Because the Earth moves on an elliptical orbit, its distance from the Sun varies by three million miles. So an accurate figure cannot be achieved.

3 Equilateral perfection The sides of the pyramid form perfect equilateral triangles.

They don't : not all the angles are exactly 60°

4 Pyramid dimensions/calendar ratio The perimeter of the pyramid indicates the length of the solar year. First suggested by Charles Piazzi Smyth in 1865, who calculated the perimeter length as 36,520 'pyramid inches', which approximates to the number of days in the year if the comma is moved forward one place and changed to a full stop.

A more scrupulous archaeologist, Flinders Petrie, later made a more accurate survey using the same unit of measurement, and found the perimeter to be 36,276 inches.

5 Earth density/pyramid ratio The coffer in the King's Chamber indicates the mean density of the earth, being 71,250 (normal) cubic inches in capacity, a figure which can be divided satisfactorily to arrive at a figure of 5.7.

The generally agreed figure for the Earth's density, according to standards currently used, is 5.41. But in any case, the pyramid mathematics involved are so abstruse that the same result could be [and has been] extrapolated from the Eiffel Tower and the Washington Monument.

6 Squaring the circle The height of the pyramid stands in the same relationship to its base area as does the radius of a circle to its area.

The magic figure of π may well have been known to the pyramid architects, but they certainly did not use it in these dimensions; to make the mathematics work, you have to multiply everything by two even to arrive at an approximation.

7 The pyramid was a secret granary *It wasn't.*

8 Numerological predictions By interpreting the measurements of the Grand Gallery and other chambers, the future can be predicted.

Piazzi Smyth and Robert Menzies both said they could 'read' in the Pyramid's dimensions the imminent arrival [in 1881] of a miracle comparable to the second coming of Christ. Others have wrongly predicted similar events in 1936 and 1953.

9 Extra-terrestrial builders Only a super-race from outer space could have achieved such an engineering miracle.

Radiocarbon dating confirms other evidence that the pyramid was built around 2500 BC, by which time Egyptian technology was comfortably equal to the demands.

10 The pyramid was merely a tomb The only reason there isn't a body is because the first workmen to enter the King's Chamber tore Khufu's mummy to shreds.

Al Mamun's expedition was a serious one attempting to find written records; there is no evidence whatsoever that they plundered the tomb.

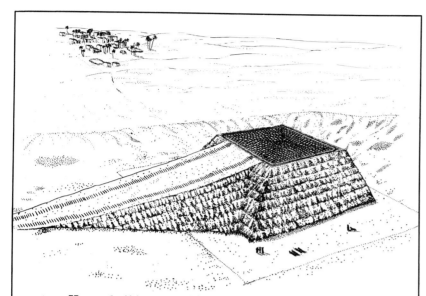

How to build a pyramid without involving spacemen

Although there is some doubt (see text) about how the blocks of stone were finally raised into place, the basic steps involved in quarrying and moving the stone for the Great Pyramids have been convincingly worked out by archaeologists. This summary is based on the account by Dr Peter White of the University of Sydney, Australia, in *The Past Is Human*.

1 *Choose the site*. On the west bank of the Nile, closest to the setting sun, on solid rock, and near to water-borne transport.

2 *Organize labour*. Gangs of 250 workmen were probably the basic unit, working mostly when not needed on farms – the equivalent of National Service, or labour in lieu of taxes. Master masons and skilled workers were needed full-time.

3 *Level the site*. Form a grid of ditches and fill them with water. Gradually drain, chiselling the floor level as you go. (Inaccuracy 0.004%)

4 *Align site*. Observe the nightly position of the Pole Star. Make fine adjustments by observing the midnight positions of other stars. Then form a square.

5 *Quarry the stone*. Use a quarry nearby for convenience – in the case of the Giza pyramids, the quarry can be seen immediately around the Sphinx. Facing stone for the pyramids came from fine white limestone in the Tura quarries on the east bank of the Nile, whose tunnels are still there today.

6 *Shape the stone*. Measure and mark with T-squares, plumb bobs, facing plates and paired rods. Cut with copper saws and chisels.

7 *Move the stone*. Place the stones, normally 2–5 tons but sometimes up to 200 tons, on sledges. Tell the labour force to chant, and pull.

8 *Build a ramp*. Remains of ramps have been found, averaging a slope of 1 : 10, forming the major supply route to one face of the pyramids. Steeper and narrower embankments surrounded the other three sides.

9 *Finish the stones*. The outside blocks were accurate to a few centimetres, and were probably cut very exactly and pre-fitted by master masons at ground level.

10 *Lever into place*. How the final positioning of stones was achieved is not known. Some sort of leverage must have been used on the narrow embankments (8 above).

the King's Chamber in AD 820, recorded by a number of Arab historians, leave no doubt that something extraordinary must have happened to the body of Cheops: either he was never put in the huge, granite sarcophagus that had apparently been designed for him, or somehow he was spirited away. Like so much that is cryptic about the pyramid, it is a conundrum that seems impossible to solve.

The chamber was discovered after a Caliph named Abdullah Al Mamun, reading Roman accounts of a secret door and passage inside the pyramid, came to believe that this must lead to a fabled library containing records of astronomical secrets. After a number of false starts, his workmen accidentally discovered the first of many passages that led maze-like to the King's Chamber; one of these, the Ascending Passage, was blocked by a number of granite plugs, each about two metres long and so tightly wedged that it must have remained there undisturbed since it had first been slid into place. The only way of going forward was to force a tunnel around the plugs, and when they finally entered the Chamber, they found the tightly jointed blocks comprising the walls and roof were utterly undisturbed.

Yet the sarcophagus was empty and its lid was missing. How could anybody, conceivably, have removed either the body or the lid, since the workmen had themselves broken through the only sealed entrance? What had happened to the skeletons of the pall-bearers who presumably had dropped the plugs into position behind them as they climbed up into the King's Chamber?

Forgotten science

Peter Tompkins, whose book *Secrets of the Great Pyramid* is the definitive modern summary of the subject, believes this to be the central puzzle. The problem of what happened to the pall-bearers may now have been solved by a theory that, having deposited the pharaoh's body, they then left the chamber and went back down the Ascending Passage, dropping the granite plugs behind them with a highly complex method of leverage. But this still leaves the question of the missing body unresolved, for everybody agrees that until the workmen broke through in 820 AD, the chamber was irrevocably sealed. So either the body was never put there, or it has literally vanished. Tompkins is sympathetic to the first idea. He believes that astronomer-priests conceived the building as something far greater than a tomb, and never had any intention of burying Cheops there; they merely promised to do so, and thus gained access to enough funds for a vast practical experiment in now-forgotten learning. During the construction of the Great Pyramid, he believes they put the final touches to an entire science that embraced astronomy, mathematics and astrology, and hid its secrets for ever within the design of the building. Or perhaps Cheops himself knew what they were doing, and arranged for his body to be buried elsewhere?

Ancient learning

The history of pyramidiocy is not reassuring, but such an idea is nowadays much less outrageous

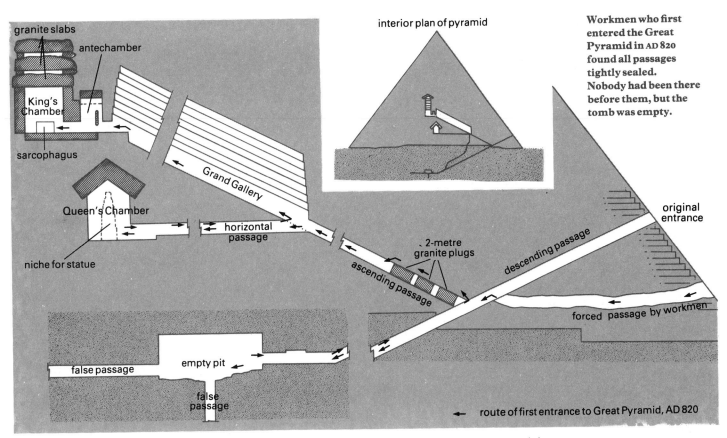

granite slabs

antechamber

King's Chamber

sarcophagus

interior plan of pyramid

Grand Gallery

Queen's Chamber

niche for statue

horizontal passage

2-metre granite plugs

ascending passage

descending passage

original entrance

false passage

empty pit

false passage

forced passage by workmen

← route of first entrance to Great Pyramid, AD 820

Workmen who first entered the Great Pyramid in AD 820 found all passages tightly sealed. Nobody had been there before them, but the tomb was empty.

than it used to be. The Great Pyramid is undeniably positioned at the exact centre of Egypt in a way that demanded finesse and deep knowledge; and this being so, it makes much more plausible some of the associated skills that have been claimed for the early Egyptians. Together with Dr Livio Stecchini, Professor of Ancient History at William Paterson College, New Jersey, who has re-examined the mathematics involved, Peter Tompkins has listed numerous achievements which are implied: 'The Great Pyramid is a carefully located geodetic marker, or fixed landmark, on which the geography of the ancient world was brilliantly constructed; it served as a celestial observatory from which maps and tables of the stellar hemisphere could be accurately drawn; it incorporates in its sides and angles the means for creating a highly sophisticated map projection of the northern hemisphere . . . the foundations were almost perfectly oriented to true north, its structure incorporated a value for π, its main chamber made use of the "sacred" triangles that were to make Pythagoras famous . . . it may well be the repository of an ancient and possibly universal system of weights and measures . . . whoever built the Great Pyramid knew the precise circumference of the planet, and the length of the year including its awkward .2422 fraction of a day . . . its architects may well have known the mean length of the Earth's orbit round the Sun, the specific density of the planet, the 26,000 year cycle of the equinoxes, the acceleration of gravity and the speed of light.'

As part of this sophisticated body of knowledge, Livio Stecchini also argues that the pyramid builders, as well as knowing that the Earth was circular, had calculated the geographical distance from the equator to the poles, and thus concluded that it was slightly flattened.
The whole, says Tompkins, added up to the fact that 'The Great Pyramid, like most of the great temples of antiquity, was designed on the basis of a hermetic geometry known only to a restricted group of initiates, mere traces of which percolated to the Classical and Alexandrian Greeks.'

Link with megaliths
The evidence for this takes many thousands of words and almost as many mathematical formulae, but what is striking is how many of the claimed achievements of the Egyptians are identical to those which have been demonstrated for the megalith builders of north-west Europe (see previous pages) at precisely the same time in man's development. Hundreds, and in some cases thousands, of years before most text-books list the fact, there was simultaneous discovery of the value of Pythagorean triangles, a precise calendar, a true compass-bearing for north, knowledge of the movement of celestial bodies (possibly including knowledge that the world was round), and a minutely accurate system of measurement.

Patterns in Peru

The largest work of art in the world, one of the most impressive and at the same time least understandable achievements of prehistoric man, was hardly noticed by anyone until 1939, for the ironic reason that it was too big. Then pilots of small aircraft flying above the desert plain of southern Peru began to send back reports of strange markings that could be seen in certain lights – a criss-cross jumble of long straight lines interspersed with strange curves and patterns.

Archaeologists imagined that they must be the tell-tale signs of an ancient irrigation system, and despatched Dr Paul Kosok, an agronomist from Long Island University, to study them. From the air they looked immense. Yet on the

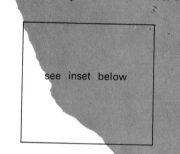

In the vastness of South America, the desert patterns were formed in a highly localized area north of the small town of Nazca.

ground the shallow indentations in the earth caused him considerable difficulty in even finding them. As another observer wrote later: 'The lines only come sharply into focus when viewed lengthways. Standing a few yards to the side makes a line invisible, but standing astride makes the faintest line show clearly.' Making his first careful survey, Kosok's puzzlement became even greater: what emerged from his plans was the perfectly formed shape of a large bird, its outline completely invisible from ground level. How could this pattern have been achieved? Kosok trudged through the desert to discover and survey the figure of a huge spider, followed by dozens more shapes, both animal and geometric. In 1946, when he passed on his notes to Dr Maria Reiche, a German mathematician interested in ancient observatories, he was still none the wiser about why or even how these vast designs had been completed; but there they were, high in the middle of nowhere, the incomprehensible work of a lost civilization.

Ancient runways?

Since then, Maria Reiche has discovered a great deal more about the way they were laid out, working continuously and almost single-handedly to record the exact dimensions of all the drawings and lines before they are obliterated by tourists and traffic. The purpose, however, is still just as obscure, except to note in passing that the one thing they definitely weren't was airstrips for passing spacecraft – as Maria Reiche put it: 'Once you remove the stones, the ground is

quite soft. I'm afraid the spacemen would have gotten stuck.'

The Peru Patterns remain one of the world's wonders. Gerald Hawkins, the astronomer who believed he had decoded Stonehenge, went there in 1972 to see if there was a significantly large number of astronomical alignments along the lines (there wasn't), and pointed out that their straightness was an almost unbelievable feat of engineering – on average they do not deviate more than two metres in every kilometre:

'That figure was the limit of capability of the photogrammatic survey. The ancient lines were in fact laid out straighter than could be measured with modern air-survey techniques. And this linearity continues for miles. It goes out beyond that circle of clear visibility set by ground-level dust haze. It picks up in the same unswerving direction on the opposite side of a gully, and can run as straight as an arrow up a hill.'

The lines are formed by a simple technique not unlike the way white horses and other hill figures were carved out of the downlands of southern Britain by removing the thin layer of topsoil and grass from the underlying chalk. Where the Peruvian desert patterns are, at Nazca, a vast level plain of yellowish-white soil is covered by a thin layer of dark stones, and when these are removed a line can be created.

Although the physical labour involved is not very great, the design work is highly complex. Maria Reiche thinks there was a fixed unit of measurement of 0.66 centimetres, similar to Alexander Thom's megalithic yard (page 61). The figures were then laid out, she believes, on scaled-down plans which were transferred to curves on the ground by using lengths of rope attached to stone markers, some of which can still be seen today. 'Length and direction of every piece was carefully measured and taken note of. An approximate estimate of

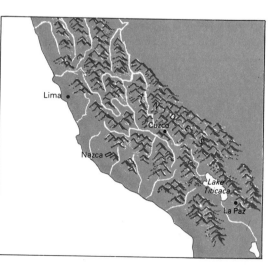

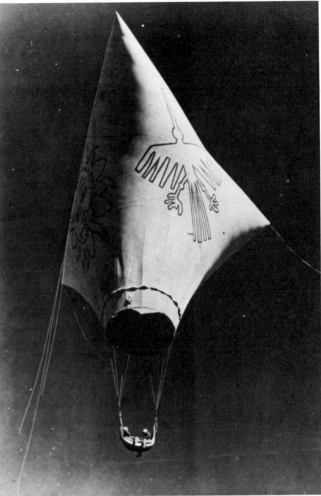

these would not have been enough to produce shapes, in which a deviation of a few inches would spoil the proportions, which as we see them on aerial photographs are perfect. Those acquainted with surveying techniques will best understand the accomplishments needed for such an undertaking. Ancient Peruvians must have had instruments and equipment which we ignore and which together with ancient knowledge were buried and hidden from the eyes of the conquerors as the one treasure which was not to be surrendered.'

Perfect proportions

She believes she has discovered so far only a fraction of this knowledge: 'What is most impressive in all the ground-drawings is their great size, coupled with perfect proportions. How they could have accomplished the animal-figures with their beautifully laid out curves and their well-balanced dimensions that are so difficult to construct, is a mystery which will take years to investigate, if ever solved.'

Maria Reiche does add one qualification to this – 'unless they were able to fly'. And this is precisely what Bill Spohrer, a US resident in Peru, and a member of the International Explorers' Society, set out to prove. The people who laid out the patterns seem to have come from two overlapping cultures known as the Paracas and the Nazca, who for many centuries before and after the birth of Christ lived a simple agricultural life.

Parachute fibre

But they had two special accomplishments, excelling in weaving and the decoration of pottery, and it was these somewhat surprising achievements that gave Spohrer his clue. Four pieces of Nazcan fabric from robbed tombs near the desert drawings were put under a microscope and were revealed to have a finer weave than present-day parachute material, and tighter than that used by modern hot-air balloonists – 205×110 threads per square inch compared with 160×90. And on pottery were numerous paintings of what may be balloons and kites, flying with trailing streamers and lines.

Following his hunch further, he discovered an old Incan legend of a young boy called Antarqui who helped the Incas in battle by flying above the enemy lines and reporting their positions. Many of the Nazca textiles depicted flying men. These legends pre-dated the many known examples of remote Indian tribes in Central and South America who to this day make

left:
**Balloon pilots
Jim Woodman (left)
and Julian Knott**

right:
**Condor I high above
the desert markings.**

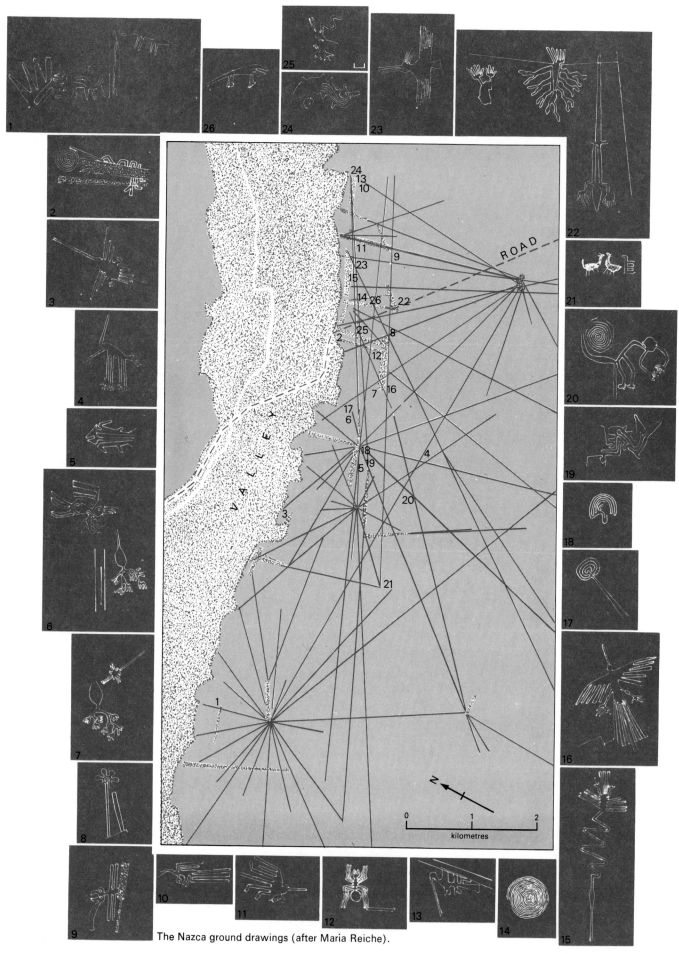

The Nazca ground drawings (after Maria Reiche).

small ceremonial hot-air balloons and release them at religious festivals; surprisingly, too, the first modern manned flight of a hot-air balloon was made in 1709 by a Brazilian priest in Lisbon, more than 70 years before the usually accredited flight of the Montgolfier brothers in France.

The final clue lay in the 'burn pits' at the end of many of the long straight tracks, circular areas upwards of ten metres in diameter containing blackened rocks. Spohrer's investigation, now involving several other members of the International Explorers' Society, analysed these stones in order to discount the theory that they were made by prehistoric extra-terrestrial rockets, and at the same time confirmed that the blackening was due to intense heat. Had this been the result of a great fire lit to warm the air inside a balloon before it was released upwards?

Balloon trial

In November 1975 the theory was put to the test. Using only materials and a level of technology that would have been available to the Nazca Indians, they built a balloon, lit a fire beneath it, and flew it some distance over the desert with two men inside a reed gondola hanging beneath. Of all the theories about how such perfectly-designed shapes and patterns could have been completed, the idea of ballooning engineers seems currently the best. But the purpose is still obscure. Perhaps dead Nazca chiefs were sent on a last journey to the Sun, as legends say, in black balloons which would rise out of sight as the balloon material gathered heat from the sun. Perhaps the birds and other great figures symbolized the life of such a chief. But why the compelling need to construct all those perfectly straight lines? There is as yet no answer – but evidence is growing that it may have been an urge among early peoples much more widespread than has been thought. As the next pages describe, there is an uncanny similarity between the long straight lines of Peru, and what had been happening on the other side of the globe a great deal earlier; Stonehenge and a great many other megalithic sites seem to be connected with geometric precision. By the time the Peruvian patterns were laid down during a few centuries either side of the birth of Christ, the tradition of megalith building had long ceased, so there is certainly no direct connection between the two cultures. But it is perhaps not too far-fetched to speculate that the levels of culture, both of them pre-literate and predominantly stone-using, were much the same; and that the urge to sculpt the landscape seems to die when writing and urban life become commonplace.

Ballast being ejected from Condor I.

Condor I landing in a cloud of dust created by ballast jettisoned a few minutes previously.

Alignments and connections

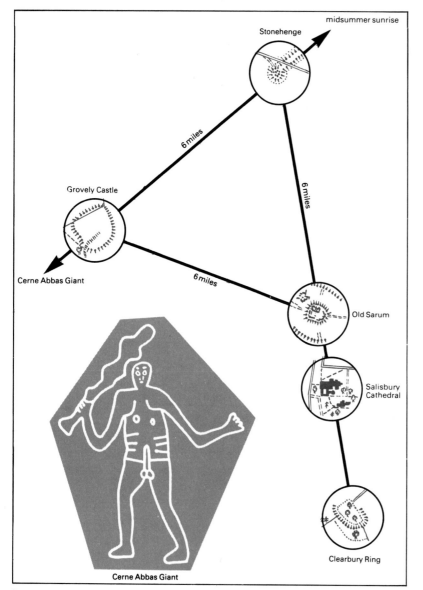

midsummer sunrise

Stonehenge

6 miles

6 miles

Grovely Castle

6 miles

Cerne Abbas Giant

Old Sarum

Salisbury Cathedral

Clearbury Ring

Cerne Abbas Giant

A near-perfect equilateral triangle based on the Stonehenge sunrise alignment, discovered by the British Astronomer-Royal Sir Norman Lockyer.

The world over, priesthoods of early societies seem to have been obsessed by the supposedly magical power of heavenly bodies. Sun-worship cults can be traced back to the dawn of civilization; pyramid builders and megalith builders alike, on both sides of the Atlantic, took infinite pains to align and construct their monuments so that they worked precisely as astronomical observatories. The knowledge and the effort involved were far beyond what would be expected – in terms of the relative sizes of population, a bigger effort even than the temple building of classical times (itself astronomically oriented) or the construction of the great mediaeval cathedrals of Europe. Just one extraordinary example out of many is the inexplicable cone-shaped mound known as Silbury Hill, in southern Britain: it has been calculated that early in the second millennium BC a total of 18 million man-hours was spent in its construction – according to the archaeologist Richard Atkinson, 'a fraction of the gross national product at least as great as that

devoted by the United States of America to the whole of its space programme.' Its importance must have been overwhelming.

Archaeological recognition for the immensity and complexity of these achievements has been slow in coming (page 58), not least because to admit them raises a number of academically embarrassing questions: in particular, is it possible that illiterate and supposedly primitive farming communities laid out their various monuments and temples in a vast co-ordinated scheme of terrestrial geometry, of which the newly-accepted astronomical function is only a part? When we visit, say, Stonehenge, are we standing at a focal point in a huge network of interconnected sacred sites, whose purpose has today been forgotten? Have we, in other words, grossly under-estimated the skills and wisdom of early people?

Stonehenge patterns

Visionary antiquarians throughout the centuries have often suggested so, without being able to offer the hard evidence that would prove them right. However, in 1909 they received the support of Sir Norman Lockyer (page 60). In the second edition of his book *Stonehenge and other British Stone Monuments Astronomically Considered*, he noted a curious geometrical pattern that had its apex at Stonehenge. He found the line of the midsummer sunrise could be traced backwards exactly six miles to the neolithic settlement/religious centre called Grovely Castle. There was an identical distance between Stonehenge and Old Sarum, a similar prehistoric hill-top site on which the original Salisbury Cathedral had been built. And when the three places were joined up on a map, a near-perfect equilateral triangle emerged. Surely this was evidence of long-distance planning? And was this knowledge still extant in historic times? For mysteriously, when the new Salisbury Cathedral was built in 1220 AD, it was placed mathematically on line, exactly two miles beyond Old Sarum.

Lockyer's speculations were derided at the time, and the objections raised against him are still made now, whether applied to his own pioneering work or that of the many fringe prehistorians who have developed and extended his ideas. Firstly, he was said to have misunderstood the nature of early society – i.e. the 'barbarians' of north-west Europe would have been incapable of such astonishing and sophisticated planning. Secondly, he was accused of statistical naïvety – an almost limitless number of meaningless patterns can be drawn on maps by joining up a number of ancient sites in straight lines.

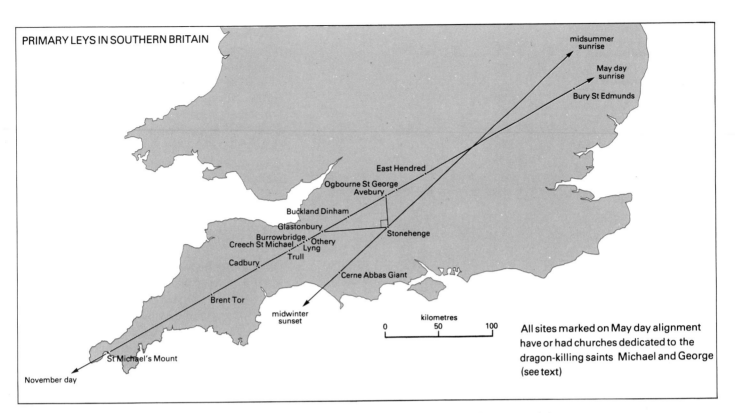

PRIMARY LEYS IN SOUTHERN BRITAIN

midsummer sunrise

May day sunrise

Bury St Edmunds

East Hendred

Ogbourne St George
Avebury

Buckland Dinham

Glastonbury
Burrowbridge
Creech St Michael · Othery
Lyng
Trull

Stonehenge

Cadbury

Cerne Abbas Giant

Brent Tor

midwinter sunset

kilometres
0   50   100

St Michael's Mount

November day

All sites marked on May day alignment
have or had churches dedicated to the
dragon-killing saints Michael and George
(see text)

The first of these objections is unconvincing today. If the megalith builders were clever enough to make Stonehenge an accurate and versatile observatory, to have a common unit of measurement throughout the huge area in which they lived, to explore geometric patterns, and to transport huge blocks of stone over many miles (all of which is accepted by many archaeologists), then there is every reason to believe that they could have laid out long alignments, if they wanted to. But did they? Here the evidence is still as strongly resisted as when Lockyer first presented it, and when in the 1920s Alfred Watkins, a worthy antiquarian in Herefordshire, began to offer his theories about a 'ley system' which had once been marked out on the face of Britain, a vein-like pattern of lines that criss-crossed each other like a geometric spider's web. Lockyer's triangle, he perceived, could be considerably elongated if the

midsummer sunrise line was taken beyond the horizons in both directions to join up with other ancient ceremonial sites. To the north-east, beyond St Peter's Mound, lay a prominent hilltop called Inkpen Beacon, and the neolithic Winterbourne Camp. To the south-west, beyond Groveley Castle, the line went through similar early settlements, crossed the enigmatic hill-figure the Cerne Abbas Giant (of great but uncertain antiquity), and finished up on the south coast of Britain at Puncknowle Beacon – in all, a dead straight line covering a distance of more than 100 kilometres.

Ley system

As Watkins explained it to local naturalists, leys such as this, some short, some long, existed in profusion all over Britain. They could be discovered by lining up on a map, and then checking on foot in the countryside, all the

A line drawn through the longest unbroken stretch of land in southern Britain coincides with the May day sunrise. Other so-called primary leys include one based on the Stonehenge sunrise alignment, which in turn seems connected to the first line by a right-angle triangle.

A typical ley formed by a line drawn between ancient sites of apparently different ages, in this case centred on Pilsdon Pen in Dorset.

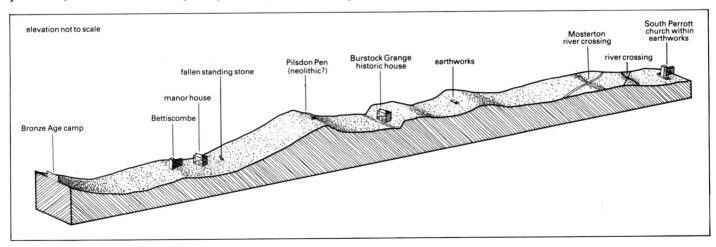

elevation not to scale

Bronze Age camp

Bettiscombe

manor house

fallen standing stone

Pilsdon Pen (neolithic?)

Burstock Grange historic house

earthworks

Mosterton river crossing

river crossing

South Perrott church within earthworks

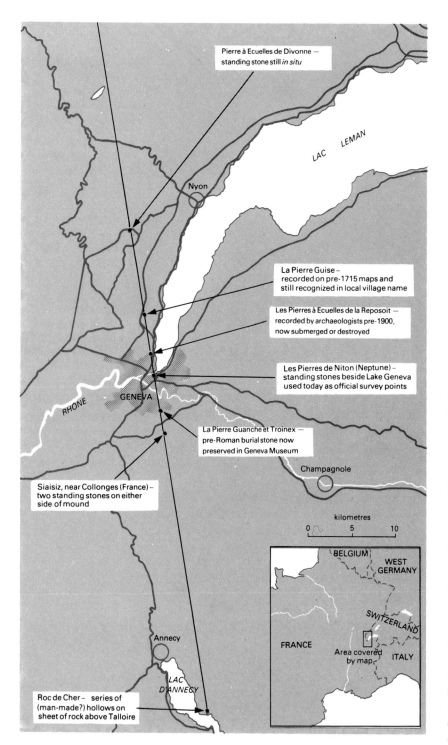

Pierre à Ecuelles de Divonne —
standing stone still *in situ*

LAC LEMAN

Nyon

La Pierre Guise —
recorded on pre-1715 maps and
still recognized in local village name

Les Pierres à Ecuelles de la Reposoit —
recorded by archaeologists pre-1900,
now submerged or destroyed

Les Pierres de Niton (Neptune) –
standing stones beside Lake Geneva
used today as official survey points

RHONE   GENEVA

La Pierre Guanche et Troinex —
pre-Roman burial stone now
preserved in Geneva Museum

Champagnole

Siaisiz, near Collonges (France) –
two standing stones on either
side of mound

kilometres
0   5   10

BELGIUM
WEST
GERMANY

SWITZERLAND

FRANCE

Annecy

Area covered
by map

ITALY

LAC
D'ANNECY

Roc de Cher – series of
(man-made?) hollows on
sheet of rock above Talloire

**Leys similar to those in
Britain have been
found in other
countries. This one in
Switzerland was
traced by antiquarian
June Knowles.**

remnants of an ancient civilization that still
showed: burial mounds, standing stones, man-
made lakes and moats, traditional holy wells and
sacred springs, the high points of mountains and
hills where beacon fires were traditionally lit, old
wayside crosses at the junction of former
trackways, churches built upon the sites of
previously pagan religious centres, notches
carved on distant hills to mark the direction of
the ley, or alongside castles and hill-forts whose
ruined walls and ditches could still be seen
silhouetted against the sky.

His lectures and research culminated in 1925
with the publication of *The Old Straight Track*,

a gentle and charming book that nevertheless
raised so much hostility in the archaeological
establishment that advertisements for it were
refused in orthodox journals. Even today, after
enthusiastic followers of Watkins have drawn up
some thousands of leys, and formed a vigorous
society in which to promote his findings, the
subject is mentioned only to be dismissed.
'You cannot argue with unreason' wrote a
reviewer of one recent book that touched on the
subject; and 'it is the point at which amateurs
and professionals part company abruptly'
according to Dr John Coles, editor of the
Journal of the Prehistoric Society.

Dating inconsistencies

It is indeed not difficult to find quick arguments
against leys. The mark-points listed by Watkins
and described above come from many different
eras – Celtic crosses and pre-Reformation
churches are millenia or centuries younger than
neolithic burial mounds and standing stones.
And since hundreds of such disparate sites exist
on most of the 1 : 50,000 Ordnance Survey
maps used by ley-hunters, it is statistically
certain that at least some of them will line up
by chance.

Yet in spite of this, could there still be a
nucleus of truth in Alfred Watkins's vision?
Leys have an uncomfortable habit of turning up
uninvited, as happened when a cautious West
Country archaeologist looked into the possibility
of a May Day sunset alignment centred upon
Pilsdon Pen, an early Bronze Age ceremonial
centre built with great earthen ramparts on one of
Dorset's highest hills. Archaeological excavation
had given tantalizing evidence of a ceremonial
way leading from the ramparts in the right
astronomical direction; today a continuation of it
leads past a fallen standing stone, a manor house,
and along a trackway to an old church – all
good Watkins ley points, supplemented by
legends and ghost stories of processions passing
along it. For those who have come to accept the
evidence of the megalith builders' astronomical
ingenuity, it is a theoretically acceptable
alignment, the supposed existence of ley points
being neither here nor there, and that was the
position the archaeologist took until he checked
it on a map. There, unbidden and unwanted, an
indisputable ley emerged; a continuation of the
alignment led in one direction to the edge of
another Bronze Age camp, exactly as Watkins
had described on many other leys; and in the
other direction ended at a Norman church built
within the visible outline of an ancient
earthwork.

This tradition of the continuity of worship in
sacred places is one of the strongest arguments

that ley-hunters have to justify their inclusion of relatively recent as well as very old sites on their lines. The earliest Christian saintly missionaries were instructed from Rome not to destroy the pagan sites that they found, but to incorporate them in their churches, and evidence for this can be seen in many churches today in the form of standing stones or the outline of the churchyard. Few records exist of why later pre-Reformation churches were placed where they are, but there is the mathematical evidence from Salisbury Cathedral that there was a definite relationship with earlier sites.

John Michell, a writer and researcher who has been at the forefront of the recent movement to gain recognition for the theories of Alfred Watkins, believes that the placing of these churches shows that the planning of leys once took place on an almost unimaginably large scale. If you take a map of southern Britain and impose on it the line of the May Day sunrise, it coincidentally marks the longest possible stretch of unbroken land; astonishingly, the megalithic surveyors may have found this out, for they put many sacred sites along it. Avebury, once more imposing and extensive than even Stonehenge, lies almost at the centre of the line; Glastonbury, its steep hill artifically shaped into a three-dimensional labyrinth, lies further to the west; and dotted along the line lie a significant number of churches that are presumably on formerly pagan sites, for they are dedicated to the dragon-killing saints Michael and George (the connection between labyrinths and dragons in ancient lore is described on pages 154 and 159).

European leys
Did something of the same sort happen simultaneously in Europe? John Michell has cited the work of the German evangelical parson Wilhelm Teudt, a contemporary of Watkins, whose book *Germanische Heiligtümer* was published in 1929 and gave details of ancient site connections called *heilige Linien* that are almost identical to the leys of Britain. Like Watkins, he soon found a following of enthusiastic map addicts who pounced upon his ideas and found many other lines. Patronized by Heinrich Himmler, his theories even became officially acceptable for a while, and although the racialist content of his writings make his work unprintable today, his astro-archaeological findings may yet prove valid.

Far more remarkable is an almost unknown work by the French philologist Xavier Guichard, who in 1936 had printed at his own expense the 558-page book *Eleusis Alesia* (complete with 555 maps). During the war, a bomb on his home at

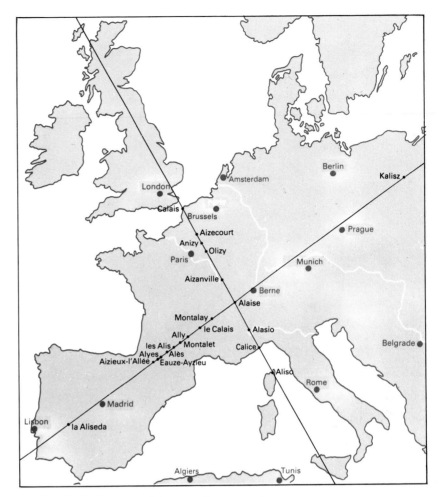

Abbeville killed him and destroyed most copies of his book, only a few of which can be found in European museums. In 1911, he had been researching the origins of ancient European place-names, and came to the conclusion that there were three basic ones: Burgus, Antium, and Alesia, of which the last was unique as never having been given to a town or village founded in historic times. In its Greek form of Eleusis it dated from legendary pre-Homeric times; in its Indo-European roots Alès, Alis or Alles meant a meeting point to which people travelled. As he pinpointed the word in all the many forms into which it had been corrupted, he found it most concentrated in his native France, but also as far away as Egypt (Eleusis on the Nile Delta), Poland (Kalisz), Italy (Alessano, on the southernmost heel) and the Spanish peninsula (la Aliseda).

His pursuit of the true meaning of the word, and the origins of the people who first used it, consumed the next 25 years of his life. As he looked more closely into the kind of place which it described, he found there were invariably two identifying features: landscaped hills overlooking rivers, and a man-made well of salt or mineral water. From this, he deduced that they had all been ancient centres where travellers could stop and drink the life-giving waters.

The French philologist Xavier Guichard published a little-known book in 1936 suggesting a link between prehistoric sites based on the word 'Alesia'. As with primary leys in Britain, a line can be traced to denote the May day sunrise.

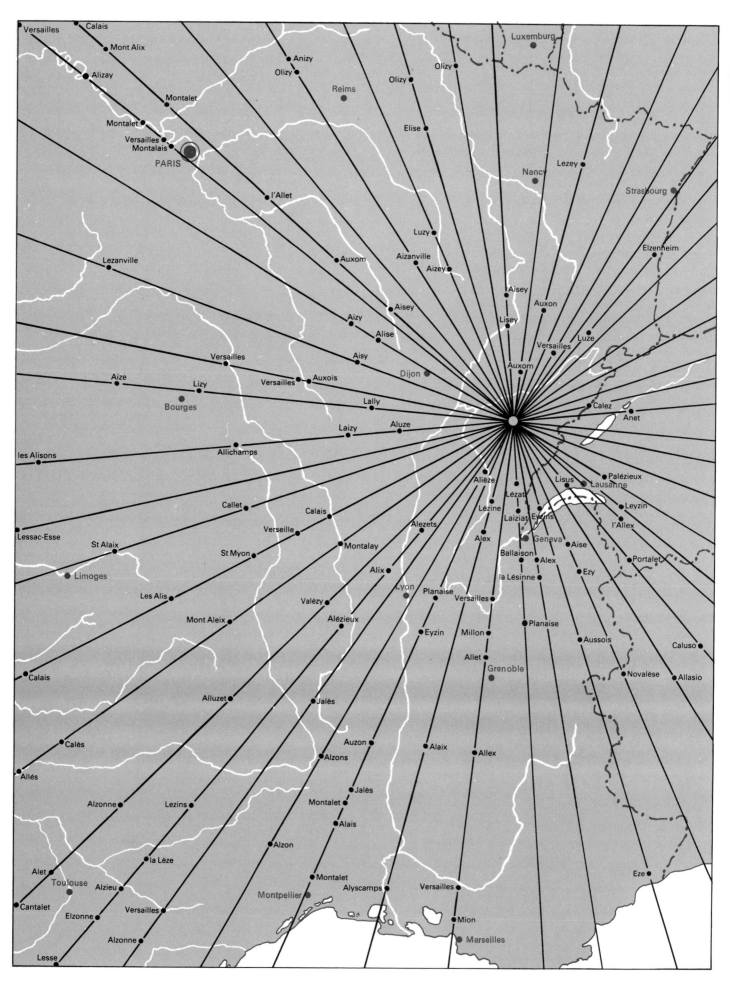

Alaise and derivative place-names throughout Europe. For details of rectangular panel see l/h page. For explanation of 'Alaise' see accompanying text on alignments.

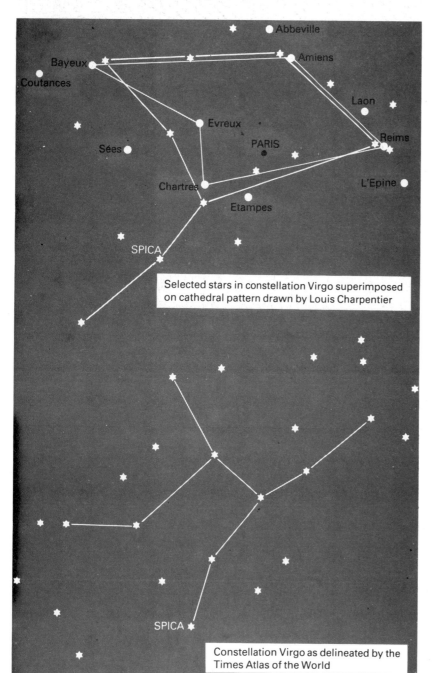

Selected stars in constellation Virgo superimposed on cathedral pattern drawn by Louis Charpentier

Constellation Virgo as delineated by the Times Atlas of the World

Some claims for Earth patterns can easily be refuted, as in the suggestion that French cathedrals near Chartres dedicated to the Virgin Mary reflect the constellation Virgo in the sky.

He found more than 400 such sites in France alone, and to his astonishment they appeared to be placed in a geodetic system so vast that, if true, it would make the most extreme speculations of old-straight-trackers look like kindergarten geography. He proposed that the whole of Europe, centred on a remote ancient site called Alaise, near Besançon in southern France, had been divided up into two *roses-des-vents* (compass cards such as those used by Greek geographers): one of 24 lines that attempted to divide the horizon into equal segments; and one of four lines that marked the meridian and the equinox, and the winter and summer solstices. This implied, he said, a knowledge of latitude and longitude, and the position of the North Pole and the Equator. Moreover, he could trace a common distance

between the sites that meant a common unit of measurement.

Guichard's book is rare by any standards, and has not been published in English; nor has it yet been subjected to academic scrutiny. When compiling the composite map on pages 78 and 79 of this Atlas, cartographers found that, perhaps because we are using a slightly different projection, some of the Alesias which he used in evidence fell a little away from the carefully drawn maps in his own book. Our judgement was that as with many ley-hunters, he had come upon a central truth but spoiled his case by taking his conclusions too far.

Heretical viewpoint

But there are compelling similarities between his speculations and those of Alfred Watkins. Without ever learning of each other's work, both men came to the conclusion that the salt trade must have been of vital importance in early trading routes. Watkins chose the word 'ley' to describe his old straight tracks because of its frequent use in ancient place names; both the consonant and the vowel sound are identical with Guichard's Alaises. Fundamentally, both men were in agreement in taking the heretical stand that the ancient sites of early man did not happen by chance, but were placed carefully in a developing pattern.

How and why such an immense operation took place seems to have been beyond the grasp of either man: Watkins's suggestion of straight paths for traders is archaeologically and geographically absurd; Guichard is even vaguer. But the more that is discovered about the relentless intellectual achievements of early man, the more likely it would seem that they were searching for something, metaphorically at least, beyond the horizon. The evidence has now been gathered in Europe, Egypt, and South America, and as John Michell has put it: 'all this could not just have been a product of the need for reckoning the time or the date, or of some abstract desire for astronomical information.' So just what was it for? Any speculation must take into account the enormous scale of what was going on. If alignments over long distances were being laid down, as they apparently were, it is difficult to imagine them not having a practical purpose; and all the elusive hints of pre-Pythagorean mathematics suggest that in some way the harmony of numbers, the movement of the celestial bodies, and the key moments in the annual cycle of the Earth's rotation could be made to combine, and to generate an energy whose force can only dimly be felt today – a science of instinct that was essential to the development of mankind.

Section four Unknown energies

There is a widespread public belief that among certain societies in the world, generally indexed in anthropological books as 'primitive peoples', such things as telepathy, black magic, and other forms of the supernatural are relatively common. Thus aboriginals in Australia 'know' what has happened – the death of a relative, for instance – many miles away seemingly by means of some kind of thought transference; medicine men in many North American Indian tribes have often been reported as having the same powers, and may also have been capable of paranormal healing; the majority of African tribes have witch doctors who use methods of divination with which to find lost objects, and the phenomenon of putting a spell on an enemy to cause his death has been frequently and reliably recorded.

These things are tiresome anomalies to anyone brought up in the school of Western rationalism; they have no scientific basis, and they do not seem to happen much in sophisticated modern societies. So they are usually pigeon-holed as superstitions that were badly observed or much exaggerated in the first place, and can therefore be ignored.

However, for anyone trying to probe the mysteries of what went on in the mind of early man, they are of the greatest importance. If extra-sensory perception, or even super-sensory perception, was widespread (as many think), then it opens a whole new area of explanation as to and why ancient sites were laid out as described in the last section of the Atlas. Some people, indeed, argue seriously that the entire network of megalithic sites was used like a cosmic power grid, through which the earth could be seasonally re-vitalized and certain people able to communicate telepathically.

The trouble is that it is difficult, if not impossible, to gain verification of all this. There are no written records of what went on in megalithic times, and the tribal evidence is so anecdotal that you can't be certain you are making a fair analogy; the vast literature of psychical research contains less than half a dozen tests with primitive people under controlled conditions.

Fortunately, however, there are some aspects of modern life where ESP, or the paranormal, still seems to surface through the gloss of Western civilization and the deadening hand of laboratory experiment. This section looks at some of the baffling examples of how all kinds of creature – humans, mammals, birds, fish, reptiles, insects – seem able to perceive things beyond the range of their normal senses. True, what they can manage with these is amazing enough; scientists have now compiled evidence beyond question that we are far more subtly influenced by minute changes in our environment than anybody had thought possible, and the section outlines how this explains a number of previously unsolved mysteries.

But beyond this, one is driven to the conclusion that something else is operating, outside the current knowledge of science. Whether it is a dowser finding water, a pet dog finding its master over the distance of a continent, or a psychic describing what is happening hundreds of miles away, some unknown energy must be allowing this to happen. And, without exception, the people today who have the gift of ESP say that it is impossible to understand what was going on in early times unless you take this gift into account.

Remote viewing

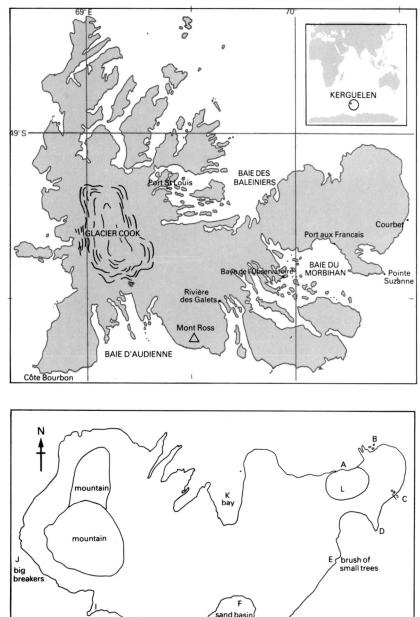

Outline of Kerguelen, a remote island in the Indian Ocean (above), with clairvoyant drawing beneath.

The New York artist Ingo Swann has one of the most extraordinary talents in the Western world today. A prosperous, dapperly-dressed man who turns out haunting, fifth-dimensional pictures from his Bowery studio, he has shown time and again, under circumstances no reasonable person would question, that he can perceive scenes and events far beyond the horizon of immediate eyesight. Most of the experiments for which he has been a subject have taken place at Stanford Research Institute in California under the eye of two physicists who have made what many believe to be a breakthrough in the technique of investigating the paranormal: Russell Targ and Harold E. Puthoff.

A detailed account of their work over a period of three years is in their book *Mind-Reach*. Repeatedly, they chronicle the ability of many people to click into a certain frame of mind and then, impossibly according to scientific laws, view actual happenings at distant sites. Not just self-proclaimed psychics have been able to do this – ordinary members of the public, and even scientists hostile to the whole idea, have been found capable of what Targ and Puthoff term 'remote viewing'.

Magnetic disturbance

However, it was Ingo Swann with whom they worked longest, and who provided them with their most astonishing yet conclusive results to date. In March 1972, Swann offered to be investigated by them, having read a scientific paper by Harold Puthoff invoking quantum physics as a possible explanation for extra-sensory perception (ESP). In the very first hour of their meeting, Swann stunned both men, and many other scientists who greeted him at SRI, by describing accurately the features of a uniquely-designed magnetometer buried six feet in concrete beneath the floor, and also, by an effort of will, affecting the output signal of the magnetometer as shown on a strip chart recorder. (The disturbed pattern on the graph paper, of a sort that has never occurred before or since, has been kept carefully in SRI.)

The initial series of formal experiments consisted of Ingo Swann trying to identify green and white cards picked at random in a distant location, and similar, somewhat elementary ESP tests. Swann insisted this was trivializing his talent, which was to use his mind's eye to visualize distant places; he claimed that if they gave him the latitude and longitude of any place on Earth, he could 'go' there, and describe the scene for them.
They were highly sceptical. As physicists, they found it difficult enough to accept the existence of telepathy over short distances, and 'knew that latitude and longitude were completely man-made constructs, adding one impossibility on top of another'. However, on Swann's insistence they set up a scheme called Project Scanate (for *scanning by co-ordinate*), and its uncanny success is still hard for many people to credit.

Co-ordinate results

In runs of ten co-ordinates, Ingo Swann was often precisely accurate eight or nine times; for example, 'two degrees south, 34 degrees east' (in fact, Lake Victoria in Africa), he instantly described as 'sense of speeding over water, landing on land. Lake to west, high elevation.' He insisted that this was the correct description, even when Puthoff and Targ told him the co-ordinates crossed on their map in the middle of the lake. Subsequent checking on a more

detailed map showed that he was right.
In scientific terms, this early test was not final proof of psychic ability: a possible explanation might have been that Ingo Swann possessed the rare and extraordinary gift known as eidetic memory, and that perhaps he had memorized from an atlas the latitude and longitude of every place on Earth. So to counter this possibility, Puthoff and Targ persuaded sceptical colleagues to choose deliberately difficult places, and asked Ingo Swann to supply details not available on maps, such as 'the locations and structural details of buildings, the shapes of structures such as towers and bridges'. One such set of co-ordinates – 49° 20′S, 70° 14′E – turned out to be a small island in the southern Indian Ocean called Kerguelen, nowadays mostly used as a base for joint French-Russian research into the meteorology of the upper atmosphere.

Swann began his commentary immediately: 'My initial response is that it's an island, maybe a mountain sticking up through a cloud cover. Terrain seems rocky. Must be some sort of small plants growing there. Cloud bank to the west. Very cold. I see some buildings rather mathematically laid out. One of them is orange. There is something like a radar antenna, a round disc.'

All this was exactly correct. Now he began to draw a map of what he was seeing in his mind's eye: 'Two white cylindrical tanks, quite large. To the northwest, a small airstrip. Wind is blowing. Must be two or three trucks in front of the building. Behind, is that an outhouse? There's not much there. It's not completely dark there, sort of orangish light. If I look to the west, hills; to the north, flatlands, and I think airstrip and ocean to the east; can't see anything to the south.'

Island outline

Starting at point A, he began to draw the coast outline: 'Point B, rocks sticking up out of the ocean, breakers on them. Point C, little cluster of buildings with wharf, boats. Point D, jetty of land sticking out. Point F is sand basin, river coming through, lots of birds. Point E, brush of small trees. This is fun; first time I've done this . . . almost a straight coastline, cuts in rocks, beach, then curves back. I see to northwest, a mountain rising, snow on top. Area G is irregular. Point H is a high cliff; Point I is a promontory. Point J has big breakers; K is a bay; L is area of airstrip and buildings.'

Puthoff and Targ have not so far offered a detailed analysis of just how close a match Ingo Swann's remote viewing map is to the actual features of the island, but even a superficial glance shows that in general terms it is excellent – the shape, the description of the terrain, the mountain with snow on top that is unmistakably

Dowsers, known since ancient times for their ability to find water, also work from maps. Standing stones in New England were pin-pointed by this method by a dowser working in south Wales.

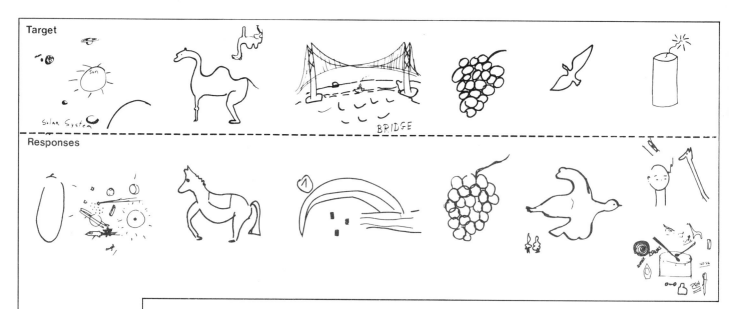

Target

Responses

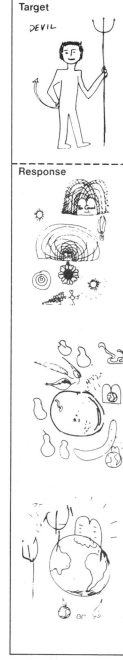

Target

DEVIL

Response

in the place where Mount Ross and Glacier Cook rise nearly 2000 metres above sea level. On an objective view, any inaccuracies are outweighed by the fact that the phenomenon exists at all, and these early feats by Ingo Swann were succeeded by a different type of remote viewing experiment in which he and others tried to see what was happening at a variety of randomly chosen sites, some as much as 5000 kilometres away. In most cases, the similarity between what was described and a photograph of the site is too striking to dismiss, even when the experiment was carried out with people who did not believe themselves to have any psychic ability. Targ and Puthoff have concluded: 'Remote viewing constitutes a robust phenomenon whereby subjects are able to describe in words and drawings, to a degree exceeding any reasonable bounds of chance correlation, both the location and actions of experimenters placed at undisclosed sites at varying separations from the subjects up to transcontinental distances.'

Map-dowsing

A similar psychic ability is the way many experienced dowsers (or water-diviners) make discoveries by using maps. This practice probably raises as many sceptical eyebrows as Ingo Swann's proven claim to be able to visualize a location just by being given its latitude and longitude; but it is now so widespread that there is a wealth of evidence, both anecdotal and statistical, showing it works. Indeed, it would be rare nowadays for a top-rank dowser to start divining without first running a pendulum, or whatever dowsing instrument he uses, over a map of the area. They do not, on the whole, believe that there is anything special that they pick up from the map itself – no rays, or emanations. What the map does (like Ingo Swann's co-ordinates) is to enable them to tune

in their minds to a certain spot on Earth, and give a description of what is there.

Missing bodies

Successful examples, ranging from the trivial to the tragic, abound in dowsing literature. The Dutch clairvoyant Gerard Croiset has had exceptional success locating the position of missing aircraft and people. In 1966 the Irish dowser Thomas Trench was asked by Belgian police, who had heard of his reputation, if he could trace the body of one of their officers, killed in a riot and taken away in a car by the murderers. Without leaving his home, Trench located the exact spot, near Blankenberghe. Police forces in Britain, too, make regular use of dowsers to trace stolen goods. Most major oil companies are believed to have dowsers working for them.

Why, then, is this well-established phenomenon of remote viewing not more widely accepted and

A series of tests on Uri Geller's claimed paranormal abilities took place at Stanford Research Institute, California during 1972. The targets were selected by placing a file card at random in a 1700-page dictionary; the experimenter then drew a picture, in silence, of the first word on the page capable of being illustrated. Meanwhile Uri Geller, sitting inside a Faraday cage (an isolation chamber with double metal walls designed to provide soundproofing and electromagnetic shielding), attempted to perceive what had been drawn. The experiment has been criticized because of the presence of Geller's companion Shipi Strang, who has said he secretly gave Geller signals on some occasions. However the two scientists involved in the experiment, Harold Puthoff and Russell Targ, are adamant that the controls on this occasion were rigorous and that the Faraday cage made it impossible for Geller to cheat by communicating with an accomplice.

used? One reason is its fallibility. Ingo Swann says that when he uses paranormal perception he has 'anything but 20/20 vision', (i.e. much less than perfect) and many of the sketches shown by Targ and Puthoff as evidence can be interpreted ambiguously. An experiment in map-dowsing under the auspices of the Society for Psychical Research in London, in which the Welsh dowser William A. Lewis was asked to locate megalithic sites in New England, showed him to be about 40 per cent accurate.

The other reason is that in spite of the rapidly accumulating experimental evidence, the existence of the phenomenon is still hotly disputed by most scientists. The work of Puthoff and Targ has been published in sober and authoritative journals such as *Nature* and the *Proceedings of IEEE* (the Institute of Electrical and Electronics Engineers), and the controls on their experiments have become steadily more fool-proof with time, but this still does not stop critics saying that every result could have occurred because of accident or fraud. Because Uri Geller is a magician, such critics flatly refuse to believe his astonishing – and to most people, conclusive – series of successful target-guessing (see opposite), in spite of Puthoff and Targ having locked him alone in a shielded

chamber while he was viewing. But then it is in the nature of scientists generally, as many stories in this Atlas show, to defend an entrenched position doggedly until sheer weight of evidence forces them to abandon it. That has not yet happened with ESP, although the time may be very near. In the meantime, perhaps the best attitude to take towards the subject for an outsider is to heed the advice of the Nobel prize-winning French phsyiologist Charles Richet about dowsing: 'It is a fact we must accept. Don't experiment to find out whether it is so. It is so! Go ahead and develop it!'

Pilsdon Pen, the prehistoric site at the centre of a ley (page 75), was excavated 1964–71; overlaid are burials that the Welsh dowser Bill Lewis expects to be found in future digs.

The migration instinct

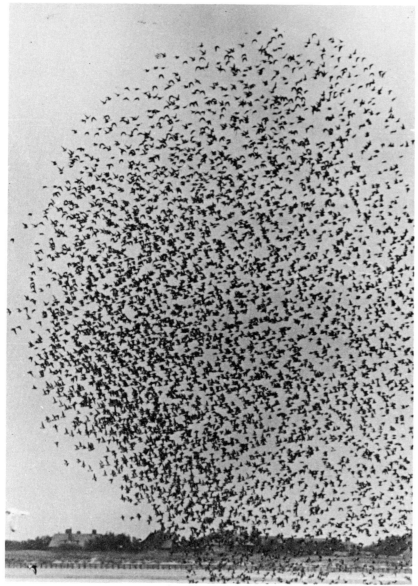

Bird flock turning simultaneously; nobody knows what method of communication they use.

(opposite) Six spectacular examples of long-distance bird migration.

Every autumn 4,000,000 seabirds of the species *Puffinus gravis*, or Greater Shearwater, gather on the coastlines of northern Europe in readiness for a migratory journey that is one of the world's annual marvels. Driven by an instinct beyond our understanding, and carried on the southerly trade winds, they head unerringly for Tristan da Cunha, a group of tiny, beautiful and remote islands in the south Atlantic. It is the only place where they nest, and by some unknown means they must be perfectly certain where they are going, for on the way they start their courtship.

Why they should be impelled to make the journey, and how they achieve such accuracy, are unanswered questions in spite of a century of research. Migrations of many kinds of creature have now been recorded, and as the French biologist Mathieu Ricard has put it, 'from the carp that oscillate from one part of the lake to the other for breeding, to the albatrosses that circle the globe, there is probably no animal which does not show some kind of rhythmic behaviour.' But why should this rhythmic urge often take such an extreme form? The Arctic Tern's annual migration takes it from its nesting place in the far north of Siberia, North America and Europe to the shores of the Antarctic, and back again, a pole-to-pole journey that means flying 24 hours a day for eight months of the year, and a total distance of around 25,000 miles. Such a journey is far in excess of any need to remain in suitable climatic conditions, the orthodox basis for explaining the phenomenon.

First migrations

The origins of migration are thought to lie in the upheavals caused by the various Ice Ages, the last of which ended around 10,000 BC. As the ice retreated northwards, a few birds perhaps made an adventurous flight out of their home territory to remain in favourable feeding conditions. On their way they would have passed other flocks not migrating, and then in the autumn when colder conditions returned, have re-joined them in their old haunts. Gradually, through a Darwinian process of selection, the robust, adventurous birds would come to dominate and absorb the more sedentary ones, until after a while all the population joined in the migration. As evidence for this explanation, it can readily be seen that the advance and retreat of such birds as humming-birds and swallows each year corresponds closely with changing temperatures; it has also been found experimentally that the sexual glands of birds subjected to an increase in the amount of radiated light, such as occurs in the spring, become stimulated so that they feel a need for greater activity.

Unanswered questions

But the theory doesn't come near to satisfying any number of awkward questions. Why didn't all birds learn to migrate? Almost half of bird species are sedentary, having stayed put and adapted to the new climate. No spell of cold weather, however severe, will persuade Arctic birds such as the great white owl or the ivory gull to leave their uncomfortable environment. And why is there such a definite time for many migrations? Some birds die of hunger and cold in their breeding environment because the fixed date for their migration hasn't yet come around; many others set off at their usual time even when there is still abundant food around.

Clearly something beyond simple explanation is at work, some internal time-clock inherited from primordial times whose mechanism has so far defied scientific discovery. And if the reason for migration is mysterious, equally so is the extraordinary skill with which migrating creatures are able to pin-point an exact

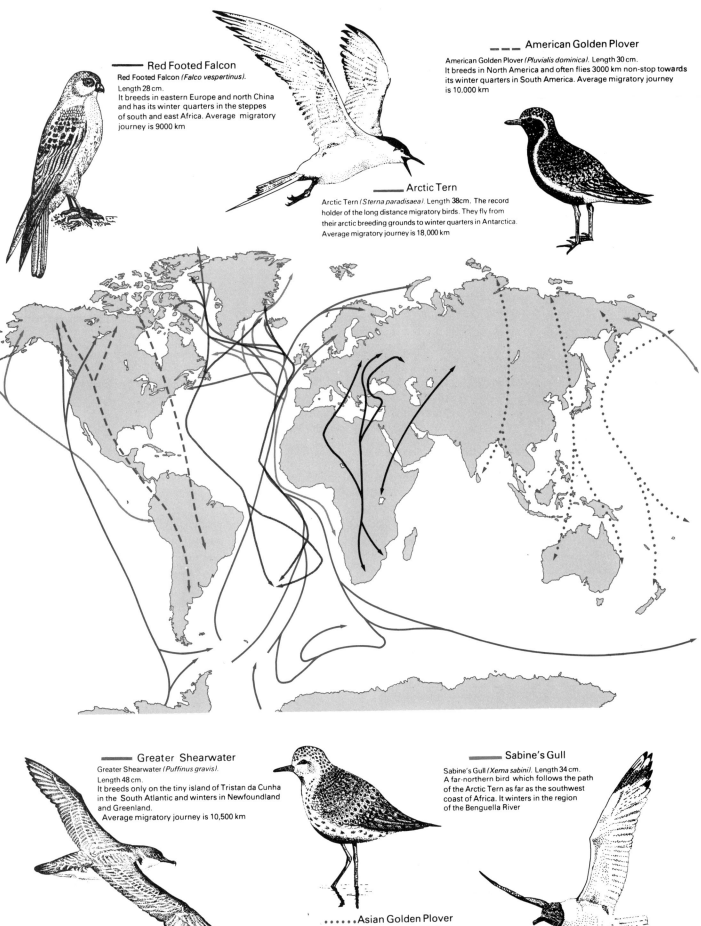

—— Red Footed Falcon
Red Footed Falcon *(Falco vespertinus)*.
Length 28 cm.
It breeds in eastern Europe and north China
and has its winter quarters in the steppes
of south and east Africa. Average migratory
journey is 9000 km

- - - American Golden Plover
American Golden Plover *(Pluvialis dominica)*. Length 30 cm.
It breeds in North America and often flies 3000 km non-stop towards
its winter quarters in South America. Average migratory journey
is 10,000 km

—— Arctic Tern
Arctic Tern *(Sterna paradisaea)*. Length 38cm. The record
holder of the long distance migratory birds. They fly from
their arctic breeding grounds to winter quarters in Antarctica.
Average migratory journey is 18,000 km

—— Greater Shearwater
Greater Shearwater *(Puffinus gravis)*.
Length 48 cm.
It breeds only on the tiny island of Tristan da Cunha
in the South Atlantic and winters in Newfoundland
and Greenland.
Average migratory journey is 10,500 km

—— Sabine's Gull
Sabine's Gull *(Xema sabini)*. Length 34 cm.
A far-northern bird which follows the path
of the Arctic Tern as far as the southwest
coast of Africa. It winters in the region
of the Benguella River

······ Asian Golden Plover
Asian Golden Plover *(Pluvialis apricaria)*. Length 30 cm.
It breeds in an area from north Eurasia to Iceland and winters
in southwest Europe and northwest Africa. Average migratory
journey is 8,500 km

Species	Characteristics of migration	Method of orientation
1 Reindeer One of the largest mammals whose migratory habits can be observed.	Reindeer spend their summers on the grassy plains where the snow has melted. In winter they descend to coasts where they live on a seaweed washed up by tides. In part of Lapland reindeer wade across the sea to nearby and more fertile islands.	The methods of navigation used by larger mammals, such as reindeer (and including dogs and cats) has not been established.
2 Turtles Herbivorous animals weighing more than 25 kilograms when fully grown.	Green turtles migrate regularly to and from beach and feeding ground, and can navigate accurately enough to find a tiny island after 2200 kilometres at sea.	The turtles may use the sun as a compass, but this does not fully explain the long-distance accuracy.
3 Lemmings Small, agile rodents, ferocious if caught. They live in underground burrows during the summer, and overground nests in winter.	The lemming migratory cycle starts with a huge upturn in the birth rate. Females produce 6–8 young with 4–5 litters a year. Burrows are soon overcrowded and birth rate of surrounding predators (snowy owls, eagles, sea-gulls, ermine and foxes) also increases. The trickle of lemmings leaving their burrows soon becomes a flood of determined migrants.	The archetypal pattern of lemming migration is from the hills to the plains and then the sea. Determined to reach their goal, they sweep through buildings and across streams. An inherited memory may be driving them towards the British Isles across the North Sea, once a land bridge; or they may have an in-built system for population control.
4 Butterflies Despite their fragility and short life span, butterflies are classified as major migrants.	Notable migrants among the species are the *Monarch* (illustrated) and the *Painted Lady*. Migration usually starts in September and builds up to a visible cloud of migrants flying south from Canada and the northern USA. Ladybirds and houseflies sometimes accompany the butterflies.	There is no conclusive evidence as to how they return to the same nesting sites year after year, but like bees they may use polarized light.
5 Seals Seals move north and south with the seasons.	Cold weather seems to be the trigger that urges both fur seals and grey seals southwards. Bulls leave before females to establish territory.	No conclusive experiments on seal migration have yet been recorded.
6 Whales The Blue Whale (right-hand illustration) is the largest living mammal, reaching a length of 30 metres plus.	Whale migrations seem to follow the movement of plankton, their main food supply.	Low frequency echo-sounding enables whales to know how deep the sea is, and how to locate their prey; their long-distance navigation methods are still a mystery.
7 Eels European and American Eels both breed and die in the Sargasso Sea.	The weed in the Sargasso Sea in which eels breed drifts from the coast of Florida, and the European Eel chooses a slightly different area from the American Eel. Both species then return to their native freshwater homes, but have an unexplained compulsion to return to the Sargasso in old age.	The eels have an acute sense of smell which enables them to navigate locally in rivers. An inherited memory seems the only explanation for their migration to the Sargasso.
8 Locusts The Migratory Locust constitutes a separate species within the locust family, and is the cause of the many historic locust invasions.	Migratory locusts follow special routes through mountain ranges, with a high mortality rate that may be a solution to over-population.	In general, heavily dependent on the direction of prevailing winds.
9 Salmon The underwater journey of the salmon from the open sea to its natal stream and back again has made observation difficult.	Salmon are at home in the open sea, but return to a particular fast-running freshwater stream to breed. Distances can be vast – Alaska to Korea in one recorded example.	For most of the journey, salmon probably use the sun as a compass, and in the final stages, their sense of smell. How they locate a particular stream is still unsolved.
10 Amphibians Toads and frogs undertake breeding migrations.	In Africa, just before the rainy season, hordes of frogs make their annual visit to a particular lake to breed.	Celestial cues such as the moon and stars.

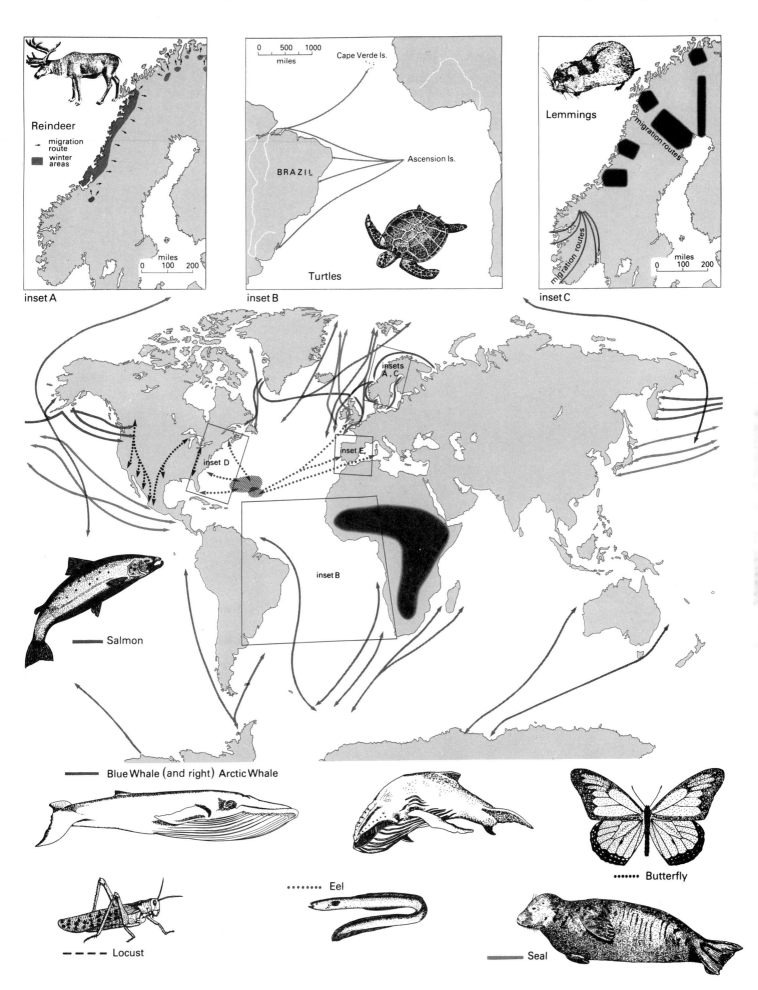

inset A

Reindeer
→ migration route
▮ winter areas

miles
0 100 200

inset B

0 500 1000
miles

Cape Verde Is.

BRAZIL

Ascension Is.

Turtles

inset C

Lemmings

migration routes

migration routes

miles
0 100 200

insets A, C

inset D

inset E

inset B

—— Salmon

—— Blue Whale (and right) Arctic Whale

········ Eel

········ Butterfly

– – – Locust

—— Seal

89

Species

Tunny fish
Weigh 600–2000 kilograms, and grow to four metres in length. They congregate and breed in well-defined areas.

Bats
Historically, bats were believed to 'disappear' in winter; in fact they hibernate or migrate to a more suitable location.

Migration characteristics

After spawning, tuna fish swim many thousands of miles in search of food, following routes which sailors and fishermen have known since antiquity.

The Mouse-eared Bat (illustrated) and the Golden-eared Bat fly long distances over the Atlantic before returning to a particular cave to breed. Local navigation in darkness is by echo-sounding; for long-distance navigation celestial clues may be used.

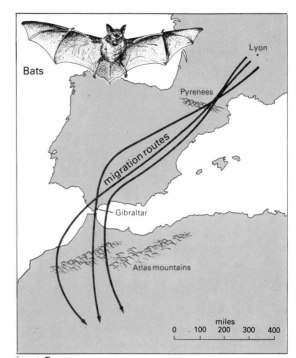

inset E

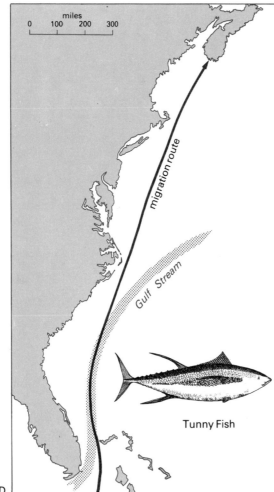

inset D

destination – the swallow to find the same nest that it used last year, the return of the salmon thousands of miles to the stream where it was born, the green turtles from the coast of Brazil which from time to time find their way across 2200 kilometres of open sea and hit their tiny target of Ascension Island just eight kilometres in diameter. For though scientists have painstakingly identified a number of ways in which orientation may be achieved, each of them a small miracle of sensitivity, none is totally satisfactory as an answer.

Sun-compass

In the northern hemisphere, the sun apparently moves across the sky during the course of a day from left to right. Any traveller wishing to use it as a directional aid needs to know exactly what time it is, and make the necessary calculation to keep himself on course. Astonishingly, many creatures are able to do this instinctively. As William T. Keeton, Professor of Biology at Cornell University, has written: 'If a pigeon is to determine a particular direction, it cannot simply select a constant angle relative to the sun. It must change the relative angle by about 15 degrees per hour, which is the average rate of change of the sun's position throughout the day. In short, the bird must have an accurate sense of time, an internal clock, and that clock must somehow be coupled with the position of the sun in the sky.' Experimentally, it has been established that this use of a sun-compass is probably the single most important sighting cue in animal navigation: many insects including ants, bees and spiders make minute and frequent adjustments of their course to take account of the moving sun, their 'straight' paths home turning out to be a series of tiny zig-zags. But how do they know where home is? William Keeton says: 'Homing requires more than a compass. If you were taken hundreds of miles away into unfamiliar territory, given only a magnetic compass and told to start walking home, you would not be able to get there. Even though you could determine where north was, you would not know where you were with respect to home, hence such compass information would be nearly useless.'

Polarized light

Another ability shared by many insects and birds (including pigeons), but not man or any mammals, is to see the sky as if through a polarized lens. To a bee, a patch of cloudless sky does not look uniformly blue, but a pattern of alternating light and dark stripes, rather like glass car windows seen through polaroid glasses. Even in overcast conditions, there is often enough light to enable the bee to calculate exactly where the sun is.

The puzzle of the way such creatures, when artificially isolated from their homes, can decide which direction to take, is still unsolved by this discovery. But orientation in bees rapidly improves with experience – a young bee quickly extends its range from a few hundred metres to several thousand. How its tiny brain is capable of such a huge number of instant calculations is beyond comprehension. Clearly, insects and birds live in a sensory world unimaginable by man.

Celestial navigation

Orientation by means of the moving sun is difficult enough; but not of the same order as the ability of many birds to use the stars. Stephen T. Emlen, Associate Professor of Animal Behaviour at Cornell University, has written: 'There is only one sun, and it moves at a regular rate, but there are thousands of stars and different stars are visible above the horizon at different times of the night and at different seasons.'

It was the German ornithologist E. G. F. Sauer of the University of Freiburg who first suggested, in the late 1950s, that nevertheless some birds had an inherited instinct that enabled them to read the map of the night-time sky. His experiments in a planetarium involved European songbirds known as warblers, which migrate annually from as far north as Scandinavia to the tip of southern Africa, particularly remarkable because 'each bird finds its own way to its destination. The warblers do not follow a leader or make the journey as a group; they navigate individually. And young birds making their first migration reach their goal as surely as the experienced travellers. Somehow, purely by instinct, the warblers know their course.'

As the warblers fly largely at night, he tested them to see if the stars could be guiding them. By using an artificial dome to shift the position of the stars and constellations, he was able to change the apparent geographical latitude, making the birds think they were farther south or north than they actually were. The direction taken by the birds corresponded exactly. He was in no doubt that 'the warblers have a remarkable

Experiments in a planetarium show that birds instantly recognize patterns of stars and use them for orientation.

hereditary mechanism for orientating themselves by the stars – a detailed image of the starry configuration of the sky.'

However, many puzzles remain. 'The birds must somehow be able to make adjustments to astronomical evolution, for in the course of time the pattern of constellations in the sky is slowly but constantly changing. Even more difficult to explain is the mystery of how the birds ever came to rely on celestial navigation and develop their skill in the first place.'

Supersenses

There is evidence that many creatures have sensory abilities far beyond those of man. Some fish can detect temperature changes of as little as 0.03° C, and it has been speculated that this is how eels keep on course from European coasts to the Sargasso Sea, a journey during which the water temperature rises from 10° C to 40° C. Several fish found in west African rivers generate their own electric field, and are highly sensitive to minute electromagnetic signals. Salmon have an exceptionally well-developed sense of smell, being able to distinguish between different types of water containing various chemical substances, sometimes apparently turning back from their run upstream if they smell a human hand placed in the water beyond them; almost certainly, this is how they are able to recognize the waters of their spawning ground – by remembering all the smells they encountered when they left it.

Perhaps the most important recent discovery is the ability of pigeons, robins and gulls – and presumably other creatures – to detect tiny changes in the Earth's magnetic field. Nobody knows how it happens, because in theory this weak magnetic flux should pass through tissue unnoticed (page 19). But William

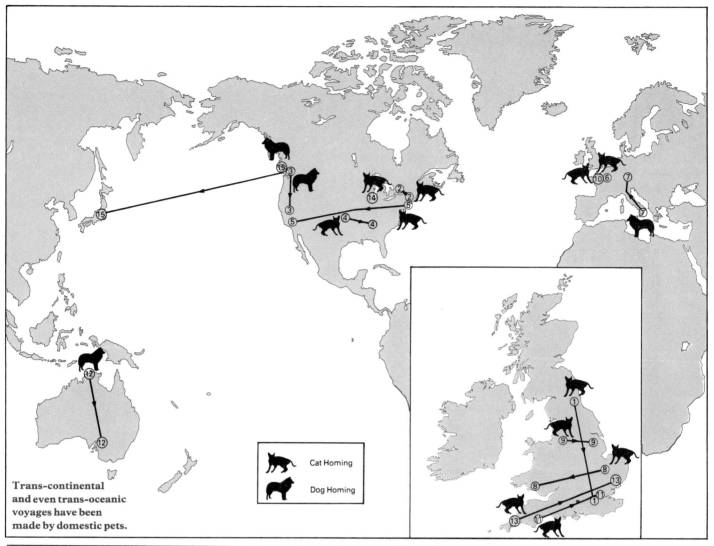

Trans-continental and even trans-oceanic voyages have been made by domestic pets.

Legend:
- Cat Homing
- Dog Homing

Records of long distance animal homing

name and species	journey	distance	date
1 Sooty/Cat	Durham to Surrey	480 km	June 1967
2 Rusty/Cat	Claremont, New Hampshire to Ontario	880 km	May 1975
3 Spook/Dog	Vancouver, British Columbia to California	1600 km	July 1977
4 Smoky/Cat	Oklahoma to Tennessee	480 km	October 1974
5 Cat	New York to California	4000 km	October 1974
6 Bobby/Cat	Paris to Orleans	96 km	October 1974
7 Barry/Dog	Southern Italy to Southern Germany	320 km	October 1974
8 Whisky/Cat	Cambridge to Swansea	240 km	August 1973
9 George/Cat	Manchester to Lincoln	144 km	December 1974
10 Chausettes/Cat	Caen to Nantes	160 km	January 1977
11 Dimples/Cat	Torquay to Clapham	560 km	June 1977
12 Whisky/Fox Terrier	Darwin to Adelaide	2880 km	July 1974
13 Bede/Irish Setter	Cornwall to Essex	480 km	July 1974
14 Gypsy/Cat	Returned home to Chicago after a two year trek	Round trip	August 1976
15 Hector/Dog	Vancouver, British Columbia to Tokyo	9600 km	April 1922

Keeton has been able to show conclusively that in overcast conditions, when pigeons were unable to use any of their normal sighting cues such as landmarks or the position of the sun, they became hopelessly disoriented if small bar magnets were attached to them in such a way as to reverse the normal direction of the Earth's magnetic field.

The cosmic theory

Current opinion is that no single method can account for all the aspects of animal homing. Pigeons, for instance, may use the sun as their principal direction beam, but switch to a magnetic compass when conditions require it, and then use direct visual observation for the last few miles of the journey. The green turtles on their extraordinary journey across the Atlantic, may use celestial cues for most of the time, and then smell Ascension Island when they approach it.

But even when all the suggested physical explanations are added up, they are inadequate to answer the fundamental question of how any creature knows where 'home' is: how do salmon know, from thousands of miles distance, which river-mouth to approach? How did a lone Manx Shearwater, taken in a darkened container by aeroplane across the Atlantic to Boston, Mass., find its way back 5000 kilometres to its nesting-place on the island of Skokholm off the coast of Wales in just twelve and a half days?

Scientists who have put forward the 'cosmic theory' propose that such feats, like all migrations, are involuntary; birds, animals and insects are in the grip of an inexplicable cosmic current that is built into them through heredity and which most are unable to resist. Thus the periodic urge by some creatures such as lemmings to embark on their suicidal migration; and the urge to start migrating on a particular day, regardless of climatic conditions.

Homing instinct

The trouble is that there is almost no concrete evidence to support such a theory, attractive though it is to imagine a combination of electric and magnetic forces that create the migratory urge, and at the same time guide the migrating creature. However, something of this sort must surely be in operation for the most baffling cases of all – the instances of pets which return to their owners over long distances. Here, as with the new-found human ability to use the mind's eye to view remote happenings (described in the previous pages), is unquestionably a phenomenon in search of a theory. Unless you look outside current scientific beliefs, it is impossible to conceive how, for example, a terrier named Hector could have made his impossible journey in April, 1922.

Hector was a ship's dog, belonging to a first officer on board the Dutch ship *Simaloer*. Accidentally left behind when the ship sailed from Vancouver for Yokohama, Hector roamed the docks before choosing to board one of five other ships remaining at the quay – as it happened, the only one also due to go to Japan. On the trip, the dog settled itself in the captain's cabin, but showed no particular attachment for anybody in the crew. Eighteen days after sailing, the ship moored at Yokohama, and Hector spotted a small boat at the wharf; he became wildly excited and barked furiously at the two men on board. The small boat came from the *Simaloer*, and one of the two men was his owner.

Similar tales appear almost daily in newspapers and magazines, all of them suggesting that something beyond electromagnetism is at work – a cosmic consciousness, perhaps, to be embraced in the cosmic migration theory which science is now investigating. Whatever it is seems to be instinctive, hereditary, and involuntary; a universal memory shared by man and his fellow-creatures alike, and still capable of being activated when circumstances demand.

Evidence for animal ESP

Dogs Whether it is a matter of foreseeing the future, or whether it is because some animals can detect tiny vibrations or changes in magnetic field strength, the ability of horses, cats, and especially dogs to act as early warning beacons for earthquakes, avalanches and other natural disasters is now well documented.

The Swiss ski resort of Cervinia has a ceramic bas-relief in memory of a dog named Bleck, a mongrel with an uncanny way of forewarning against avalanches, and of baying pitifully all night if in spite of its 'advice', anybody was killed.

In February, 1939, St Bernard dogs in the Swiss Alps refused, for the first time ever, to go for their morning walk with the monks. An hour later an avalanche engulfed the part of the track that they would have been on in normal circumstances.

J. D. Carthy in *Animal Navigation* tells of a German experiment in animal homing. A Scottish sheepdog named Maxl was taken by a roundabout route to a place six kilometres away from his master's home. He was released next morning, and after half an hour's aimless wandering, seemed to sense the direction he should go in, and arrived back after 78 minutes. 18 days later, the test was repeated; this time Maxl spent only five minutes orienting himself, and covered the journey by a more direct route in just 43 minutes.

A later experiment over an 8.5-kilometre distance with another dog showed a similar improvement in time on the dog's second journey, even though it took a different route and was therefore not using remembered visual landmarks.

Cats The French Consul-General in Istanbul recorded the curious story of a dozen cats lent by their owners to deal with a plague of rats on a merchant ship that called at the port there. At the end of the voyage, they were returned to their owners; but each time the ship returned to port, unscheduled and unannounced, the cats turned up on the wharf to greet her, seeming always to know at which point she would be moored.

Experimentally, it has been established that the oft-recounted episodes of cats homing over many kilometres to rejoin their owners in a new home is because of some unknown, but inherent, sense of direction. Matthieu Ricard in *Mystery of Migration* has written how 'cats were taken from a town and placed in darkened containers and then transported some miles away after a most complicated journey full of detours and retracing of steps. There was no possibility that the cats could use their memory of the route for this experiment. The cats were then taken from the containers and placed in the centre of a large maze with 28 exits. The great majority of cats chose the exit that was in the direction of their home.'

Horses Horses have been shown experimentally to have exceptional memory; their ability to remember a route home is said to have saved the life of many a wounded cavalryman.

J. D. Carthy reports that on at least one recorded occasion a horse's memory was used in crime detection: a thief near Marburg, Germany, had robbed a farm and at the same time taken a horse and cart to transport the stolen goods, which he then hid in a bunker near some woods. The horse and cart were found abandoned some miles away in the town, and the horse, unaided, led police directly to the bunker.

Underground streams

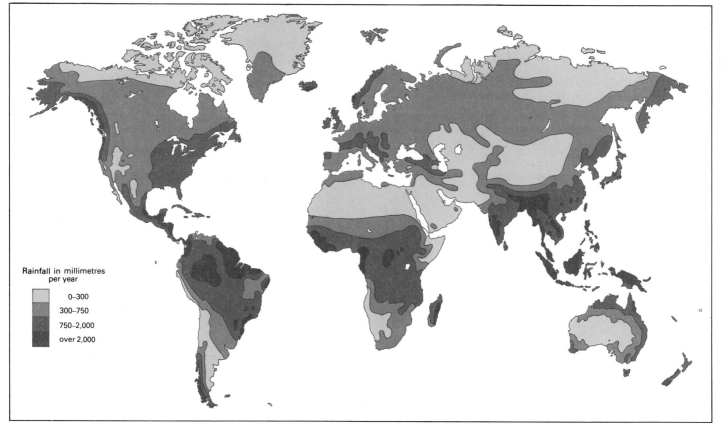

Rainfall in millimetres per year

- 0–300
- 300–750
- 750–2,000
- over 2,000

Rainfall collects in a water table beneath the Earth's surface at varying depths; many people such as Australian aboriginals have a natural ability to sense how deep it is.

We have an affinity with water. It pulses through us constantly, making up more than three-quarters of our weight. Deprived of it, we die at least ten times faster than if we lack food. From earliest times, we have built our most sacred places where water wells up, mysteriously, from deep in the rocks beneath. One of America's great naturalists, the late Loren Eiseley, wrote: 'Its substance reaches everywhere; it touches the past and prepares the future; it moves under the poles and wanders thinly in the heights of air . . . If there is magic on this planet, it is contained in water.'

Small wonder that a substance with such mystic associations should float with questions still unresolved by scientific enquiry. Where does it come from? Why is there so much of it? Why can dowsers and many animals find its source so readily? What subtle effects can it have on the human body? Why the persistent belief in healing springs whose effect resists chemical explanation? Did the priests and seers of prehistoric times understand more about it than we do now?

Too much water

The first great problem for science has been to account for the sheer volume of water in the oceans that cover two-thirds of the world's surface – at latest estimate, some 1370 million cubic kilometres. The old idea that water vapour surrounding the planet gradually condensed and fell as rain (as, legendarily, in the 40 days of rain during the biblical Deluge) is now discounted as being mathematically impossible; the Earth's present gravity can only hold on to an atmosphere some 100,000 times less than would be needed to contain such an amount of water vapour. Moreover, although some of the sea's saltiness comes from minerals washed from the surface of mountains and hills, sea-salt also contains chemicals that are only found in volcanoes. So the latest theory is that water is formed constantly as a by-product of continental drift (page 14). The rift in the Earth's mantle that wanders 65,000 kilometres beneath all the major oceans, and which marks the boundaries where the continental plates grind against each other, is a scene of almost perpetual underwater volcanic activity. Here, it is thought, fresh basalt flows upwards 600 kilometres or more from the Earth's semi-molten mantle, accompanied by what is called 'juvenile water' – elements of water that have never before combined in liquid form. It is calculated that as this hot amorphous matter is released into the oceans, about 100 cubic metres of water a year is created, although the rate has probably varied enormously during geological history. Certainly, there have been catastrophic changes in the level of the sea. As recently as six million years ago the Mediterranean outlet to the Atlantic was blocked and the Mediterranean Sea was dry; when the breach came, the torrent of water forcing its way through must have made the Niagara Falls look like a bath-tap.

Unsolved problem

However, although creation of water almost certainly happens from deep within the Earth's interior, nobody knows quite how. 'The origin and rate of collection of this water into the ocean receptacles is still an unsolved problem' according to C. A. M. King, Professor of Physical Geography at Nottingham University in England. Ferren MacIntyre, research associate in the Marine Science Institute of the University of California, has written: 'The chemistry of the sea is largely the chemistry of obscure reactions at extreme dilution in a strong salt dilution, where all the classical chemist's "distilled water" theories and procedures break down.'
But assuming that the basic thought is right, and that water is indeed created from within Earth itself, it may be more than an oddity that dowsers have been saying so for years. It is possible, in other words, that the current theoretical findings of geologists now support dowsing in its long dispute with hydrology (the scientific study of water, itself a branch of geology).

At the centre of the dispute is the question of whether dowsers can or cannot detect subterranean passages carrying a special kind of water. 'Normal' water, both sides agree, consists of rainfall which is collected by plants and returned to the atmosphere by transpiration, or which percolates through the ground to form a water 'table' of varying depth depending on the rock formation in the particular area. This water is what most people in industrialized societies have learned to live with, collected in reservoirs above and below ground, and piped through a communal water system. Hydrologists are trained to study geological formations, and to predict in a general way whether enough such

Nature's water diviners

What is remarkable about the animal world's attitude to water is the way so many creatures manage to survive long periods with only minimal quantities and even do without it. The Black Rhinoceros of Somalia does not drink for several weeks at a time; a breed of antelope on an island in the Red Sea, entirely without surface water, has never been observed drinking and it is assumed they glean water from plant life. Experimentally, several varieties of small mammal in North America have adapted to living solely on dry seeds, apparently producing within their bodies a type of 'metabolic water'.
A standard text-book on the subject says that 'most animals, however large, can adapt themselves to waterless conditions for at least ten days, sometimes for as many weeks.' Elephants, however, are uniquely accustomed to finding water in times of drought in much the same way as a human water diviner. There are many recorded instances of them roaming far from their feeding grounds and making a drill-hole with their trunks in places where there is no apparent surface indication of water beneath. Having found it, baby elephants are allowed first drink, followed by the females and finally the males. In India, male elephants have been seen to allow other species of animals, desperate for water, to have precedence. In Africa, elephants are known after drinking to block water-holes with plugs of chewed bark, presumably to prevent them becoming silted up or contaminated.

water exists locally to make it worth the expense of drilling.

Primary water

Dowsers have another belief about water. They say that there is an additional, virtually inexhaustible supply of 'primary' water that is independent of rainfall. Like the geologists' juvenile water, it comes from the depths of the earth. Carried along underground channels, natural pressure forces it upwards towards the surface of the ground, often in places impossible to predict by geological methods. Dowsers perceive this water as flowing through a vast network of vein-like faults in rock, occasionally rising even to the tops of hills in natural pipes, and then spreading out in a dome like the spokes of an umbrella.

In conventional geology books, there is nothing to support this. Nevertheless, inexplicable sources of water have occasionally been noted. In 1957 the journal *Engineering News-Record* told of a huge gush of water that spurted from the ground when builders were digging the foundations of an extension to Harlem Hospital

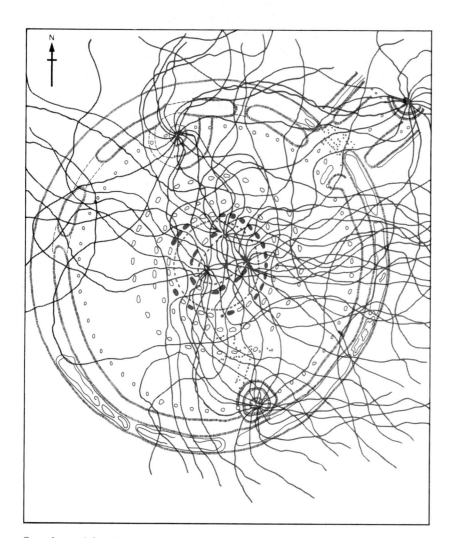

Stonehenge (above) and
Avebury (opposite) both
show labyrinthine
patterns of underground
water traced by map-
dowsing methods.
Similar patterns are
said by dowsers to exist
beneath all ancient sites.

in New York. It flowed continuously at a rate
of 8000 litres per minute, and throughout a
bitterly cold winter its temperature held steady at
20°C. Officials from the Department of Water,
Gas and Electricity were never able to trace its
origin, in spite of pumping green dye into nearby
sewers and reservoir outlets to see if it would
appear in the gush. Hospital chemists who
analysed the water found it so pure that it tasted
as fresh as any mountain spring.

In the end, the outlet was plugged with massive
concrete blocks, and the building's shell had to be
specially reinforced to cope with the water
pressure. Christopher Bird, a trustee of the
American Society of Dowsers, thinks the only
reason why this plentiful supply was not diverted
and used by the hospital must be 'the
unreasonable fears associated with the
mysterious water, grounded on the fact that, like
dowsing, its existence confounds conventional
hydrologic practice.'

Dowsing accuracy

What the best dowsers can achieve is certainly
beyond scientific explanation. Compared with
the rough and ready predictions of a geologist
hoping to strike a water table at approximately
a certain depth, a top dowser will insist on the

drill hole being placed in a precise position above
where he senses a water vein, to an accuracy of
less than ten centimetres. He will also invariably
predict the exact depth in feet or metres, the
number of litres per hour to be expected, and
the quality of the water. To be able to divine
such information correctly smacks of second-
sight or magical practice, and it is perhaps not
surprising that in the United States dowsing is
widely known as water-witching.

Dowsers themselves do not know where their
knowledge comes from, although in general
terms they sense that in acquiring it they are
somehow plugging into a cosmic pool of
omniscience, perhaps in much the same way as
a clairvoyant can see remote places with the
mind's eye, or a pet cat is inspired to find its way
home across the breadth of a continent. Nor do
they seem to worry about it – indeed, instead of
theorizing, most lectures and discussions at
dowsing conferences are refreshingly practical:
how to get better at it, rather than why they can
do it at all. Predicting the depth of a water vein
correctly, for instance, they see simply as a matter
of asking questions – is it more than ten metres?
more than 20 metres? more than 30 metres?
and so on, until their rod gives a twitch or their
pendulum a turn. Quantity and quality are
discovered by the same question-and-answer
method.

Outside scientific comprehension it may be, but
it works. Jack Livingston, a renowned dowser
who lives in the Sierra foothills of California,
has kept a careful record of depth and flow for
every well that he has ever dowsed – now more
than a thousand. Only about a dozen are
substantially at variance with what he predicted.
The great drought of 1976–77 gave him and a
number of other good dowsers on the West Coast
an opportunity to prove that, in competition with
orthodox water-finding techniques, they could
succeed even when reservoirs run dry and the
water tables are diminished. Livingston himself
is particularly proud of a well in a location he
found in the public park of Pine Grove, a small
town near his home, in 1965. Two wells sunk
on the advice of an engineer and a geologist in
a hill by the town had proved dry. At Livingston's
chosen spot, he predicted 150 gallons (550 litres)
a minute at 130–140 feet (41 metres), and even
more lower down. To his delight, when the drill
hit that level, the water spurted high in the air,
soaking all spectators. In the summer of 1977,
Christopher Bird reported the local water official
as saying that alone among 250 neighbouring
communities, Pine Grove was the only one
without water rationing: Livingston's well
seemed inexhaustible.

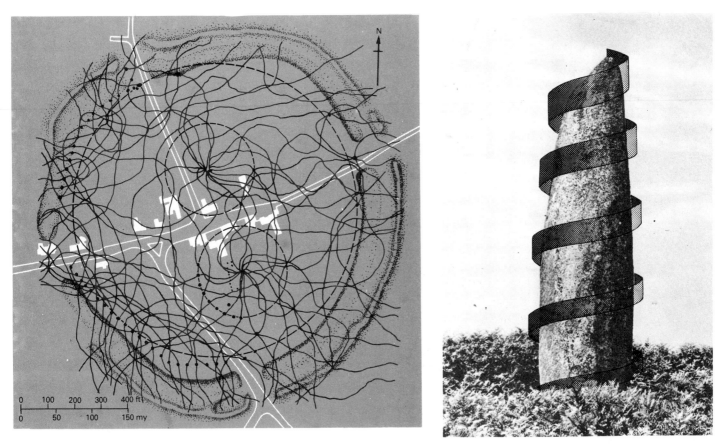

Bird has collected a great deal of evidence for his society that California dowsers succeeded in extremely unfavourable conditions, and there are so many similar stories from all over the world that no open-minded person can doubt good dowsers are successful far more often than chance alone would permit, which is the standard way of dismissing their work. Why then are geologists so reluctant to give them credit? Partly because the phenomenon cannot be properly explained, no doubt; but also because not all that many people are good dowsers, geologists included. For while it is widely believed in dowsing circles to be an almost universal gift of mankind that can be re-awakened with practice, it is evident that the near-infallibility of a Jack Livingston is very rare. So for every one of his achievements, any geologist can quote you a dozen where a less-good dowser has failed.

Harmful water

Beyond this, the extreme sensitivity of good dowsers has led them into areas where proof is much more difficult to come by than in water-finding. Map-dowsing is not the only thing that outsiders find incredible; there is also their belief that invisible emanations from underground water can have harmful or helpful effects on human health. Dowsing literature contains a great deal about 'black streams' that can trigger off arthritis and cancer, whose effects dowsers try to neutralize in various ways. A family doctor in Arlington, Vermont, Dr Herbert Douglas, was at first extremely sceptical about the supposed connection. However, having had it proved to him in 1965 that he was a capable dowser, 'I walked around the beds, chairs and couches of arthritic people to see if dowsing reactions or underground flowing veins were really present. To my astonishment I found they were. At first I felt it to be coincidental. It was too crazy to believe. But I repeated the test around these beds in 55 consecutive cases. Each time, without a single exception, there were intersections of dowsing reaction lines, presumably caused by underground veins of water and generally underneath that part of the bed where the person usually lay. Over a period of time 25 of these people agreed to move to a different bed or place to sleep, one free of underground irritation points. Strangely enough, all 25 improved substantially or were completely free of pain.'

Soil influences

Subsequent research with 16 cancer patients has led him to believe that this disease, too, is connected with a certain kind of underground water. He admits that there is 'no scientific explanation for the relationship between arthritis and underground forces', but points to related work by Swiss, German and Austrian scientists on 'illness caused by soil influences'. His findings might be no more than a curiosity. But just about every first-class dowser in the world supports what he has to say, and can sense instinctively the same subtle forces. As additional evidence

The Welsh dowser Bill Lewis (see pages 83 and 85) can sense a spiral force around ancient standing stones, derived from its position above the crossing of streams immediately beneath.

St Michael's Mount,
sited in a bay on the most
southerly point in
Britain, has a natural
spring rising in a 'dome'
as described by dowsers.

that usually prove too elusive to measure. A part of what Lewis feels – a growing magnetic strength towards the top of a standing stone – was confirmed by Professor John Taylor of Kings College, London, in a careful series of measurements with a portable magnetometer. An Italian chemist, Giorgi Piccardi, has also demonstrated that the molecular structure of water is affected by sunspot activity, so it is perhaps not too fanciful to believe that what goes on in outer space may have unsuspected consequences on Earth. We know, too, that minute changes in magnetic fields (page 17) also have inexplicable effects on human life.

Historically, the evidence of belief in the healing powers of water is overwhelming. The hill-tops and mounds on which ancient ceremonial sites were placed, and where many Christian churches dedicated to St Michael or St George, the dragon-killing saints, can be seen today (page 94) almost invariably contain wells, springs and streams that dowsers recognize as domes of primary water. More than 300 early Greek medical centres dedicated to the God Aesculapius, a twin spiral as his symbol, were placed at water sources where elaborate rituals took place invoking its magical (or nowadays we might say chemical) properties.

Prehistoric ceremonies
It is hard to resist the idea that water is the key to many of the mysteries of ancient and forgotten knowledge that have been touched upon in many parts of this Atlas. The homeopathic doctor today who dilutes his herbal remedy to one part in 100 of water, shakes the bottle vigorously, then in turn dilutes this solution to one part in 100, and so on perhaps a dozen times until the original herbal ingredient is absolutely undetectable, is the inheritor of practices dating back far into the mist of prehistory. For such a remedy to be effective, something outside scientific analysis must be operating; perhaps the molecular structure of the water is subtly changed when it is shaken, as it apparently is when the level of cosmic radiation changes. Since much of this is not susceptible to measurement, it cannot yet be proved. But to one observer at least, water is the unifying reason why early people held their sacred ceremonies at seasonally crucial moments of the year, in places specially chosen because an earth force there was felt to be at its most powerful. According to tradition, at such times a vital life-stream was activated and re-generated, temporarily proving a universal communion between mankind and a cosmic force whose nature we can now only glimpse by piercing the barrier of rationalist belief.

that the mysterious quality of primary water has had a crucial effect on the evolution of human life, they point to the way that ancient sacred sites were always placed above a significant underground water pattern.

Dowsers at megalithic circles and standing stones invariably discover an intricate network of meandering underground veins. Churches built on early pagan sites have a crossing of streams in front of the altar. William Lewis, the Welsh dowser involved in the experiment described on page 82, has made a detailed study of the way single megaliths are affected by the water beneath them. He can detect an energy, partially magnetic in nature, that emerges in spiral form from the stones, which seem placed deliberately to act as amplifiers for an earth force that waxes and wanes with the lunar cycle. This energy gathers strength as it rises up through the stone, and can frequently be felt physically as a tingling when touched with the fingertips, or as a loss of equilibrium if the palms of the hands are placed on the stone.

Magnetic forces
For scientists, the difficulty is to know what credence to place on sensations and vibrations

Feng-shui

Even today there are places in the world where people's lives are partly run according to the scientific principles hinted at in many of the subjects in this Atlas: an ancient sensitivity to magnetic forces; an ability to activate what has been called the earth spirit; a natural energy that makes people decide where is the right place to site their sacred buildings. To the Chinese, this art is known as *feng-shui*, and although officially discouraged on the mainland following the victory of Chairman Mao, it still operates in Taiwan and Hong Kong, where baffled foreign businessmen are liable to come up against the kind of attitude described in 1873 by E. J. Eitel, an earnest Church of England missionary:

'When purchasing a site, when building a house, when pulling down a wall, or raising a flagstaff, residents in the Treaty Ports have encountered innumerable difficulties, and all on account of Feng-shui. When it was proposed to erect a few telegraph poles, when the construction of a railway was urged upon the Chinese Government, when a mere tramway was suggested to utilize the coal-mines of the interior, Chinese officials would invariably make a polite bow and declare the thing impossible on account of Feng-shui. When the Hong Kong Government cut a road, now known as the Gap, to the Happy Valley, the Chinese community was thrown into a state of abject terror and fright, on account of the disturbance which this amputation of the dragon's limbs would cause to the Feng-shui of Hong Kong... When Senhor Amaral, the Governor of Macao, who combined a great passion for constructing roads with an unlimited contempt for Feng-shui, interfered with the situation and aspects of Chinese tombs, he was waylaid by the Chinese, his head cut off, and the Chinese called this the revenge of Feng-shui.'

Wind and water

Literally translated, feng-shui means 'wind and water', and Eitel expressed a heartfelt anguish about the difficulty of understanding its principles by quoting his houseboy: 'It's a thing like wind, which you cannot comprehend, and like water, which you cannot grasp'. Certainly for any Westerner unsympathetic to beliefs beyond those of modern science, the art of feng-shui is obscure and irrational. It is an attempt to balance the forces of *Yang* and *Yin*, the positive and the negative, whenever the landscape of the earth has to be altered for human need, 'the art of adapting the residences of the living and the dead so as to co-operate and harmonize with the local currents of the cosmic breath,' as it has been described. In Chinese thought, all things are supposed to have an essence that makes them live,

drawn from the breath of Heaven (Yang) and the breath of Earth (Yin). According to Steve Moore, a young London-based scholar, 'productivity is caused by the breath of Heaven descending and mingling with the breath of the Earth. The most auspicious spots are those obtaining a maximum of heavenly breath, and so the configuration of the landscape is important.'

Allied to this is the concept of dragon paths, or *lung-mei*, along which currents of vital power flow. Yin (female) current flows along mountainous ridges and ranges of hills. Yang (male) current runs along valleys and through subterranean channels. John Michell, the British antiquarian who has written about the subject at length, says that 'the former ought always to be to the left, and the latter to the right, of any town or habitation, which should preferably be protected by them, as if in the crook of an elbow. But this was only the beginning of the complexity, since high and abrupt escarpments were considered Yang, and rounded elevations Yin.'

Many other factors, particularly astronomical ones, were taken into consideration, and all these influences had to be balanced according to the nature of the site – for instance three-fifths

Anonymous 18th-century Chinese landscape portraying the ideal harmony of landscape aimed for in *feng-shui.*

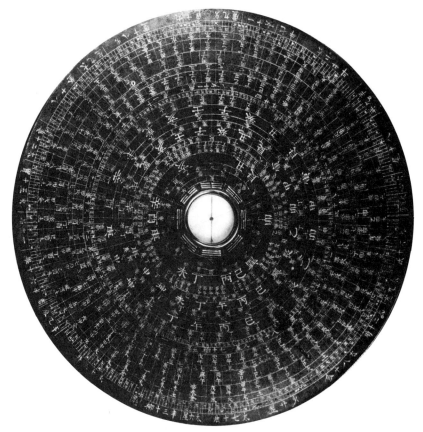

Compass used by Chinese geomancer (courtesy Science Museum, London). Magnetic and magical forces are involved. (above right) Geomancer at work during time of Ching dynasty.

Yang to two-fifths Yin – in order to obtain maximum benefit from whatever was being constructed there. A famous legend tells of how Chao Ming went from poverty and obscurity to become founder and Emperor of the Sing dynasty after re-interring his father's bones in a place favoured by lung-mei. Whatever its direct effect on human life, every observer believes that the marvellous harmony and internal symmetry of Chinese landscaping derives from feng-shui.

Instinctive understanding

John Michell presumes that 'the perception of the earth spirit as the ruling factor in life' was in the first place instinctive. The Chinese geomancers who today still advise on how buildings should be sited, using geomantic compasses much like the one preserved in the Science Museum in London, are following a relatively recent tradition based on the teachings of Choo-he and others, who lived under the Sung dynasty, AD 1126–1278. It is the responsibility of the geomancer to ensure 'that no changes are made to the shape and appearance of the landscape that might disturb locally the harmonious flow of the earth's vital energy. More than that, he may actually improve the landscape, manifesting its latent powers and making the pattern of its energy field conform more closely to the ideal requirements of its inhabitants. This he does by judicious siting of all buildings, tombs, walls and roads, with the addition of pillars, temples and monuments at the spots designed by nature to receive them.'

E. J. Eitel, in spite of his missionary beliefs, regretted the fact in words that a century later ring true: 'Would God that our own men of science had preserved that child-like reverence for the living powers of nature, that sacred awe and trembling fear of the mysteries of the unseen, that firm belief in the realities of the invisible world and its constant intercommunication with the seen and the temporal, which characterize these Chinese gropings after natural science.' It is a habit which industrialized countries, including most of China, have lost.

Section five
Lost achievements

The most significant archaeological upheaval in the last decade or so has been a steadily increasing respect for the abilities and achievements of ancient societies; at the same time, the dates for various crucial steps in man's development have been pushed ever further backwards. During the 1950s the majority of standard text-books put the development of agriculture at around 4000 BC; in 1978 most prehistorians agree that animal herding took place in northern Iraq as early as 9000 BC, and domestication of wild grain happened about 7500 BC. In the United States, the change in thinking about prehistoric antiquity has been even more remarkable. Until World War II, US archaeology was dominated by Aleš Hrdlička, a ferocious scholar under whom it was not permitted to discuss openly the possibility of *anybody* having arrived in the Americas before 2000 BC; agriculture was supposed to have sprung up around the time of Christ's birth. Nowadays everybody agrees a figure of 30–25,000 BC for fossils of early man in the New World (perhaps even 50,000 BC), and cross-bred maize was being grown in 5200 BC. In other fields the re-evaluation is similarly dramatic. Professor Alexander Thom, who first authenticated the extraordinary skills of the megalith builders, is one of a growing number of people who think that as these ancient navigators were capable of sailing the storm-chopped waters of northern Scotland, there is no reason why they should not have sailed to America as long ago as the third millenium BC. Modern experiments with small boats have shown that neither the Atlantic nor the Pacific were the barriers to early crossings that have usually been imagined.

Many societies, in their own ways, also became technologically adept. The stone sickles of early farmers were sharper than modern razor-blades; self-sharpening, too, since every flake chipped away left a new fine edge. Their engineering with large blocks of stone was just as satisfying. The careful mortice-and-tenon joints at Stonehenge needed craftsmanship of a very high degree; the one-and-a-half ton blocks of limestone used in the Great Pyramid were prepared so carefully that nowhere is there a gap between them of more than a few millimetres; the asymmetrical jointing of the massive stone blocks at Sacsahuan still defies belief.

Against the background of a growing respect for what early societies were able to achieve, this section of the Atlas looks at the question of whether other, largely forgotten, abilities may also have been involved. Levitation, or use of a contra-gravitational force, may have been more common in the past than now. The kind of psychic viewing described in the previous section may have been an aid to map-making and navigation. A number of ancient artifacts in various museums hint at a knowledge of electrical forces. The date for the first use of writing, held to be around 3500 BC in Mesopotamia, may have to be pushed back at least another 1000 years to a different part of the world. For none of these is an extra-terrestrial explanation essential. What archaeologists are newly discovering is the almost limitless capacity of man's own mind.

The gravity enigma

Daniel Dunglas Home,
19th-century
'medium' whose
levitations were
observed on several
hundred occasions.

Levitation may be easier than we think;
irresistible, even. It certainly came as a surprise
to the group of house guests gathered in the
Connecticut home of silk manufacturer Ward
Cheney in August 1852. In the fashion of the
time, they had arranged a séance, hoping for
evidence of the after-life by way of spirit
manifestations – table-rapping, ghostly lights,
ectoplasm, or the like. Instead, Daniel Dunglas
Home, the 19-year-old medium whom they had
invited to be at the centre of activities,
experienced something that had never happened
to him before, and which none of the people
present were ever to witness again: he floated
involuntarily from the ground. As good fortune
would have it, the incident was observed and
recorded by a hard-headed reporter – F. L. Burr,
editor of the *Hartford Times*: 'Suddenly, without
any expectation on the part of the company,
Home was taken up in the air. I had hold of his
hand at the time and I felt his feet – they were
lifted a foot from the floor. He palpitated from
head to foot with the contending emotions of joy
and fear which choked his utterances. Again and
again he was taken from the floor, and the third
time he was carried to the ceiling of the
apartment, with which his hands and feet came
into gentle contact.'

D. D. Home subsequently learned to levitate
voluntarily, and performed the feat in front of
hundreds, perhaps thousands, of witnesses, by
turn eminent, sceptical and amazed: Thackeray,
Bulwer Lytton, Emperor Napoleon III, Ruskin,
Rossetti, Mark Twain – these and many others
saw the gravity-defying phenomena that
surrounded him wherever he went. As well as
being able to lift himself above the ground, tables
tilted and rose, (though objects upon them
remained stationary as if glued); heavy pieces of
furniture (on occasions, even grand pianos)
moved weightlessly across the room; bells rang,
music played (notably an accordion while its
bellows were motionless), bird noises sounded,
spirit voices sang out; an evening with
D. D. Home was an evening of psychic mayhem.

Absence of fraud

What makes him unique in the history of
levitation is the sheer volume of testimony.
The manifestations occurred over a period of
some 40 years, often in broad daylight and in
full view of everyone around him. In spite of
extreme hostility by such critics as the magician
Harry Houdini, who claimed without ever
attempting to prove it that he could duplicate
all of Home's feats, he was not once shown to
be fraudulent. In July 1871 he received the
approval of William Crookes, one of the era's
renowned scientists, later to be knighted and
become President of the British Association for
the Advancement of Science. He wrote in the
Quarterly Journal of Science: 'The phenomena I
am prepared to attest are so extraordinary, and so
directly oppose the most firmly-rooted articles of
scientific belief – amongst others, the ubiquity
and invariable action of the force of gravitation –
that, even now, on recalling the details of what
I witnessed, there is an antagonism in my mind
between *reason*, which pronounces it to be
scientifically impossible, and the consciousness
that my senses, both of touch and sight, are not
lying witnesses.'

Weightlessness of Christ

The reaction of the scientific establishment was
to denounce his observations; Darwin said that
he could neither disbelieve in Crookes's
statements, nor believe in his report. Yet seen in
perspective, Home's activities were merely a
spectacular demonstration of something that has

1. Henry C. Gordon levitated in New York City, 1858.
2. Charles Cathcart's son was lifted above the ground by a mysterious force in Indiana, 1858.
3. Father Suarez levitated at Santa Cruz, 1911.
4. Mary London levitated in Cork, 1661.
5. David Dunglas Home levitated in Manchester, 1852.
6. Henry Jones levitated at Shepton Mallet, 1657.
7. St Edmund, Archbishop of Canterbury, levitated at Canterbury, c.1242.
8. St Teresa levitated in Madrid, 1680.
9. Nana Owuku levitated in Togo, Africa, May 1975. The incident was recorded on film.
10. St Joseph of Copertino levitated many times in the area from which he took his name, 1603–1663.
11. Member of the congregation of the church of St Mary's, Vienna, 1861.
12. N. P. Damascolluf levitated in Warsaw, 1933.
13. An African witchdoctor was seen causing the levitation of an adolescent boy in Durban, 1870.
14. Sister Mary, an Arabian Carmelite nun, levitated in Bethlehem, c.1700.
15. A boulder in Shivapur, India, is regularly levitated by a group chanting the words 'Qamar Ali Dervish' in loud ringing tones.
16. Sabbyar Pullavar levitated in Southern India, 1936. The incident was recorded on film.
17. William Eglinton, an internationally renowned medium, levitated in Calcutta, 1862.
18. A fakir, whose name was not recorded, levitated in front of the Prince of Wales in Calcutta, 1862.
19. Emperor Cheng Tang ordered Ki-Kung-Shi to build a flying chariot in 1766 BC. The chariot was later destroyed by Imperial edict.
20. The Chinese poet, Chu Yuan, wrote of his flight in a jade chariot in 300 BC.

a long tradition, however sporadically it may happen. Levitation has been recorded at all times among all people: the miracle of Christ walking on the water involved no more weightlessness than when 12-year-old Henry Jones, from Shepton Mallet in the west of England, was 'bewitched' in 1657; on many well-observed occasions during that year he rose unaided and placed the flat of his hands on the ceiling, and once flew 30 yards over a garden wall.

Shortly after Home retired, an equally renowned medium named Eusapia Palladino achieved the same sort of anti-gravitational chaos that he had, again under the strictest experimental supervision, being bound to her chair and held firmly by a variety of doubting investigators who afterwards swore that they had truly seen all manner of objects in the room waltzing weightlessly about, and on one occasion herself rise in the air. An amiable peasant woman from Naples, she triumphantly passed a series of such tests over a period of several years. At the end, however, she was deliberately given the opportunity to cheat in less rigorous circumstances, and took it; because of this, all her undoubtedly successful earlier feats have been discounted by the Society for Psychical Research.

Saint Teresa

Out of the 230 Catholic saints to whom levitation, voluntary or otherwise, is attributed, some at least seem beyond question. Teresa of Avila was canonized because of it, and her official biography, written during her lifetime, records her feelings: 'It seemed to me, when I tried to make some resistance, as if a great force beneath my feet lifted me up ... I confess that it threw me into great fear, very great indeed at first; for in seeing one's body thus lifted up from the earth, though the spirit draws it upwards after itself (and that with great sweetness, if unresisted), the senses are not lost; at least I was so much myself as to be able to see that I was being lifted up ... After the rapture was over, I have to say my body seemed frequently to be buoyant, as if all weight had departed from it, so much so that now and then I scarcely knew that my feet touched the ground.'

Saint Joseph

St Joseph of Copertino (1603–1663) led an even more charmed life. A feeble-minded boy from Apulia, Italy, he seems to have spent most of his teenage life trying to induce a state of ecstasy in himself by various forms of self-torment such as flagellation and starvation. Accepted with some reluctance as a Franciscan priest at the age of 22, it was not long before he achieved ecstasy during prayers after Mass, and promptly flew off the ground and landed on the altar, to be burned by candle flames. After this, his readiness to repeat the feat became something of an embarrassment to the church authorities, so promptly and frequently did it occur – every time, in fact, the young man became dangerously delighted by some new event in his life. Seeing

Throughout history, as the above map shows, the ability to levitate has been widespread.

Followers of the Maharishi Mahesh Yogi (above) claim that by following his teachings, levitation can be readily achieved today.

the Pope for the first time, he rose several feet in the air. A fellow monk once rashly observed that God had sent them a beautiful day; St Joseph uttered a shriek of joy and flew to the top of a tree. More than 100 such incidents were attested by scholars before his sainthood was granted. For much of his life, his superiors required him to worship in private, so disrupting to congregations and other gatherings were his well-meaning ecstatic flights, during which he would often offer kindly to carry people's belongings.

Hilariously though the events read to modern eyes, they are important simply because they happen to be true. People as eminent as Princess Maria of Savoy and King Casimir V of Poland testified under oath to his feats, and if levitation could happen then, there is no good reason why it should not now. In fact, Transcendental Meditation followers of the Maharishi Mahesh Yogi say that after a course of instruction at TM's headquarters in Switzerland, they are able to do so at will. One such graduate was quoted in the London *Evening Standard* as saying: 'The first time we started to practise none of us moved – we were too busy laughing at the instructors who were sort of hopping and leaping about the room. Then, gradually, we started to do it ourselves. People would rock gently, then more and more, and then start lifting off into the air. You should really be in a lotus position to do it – you can hurt yourself landing if you've got a dangling undercarriage. To begin with it's like the Wright Brothers' first flight – you come down with a bump. That's why we have to sit on foam rubber cushions. Then you learn to control it better, and it becomes totally exhilarating.'

The obstacles to belief in such descriptions are the usual ones: you won't believe it until you see it with your own eyes, and even then it's probably trickery because there isn't a scientific explanation for it. Of course, fraud exists, and so does self-delusion. But a number of writers who have investigated the most widespread contemporary reports of levitation – among Eastern mystics – have come back convinced that alongside the deceit a small number of genuine cases occur. John Keel told in his book *Jadoo* how his journey across India and Tibet during the 1950s had shown even the most renowned of miracle-working holy men usually to be nothing more than expert magicians. However, he also interviewed a Tibetan lama named Nyang-Pas in Sikkim, who levitated for him during their conversation. The lama 'struggled to his feet, pressed one hand on top of his stick, a heavy branch about four feet long, frowned a little with effort, and then slowly lifted his legs up off the floor until he was sitting cross-legged in the air . . . There was nothing behind him or under him. His sole support was his stick, which he seemed to use to keep his balance.'

Photographic evidence

It seems that such people make universal use of a stick in this way, sometimes wrapped ritually with a cloth, and because of this the usual explanation of their feats is that a series of metal rods must be hidden in their clothes. If the many 19th-century engravings showing cross-legged levitation are accurate, this would seem dynamically impossible – the centre of gravity would be in the wrong place; and in any case there is the set of photographs taken in 1936 by P. T. Plunkett and published in the *Illustrated London News* that seems conclusive. The event took place in southern India, and was described by Plunkett in careful detail. 'The time was about 12.30 p.m. and the sun directly above us so that shadows played no part in the performance . . . Standing quietly by was Subbayah Pullavar, the performer, with long hair, a drooping moustache and a wild look in his eye. He salaamed to us and stood chatting for a while. He had been practising this particular branch of yoga for nearly 20 years (as had past generations of his family). We asked permission to take photographs of the performance and he gave it willingly, thus dispelling any doubt as to whether the whole thing was merely a hypnotic illusion.'

Having mustered about 150 witnesses, Plunkett then watched the fakir pour water in a circle round a small tent in which the levitation itself was about to take place, unseen by outsiders. Nobody with leather-soled shoes was allowed inside the circle. Some minutes later the tent was

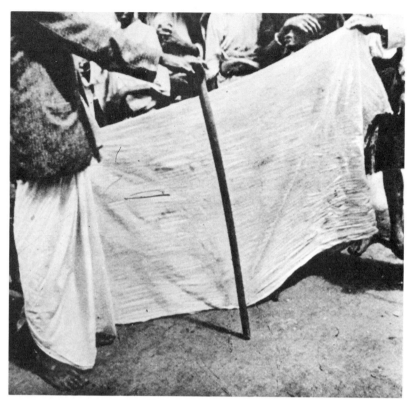

Perhaps the most convincing pictures of a levitation ever taken published in the *Illustrated London News* of 6 June 1936. (above) The stick used apparently for balancing is shown before being wrapped.

removed, and Plunkett and a friend watched carefully from either side as the airborne fakir was revealed. They took their photographs, prodded the space around him, and concluded that 'the man had no support whatsoever except for resting one hand lightly on top of the cloth-wrapped stick.' He remained horizontal in the air for about four minutes, after which the tent was put back over him to enable him to return to the ground concealed from public view.

However, the tent walls were so thin that Plunkett could still see what was going on. 'After about a minute he appeared to sway and then very slowly began to descend, still in a horizontal position. He took about five minutes to move from the top of the stick to the ground,

a distance of about three feet. Evidently we were not meant to see this part of the performance or it would have been done in the open. When Subbayah was back on the ground his assistants carried him over to where we were sitting and asked if we would try to bend his limbs. Even with assistance we were unable to do so.' It took some five minutes of massaging and cold water douches before the man returned to normal, and Plunkett ended his account by declaring that 'as I have witnessed this performance with several of my fellow planters on several occasions, I am quite convinced of the total absence of tricking.'

Local phenomenon

Some of the facts that are common to all observed levitations of the kind so far described are that they are short-lived, and relatively localized – metres rather than kilometres. This would seem to rule them out as explanations for why many man-made structures on Earth seem designed only to be seen from above – the serpent mound in Ohio, the desert patterns in Peru (page 70), certain hill figures on the chalk downland of southern Britain.

Here, something more extensive would be called for: either physical forms of early flying such as hot-air ballooning, or psychical projection of the mind as in the various forms of remote viewing. Indeed, levitation seems very close to one of these, the sensation known as an out-of-body experience (OOBE) that has been widely recorded in both psychic and orthodox medical journals and may happen to as many as one person in 20. During an OOBE, the person has the vivid feeling of being some distance away from his or her physical body, which can be viewed with an air of detachment; often, the experience happens during the crisis between life and death that follows a severe accident or a near-fatal emergency during hospital surgery, but it is also a psychic experience which some people say they can achieve at will, and in which they can travel dream-like to far distant places and view their surroundings with perfect clarity. Tibetan lamas have been reported as saying that this, rather than physical movement, is the explanation for all the stories about how they can levitate across hundreds of kilometres of mountains and gorges. There may be a connection, too, with all the unobserved but widely believed stories of witches in mediaeval times flying on broomsticks. In recent times there is the confrontation between Carlos Castaneda and his 'Don Juan', the apocryphal Yaqui Indian man of knowledge with supernatural powers. Under the influence of hallucinogens, Castaneda finds he has inexplicably travelled through the air half a mile.

Trying to reassure himself, he says to his master: 'I really didn't fly, Don Juan. I flew in my imagination, in my mind alone. Where was my body?' The answer comes: 'You don't think a man flies; and yet a *brujo* (witch) can move a thousand miles in one second to see what is going on. He can deliver a blow to his enemies long distances away. So does he or doesn't he fly?'

Causes of levitation

Such ambiguities and enigmas apart, there can only be two causes of classic levitations (one may lead to the other): exceptional control of the body, or a temporary dislocation of gravitational forces. There is overwhelming evidence for the first. D. D. Home, later in his life, was able to handle red-hot coals without being burned, in much the same way as firewalkers can go over a pit of hot embers without damaging the soles of their feet. Alexandra David-Neel, a French explorer who spent 14 years in Tibet before publishing *Mystiques et Magiciens du Tibet* in 1929, gave many instances of how hermits were able to generate a mysterious inner heat called *tumo* by a certain method of yogi-like concentration, enabling them to withstand sub-zero temperatures clad only in a thin cotton garment. She described a lama in northern Tibet moving in a way that sounds almost like the ballet dancer Vaslav Nijinsky's legendary jumps, where he appeared to remain motionless at the highest point of elevation: 'The man did not run. He seemed to lift himself from the ground proceeding by leaps. It looked as if he had been endowed with the elasticity of a ball and rebounded each time his feet touched the ground. His steps had the regularity of a pendulum.' In this way the man could cover hundreds of miles, his eyes transfixed on a distant object.

Anti-gravity

But true levitation – the rising of human beings into the air for some minutes – goes beyond that. Something to cancel the gravitational force has to happen, and it may be reassuring to know that the fundamental characteristics of gravity still elude analysis by modern physics. It is, after all, an extremely weak force: every time a child lifts a spoon to its mouth, it is defeating the gravity of the entire Earth. Some of the best-attested psychical experiments involve proof that weight can be changed by will-power; total weightlessness is just one step further. Perhaps the biggest mystery is why it doesn't happen to more of us more often – and should it do so, we can take comfort from D. D. Home's description of what it feels like: 'I feel no hands supporting me, and, since the first time, I have never felt fear; though, should I have fallen from the ceiling of some rooms in which I have been raised, I

The actual levitation took place inside a tent which was removed to reveal the yogi horizontal in the air, in a state of trance. Photographs were freely taken at close range and from all angles.

could not have escaped serious injury. I am generally lifted up perpendicularly; my arms frequently become rigid, and are drawn above my head, as if I were grasping the unseen power which slowly raises me from the floor.'

Early astronomers

The primitive tribe of Dogon people in the southern Sahara draw sand pictures of the halo that surrounds Saturn and of the four moons circling Jupiter.

Galileo's announcement on 7 January 1610 that his new-fangled invention, the telescope, had enabled him to identify four moons revolving round the planet Jupiter was hotly disputed. He was already a controversial figure, and the accuracy of his telescope and his judgement were attacked and a pamphlet published against him. The authorities were concerned that, should he be right, it would have thrown into doubt the prevailing concept that the Earth was the centre of the Universe. A variety of counter-suggestions were put forward to 'explain' what he had seen – optical illusions, haloes, reflections, luminous clouds, self-delusion. As Arthur Koestler remarked in *The Sleepwalkers*, the furore had all the elements of a similar controversy 300 years later concerning the existence of flying saucers: 'The Jupiter moons were no less threatening to the outlook on the world of sober scholars in 1610 than, say, extra-sensory perception was in 1960.'

We know now that Galileo was right, and with even limited understanding of the force of gravity and its effect on the movement of the celestial bodies, we have no intellectual difficulty in accepting that not only Jupiter, but most other planets, have satellite moons revolving around them. But was Galileo the first to perceive this? And is a telescope the only means of seeing distant moons? Beyond easy explanation, a number of primitive tribes and early societies seem to have gained a knowledge of the Universe that greatly exceeds the bounds of normal sight. The preoccupation of emerging civilizations with the movement of celestial bodies (page 58) is itself a wonder; it is almost beyond belief that a few people could identify small globes as they invisibly orbited pinpoints of starry light in the sky.

Pygmies from the Ituri forest of central Africa know about the moons of Saturn.

Ituri pygmies

Yet that is what, for instance, the Pygmies of the Ituri Forest in Central Africa can do. Jean Pierre Hallet, a French anthropologist who became an honorary member of the Efé tribe and lived with them for 18 months, was astonished to find that they traditionally called Saturn *Bibi Tiba Abutsiua'ani* – 'the star of the nine moons'. This arcane astronomical fact was at the time of Hallet's visit a little-known truth, Saturn's ninth planet having been discovered by the American, W. H. Pickering, in 1899. In 1966 a tiny tenth moon, about 200 kilometres in diameter, was discovered by the French astronomer Audouin Dollfus, but this hardly detracts from the pygmies' achievement. Hallet summed up: 'I have never encountered a Bantu or Sudanese who credits Saturn with any moons, much less nine. Most Americans and Europeans are no better informed concerning the existence and number of Saturn's satellites.'

The Dogon

South of the Sahara desert live four related tribes of Africans whom the French anthropologists Marcel Griaule and Germaine Dieterlen studied from 1946–1950, living mainly with the Dogon people and inspiring such confidence that four of their head priests were persuaded to reveal their most secret traditions. There is no doubt that what the two scientists were told was authentic; so highly were they respected by the Dogon that when Griaule died in 1956, 250,000 Africans from the area gathered in tribute for his funeral in Mali.

Drawing patterns and symbols in the dusty soil, Dogon priests showed that they had inherited from ancient times a knowledge of the universe that was unbelievably accurate. The focus of their attention was the star Sirius, the brightest in the sky – in fact, a binary star; around Sirius A, the star we can see, revolves Sirius B, a 'white dwarf' star of great density which is totally invisible to the naked eye, and was seen for the first time in 1862 by the American Alvan Clark when he peered through the largest telescope then existing, and spotted a faint point of light; being 100,000 times less bright than Sirius A, it was not possible to capture it on a photograph until 1970. Yet the Dogon not only knew about this star, but also many of its characteristics. They knew it was white, and that although it was 'the smallest thing there is', it was also 'the heaviest star', made of a substance 'heavier than all the iron on Earth' – a good description of Sirius B's density, which is so great that a cubic metre weighs around 20,000 tons. They knew correctly that its orbit round Sirius A took 50 years, and was not circular but elliptical (true of the movement of all celestial bodies, but not

widely known outside the world of trained astronomers); they even knew the position of Sirius A within the ellipse.

Their knowledge of astronomy in general was no less astonishing. They drew the halo that surrounds Saturn, which is impossible to detect with normal eyesight; they knew about the four main moons of Jupiter; they knew that the planets revolved around the sun, that the Earth is round and that it spins on its own axis; incredibly, they were sure that the Milky Way is a spiral-like shape, a fact not known to astronomers until well into this century. They also believed (page 150) that their knowledge was obtained from extra-terrestrial visitors.

The Maoris

Though not in the same class as the Dogon, the Maoris of New Zealand were also found by early travellers to have a rich and extensive lore about the stars and planets, reputedly having used astronomical methods when they sailed from their unknown place of origin through the Polynesian Islands – a formidable feat of neolithic navigation. According to one explorer in 1814: 'They have given names to certain stars and constellations, and have likewise connected with them some curious traditions, which they hold in superstitious veneration. It is usual with them in the summer season to remain awake during the greater part of the night watching the motions of the heavens, and making inquiries concerning the time when such-and-such a star will appear.' The most important apparently paranormal observation that the Maoris made was that one of the planets, which they called Parearu, was surrounded by a ring. Whether they meant the rings of Saturn or the bands of Jupiter is not clear from their legends, but neither can nowadays be seen with the naked eye.

Early telescopes

So where did all this extraordinary tribal knowledge come from? Perhaps in the case of the Maoris, superhuman eyesight cannot be ruled out. Telescopic vision; the presence of magnifying atmospheres; larger, more marked bands and rings seen through a clearer atmosphere; a time in history when the planets were closer to Earth than now; all these have been put forward as unlikely but not absolutely impossible ways of obtaining information. But the Dogon and the Ituri Pygmy knowledge is in a different class. The two French anthropologists understated the problem when they said the difficulty was to discover 'how, with no instruments at their disposal, men could know the movements and certain characteristics of

virtually invisible stars'; what the Dogon and the Ituri knew is not virtually invisible, but totally invisible.

The possibility is that they learned their astronomy from somebody else – not recent European explorers, for the traditions go back to much more distant times, but perhaps from contact with ancient Mesopotamia, Egypt or Greece. This is distinctly more likely. Although Galileo is usually credited as being the first person to use a telescope methodically, it is certain that cruder versions were available long before his time. The first man-made glass is dated to around 3500 BC in Egypt, and primitive lenses made about 2000 BC have been found in Crete and Asia Minor; it is a short and simple step to place one lens in front of another to make a basic telescope, and the chances are it must have

The tiny dot to the lower right is Sirius B, a star known to the Dogon tribe; it is dwarfed by Sirius, and was not photographed until 1970. Other small dots on the photograph are multiple images of Sirius.

Only a powerful telescope can enable people to see the bands that form a halo round Saturn.

Possible route of Dogon Africans in ancient times from north Africa to their present homeland.

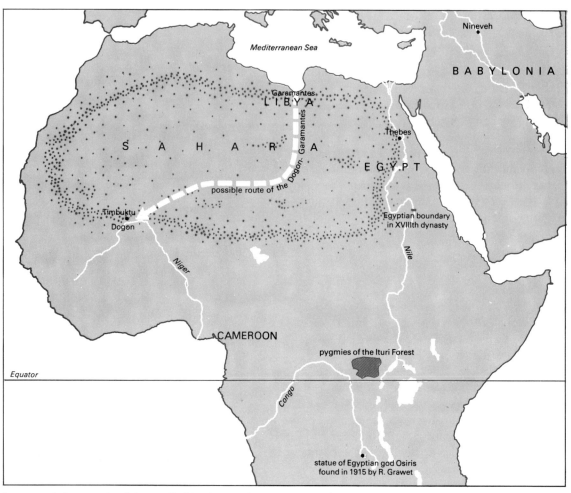

Was the astronomical knowledge of primitive African tribes diffused from Egypt? Pygmies (below) occur often in Egyptian reliefs.

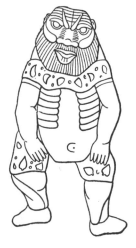

happened thousands of times. Galileo himself noted that the 'ancients' were aware of telescopes. By the Third Century BC Euclid was laying down the principles of light refraction and magnification, and there is evidence in Greek drama of magnifying glasses made of globes filled with water. Later Nero (who was extremely short-sighted) used a telescope made of emerald lenses to watch the Roman Games.

The crucial question is just how good these telescopes may have been, and how much knowledge the astronomer-priests of early civilizations were able to obtain. Babylonians certainly knew of the phases of Venus, and possibly observed the moons of Jupiter and Saturn, although they thought Saturn had seven of them rather than nine. If the secrets of the Great Pyramid have truly been decoded at last (page 65), Egyptian knowledge went much farther than this, embracing truths about the nature of the Universe that were later taken up by Pythagorean and Platonic schools of philosophy to form the basis of civilized thinking for more than a thousand years. Such knowledge certainly would perhaps have included everything that the Dogon and the Ituri Pygmies know now, and more.

The American historian Robert Temple has

argued persuasively in *The Sirius Mystery* that this is what happened. (His proposal that beings from a Sirian planet brought the knowledge in the first place is examined on pages 150–152 of this Atlas.) He has traced the origins of the Dogon to the Garamantes people of Libya, Egypt's neighbour; in any case, Egyptian influence through the African continent was wider than is normally assumed. The Pygmies were well-known to the Egyptians, who employed the little folk as clowns and dancers at court, where they were highly valued. Egyptian – Pygmy contacts were established at least as early as the Old Kingdom (*c.* 2300 BC), and at some date Egyptian influence spread even further, for a statue of the god Osiris was found well to the south of the Ituri forest. It has even been suggested that the mysterious homeland of the New Zealand Maoris was among a Libyan people known as 'Ma'. The Egyptian sun-god Ra is paralleled by use of the same word for the same god throughout Polynesia and New Zealand.

If there is a common source for the astronomical understanding of all three tribes, Temple's is undoubtedly the neatest solution. The problem is whether the Babylonians and Egyptians really knew the details about Sirius; his evidence relies on hieroglyphic texts which everybody agrees are

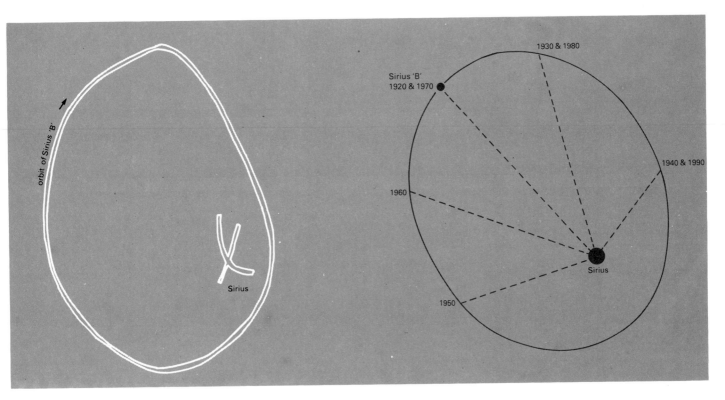

notoriously difficult to interpret. It is curious, to say the least, that the Dogon are able to explain everything so precisely when the written evidence from ancient civilization is so obscure.

Recent experiments into remote viewing and extra-sensory perception (page 82), suggest one other possible explanation. In the extraordinary world which modern psychics such as Ingo Swann seem able to penetrate, distance makes no difference. With another subject, Harold Sherman, he recorded his impressions of what it was like to 'view' the surface of Jupiter and Mercury in advance of the *Pioneer 10* and *Mariner 10* rocket probes. What the two men described was remarkably similar in detail – on Jupiter, eerily coloured thick cloud, blue ice crystals, tornado-force winds; on Mercury a thin atmosphere, a small magnetic field, and a helium tail streaming out from the planet away from the sun (all unsuspected by astronomers but later confirmed by *Mariner 10*). The degree of Dogon knowledge is hardly more accurate than this, and intriguing though it is to see them as the last inheritors of an ancient

wisdom brought from outer space, the reality is that everything they know could have come from one wise old tribal seer, projecting his mind from his body towards the brightest star in the sky, and describing with wonder what he saw there.

Dogon sand drawings showing details of the orbit of Sirius B around Sirius.

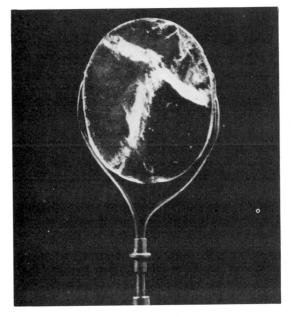

Ground glass in the British Museum, probably used as a lens *c.* 8th Century BC.

Gulliver's moons

Jonathan Swift (left) probably researched all his supposedly uncanny knowledge about the moons of Mars (e.g. Phobos, below right) from Johannes Kepler.

Books about supposed visitors from outer space, and the knowledge they brought with them to enlighten us earthlings, are fond of quoting the 'prediction' by Jonathan Swift in *Gulliver's Travels* (1726) that Mars would turn out to have two moons, at a distance of three and five diameters from Mars respectively, the nearest one revolving in ten hours and the outermost in $21\frac{1}{2}$ hours. This statement, insignificantly placed in the middle of a long satirical allegory about Anglo-Spanish relations at the time (disguised as 'Lilliputians'), is seemingly a remarkable one. The existence of the moons was not established until August 1877, when Asaph Hall, an astronomer at the US Naval Observatory in Washington, DC, saw them, with difficulty, through a 26-inch refracting telescope. They were tiny – mere chunks of rock in the sky: the outer $20 \times 23 \times 28$ kilometres, the inner $10 \times 12 \times 16$ kilometres. Their distance from Mars, and the length of their orbits, also corresponds closely to what Swift suggested. In particular, the inner moon moves with startling rapidity, just as he said. The US psychologist Martin Gardner, an arch-sceptic of any psychic happening, wrote in *Fads and Fallacies in the Name of Science* that this inner moon is 'the only known body in the universe that revolves around a central body *faster* than the central body rotates, yet this fact also is included in Swift's brief description!'

Extra-terrestrial suspicions

Other writers have frequently taken up the point, generally implying that Swift could not have known what he did with extra-terrestrial or supernatural help. Erich von Däniken in *Chariots of the Gods*: 'How could Swift describe the Martian satellites when they were not discovered until 150 years later? Undoubtedly the Martian satellites were suspected by some astronomers before Swift, but suspicions are not nearly enough for such precise data. We do not know where Swift got his knowledge.' R. De Witt Miller in *Impossible – Yet It Happened*: 'Where Jonathan Swift got the astronomy in his *Gulliver's Travels* is a problem.'

Where he got it from is almost certainly now known: from Johannes Kepler, the 17th-century mathematician, savant, astrologer, and discoverer of the laws of planetary motion. Kepler, a passionate astronomer in the tradition of Pythagoras and Plato, believed in a harmonious universe based on the rhythmic symmetry that can be produced by numbers. Learning of Galileo's telescope through which four moons had been observed round Jupiter, he made efforts to borrow it; although Galileo, jealous, at first refused, Kepler eventually had use of it and saw for himself that the moons existed. He deduced (wrongly) that there must be a geometrical progression in the number of satellites orbiting each planet – none for Venus, the Earth with one, Mars two, and Jupiter four.

Planetary laws

Wrong though he was, Kepler's eminence as an astronomer made his beliefs generally accepted, and in fact his planetary laws still stand today. So when Swift was writing *Gulliver's Travels* and wished to include a piece of imaginative but feasible science fiction, there is no doubt he was well aware of Kepler's calculations; among Swift's sources were the *Philosophical Transactions of the Royal Society*, which still regarded Kepler as having spoken an irrevocable truth. Even rudimentary calculations using Kepler's third law of planetary motion would have given Jonathan Swift a figure very close to the uniquely rapid orbit of the inner moon of Mars. Alas for those who want to use this oddity as a piece of evidence for extra-terrestrial intervention, it isn't valid. As the US astronomer Carl Sagan wrote in *The Cosmic Connection*: 'There is an entire genre of writing on how it was that Swift knew about the moons of Mars, including the suggestion that he was a Martian. Internal evidence suggests that Swift was no Martian, and the two moons can almost certainly be traced back to Kepler's speculation.'

Early navigators

Seamanship is one of the oldest of man's skills. Long before there were shepherds or farmers, there were sailors, launching themselves across rivers, then lakes, and finally oceans in pursuit of new horizons; the feats of these early navigators are a testimony to man's restless ambition. Nobody knows for sure who the first sailors were, but the urge and ability to sail may well have happened simultaneously with the mysterious emergence of modern man from an unknown birthplace (page 43).

Homo sapiens sapiens arrived in Australia at least 30,000 years ago, very shortly after his appearance on the archaeological map of Europe. Even though, because of lower sea-levels, Borneo and much of Indonesia were then joined to south-east Asia, and New Guinea was linked to the Australian continent, there were gaps between islands that could not have been crossed on foot: if boats were not used, then floats or rafts certainly were. Somehow, the earliest Aboriginals managed to cross large stretches of water at the very dawn of humanity.

By the end of the last Ice Age, from 10,000 BC onwards, the swelling oceans severed many land connections, and prompted further voyaging. A hand-made paddle dated at 7500 BC was found at Star Carr in Yorkshire, used by a tribe of hunter-fishers who went there seasonally and camped by the lakeside. At about the same time, active sea-faring was taking place in the Aegean Sea. A strata of debris in the Franchthi cave in the Peloponnese islands contains a mass of fish-bones, proving that the inhabitants of the cave had turned to the sea as a food source. There is also a quantity of obsidian, a black volcanic glassy rock much prized by prehistoric man for its beauty and workability. It comes from the island of Melos, some 120 kilometres away, and is the earliest evidence so far for the transport of goods by sea.

Type of boat

The first boat known is a wooden dug-out canoe from Pesse in Holland, dated to around 6400 BC. But boats rot, and most archaeologists believe that other types – skin-covered, or rafts of logs – were also used, and may be discovered one day beneath the sand and mud of the sea bed. The American archaeologist Alice B. Kehoe thinks that the Celtic tradition of skin-boats, such as the Irish and Welsh currachs, were modelled on those from neolithic times. The few small modern ones still used by fishermen today are feeble copies of the imposing vessels described in classical and pre-medieval literature: some Irish boats of those times were large enough to support a mast and hold 20 men, and were in some ways more seaworthy than heavy keeled ships that rely on ballast to keep

stable. Although a currach may capsize, it rides the waves and is essentially unsinkable; it is likely that at least from 4500 BC onwards, the western European megalith builders (page 58) were using them from Iberia in the south to the Western Isles of Scotland.

Mesopotamian voyages

In the Arabian Gulf in the same period, voyages on a similar scale were beginning. At Eridu, the earliest settlement site in Mesopotamia, a clay model of a sailing vessel was found, probably dating from the fifth millenium BC. Its broad oval shape suggests a skin-covered boat. The familiar high-prowed and high-sterned boats, probably made of reeds, of the shape that became characteristic of Mesopotamian and Egyptian ships, are portrayed on tablets from the second half of the fourth millenium BC. From 3000 BC onwards, the sea routes used were probably not much different from those now sailed by Arab dhows ranging along the Arabian, African and Indian coasts; traders' seals show that in 2350 BC there was a thriving two-way traffic between the young civilizations in the Indus Valley and the older-established Sumerians in Mesopotamia.

Skin-covered boats of the type known as currachs are virtually unsinkable; larger versions than this modern fishing currach existed in ancient times, and may have been used to cross the Atlantic.

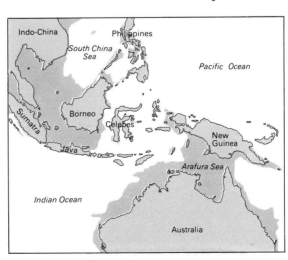

Although the sea level was lower in 30,000 BC early man must still have made island-hopping voyages to reach Australia.

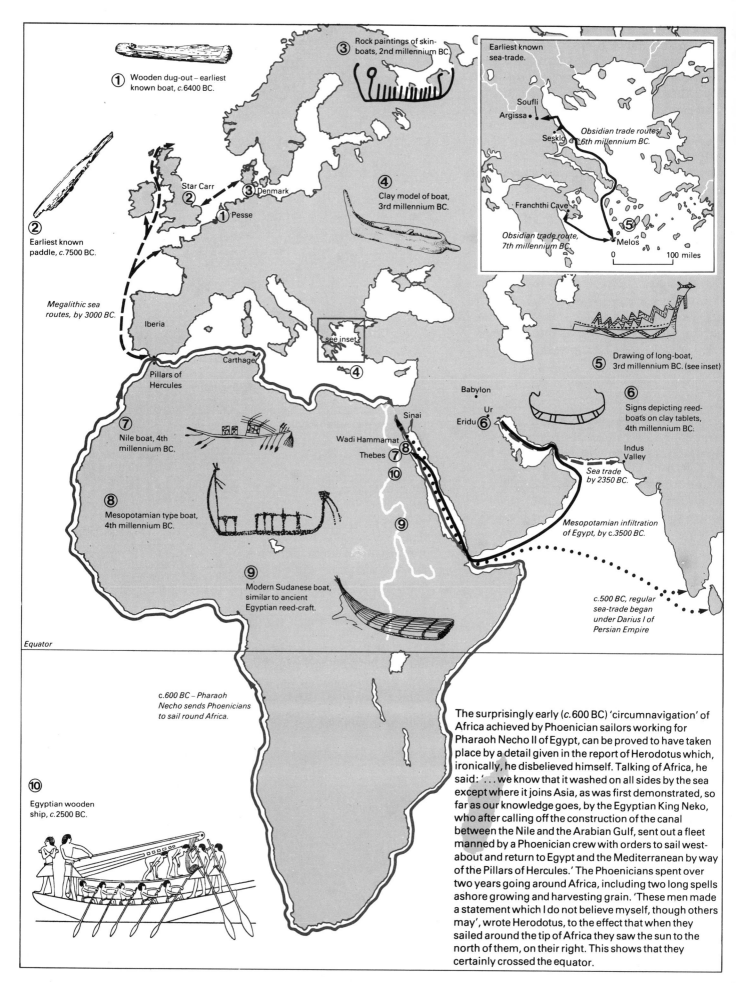

① Wooden dug-out – earliest known boat, c.6400 BC.

② Earliest known paddle, c.7500 BC.

③ Rock paintings of skin-boats, 2nd millennium BC.

Star Carr

② ③ Denmark

① Pesse

Megalithic sea routes, by 3000 BC.

Iberia

Carthage

Pillars of Hercules

④ Clay model of boat, 3rd millennium BC.

see inset

④

Earliest known sea-trade.

Soufli
Argissa

Sesklo

Obsidian trade routes, 6th millennium BC.

Franchthi Cave

⑤

Obsidian trade route, 7th millennium BC.

Melos

0   100 miles

⑤ Drawing of long-boat, 3rd millennium BC. (see inset)

⑥ Signs depicting reed-boats on clay tablets, 4th millennium BC.

Babylon

Ur
Eridu ⑥

Sinai

Wadi Hammamat
Thebes ⑦ ⑧

⑩

⑨

⑦ Nile boat, 4th millennium BC.

⑧ Mesopotamian type boat, 4th millennium BC.

Indus Valley

Sea trade by 2350 BC.

Mesopotamian infiltration of Egypt, by c.3500 BC.

c.500 BC, regular sea-trade began under Darius I of Persian Empire

⑨ Modern Sudanese boat, similar to ancient Egyptian reed-craft.

Equator

c.600 BC – Pharaoh Necho sends Phoenicians to sail round Africa.

⑩ Egyptian wooden ship, c.2500 BC.

The surprisingly early (c.600 BC) 'circumnavigation' of Africa achieved by Phoenician sailors working for Pharaoh Necho II of Egypt, can be proved to have taken place by a detail given in the report of Herodotus which, ironically, he disbelieved himself. Talking of Africa, he said: '... we know that it washed on all sides by the sea except where it joins Asia, as was first demonstrated, so far as our knowledge goes, by the Egyptian King Neko, who after calling off the construction of the canal between the Nile and the Arabian Gulf, sent out a fleet manned by a Phoenician crew with orders to sail west-about and return to Egypt and the Mediterranean by way of the Pillars of Hercules.' The Phoenicians spent over two years going around Africa, including two long spells ashore growing and harvesting grain. 'These men made a statement which I do not believe myself, though others may', wrote Herodotus, to the effect that when they sailed around the tip of Africa they saw the sun to the north of them, on their right. This shows that they certainly crossed the equator.

Egyptian stay-at-homes

By contrast, the Egyptians during the same period showed little inclination to move far beyond their borders. They have left us with many attractive pictures of a wide range of boats, from wooden vessels with sails and oars to the papyrus boats made famous by Thor Heyerdahl's *Ra* expeditions; but there is very little evidence that they used such vessels except in the Nile itself. How little experience the Egyptians had on the open sea can be judged from the expedition organized by Queen Hatshepsut (*c.* 1500 BC) to the mysterious 'Land of Punt'. Her own records laud the event as a major naval achievement, and many historians have cited it as another of ancient Egypt's high achievements. The truth, as established recently by the Egyptologist Alessandra Nibbi, is somewhat more pedestrian. Pointing out that the Egyptians did not have a sea god, and may not even have had a word for 'sea' until they adopted the Semitic word *yam*, she has established the location of the Land of Punt as the Sinai Peninsula, immediately the other side of what is now the Suez Canal. Queen Hatshepsut's entire voyage may only have been a total of 700 kilometres, vastly less adventurous than those regularly sailed by the megalithic Europeans or the Mesopotamians (page 113).

Long-distance navigation

These newly-established facts are crucially important in trying to come to terms with the two great puzzles surrounding early sailors: just how far did their voyages range? How did they manage to navigate accurately? For as the next pages describe, it seems certain that a number of intrepid travellers not only crossed the Atlantic but perhaps went as far south as the Antarctic continent, and while they were there made maps of startling accuracy. Archaeologists have concentrated on four possible methods of navigation:

Compass Although the legendary 'south pointing chariot' of China in 2634 BC is often cited as the first use of pole-seeking magnets, it was almost certainly no more than a mechanical device; the properties of the compass were known to the Chinese in AD 1093, but were not put to practical use for a further

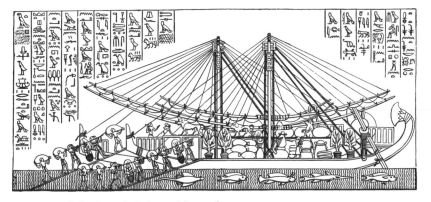

200 years. The first definite evidence for compass use in Western Europe is AD 1187.

Cordierite crystals Vikings around AD 1000 used 'sunstones' of cordierite crystals that occur naturally as pebbles on the coast of Norway; they refract light so that even in overcast weather it is possible to tell the position of the sun, and may well have been used by neolithic navigators.

Bird orientation The homing ability of birds (page 86) was widely used by early sailors (including Noah who released a raven and a dove) to tell them in which direction to sail; migratory patterns could have served the same purpose.

Mental orientation Keith Oatley, a psychologist at Sussex University, has observed how Pacific Islanders retain a mental map of 'the exact position of the canoe at all times in relation to the known islands in the archipelago' by observing such things as the wake of the boat, the strength of the wind, the position of the sun, the stars, and other natural phenomena. Beyond Oatley's suggestions, some people are able to harness an instinctive gift for direction-finding and for mentally viewing distant locations (page 82).

Although these are only partial answers, they are the jumping-off point for finding out just which ancient mariners are candidates as the extraordinary map-makers of far-distant coastlines, and this is where the mystery and the controversy begins. Once in the Atlantic and carried on the right current, no special skills or instruments were needed to cross the Ocean in the sort of boat available in prehistoric times. The question is: how many people *intended* to get there – and back?

Boats are frequently depicted on Egyptian reliefs; however Egyptians were not adventurous sailors, often employing others to trade abroad.

Early cartographers

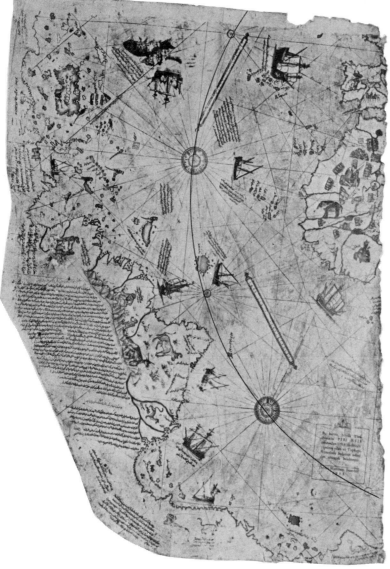

Map compiled by the Turkish admiral Piri Re'is in 1513; its detail is in striking contrast to typical maps of the period such as that by Robert Thorne below.

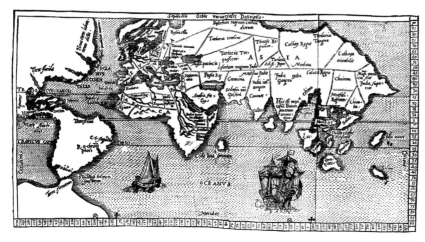

At first glance the coast-line map of the Atlantic, drawn on gazelle skin by the Turkish admiral Piri Re'is in 1513, is a whimsical and mystifying blend of artistry and imagination, overlaid with a series of incomprehensible grid-like lines that lend it a quaint authenticity. Piri Re'is himself thought it better than this, boasting in a footnote that 'in this century there is no map like this in anyone's possession.' In compiling it, he wrote, 'I made use of about twenty old charts and eight Mappa Mundis', i.e. of the charts called *Jaferiye* by the Arabs and prepared at the time of Alexander the Great and in which the whole inhabited world was shown.

The puzzle is this: if Piri Re'is was telling the truth (there is no reason at all to believe otherwise) the ancient maps he drew on show a detailed knowledge of the world's geography dating back to a time before civilization. According to Professor Charles Hapgood of Keene State College, New Hampshire, who spent seven years interpreting the Piri Re'is map and a handful of other near-contemporary ones that have survived, they constitute 'the first hard evidence that advanced peoples preceded all the peoples now known to history . . . The ancient voyagers travelled from pole to pole. Unbelievable as it may appear, the evidence nevertheless indicates that some ancient people explored the coasts of Antarctica when its coasts were free of ice. It is clear, too, that they had an instrument of navigation that was far superior to anything possessed by the peoples of ancient, mediaeval, or modern times until the second half of the 18th century.'

Enormous implications

These enormous claims were made by Hapgood in 1966 in his book *Maps of the Ancient Sea Kings*, and in spite of their profound, even revolutionary, implications for prehistory as it is taught, they have not been decisively refuted. The judgement of several senior geographical experts who are quoted in the book still stands. Lieut. Colonel Harold Z. Ohlmeyer, at that time serving with a Reconnaissance Technical Squadron of the United States Air Force, wrote of the Piri Re'is map: 'The geographical detail shown in the lower part of the map agrees very remarkably with the results of the seismic profile made across the top of the cap by the Swedish-British-Norwegian Antarctic Expedition of 1949. This indicates the coastline had been mapped before it was covered with the ice cap. The ice cap in this region is now about a mile thick. We have no idea how the data on this map can be reconciled with the supposed state of geographical knowledge in 1513.' Similarly Captain Lorenzo W. Burroughs, Chief of the cartographic section of the same squadron, wrote to Hapgood: 'It is our opinion that the accuracy of the cartographic features shown in the Oronteus Finnaeus Map (1531) suggests, beyond a doubt, that it also was compiled from accurate source maps of Antarctica, but in this case of the entire continent. Close examination has proved the original source maps must have been compiled at a time when the land mass and inland waterways of the continent were relatively free of ice.'

Professor Hapgood arrived at his conclusions after an exhaustive search through hundreds of other maps from the period, and then conducting a remarkable piece of detective work which enabled him to re-plot the important ones on a modern projection. He found only a few worth considering, for the state of the art of map-making in Piri Re'is's time was on the whole very primitive. The Age of Exploration, whose starting date is generally taken as the arrival of Columbus in the New World in 1492, was just getting under way, and although the general shape of the continental land-masses was known, the proportions were often wildly out of scale. Robert Thorne's map of 1527 (opposite below) is typical, as a later publisher apologized in a footnote: 'The imperfection of which mappe may be excused by that tyme; the knowledge of Cosmographie not then beyng entrd among our Marchauntes, as nowe it is.'

Longitude problem

The main problem was in finding longitude (the vertical lines on a map that let you know how far east or west you are). Latitude could be fixed fairly readily by reference to the stars, but longitude needed the invention of an accurate method of telling the time, and the first chronometer was not invented until more than two centuries later. The great majority of maps in the time of Piri Re'is make large errors in the east–west placing of land; Columbus himself, using a map of the Atlantic and West Indies which is now lost to us (but which Piri Re'is claimed to have incorporated), mistakenly believed he had reached Asia when he first sighted the Canary Islands, some 1000 miles short of his destination.

Ancient grids

However, a handful of maps were exceptions. For 200 years, mediaeval sailors in the Black Sea and Mediterranean had used reasonably accurate maps based on portolans, the grids that radiate like spokes on a wheel, sometimes 16 and sometimes 32, resembling the pattern of a mariner's compass. Their origin is a mystery. The great 19th-century Swedish scholar of ancient maps, A. E. Nordenskiöld, pointed out that the maps did not improve in accuracy during the two centuries, and surmised that they must all be various copies based on a single, much more ancient source. How the portolans were intended to be used was also unclear – were they an aid to navigation for sailors, or an aid to mapping for cartographers?

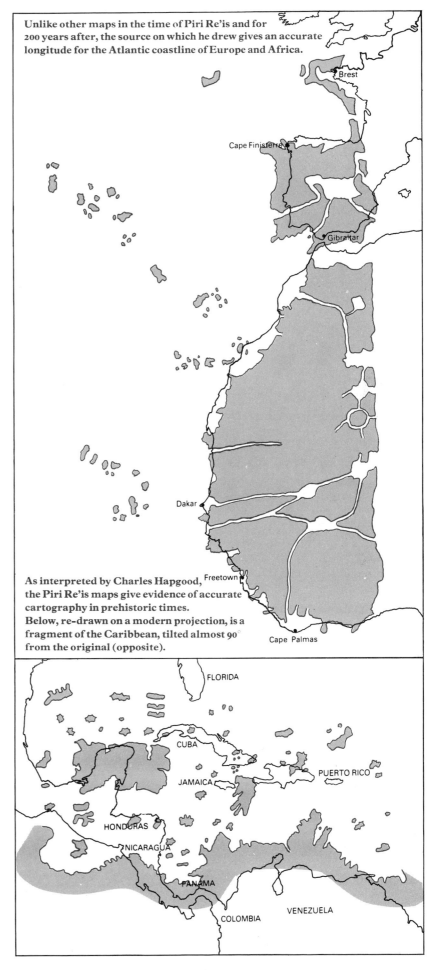

Unlike other maps in the time of Piri Re'is and for 200 years after, the source on which he drew gives an accurate longitude for the Atlantic coastline of Europe and Africa.

As interpreted by Charles Hapgood, the Piri Re'is maps give evidence of accurate cartography in prehistoric times.
Below, re-drawn on a modern projection, is a fragment of the Caribbean, tilted almost 90 from the original (opposite).

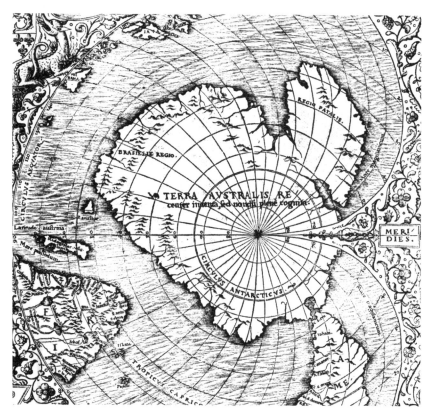

establish that the centre of this circle was the intersection of what we now know to be two major co-ordinates: longitude 30°E, which passes through Alexandria, the ancient centre of knowledge from which Piri Re'is said he had derived some of his original maps; and latitude $23\frac{1}{2}$°N, the Tropic of Cancer. With this information, Richard W. Strachan of the Massachusetts Institute of Technology was able to use trigonometrical methods to find precisely whereabouts in the Atlantic the five portolan centres lay, and this in turn allowed the Piri Re'is map to be re-drawn using modern grids on which its accuracy could be checked.

Startling results

What emerged was startling. Piri Re'is, as he said, had indeed drawn on a number of ancient sources, and some of these were of a precision far beyond the map-making ability of his time. The western coasts of Africa and Europe, and the north Atlantic islands (with the exception of Madeira) were all in their correct longitude; even more remarkably, they stood in their proper longitudinal relationship with the coasts of South America and Antarctica.

The Caribbean, too, fell into place once Hapgood had realized that by a peculiarity arising from the use of portolans, it was tilted at the wrong angle. This part of the Piri Re'is map was drawn, it seems, from an original that had Egypt at the centre of a spherical projection. Of the Amazon and the island of Marajo, Hapgood concluded that 'the excellent representation of the Island of Marajo is quite unique. Nothing like it can be found on any map of the 16th Century until after the official discovery of the island in 1543.' The southern part of South America was drawn accurately to an average error of less than one degree, but left blank of explorers' names for the simple reason, Hapgood wrote, that 'There were no explorers' accounts.' The Falkland Islands

Mystifying though the map first appears (above) Charles Hapgood was able to re-draw the Oronteus Finnaeus Antarctic map to show a surprising match with the sub-ice coastline (below). The Piri Re'is map of the Brazilian coastline also seems accurate over a smaller area.

The great contribution of Professor Hapgood and his team of students was to interpret the way that Piri Re'is seems to have used them to draw up his map. The key lay in the fact that the centres of the five portolans lie on the circumference of a circle. After three years painstaking trial and error Hapgood was able to

appear on this section of the map at the correct latitude relative to this lower east coast, but there is an error of about 5° in longitude. The Falklands are supposed to have been discovered by John Davis in 1592, nearly eighty years after Piri Re'is made his map.

Antarctic maps

So far, the criticism of Hapgood might be that he was making a fanciful and over-blown interpretation of a single enigmatic map. He himself wrote: 'If the Piri Re'is map stood alone, it would perhaps be insufficient to carry conviction. But it does not stand alone.'

Moreover, the part of it which is independently confirmed is the most remarkable of all – the outline of Antarctica. It was a radio discussion of this possibility that first led Hapgood to his long research project, for if it could be proved it would be 'no slight matter. Important questions, for geology as well as for history, depend on it.' Antarctica was officially 'discovered' in 1818; although a huge land-mass in the approximate area is often shown on ancient maps, this had long been thought imaginary, particularly after Cook's 18th-century voyages failed to find it.

The Piri Re'is map shows only a small portion of the northern coastline known as Queen Maud Land, but is nevertheless of the same order of accuracy as other portions of the map drawn from ancient sources. A slightly later map drawn in 1531 by Oronteus Finnaeus is even more spectacular evidence. The coast-line of Antarctica, covered with ice since at least 4000 BC, is shown in detail, with rivers pouring out to sea from mountain ranges, and a blank interior suggesting that when the original source maps were made, there was already a central ice cap. Again, Hapgood had to make certain assumptions and adjustments before arriving at his definitive re-projection on a modern scale, but these are carefully argued in his book and have not been subsequently disproved.

So Hapgood's case seems conclusive. The art of map-making reached an ancient pinnacle, and then steadily declined through classical and mediaeval times. These maps were lodged as part of the vast body of ancient knowledge contained among the million books in the Alexandrian library before its final destruction by fire in the seventh century AD, and Piri Re'is drew on fragments of them to compile his own world map (of which we ourselves now only have a fragment). But who could these mathematicians

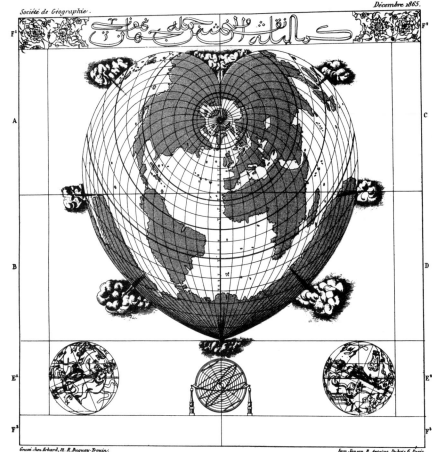

and navigators have been, and when did they sail and map the globe?

Apart from Hapgood's own solution of a lost people dating from the Ice Age (i.e. pre–10,000 BC), for which there is not a shred of archaeological evidence, there seem to be only three possible solutions, all difficult, with the third perhaps the least unlikely. (1) the geologists' date for the Antarctic ice cap is wrong by some 3000 years, which would allow Minoan or Phoenician sailors to have observed the outline of the continent. (2) The megalith builders (or their possible Atlantean predecessors, page 140) sailed in their skin boats more widely than has been thought, and with their superb knowledge of astronomy were able to draw accurate maps; but not a single written document has been found to support this theory. (3) The arcane body of wisdom built up in Classical and Alexandrian times from many sources, certainly including accounts from early voyagers, and perhaps even embodying knowledge from an extra-terrestrial source (pages 144–152), included a form of divination that allowed cartographer-priests to draw up, as map-dowsers do today, a portrait of the world's geography beyond the range of normal sight.

A Turkish map of 1559, drawn by Hadji Ahmed, shows incredible accuracy for America's west coast, at that time scarcely visited, let let alone surveyed.

Who discovered America?

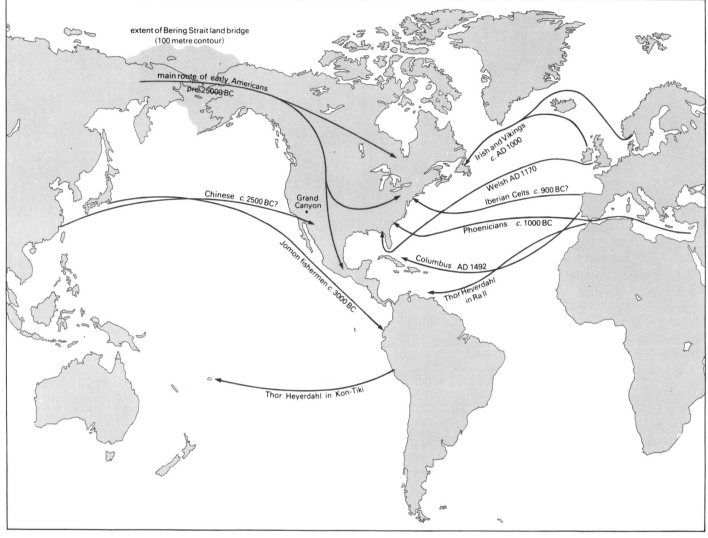

extent of Bering Strait land bridge
(100 metre contour)

main route of early Americans
pre 25000 BC

Irish and Vikings *c.* AD 1000

Welsh AD 1170

Iberian Celts *c.* 900 BC?

Chinese *c.* 2500 BC?

Grand
Canyon

Phoenicians *c.* 1000 BC

Jomon fishermen *c.* 3000 BC

Columbus AD 1492

Thor Heyerdahl
in Ra II

Thor Heyerdahl in Kon-Tiki

Some of the many routes now thought to have been made to America by early navigators. Megalithic sites in New England like this 'chambered tomb' (below) are hotly debated.

Reading standard text-book accounts of how man arrived in the New World, you might imagine that his only mode of transport was by foot. We are asked to believe that a trickle of migrants, 30,000 years ago or more, made their way across a green and fertile Bering Strait land bridge, and steadily moved southwards. These mongoloid people formed a nucleus that split up into many different sorts of societies under the influence of local conditions; the vast range of physical types of native Americans is explained by the working of natural selection and genetic drift. With the exception of the Vikings, no pre-Columbian outsiders arrived to disturb this isolated evolution. Gordon R. Willey and Jeremy A. Sabloff of Harvard University, in their definitive *History of American Archaeology*, say that the thinking of most of today's archaeologists is dominated by 'the tradition of American culture history as an essentially self-controlled one, without important contacts or relationships to the Old World.'

They themselves subscribe to this. Their book makes no mention of the possibility of early trans-Atlantic voyages, nor even of the experimental crossing by Thor Heyerdahl and Santiago Genoves in *Ra* that proved such voyages feasible; they limit the early trans-Pacific possibilities to an insignificant two.

Doctrinal basis

This view of man becoming civilized independently, not just in America but in several different parts of the world, represents a violent swing of the pendulum away from archaeological

theory in the 1920s and 1930s, when it was widely held that 'civilization' was an event which had only happened once, somewhere in the Near East, and had diffused outwards from there to the rest of the world. 'Hyper-diffusionists' of those times are now scornfully attacked. 'Why does the world tolerate this academic rubbish?' Britain's most influential archaeologist, Professor Glyn Daniel of Cambridge University, once asked, giving his own answer that it was because most people sought an over-simple answer to problems of prehistory. He himself has developed the theory of 'multilinear evolution' in which a favoured few societies encountered conditions that enabled them to make the jump from village to city life: notably those in Mesopotamia, Egypt, India, China, and three separate areas of America. He does not deny the possibility of a few minor shipwrecks, but 'any contacts trans-Atlantic or trans-Pacific that may have occurred were slight and very infrequent and had little effect on the native development of pre-Columbian American culture.'

Challenge to theory

However, this isolationist view is now increasingly under attack for being too limited in its approach. As Glyn Daniel himself predicted in quoting a friend's warning ('Mark my words, there will be a swing of the pendulum. The Egypt theory will be back in favour again, no matter what you may say'), all manner of early sea-borne influences on the evolution of American people have now been suggested; according to Professor Roger Wescott of Drew University, no fewer than 25 Old World peoples have made their mark on the New.

A number of these were put forward at an important 1970 symposium, *Man Across the Sea*. The American archaeologist Robert A. Kennedy suggested why they were not so far incorporated in the text books: 'Diffusion by land is still easier to accept than that by sea. The reason is, quite simply and bluntly, that precious few prehistorians are small-boat sailors, let alone experienced in the navigational conditions and seas familiar to men during that truly great period of voyaging four to five thousand years ago.' The American archaeologist Alice B. Kehoe told the same gathering: 'That the Atlantic could have been traversed before the development of the 15th-century caravels is amply proven by hundreds of authenticated crossings in small boats of every description. At least two rafts, two dug-out canoes, two dories propelled only by oars, several dories fitted with sails, conventional sailboats as small as five feet eleven inches in length, and unconventional boats including kayaks, folding boats, and an

'dog bone' motif

parallel lines and zig-zag incising

clay dragged and jabbed alternately by multiple-edged tool

grooves formed by potter's fingers

amphibian jeep have successfully floated across the ocean.'

Japanese pottery

So the questions nowadays tend to be not whether trans-oceanic contacts took place, but how early, how often, and how important their effect. For instance most people agree that the case of pottery which suddenly arrived around 3000 BC on the Valdivian coast of Ecuador is almost certainly Japanese in origin. It is decorated and incised in exactly the same way as pottery from the Jomon area of Japan, and is not preceded in Ecuador by plainer and simpler bowls and urns. The only likely explanation is that a Japanese fishing boat was caught in a storm, and subsequently drifted the 8,000 miles to Ecuador, a journey that lasted several months, during which the crew collected rainwater to drink and caught fish to eat, carrying on board by chance someone who had learned the art of pottery.

Several other intriguing Pacific voyages have been suggested. The Austrian ethnologist Robert von Heine-Geldern is convinced that the Chinese, around 2000 BC, had a profound effect

Similarity of pottery fragments from Japan (left) and Ecuador leave little doubt that there must have been contact between the two countries around 3000 BC.

Pottery figurines from western Mexico showing indisputably Semitic faces, all dating from before 300 BC.

on the development of civilization in middle America and Peru. The Hopi Indians in Arizona have a seminal legend about being the first inhabitants of America, arriving there by means of 'stepping-stones' (islands) on the way. The oldest Chinese classic, the *Shan Hai King* of *c.* 2250 BC, contains what seems to be an accurate description of the Grand Canyon.

Atlantic crossings

In the Atlantic, too, there seems no good sea-faring reason to go on believing that America remained isolated. In the north, there is the Irminger Current that flows from Scandinavia via the Faroe Islands, Iceland, and Greenland, where early sailors may have stopped off for provisions. In the other direction, the Gulf Stream could have carried boats back to Britain via Nova Scotia, or more directly to Iberia. Alice Kehoe has suggested two archaeological oddities in north-east America that can perhaps be best explained by the idea of very early two-way trans-Atlantic trade. The first is the appearance, around 2500 BC, of wood-working tools and fishing gear in the Great Lakes area, and shortly afterwards, ground slate knives in Scandinavia and the Baltic countries; she thinks that cod fishermen may have strayed across the Atlantic, and brought back the new, more efficient slate for gutting their catch. Her other example is some distinctive pottery of the Early Woodland period in America around 1000 BC that closely matches Baltic pottery of the same age. Although most archaeologists suppose it to have been brought in orthodox fashion by land from Asia, she says that if so, it 'hid all traces of its passing'. In spite of this, 'archaeologists still envision hunters trudging with unbroken pots across the Straits and 2000 miles of Arctic coast or boreal muskeg. A far more comfortable hypothesis is that the pots skimmed over the Atlantic in fishermen's curraghs.' Another archaeological dispute in north-east America

centres on the enigmatic standing stones and 'burial mounds' of New England; some hundreds of these have been discovered, in shape and appearance similar but not identical to European megaliths. Local official guides describe them, improbably, as colonial bee-hives or pig-pens. Local antiquarians are convinced that they are far more ancient, and evidence of trans-Atlantic colonization.

Middle Atlantic

As for more southerly crossings over the Atlantic, between the Mediterranean and north Africa on one side and central America on the other, so many have now been suggested that their importance can no longer be denied. Again, in sea-faring terms, there is nothing inherently unlikely. As the builders of *Ra* pointed out, a combination of wind and current meant that 'the raft went to America whether the crew wanted it or not.' Historians such as R. A. Jairazbhoy are convinced that an influx of Egyptian, Negro, Jewish and Chinese immigrants were together responsible for the sudden rise of the Olmec civilization in Mexico in 1200 BC. Phoenicians, according to interpretations of texts by Plato and Diodorus, traded with America around 1000 BC. Professor Alexander von Wuthenau, of the University of the Americas in Mexico, has spent 50 years collecting evidence of sculpted heads dated from 1500 BC–1500 AD that show unequivocally bearded Jews (American Indians are beardless), African negroes, and other distinctive racial types. Thor Heyerdahl believes that the pyramid cult of various American civilizations, though different in detail from Egypt, has too many basic similarities to be explained except by the influence of Mediterranean voyagers.

It is not over-simplistic, as Glyn Daniel suggests, for all these scholars to be searching for evidence of trans-oceanic diffusion that once nudged the development of civilization in America. Rather the reverse, for it is even more complicated to penetrate the obscurity of the past when ancient sea adventurers are brought into the picture than when they are ignored. Certainly Hernando Cortes, when he landed in Mexico in 1519, was in no doubt that someone had preceded him long ago. He was welcomed to the court of the Aztec Emperor Montezuma, and there told by priests that he was the reincarnation of their fair, bearded god Quetzalcoatl, who had long ago brought civilization 'from the sunrise' and then departed, promising to return. Why should a dark-skinned, beardless people worship a fair, bearded deity unless something of this sort had once been the living focus of their religious life?

Ancient anomalies

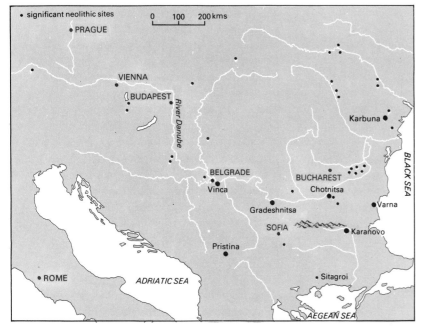

significant neolithic sites

PRAGUE

VIENNA

BUDAPEST

River Danube

BELGRADE
Vinca

BUCHAREST
Chotnitsa

Gradeshnitsa

Varna

Karbuna

SOFIA

Karanovo

Pristina

ROME

ADRIATIC SEA

Sitagroi

AEGEAN SEA

BLACK SEA

0 100 200 kms

Around 4500 BC, the Karanovo people of the Balkans reached a level of wealth unmatched anywhere in the world, pre-dating Near Eastern civilization by more than a millenium.

In the summer of 1977 a progress report was released concerning the contents of 81 graves on the Black Sea Coast in Bulgaria, all of them dating back to around 4500 BC, a time when the technological achievements of man are generally characterized by a variety of stone tools, mud or wooden huts, and simple earthenware pots. The archaeologist describing the cemetery, the Lithuanian-born Professor Maria Gimbutas of the University of California in Los Angeles, was so impressed that she was moved to use a rare academic term: the graves, she wrote, 'are *sensational* for the extraordinary richness in gold, copper, marble, obsidian, flint, various semi-precious stones and Aegean shells, as well as in their technological achievements – including graphite and gold-painted ceramics.'

Once again, archaeological discovery was catching up with antiquarian romance; a lost civilization far in advance of its times flourished long ago in the heart of Europe. Independent and different from the megalith builders on one side, and the new agriculturalists and city-builders of the Near East on the other, the Karanovo people seem to have lived an idyllic life, prosperous but at the same time egalitarian (only five of the graves were without rich belongings). The most spectacular was that of a rich man buried with a profusion of gold jewellery – three golden necklaces, three massive gold arm-rings on each arm, two golden ear-rings, delicately made of wire with a rectangular cross-section, six small gold hair-rings, and various golden discs that had once been sewn to his clothes. By his shoulder lay what Maria Gimbutas described as 'a stone axe of superb workmanship with a shaft in a golden tube', and along the other side of his body was a copper spear, the shaft of which was also wrapped in gold.

Technological achievements

Dazzling as this discovery is, it can been seen as part of an awakening recognition by prehistorians that the capabilities of early people, both intellectually and technologically, have been much under-estimated. A capacity for abstract thought of a high degree is shown by stone-age astronomy, mathematics, and cartography (pages 108 and 116); considerable technical skills are involved in flint tool-making, in massive stonemasonry and architecture (page 58), in seamanship (page 113) and in metallurgy, of which the buried treasure of Karanovo is just one recent example. Early in 1977 Professor Beno Rothenberg, director of the London-based Institute for Archaeo-metallurgical Studies, announced discoveries of copper mines and copper smelters in Israel and Spain dated at 4000 BC. In pushing back the date of the first known copper mining by a full 2000 years, he said it meant 'a complete revolution in our ideas about early mining technology'.

In southern Africa, the archaeologists Adrian Boshier and Peter Beaumont meanwhile found evidence of ochre mining that dwarfs these near-Eastern and European dates. Carbon tests at Gröningen University in Holland showed one mining complex to have been in active use 26–20,000 BC, with a possible pre-40,000 BC start; another mine disclosed notched bones 50–35,000 years old which 'indicate man's ability to count at that remote period'. Scarcely able to believe their own findings, the two scientists reported they were forced to the conclusion that the 'true age of the onset of mining in Swaziland is more likely to be in the order of 70,000–80,000 BC.'

Marvels of man

Discoveries such as these are bound to have a profound effect on two separately entrenched groups of prehistorians. On the one hand there are the orthodox archaeologists, disciplined in a time when it was heretical to believe in anything except the gradual diffusion of civilization from the near East during the years following the invention of writing around 3000 BC; to this dwindling band, and even to those who have modified their views and agree that the process of civilization must have happened independently at several different centres, any very early oddities such as writing tablets or lightning rods are *prima facie* a fraud, or a misinterpretation, or an anomaly due to faulty dating. On the other hand are the fringe writers who tend to believe that any marvellous-looking antiquity, be it a giant sculptured head,

a pyramid, or even a wheel, is an example of extra-terrestrial intervention and/or a sophisticated lost technology that existed in some unspecified former time. For both groups, the new discoveries are a chastening reminder of what marvels man can achieve on his own, without invoking help from either voyaging Egyptian priests or creatures from outer space.

Ancient electricity

The early use of electricity is an example. While earth-moving operations were being carried out near Baghdad in June 1936, railway construction workers came across an ancient grave covered with a stone slab. During the next two months the Iraq Antiquities Department extracted a wealth of artifacts from it dating to the Parthian period (248 BC–226 AD) – in all, some 613 beads, clay figurines, engraved bricks, and so on. But among them was an object of unique interest: a copper cylinder and an iron rod which the German archaeologist Wilhelm König, then in charge of the Iraq Museum Laboratory, soon identified as probably being a primitive electric cell. Back in Germany at the Berlin Museum, he related the discovery to similar Iraqi cylinders, rods and asphalt stoppers, all corroded as if by some acid, and to a few slender iron and bronze rods found with them. As many as ten batteries, he concluded, had been joined up in a series in order to increase the voltage output, and the immediate purpose was to provide current for electroplating the excellent local gold and silver jewellery.

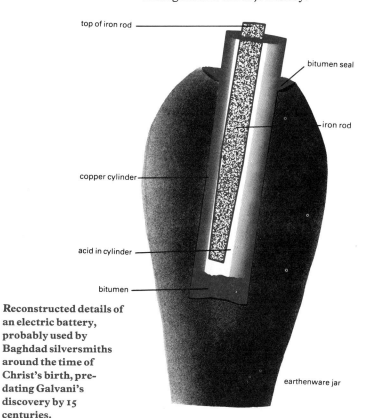

top of iron rod

bitumen seal

iron rod

copper cylinder

acid in cylinder

bitumen

earthenware jar

Reconstructed details of an electric battery, probably used by Baghdad silversmiths around the time of Christ's birth, pre-dating Galvani's discovery by 15 centuries.

This remarkable conclusion received very little attention, for reasons which the chemist and physicist Walter Winton, a keeper at the Science Museum in London, explained when he went to Baghdad in 1962 to re-organize the Iraq Museum in new buildings. 'Tell any physicist,' he said, 'that electrical current was being used 15 centuries before Galvani and his frogs' legs, and "Fiddlesticks! Ridiculous notion! Impossible!" he will declare. This was my own reaction too when I first heard of it. I was extremely suspicious. A misinterpretation of facts, a hoax, a forgery, another grinning Piltdown skull. Why, if this were true it would be the biggest news ever in the history of science.'

Primitive battery

However, on seeing the battery he immediately recognized it as being a primitive cell. He says today that 'not being an archaeologist, I jumped straight to the easiest scientific solution. I still can't see what else it could have been used for, and if there has been a better suggestion, I haven't been told it. For absolute proof you would need some accessory like connecting wires, and I thought it important to make my interpretation public so that archaeologists would start looking for this in addition to the usual buried material with which they are familiar. Is a practical knowledge of current electricity at this period so unthinkable? I am sure the ability of early people is much under-rated. Perhaps the incredibility is in the mind of the unbelievers, and arrogant pride in our modern scientific achievements makes us unwilling to believe that the effects of current electricity could be known to our Mesopotamian ancestors 2000 years ago.'

Voltage experiment

Two separate experiments in the United States with replicas of the cells have produced a $\frac{1}{2}$-volt current for as long as 18 days from each battery, using as an electrolyte 5 per cent solutions of vinegar, wine, or copper sulphate; sulphuric and citric acid, available at the time, would have worked equally well to operate the cells. Beyond reasonable doubt, then, this is their purpose; and once you accept the use of electricity in those times, a new area of possibilities is opened up. Plating of gold and silver in Mesopotamia goes back 2000 years before then, and in the new Bulgarian find more than 4000 years. How early was the technique used? Is it the original basis for the ancient art of alchemy, the practice of turning base metal into gold? The probable answer is yes.

Nor does the apparently zany suggestion that the Egyptian pyramid builders used electric light now seem quite so speculative. There is a genuine

puzzle here, noted in the 19th Century by Sir Norman Lockyer. Deep within the pyramids, in pitch blackness, intricate and detailed paintings are etched into solid stone. Obviously the artists needed illumination of some sort, yet there is no sign of the blackened carbon on the walls that would have been left there by even well-trimmed torches and oil lamps of the kind normally used. Could they have used battery-powered lights? Engravings on the tomb walls of Dendera show devices that look curiously like electrical insulators and electric lights, and although the physical remains of these have not yet been found, it could be that as with the Baghdad batteries, it is a rare archaeologist who would recognize them.

Other anomalies from recent prehistory frequently quoted in fringe literature, also offer evidence of practical experiment in the mechanical application of science. Wooden flagstaffs about 30 metres tall, placed in front of Egyptian temples and capped with a sheath of copper were described in a Ptolemaic inscription of about 320 BC as intended to 'cut the lightning out of the sky'. A model glider from Saqqara, site of the first step pyramid, and probably about the same date as the lightning conductors, has a wing span of 18 centimetres and shows a degree of aerodynamic sophistication. Whether it is a scale model of a larger aircraft is much more doubtful; most commentators compare it to Leonardo da Vinci's designs for winged flight – theoretically just possible but never practically achieved. A corroded fragment of a metallic device found by sponge-divers near the island of Antikythera turned out after cleaning to date from around 65 BC, and to be a complicated construction of dials and gears. In 1959 its purpose was decoded when Derek J. de Solla Price, of the Institute for Advanced Study at Princeton, New Jersey, proved it to be a basic form of analogue computer that was used to short-cut astronomical calculations. He commented in *Scientific American* that he found it 'a bit frightening to know that just before the fall of their great civilization the ancient Greeks had come so close to our age, not only in their thought but also in their scientific technology'.

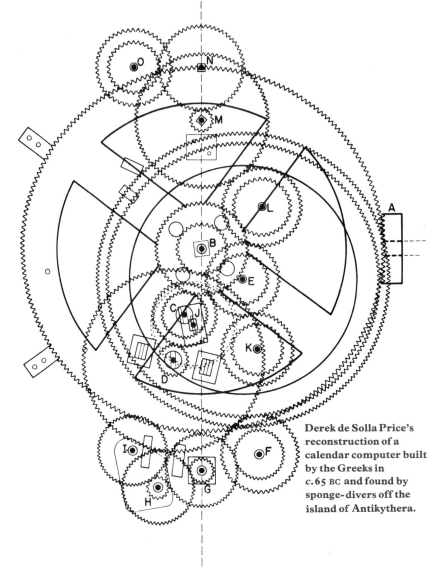

Derek de Solla Price's reconstruction of a calendar computer built by the Greeks in *c.*65 BC and found by sponge-divers off the island of Antikythera.

Inventive skills

Such finds (and doubtless there would be more if they were actively sought) do not add up to a wholesale re-writing of the history of science; more to a re-evaluation of man's inherent genius. However, as genuine inventive anomalies, they are of great significance as background to the next subject: the disputed finds of early writing. If early people, by trial and error, could discover how to use electricity and guess at the nature of heavier-than-air flight, who are we to put a limit on their other attainments, however unlikely they may at first seem?

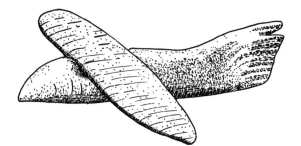

Artist's drawing of a glider found near the step-pyramid of Saqqara, approximately one-third real size.

Undeciphered writing

Emile Fradin, the farm labourer who started half a century of archaeological controversy with his 1924 discoveries. (right) With his friend and mentor Dr A. Morlet examining the excavated site.

Who discovered writing, and when? The text-book answer can readily be found: the bureaucrats of ancient Sumer, around 3500 BC, who developed it in response to the needs of an organized urban society. With writing, they were able to record ownership of property, distribute goods and rations to workers in an economical way, and perform similar time-consuming and presumably essential functions much in the manner of state employees today. Egyptian priests then borrowed the idea from Sumer (although their hieroglyphs bear no resemblance). Later the Hebrews and Phoenicians developed their alphabets (essentially identical); and the lettering on this page, the Latin alphabet, is derived from the Phoenicians through the Greeks. The Chinese are also thought to have developed their script under the influence of the Near East.

However, the origin of writing now looks a good deal more complicated than that. New World civilizations show a different form of literacy. The Incas had no writing, in our sense of the word, but effectively used *quipus* of knotted string to record information (although the way they did so has still not been deciphered). Nor is writing invariably an automatic response to certain mundane requirements of urban societies, as it was in Sumer. The Mayans and Aztecs used their pictographic writings for religious, calendrical and ritual purposes, not for accounting. Egyptians, too, used their earliest hieroglyphic script for inscriptions of state and religious importance, not for day-to-day business records.

Doubts on Sumer

Added to these complications is a doubt – or rather, several doubts – about Sumer's claim to be the origin of writing. To an outsider, this might seem obvious, reading what has lately become known about the achievements of early man; it is certain that the intellectual capacity for abstract thought has made writing a possibility for at least the last 40,000 years or so, the only question being whether circumstances in a particular region sparked it off.

Calendrical markings on early stone-age bones

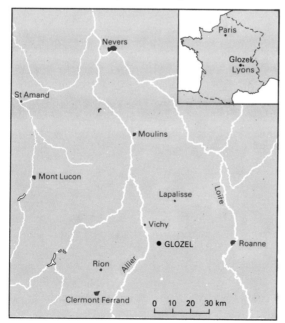

Location of Glozel. No site like it has been found elsewhere.

have led the writer Alexander Marshack to conclude that they stem from 'an earlier symbolizing tradition, one that was at least 25,000 years old'. Enigmatic markings can be found on pebbles from Mas d'Azil in France of around 10,000 BC. The astronomical observations of megalithic times, and the map-making of early navigators, are difficult to believe unless some form of written recording also took place. All in all, it seems unlikely that the idea of writing did not occur to anybody between, say, 35,000 BC and 3500 BC; rather, that we have not yet identified it.

Our failure to do so may be partly to do with the furore created by the most bizarre archaeological mystery of this century: the extraordinary hoard of artifacts, including tablets of undeciphered writing, that emerged from a field at Glozel, near Vichy in southern France, during the 1920s. It became an affair of high archaeological scandal, with experts on either side of the English Channel either proclaiming that the objects were of revolutionary significance to the study of prehistory, or on the other hand complete fakes. In the debate that followed, closely reported by the media, those who believed in fraud seemed total victors; yet in the 1970s, advances in scientific dating of early pottery re-opened wounds that had never properly healed, since when there has been an obstinate refusal to admit what now looks like a grave academic mistake.

'Not quite right'

The way this judgment came about and has since been perpetuated is a salutary example of how a wrong assumption can get into archaeological text-books and be vehemently defended against later evidence to the contrary (a similar story surrounds the dating of Egyptian and Greek history, described on page 168). At Glozel, the main archaeological problem is that nothing like it exists anywhere else. A host of strange objects, including more than 300 ceramics, were found in a single field, the *Champs des Morts*, and are now preserved in the local museum. They are an amazing mixture: crudely fired pottery (face urns, lamps, phallic symbols and clay tablets), carved bones, engraved pebbles and various tools of stone and bone. Some of them are indisputably ancient, such as a polished stone axe, and some only a few hundred years old, such as pieces of glass probably fired in a mediaeval kiln. But the bulk of the objects are of completely unknown origin and, although recent scientific dating tests have shown them to be around 2000 years old, why were they found buried in the ground in isolation? None of the everyday things of the period that excavations usually bring to the surface – for example broken

pottery and coins – have ever been found. To an archaeologist, this is highly suspicious. As Professor Colin Renfrew of Southampton University wrote after a conference on the matter in 1975, 'to use the jargon of the dealer, there is something about Glozel which is "not quite right".'

Unique features on a sculpted face. The symbols on the lower ceramic have proved impossible to interpret.

First finds

The fact that Glozel was never competently excavated adds to the archaeological problem. The original discovery of the site was made by a young farm boy called Emile Fradin, who was ploughing the field with some oxen when one of them stepped into a shallow pit, nearly three metres in length and 50 centimetres deep, lined with glass-covered stones and tiles, and later identified as a glass kiln or factory. On the tiled floor were pieces of ceramics and a polished stone axe-head. Encouraged by his schoolmistress, the youth dug in the surrounding field during the next few weeks, uncovering the rich beginnings of his treasure trove.

The nature of these early finds is highly relevant to the story, for it has become an article of faith among anti-Glozelians that nothing of importance was discovered to begin with and that only after Fradin came under the Svengali-like influence of a local schoolteacher, M. Clément, did anything unusual, particularly the unknown writing, appear. M. Clément himself claimed that he had shown Emile Fradin

Examples of undeciphered text found at Glozel. One suggestion is that they are occult symbols used in pagan ceremonies.

A committee of investigation consisting of French archaeologists found Glozel authentic. A British investigation disagreed.

LES DISPUTES DES VIVANTS AUTOUR DU CHAMP DES MORTS

GLOZEL EST AUTHENTIQUE

Telle est la conclusion des savants qui viennent d'y pratiquer des fouilles

[DE NOTRE ENVOYÉ SPÉCIAL]

VICHY, 15 avril. — Par téléphone. — Le comité d'études glozélien a terminé vendredi ses fouilles dans le champ les morts.

Cette dernière journée, qui a amené d'intéressantes découvertes, fut marquée par un curieux incident. Devançant leurs collègues, quatre membres du comité s'étaient, dès sept heures du matin, acheminés vers le champ des morts et s'étaient mis au travail avec la collaboration des deux terras-

LES FOUILLES DU COMITÉ DANS LE CHAMP DES MORTS
Au bord de la tranchée, on reconnaît : MM. FOAT (1) et SODERMAN (2), le docteur ARCELIN (3), MM. LOTH fils (4) et LOTH père (5).

illustrated archaeological books before any inscribed tablets were found and most investigators seem to have taken him at his word. For instance Professor Dorothy Garrod, the English member of the Glozel Commission of 1927, wrote in a memoir in 1968 that after Clément's arrival Fradin 'began to produce strange things which didn't fit in at all with what had been found before'.

Clément's statement conflicts with contemporary evidence. Emile Fradin made his original discovery on 1 March 1924 and Clément did not appear on the scene until four months later, on 9 July. In the meantime, many local people visited the site and no less than 43 of them later went on record in journals and court depositions as saying that at least one inscribed tablet had been amongst the first discoveries. This must, therefore, have been genuine, or at worst forged by Fradin working on his own. The pieces of glass-covered ceramics which he found at the bottom of the glass kiln on the very first day are also significant, because they are similar to some of the later finds which he was supposed to have forged under tuition.

After M. Clément, two new figures appeared on the scene, each of them according to anti-Glozelians deluded or fraudulent. The first was the distinguished director of the French Museum of National Antiquities, M. Salomon Reinach, who heard of Fradin's discoveries and thought them potentially significant. To encourage Fradin's interest, he sent him various books and documents which, wrote Dorothy Garrod, 'had the effect of launching him on a career of organized forgery'. The second was a schoolteacher from Vichy, Dr A. Morlet, who in the English writing on the subject has now become cast as the main villain of the piece; according to Glyn Daniel, who succeeded Dorothy Garrod as Professor of Archaeology at Cambridge, he was the '*cerveau de l'enterprise*' who now, having died in 1965, 'lies with his evil secrets in a cemetery in Vichy'.

This was the opinion of the 1927 Glozel Commission, which consisted of eight archaeologists chosen by the Bureau of the International Institute of Anthropology who, after a somewhat cursory four-day visit to the site in November of that year, came unanimously to the conclusion that all of the objects which they examined were forgeries, with the exception of some polished stone axes and some fairly recent pottery and glass associated with the kiln.

Silent inquiry

Dorothy Garrod's account of the investigation tells of going straight from Vichy to the site, where they found many trenches already dug by

various important personages, including the King of Rumania. Having chosen a spot at which to dig, they worked for three days in total silence to the annoyance of dozens of newspapermen and photographers who crowded around them. In the evenings they locked themselves in the hotel sitting room to discuss what had happened, periodically interrupted by one of the three French archaeologists, M. Peyrony, springing to his feet to fling open the door and try to catch unawares anybody trying to eavesdrop on the conversation.

He never discovered anybody nor, on the first day of the dig, did they uncover any Glozeliana – because, wrote Dorothy Garrod, 'the hoaxers had not yet had time to furnish our hole with the necessary finds: indeed they did not know that first day where we were going to dig. But on the second day finds began to appear, typical Glozelian objects. We found a little round piece of bone with scratches of Glozelian characters on it, and then we found one of the famous tablets. These tablets of clay were not big, they were quite soft, and had on them extraordinary scratches in which Phoenician letters alternated with various meaningless signs – the whole making up what were referred to as "inscriptions".'

Tablet uncovered
Quite apart from its unique characteristics, the tablet seemed to the Commission suspicious because the ground around it had apparently been disturbed. Emile Fradin himself was allowed to make the final thrust of the spade that dug it out and as he carried it through the crowd with cries of 'Make way! Make way!' most onlookers were sure Glozel's authenticity had at last been settled. However, the Commission remained silent and in the evening, unknown to Morlet or Fradin, they powdered the site with plaster so that they could tell if it had been interfered with overnight.

When Morlet saw this the next morning, Dorothy Garrod was already checking the coded pattern made in the plaster. He shouted furiously at her that she was trying to 'salt' the site in order to discredit him. Although there was a reluctant reconciliation between the two that allowed digging to continue, no more finds were made. In the New Year, the Commission announced its verdict: the objects, including the tablets, were forged.

In Cambridge, O. G. S. Crawford, the editor of *Antiquity*, was delighted. Always an opponent of Glozel's authenticity, he wrote that 'after a short but gay life it is dead. On the field of battle lie the corpses of several learned reputations . . . We shall not refer again to Glozel – unless greatly provoked.'

Dr Salomon Reinach, a distinguished French museum director, on his way to the site. He thought the finds dated to *c.* 4000 BC.

However his was not the last word. In 1928 a French Commission, headed by Salomon Reinach, re-investigated the site and came to the opposite conclusion. Several objects were discovered in undisturbed soil, including a clay tablet that had a fingerprint on it; the fingerprint failed to match any of Fradin, his family or associates. In the years that followed, Fradin and Morlet were also conclusively cleared of fraud in three protracted court proceedings, two of which went to appeal. But Anglo-Saxon opinion remained largely unchanged and in 1974 Glyn Daniel, who had succeeded Crawford on *Antiquity*, wrote that 'hardly anyone has any doubt that most of the Glozel material was fabricated 1924–1927'.

His provocation for re-opening the debate into 'this fascinating problem' in 1974 was the finding by four physicists that thermoluminescence dating of a number of objects found at Glozel by Fradin and Morlet showed them to have been manufactured in the period 700 BC to AD 100. Like all scientific dating techniques, TL dating is a recent development and difficult for non-scientists to understand, but at the same time has become widely accepted as an accurate way of discovering when ceramic objects were fired. Glyn Daniel immediately perceived the challenge that the new findings made: 'One thing is certain: somebody is wrong. Either there is something unexplained about these TL dates, and all our scientific colleagues assure us that there cannot be anything wrong with the TL technique, or the many distinguished archaeologists from 1925 onwards who have pronounced the Glozel finds as palpable forgeries are wrong . . . This paper is a major document in the resolution of L'Affaire Glozel and as we publish it we wonder if Crawford is turning restlessly in his grave. Was the 1927 anti-Glozelian Commission which said everything was a forgery mistaken?'

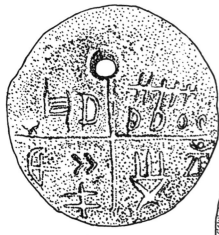

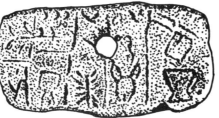

Writing on the Tartaria tablets (above) seems to pre-date the first known writing in the world, from Jemdet Nasr in Sumer (beneath). There are obvious similarities in the characters.

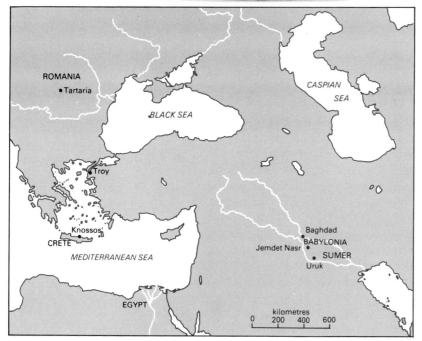

Subsequent TL tests have shown that, on scientific evidence alone, the answer is yes. There is now an impressive unanimity from a number of laboratories that 27 ceramic objects chosen at random from the 300 plus at the Glozel museum fall in the range 350 BC to AD 250, with an average date of 120 BC. A radiocarbon date on ox-teeth found inside one of the decorated urns is consistent with this. One tablet with 'writing' on it is coated with glass fired in the 18th Century, proving that it could not have been carved on the tablet in the 1920s.

The scientific evidence, in other words, is conclusive. As Dr Hugh McKerrell, one of the four scientists, wrote in 1977: 'We have now gone into every possible aspect of forgery or accidental deception of the TL process and can happily dismiss them all. Every piece we have examined by TL dating is certainly *not* modern forgery.'

Glyn Daniel, although resolutely refusing to change his mind, has not adequately contested this, seeming content to write vaguely that the scientists 'are confused and produce confusing results' (to which Dr McKerrell replied: 'Perhaps it is you who are confused because the dating results to which you refer are manifestly straightforward'), and once more Glozel is banned from the pages of *Antiquity*.

Early proto-writing
The writing on the Glozel clay tablet is still undeciphered and the most likely theory so far put forward is that it consists of a number of magical signs, used locally in some magician's or witch's den, most of which are not even intended as writing. Its importance lies more in the archaeological establishment's resistance to a scientific finding than in its intrinsic interest, for it is certainly not, as Reinach and Morlet once hoped, the world's first writing. For this, a new candidate has emerged – the Tartaria tablets of Bulgaria, which everybody agrees to be genuine and to have obvious similarities with the proto-writing of Sumer as represented by the Jemdet Nasr tablets now in Oxford's Ashmolean Museum.

As with Glozel, they are disturbing for text-book archaeology. They are at least 1000 years older than Jemdet Nasr, showing once again that the 'barbarians' of neolithic Europe had skills and knowledge before they are supposed to. Tartaria, like Varna where graves described in the previous pages revealed such astonishing quantities of gold, is part of what is known as the Vinça culture; by 4500 BC its people grew all the crops then known to man, bred all the animals and sailed the Black Sea, the Aegean and the Mediterranean. Until perhaps some even earlier script is found in megalithic Europe, here is where man first learned to write.

Section six
Before civilization

Throughout the previous sections we have traced the outline of a new way of looking at prehistory. It is somewhat more complicated and imprecise than the conventional view, involving as it does the idea of unpredictable and unrecorded catastrophes punctuating life on earth; of early man possessing a psychic sensitivity which he used to discover and harness earth forces of which we are no longer aware; of stone-age people, perhaps even before they knew how to write, exploring the farthest corners of the globe, and mapping the oceans and the skies.

Much of this is still far from being accepted in orthodox circles, although the use of scientific dating techniques has brought a general understanding that man achieved many things earlier and more widely than had been thought. However, there is an even more radical view which no Atlas of mysteries ought to ignore – or rather, two views, which in most believers' minds seem somehow to be connected. The first is that the civilization we see now is only the most recent of many, just as advanced, that have thrived and perished during Earth's history; the Golden Age, or the Garden Age of Eden, were once realities, and all of us today have a shared folk-memory of this distant time. The second is that the development of life on Earth, particularly that of mankind, has been interrupted and shaped by extra-terrestrial intervention.

Surprisingly neither idea, particularly the first, is quite as impractical or crazy as it first sounds. In our present form, we have been around for at most 50,000 years, and the significant development of civilization has taken only the last 10,000 of those. Yet there has been life of some sort on Earth for at least 500 million years. How often during that period could a society have followed the cycle of growth and destruction as described by Plato and the pagan philosophers? According to the extreme catastrophist view, the answer is many times. Immanuel Velikovsky, for instance (page 30), has no doubts about this: 'Before this present Earth Age existed, several times the *same* Earth was created, then levelled and recreated. These civilizations are now buried so deeply within the lower strata of the Earth that we simply do not have archaeological evidence of their existence.' Without evidence, it is of course impossible to say whether he is right or wrong, and the geological debate about whether catastrophes have upheaved the Earth's surface occasionally to produce massive fossilized extinctions is as much a matter of philosophy and logic as of science. Certainly in many parts of the world there are tantalizing 'human' or 'giant' footsteps imprinted on rock seemingly hundreds of millions of years old, but there are not enough to form a convincing or coherent pattern. However, Plato and the catastrophists agree on one lost civilization recent enough to be examined – Atlantis; and rather than become embroiled in a geological argument unprovable one way or another, the next section of the Atlas concentrates on how Atlantis fits the changing view of prehistory.

As for extra-terrestrials, the evidence is much thinner. Almost everything usually put forward in their favour is more readily explained by man's own genius. *Almost* everything; there is just one possible time in recorded history as interpreted by the writer Robert Temple when beings from the Sirius star system might have had a direct influence on the development of civilization; new facts presented in this section tend to support what he has put forward. Probably a single act of vandalism has prevented us ever being certain about this, or about Atlantis. The great Library of Alexandria once contained one million volumes in which the entire science, philosophy, and mysteries of the ancient Western world were recorded, including whatever knowledge the Sirian amphibians may have left behind. In the 7th Century it was burned to the ground by Arab soldiers, who supposedly used the priceless parchments to heat water for themselves in the city's Roman baths.

Atlantis solved?

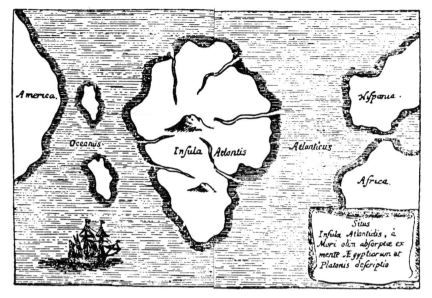

The 17th-century scholar Athanasius Kircher was one of the first to re-open enquiry into the location of Plato's Atlantis.

The primary evidence for Atlantis is in Plato's books *Critias* and *Timaeus*, written around 355 BC. Then in his seventies, Plato chose the literary device of writing as though he was a young pupil listening to Socrates discussing various philosophical matters with a group of friends; you can never be certain which idea originates with Plato and which with Socrates, and indeed much of the time it is difficult to sort out what is fact and what is invention. In the case of Atlantis, the story is attributed to one of the friends present, Critias, who says it is 'derived from ancient tradition'.

It is exaggerated, mythical, and ruminative, as in all the Socratic dialogues. Aristotle, for one, believed that Plato had made Atlantis up, and this doubt has continued over the centuries. The prevailing archaeological view is either that Atlantis never existed, or that it refers in an allegorical way to the splendours of Minoan civilization in Bronze Age Crete. Derek Ager, Head of the Department of Geology at Bristol University, wrote a letter to *Catastrophist Geology* objecting among other things to the mention of Atlantis in its literature: 'Take "Atlantis", for example. I have no doubt at all that there never was such a land-mass (at least not in man's time) beyond the "Pillars of Hercules". The subject is just not worth discussing. On the other hand I think it quite possible, even probable, that the legend refers to the destruction of the Minoan civilization by the volcanic processes.' L. Sprague de Camp, in his scholarly *Lost Continents*, analysed the evidence carefully and convinced himself that 'the most reasonable way to regard Plato's story, then, is as an impressive if abortive attempt at a political, historical, and scientific romance – a pioneer science-fiction story'; he thought that like Thomas More's *Utopia*, it described an ideal community as preconceived by the author.

Plato's truth

However, more than 2000 books on the subject disagree, and while it may be comfortable to take the orthodox line, the chances are that Atlantis actually existed, and that it wasn't Crete. For Plato goes out of his way to report exactly what were the origins of the Atlantis tale: Solon, a famous Greek elder statesman, had been given the story by the Egyptian priests of Sais, and had planned to write a poem on the subject. He told what he knew to an equally renowned Greek, Critias, whose grandson was the friend of Socrates and narrated the story in Plato's books. These were all highly eminent people. Also, Plato affirmed flatly four times that the story was true. He was definite about this: 'The fact that it is not invented fable but a genuine history is all-important.'

Historically, too, there is no doubt that after Solon's retirement from public life he travelled the Mediterranean as a businessman, and there are a number of contemporary witnesses of his visit to Egypt at the time in question (around 600 BC); the Roman historian Plutarch later quoted a fragment of his poetry that describes the Nile. As one of Greece's 'seven sages' Solon would almost certainly have met the Egyptian priests, one of whom Plutarch identifies as having the name Sonchis. So much the most reasonable interpretation of Plato's story is that Solon gave a factual account of what the Egyptians told him: Atlantis was a genuine Egyptian tradition, not a philosophical fable.

Beyond Gibraltar

But if so, where had it been located? Plato is unambiguous, you might think. 'Beyond the Pillars of Hercules' can only mean passing through the Straits of Gibraltar (on either side of which the pillars stood) and out into the Atlantic Ocean. So powerfully does the idea of Atlantis work on people's minds that Plato's invitation has led investigators to all manner of unlikely sites. As T. H. Martin wrote in *Etudes sur le Timée de Platon* in 1841 'many scholars, embarking upon the search with a more or less heavy cargo of erudition, but with no compass other than their imagination and caprice, have voyaged at random. And where have they arrived? In Africa, in America, in Spitzbergen, in Sweden, in Sardinia, in Palestine, in Athens, in Persia, and in Ceylon, they say.' In general, however, the search has become concentrated on just two areas that might approximate to Plato's overall description: a sunken continent in the Atlantic, or (ignoring the Pillars of Hercules) a lost civilization in the Mediterranean Sea.

Garden of Eden

Plato's image of Atlantis as representing a

Plato's description of the Atlantean metropolis

'At the centre of the island, near the sea, was a plain, said to be the most beautiful and fertile of all plains, and near the middle of this plain about fifty stades inland a hill of no great size . . . There were two rings of land and three of sea, like cartwheels, with the island at their centre and equidistant from each other . . . In the centre was a shrine sacred to Poseidon and Cleito, surrounded by a golden wall through which entry was forbidden . . . There was a temple to Poseiden himself, a stade in length, three hundred feet wide and proportionate in height, though somewhat outlandish in appearance. The outside of it was covered all over with silver, except for the figures on the pediment which were covered with gold . . . Round the temple were statues of all the original ten kings and their wives, and many others dedicated by kings and private persons belonging to the city and its dominions . . . The two springs, cold and hot, provided an unlimited supply of water for appropriate purposes, remarkable for its agreeable quality and excellence; and this they made available by surrounding it with suitable buildings and plantations, leading some of it into basins in the open air and some of it into covered hot baths for winter use. Here separate accommodation was provided for royalty and commoners, and, again, for women, for horses, and for other beasts of burden . . . The outflow they led into the grove of Poseidon, which (because of the goodness of the soil) was full of trees of marvellous beauty and height, and also channelled it to the outer ring-islands by aqueducts at the bridges. On each of these ring-islands they had built many temples for different gods, and many gardens and areas for exercise, some for men and some for horses . . . Finally, there were dockyards full of triremes and their equipment, all in good shape . . . Beyond the three outer harbours there was a wall, beginning at the sea and running right round in a circle, at a uniform distance of fifty stades from the largest ring and harbour and returning in on itself at the mouth of the canal to the sea. This wall was densely built up all round with houses and the canal and the large harbour were crowded with vast numbers of merchant ships from all quarters, from which rose a constant din of shouting and noise day and night.'

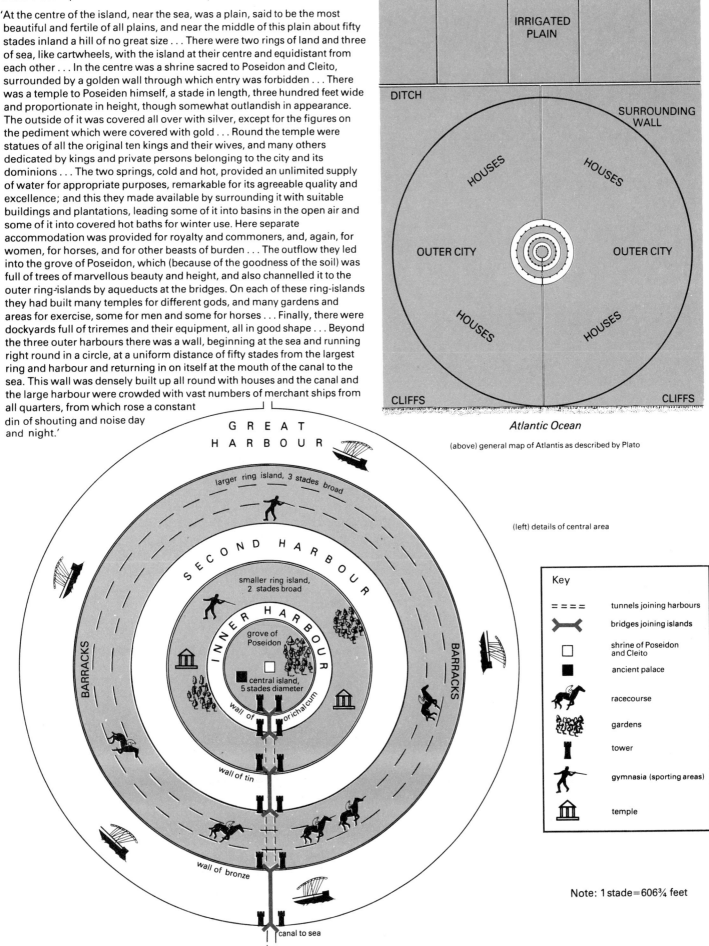

Atlantic Ocean

(above) general map of Atlantis as described by Plato

(left) details of central area

Key

= = = =	tunnels joining harbours
	bridges joining islands
□	shrine of Poseidon and Cleito
■	ancient palace
	racecourse
	gardens
	tower
	gymnasia (sporting areas)
	temple

Note: 1 stade = 606¾ feet

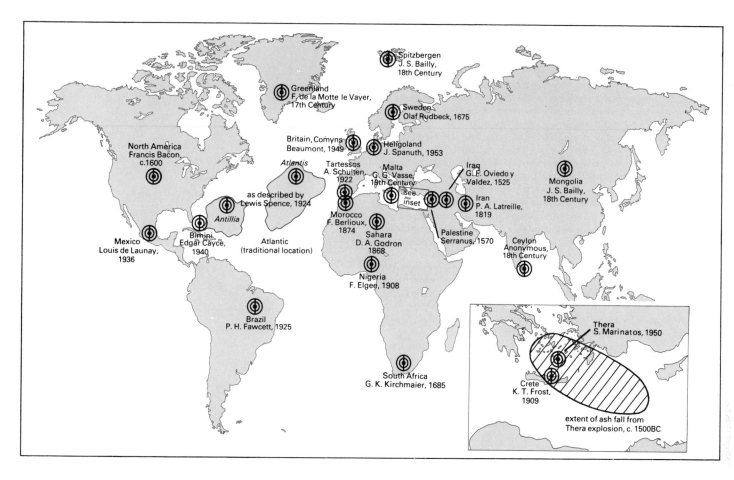

Of the many eccentric suggestions for where Atlantis may have been, most archaeologists today think Plato was referring to the Minoan civilization in Crete.

Golden Age of mankind, an earthly paradise before the Fall, in Biblical terms the original Garden of Eden, is so seductive and persuasive a thought that speculation about it has continued more or less uninterruptedly from the moment he first brought the subject up. Serious research began in the 17th Century, but it was the end of the 18th Century before the new Atlanteans found their prophet: Ignatius Donnelly. Rather like Solon, he was an outstanding public figure as well as being a scholar. A lawyer at 22, he became Lieutenant-Governor of Minnesota six years later, and at 34 was a member of Congress,

where because of his endless studying in the Congressional Library he was characterized as 'perhaps the most learned man ever to sit in the house'. In 1882 and 1883, when he was in his fifties, his two masterpieces were published: *Atlantis, the Antediluvian World*, and *Ragnarok, the Age of Fire and Gravel*. Both were immediate best-sellers. Drawing on a huge number of deluge myths to support Plato's account of how Atlantis disappeared in 'violent earthquakes and floods in a single day and a night', he believed that it had existed as a mid-Atlantic continent before 9600 BC

Archaeological periods

However, the theory that Minoan civilization was destroyed by the explosion of Santorini is contradicted by dating of pottery styles. This shows that the major Cretan sites were not destroyed until some fifty years after the explosion of Santorini; Knossos, the capital city, was destroyed more than a hundred years later.

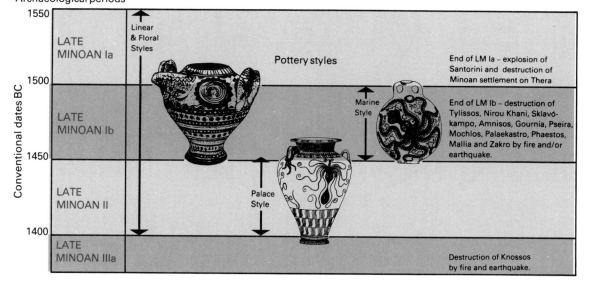

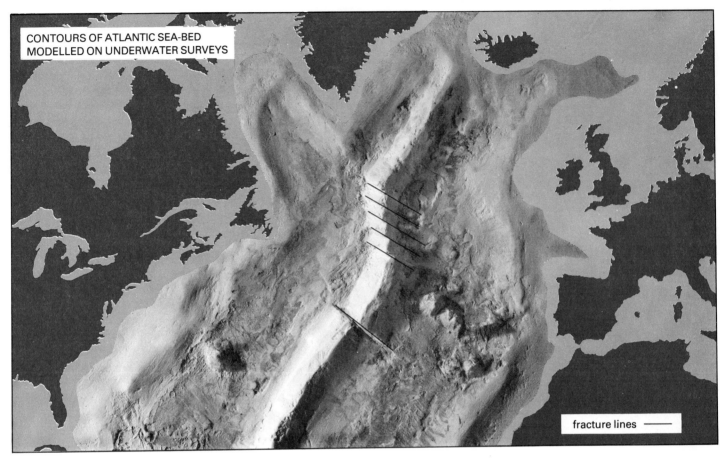

CONTOURS OF ATLANTIC SEA-BED
MODELLED ON UNDERWATER SURVEYS

fracture lines ———

(Plato's date), and was the first highly-advanced metal-working culture in the world. All the main features of civilized societies had originated there: the invention of writing, the discovery of the compass, the development of navigation, the discovery of gunpowder, paper, silk manufacture, astronomy and agriculture.

Outdated theories

His massive documentation is the starting-point for all later books that seek a mid-Atlantic solution to Atlantis. Unfortunately, our new-found knowledge of sea-floor spreading and continental drift (page 14), and other scientific advances, have weakened most of the arguments put forward. *Plants and animals are common to both sides of the Atlantic; therefore there must have been a land bridge between them.* Not so. Birds migrate, seeds are carried long distances on the wind or on floating ocean debris. *Eels migrating to the Sargasso Sea probably have a racial memory of a freshwater source that was once there; nor can the area's four million square kilometres of weed be explained.* It can, now; the weed is carried by swirling currents from Florida. And although racial memory may play a part in migration (page 86), eel migration is no more a mystery than many others. *The many cross-Atlantic cultural similarities [e.g. pyramid building, mummification] must be derived from a central source.* Or because early people were much better navigators than had been supposed

(page 113). *Greeks, Egyptians, Celts and other Europeans all had legends of fairy-tale land-masses in the Atlantic; the Aztecs of Mexico believed they had migrated there from an island called 'Aztlan' – very close to the word Atlantis.* Impossible to deny this evidence, which remains the strongest corroboration of Plato. However, some of the legends seem to be purely symbolic, and the Celtic paradise islands may well have been the Canaries. The Aztecs themselves dated their departure from Aztlan to 1168 AD, and whatever date you put on Atlantis (see below) it requires the Aztecs to wander around for several thousand years before their arrival in the American archaeological record.

Mid-Atlantic ridge

The Mid-Atlantic Ridge, the great chain of jagged underwater mountains whose peaks can still be seen in some places such as the Azores, is the visible proof of a sunken continent. It is a geophysical impossibility for such a continent to have existed as recently as Plato's Atlantis. In fact, the ridge is getting steadily larger as new material pours out from the Earth's interior as a consequence of continental drift. *The end of the Ice Age coincides exactly with Plato's date for the end of Atlantis, when the sea-level the world over rose by ten metres.* Many deluge legends seem to have their basis in this event (page 163); but how did the Egyptian priests of 600 BC have

The steep sides of the mid-Atlantic ridge, similar to the Rockies or the Alps, make it impossible for a lost continent to have existed there.

Ignatius Donnelly drew this impression of the eruption of Vesuvius in 1737 to suggest how Atlantis had perished.

the means of accurately dating what went on some 9000 years earlier?

The Minoan theory

Around 1500 BC, a volcanic eruption of almost unimaginable proportions destroyed the island of Thera in the southern Aegean Sea. Its nearest modern equivalent would be the 1883 eruption of Krakatoa in the Pacific, which set off a series of tidal waves 15 metres high that devastated neighbouring islands, unleashed an enormous cloud of ash and colossal volumes of lava that covered the whole island and killed 37,000 people; it was so deafening that the explosion could be heard 6300 kilometres away in Australia – the loudest historically verified sound in Earth's history.

Cataclysmic as this explosion was, the one on Thera may have been *four times* as violent, according to calculations by the renowned Greek archaeologist Spyridos Marinatos, who in 1939 first set out in *Antiquity* the detailed reasoning through which Plato's Atlantis should be placed not in the Atlantic but in the Mediterranean. In essence, he proposed that tidal waves and debris from the Thera eruption quickly travelled the 100 kilometres from there to Crete, where they 'caused enormous havoc on the low-lying land' and destroyed the rich and powerful Minoan civilization living on it. The Minoans, he argued, who dominated that part of the world until then, and whose sea-faring trade links stretched into north Africa and southern Europe, could easily be equated with the 'great and wonderful empire' written about by Plato. As for the date, by knocking a nought off Plato's 9000, and adding this figure to the time when the Egyptian priests told Solon the story (around 600 BC), you have 1500 BC – near enough the time when Thera erupted and the Minoan civilization disappeared from the archaeological record. He summed up: 'Thus the myth about Atlantis may be considered as historical tradition which, in the manner typical of the distortion of such events, grew from the fusion of various disparate episodes. The destruction of Thera, accompanied by terrible natural phenomena felt as far away as Egypt, and the simultaneous disappearance of the Cretans trading with Egypt, gave rise to a myth of an island, beyond all measure powerful and rich, being submerged.'

Theran errors

Other archaeologists have subsequently developed this theory. Angelos Galanopoulos, for instance, a Greek seismologist who restated the case in a paper to the International Union of Geodesy and Geophysics in 1960, listed 19 'factual' statements about Atlantis by Plato, most of which could be related to Minoan Crete. Dorothy Vitaliano, a geologist who summarized these points in her book *Legends of the Earth*, found six of them 'fully consistent' and eight that 'can be made to fit'. This seems over-generous. Peter James, a young archaeologist and the chief researcher for this Atlas, has studied the Atlantis legend for the last six years, and rates only three as positive indications, six as negative, and the rest as inconclusive. In fact the whole Cretan answer may have been accepted without critical enough scrutiny, particularly in the light of some damning evidence which emerged in 1977 showing that the eruption of Thera was much earlier than the decline of Minoan civilization on Crete. After a careful study of volcanic debris, two German scientists, Hans

Feature	Plato's statement	Commentary on Plato's writings
1 The date	Nine thousand years before Solon (c. 600 BC)	Vitaliano: If there is one nought too many, the date is correct. James: *Arbitrary; not consistent with internal evidence.*
2 Location	'In those days the Atlantic was navigable; and there was an island situated in front of the straits which are by you called the Pillars of Heracles.'	V: Plato's Atlantis was too big for the Mediterranean, so he moved it to the Atlantic. J: *Quite so. Plato definitely wasn't talking about the Mediterranean. – And the Egyptians of c. 600 BC knew where the Pillars of Hercules were* (page 114).
3 Islands beyond	'The island . . . was the way to other islands, and from these you might pass to the whole of the opposite continent which surrounds the true ocean' (as opposed to the Mediterranean, which he describes as a 'harbour', not 'real sea').	V: The description of the islands refer to Crete as the gateway to the Cyclades and mainland of Greece (the 'continent'). J: *But Plato specifically excludes the Mediterranean as a location.*
4 Great Empire	Atlantis was 'a great and wonderful empire which had rule over the whole island and several others, and over parts of the continent,' in Europe reaching Libya and northern Italy.	V: An accurate description of the sphere of Minoan political and economic influence. J: *It is by no means certain how far the Minoan 'empire' extended.*
5 End of Atlantis	'There occurred violent earthquakes and floods; and in a single day and night of misfortune the island of Atlantis disappeared in the depths of the sea.'	V: Describes the eruption of Thera. J: *Or any earthquake or volcanic eruption anywhere.*
6 Mud shoals	'The sea in those parts is impassable and impenetrable, because there is a shoal of mud in the way; and this was caused by the subsidence of the island.'	V: Perhaps a description of floating pumice following the volcanic eruption. J: *There are no shoals of mud around Crete; pumice is an* ad hoc *invention.*
7 Ruling caste	Ten sons of Poseidon, the leading sea-god, inherited Atlantis and divided it up and ruled it as a confederacy of kings.	V: Completely consistent with Minoan priest kings subject to a supreme ruler at Knossos. J: *And with many other ancient kingdoms, including the British Empire.*
8 City and plain	The city was circular, and about 15 miles in diameter. A canal of enormous size ran through the city, connecting with a 'great rectangular irrigated plain 230 × 340 miles in size'.	V: Probably a description of the relationship of Thera to Crete. J: *No matter how you juggle with the dimensions, they cannot be made to fit either island.*
9 Hot and cold springs	The central hill in the city was supplied with hot and cold fountains from underground streams.	V: Hot springs are commonly associated with volcanic areas. J: *And also exist in many non-volcanic areas.*
10 Flora	The island grew 'whatever fragrant things there now are in the earth . . . all these that sacred island brought forth fair and wondrous and in infinite abundance.'	V: Admittedly not much like the relatively barren modern Crete. J: *Even hard-core Thera supporters admit this description doesn't fit.*
11 Fauna	'There was a great number of elephants in the island', and enough food for all sorts of animals from 'lakes and marshes and rivers' as well as mountains and plains.	V: The basis for this may be that Minoans imported ivory. J: *So did everyone in the Near East; nor do lakes and marshes (nor elephants) exist on Crete.*
12 Mineral resources	The Atlanteans mined in such quantity that they were able to cover the inner enclosure of their Metropolis with gold, and the surrounding walls with brass, tin, and orichalcum.	V: Minoans must have imported most of the metals they needed – Plato's is not a likely description. J: *Agreed.*
13 The palace	The royal palace was successively adorned and augmented by its kings and became 'a marvel to behold for size and beauty'.	V: The sumptuous royal palace is Knossos 'to a T'. J: *And any other palace 'to a T'.*
14 Coloured stone	White, red and black stones were used to build Atlantean walls.	V: These colours were widely used in Aegean islands. J: *They were also used in the Azores and elsewhere.*
15 Religion	Over the sacred spot where Poseidon had dwelt, there was a temple surrounded by a golden wall; other temples were also lavishly decorated and furnished with golden statues.	V: Not a good match; Minoans did not build temples as Plato describes, nor make huge gold statues. J: *Agreed.*
16 Baths	Atlanteans were fond of warm baths in winter. 'There were the king's baths, and the baths of private persons, and there were baths for women'.	V: The Minoans' fondness for bathing is well known. J: *Agreed. A point in favour of Thera.*
17 Canal system	As well as the central canal, an elaborate system of great irrigation ditches surrounded and traversed the plain.	V: No trace of an early irrigation system has been found in Crete. J: *Agreed.*
18 Military strength	The kings of Atlantis, when they went to war with ancient Athens, were able to call on 10,000 chariots and 1200 ships.	V: Again the numbers are realistic for Crete if a nought is taken off. J: *Number-juggling.*
19 The bulls	The kings met every fifth or sixth year for consultation, and sacrificed a bull to mark the event; the bull was captured with staves and nooses before having its throat cut.	V: Strongly backed by Minoan friezes showing evidence of a cult involving public bull-games. J: *The Minoan friezes are vivid, but bull-cults are widespread. The earliest ones may even date from Cro-Magnon times.*

Pichler and Wolfgang Schiering, reported in *Nature* that the Thera explosion had hardly affected Crete, and it was not until 1450 BC that the Cretan coastline was struck by a 'catastrophic regional earthquake, similar to that of AD 1926'. Even afterwards, Minoan civilization continued around the palace of Knossos until 1380 BC. Peter James puts it: 'The Minoan centres of Crete survived Thera by about 50 years, and in the case of Knossos, by over 100 years. The basic archaeological premise for the Crete/Thera/Atlantis has therefore been proved shaky, quite apart from all the other weaknesses in the evidence. The original story of Atlantis as told by the Egyptian priests can't have been about the destruction of Minoan civilization by a volcano on Thera, because no such thing happened.'

It is still possible to argue that Plato's legend compressed the two events into one, but even if this is so, James has a telling criticism to make about the way that the Thera hypothesists arrived at their date of 1500 BC (or thereabouts) so that it conveniently matched the Thera eruption: it is both arbitrary and wrong, he says, to 'knock off a nought' from Plato's date. Velikovsky was one who did this, so that the end of Atlantis fitted his date for the chaos caused by the approach of the planet Venus to Earth (page 26). Other archaeologists have suggested that Solon made a mistake when 'transcribing the Egyptian Writings', or that 'the symbols for 100, 1000 and 10,000 in Cretan scripts are very similar'.

Great antiquity

Peter James insists all this is highly unconvincing, and that the internal evidence of Plato's account makes it clear that the Egyptian priests were talking about a period of great antiquity – certainly more than 900 years before their conversation with Solon: 'many great deluges have taken place during the last 9000 years, for that is the number of years that have elapsed since the time of which I am speaking...' A figure of 900 years would have taken the Egyptian priests back only to the relatively recent and well-recorded XVIIIth Dynasty, whose details they would certainly have known. Their date refers to a dimly-remembered period when a war 'was said to have occurred between all those who dwelt outside the Pillars of Hercules' (i.e. the Atlanteans) 'and those who dwelt within them' (i.e. the Greeks); the account goes on to state that this war took place 1000 years before the 'institutions' (or 'constitution', in another translation) of Egyptian civilization were founded.

This is a crucial statement, for it refers to a known quantity – the beginning of Egyptian civilization. Atlantis existed (and perished) before that. The figure for Egypt's antiquity that nearly all modern Egyptologists agree on is 3100 BC plus or minus 150 years. Therefore, if the Egyptian priests told a true fact, the date for the end of Atlantis would be $3100 + 1000 = 4100$ BC.

But of course they didn't say this – they said 9600 BC. Why the discrepancy? Peter James has neatly resolved the problem by pointing out that all the ancient kingdoms were fond of exaggerating their antiquity in competition with each other (page 45); Egyptians, Babylonians, Phrygians, Jews and others all did so. The Egyptian method was by adding up the number of years in the reigns of all their kings, as preserved in the king-lists; as several kings had reigned simultaneously in various parts of Egypt on many occasions, this totting-up led to wildly inaccurate figures; the Greek historian Herodotus, visiting Egypt a mere 150 years after Solon, was given by this method an

Typical stone circle in Britain, representing the genius of the megalith builders. Their empire may have started the legend of Atlantis.

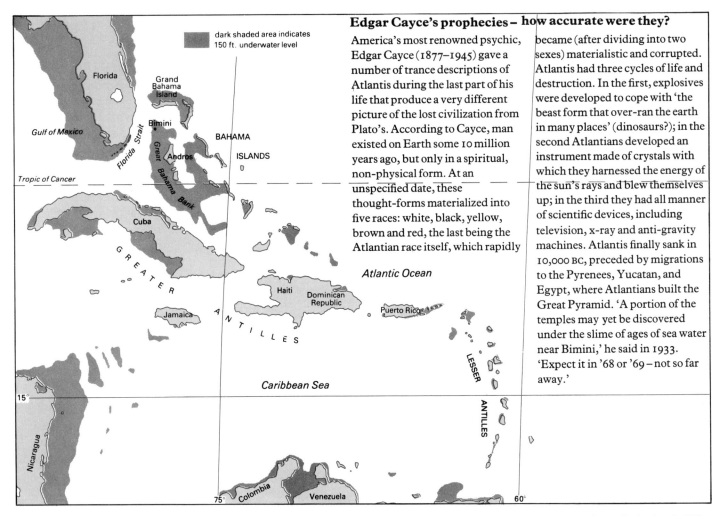

America's most renowned psychic, Edgar Cayce (1877–1945) gave a number of trance descriptions of Atlantis during the last part of his life that produce a very different picture of the lost civilization from Plato's. According to Cayce, man existed on Earth some 10 million years ago, but only in a spiritual, non-physical form. At an unspecified date, these thought-forms materialized into five races: white, black, yellow, brown and red, the last being the Atlantian race itself, which rapidly became (after dividing into two sexes) materialistic and corrupted. Atlantis had three cycles of life and destruction. In the first, explosives were developed to cope with 'the beast form that over-ran the earth in many places' (dinosaurs?); in the second Atlantians developed an instrument made of crystals with which they harnessed the energy of the sun's rays and blew themselves up; in the third they had all manner of scientific devices, including television, x-ray and anti-gravity machines. Atlantis finally sank in 10,000 BC, preceded by migrations to the Pyrenees, Yucatan, and Egypt, where Atlantians built the Great Pyramid. 'A portion of the temples may yet be discovered under the slime of ages of sea water near Bimini,' he said in 1933. 'Expect it in '68 or '69 – not so far away.'

A prediction by the US clairvoyant Edgar Cayce has led to intense underwater exploration around Bimini in the Bahamas.

authoritative date of 12,040 BC for the founding of Egyptian civilization.

The right date

Given that what the Egyptian priests told Solon was similarly exaggerated, it would seem possible at last to arrive at a sensible date for the destruction of Atlantis: 3100 BC (the archaeological date for the beginnings of Egyptian civilization) plus about 500 years (halving the priestly '1000 years'). As Peter James puts it: 'A date in the middle of the fourth millenium BC is absolutely consistent with the textual and historical evidence.'

Site of Atlantis

If so, where could the legendary Atlantis have been sited, and how far did its influence spread? Assuming that the Egyptian habit of exaggerating, rather than lying, included geographical size, we can look beyond the Straits of Gibraltar for somewhere rather smaller than a lost continent in the Atlantic, or as Plato describes it 'an island larger than Libya and Asia combined'. A lost work by the Greek geographer Marcellus written in the first century AD and containing the first independent reference to Atlantis after Plato, said that it consisted of 'seven islands . . . and also three

others of immense extent', the middle one of which was dedicated to the Atlantean god Poseidon. The magnitude of this island was 'a thousand stadia', and the inhabitants of it 'preserved the remembrance of their ancestors, or the Atlantic island that had existed there, and was truly prodigiously great; which for many periods had domination over all the islands in the Atlantic Sea.'

The historian Lewis Spence, whose contribution to Atlantean scholarship equalled Ignatius Donnelly's, suggested in 1912 that the remnants of this island formation 'still persists fragmentally in the Antillean group, or West Indian Islands,' and today this still looks the most likely place. The sea around them is shallow, and given the rising sea level since the last Ice Age ended (page 142), a much larger land area would have been above the surface. The continuing Bimini explorations, described on the next pages, may already have given evidence that a civilization was once here. By Mediterranean standards, the three main islands of Cuba, Haiti and Puerto Rico are all large. Haiti, the middle one, is even the size that Marcellus reported – about a hundred miles from side to side, the equivalent of 1000 stadia.

Maes Howe
2800 BC

Raigmore
3000–2700 BC

Monamore
3700 BC

Lochhill
3700 BC

Jordhoj
3350 BC

Knowth
3300 BC

Newgrange
3350 BC

Tara
3000 BC

Tustrup
3300–3000 BC

London

Amsterdam

Atlantic Ocean

Île Carn
4200–4000 BC

Île Gaignog
4500 BC

Barnenez
4600 BC

Brussels

Frankfurt

Paris

Berne

Carapito
3700 BC

Carenque
3900 BC

Lisbon

Madrid

Gorginos
4500 BC

Poço da Gateira
4500 BC

Rome

Los Millares
3300–3000 BC

Malta
3500 BC

Distribution of megalithic burial chambers in western Europe (shaded grey), showing earliest dates on the Atlantic coast.

Atlantean America

Without archaeological evidence, guessing the site of Atlantis is armchair detective work; but in the light of current knowledge, this area seems the most coherent and intriguing solution.
It gives a good interpretation (America) for Plato's enigmatic use of the word 'continent' in his account that Atlantis was 'the way to other islands, and from these you might pass to the whole of the opposite continent which surrounds the true ocean.' On another occasion he wrote: 'On this island of Atlantis had arisen a powerful and remarkable dynasty of kings, who ruled the whole island, and many others as well and parts of the continent; in addition it controlled, within the strait, Libya up to the borders of Egypt and Europe as far as Tyrrhenia.' (Tyrrhenia was the Greek term for Etruria in central Italy.)

So if America was the 'continent', what was going on in the part of western Europe and

north Africa that, granted some exaggeration, could have fitted Plato's description of a highly civilized people who had organized agriculture, a developed hierarchy with leisure time, writing, and metal-working? The answer is the society of the megalith builders, flourishing much earlier than Egyptian civilization, with its own advanced astronomers and mathematicians, agriculturalists, and early copper-users. It is only recently that these achievements have been archaeologically proved (page 58), but the implications are that this megalithic society must have been organized in a way akin to Plato's description of a 'powerful and remarkable dynasty of kings'. Doctor Euan MacKie of the Hunterian Museum has suggested in *The Megalith Builders* that instead of the primitive tribal society usually imagined, we should think of megalithic civilization as something like that of the Mayans in central America 'in which a small elite class of professional priests, wise men and rulers was supported with tribute and taxes by a predominantly rural peasant population.'

Neolithic writing?

The megalithic empire, or influence, certainly spread as far as Libya and Italy. It fits Solon's description of having existed before Egyptian civilization; copper-working took place in Iberia and Malta in the fourth millenium BC; no example of writing exists, but unless the Tartaria tablets (page 103) are an isolated case, it is by no means impossible that some form of writing was used to keep records on perishable materials (easier, indeed, to suppose this than to imagine the vast body of astronomical knowledge in megalithic times being compiled *without* records of some kind).

What is more, a large number of radiocarbon dates now consistently support Peter James's approximate date for the existence of Atlantis, and the idea of civilization being diffused from The Atlantic eastwards. Simple Neolithic farming communities existed in the sixth millenium BC, and then rather suddenly, about 4500 BC, megalithic burial chambers appear on the coastlines of Iberia and Brittany. Soon eastern Ireland and the Western Isles of Scotland had them too. By 3500 BC megalithic culture was widespread, and there were probably hierarchical societies with astronomer-priests governing their activities.

'All of this was told to Solon by the Egyptian priests,' says Peter James. 'Rightly or wrongly, the Egyptians believed that these ancient European societies were colonies from Atlantis, an island situated in the Atlantic.'

In other words, Atlantis is a genuine possibility as the legendary home of the megalith builders, and the origin of their skills.

Bimini revealed

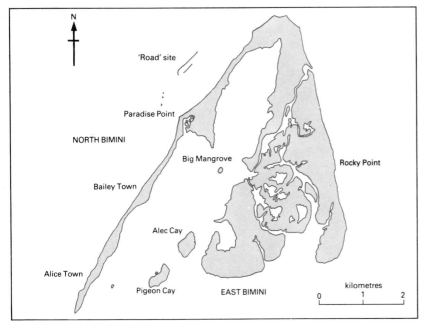

Rising sea-level submerged the rocks off Bimini about 3000 BC; before that the island land-mass was much larger.

John Steele is a Californian now lecturing mostly in London. In 1975 and 1977 he was the archaeologist among a team who formed the *Poseidia '75* and *Poseidia '77* expeditions to discover more about a curious rock formation off the coast of North Bimini, a small island in the Bahamas. Many years earlier the US clairvoyant Edgar Cayce had predicted (page 137) that 'a portion of the temple of Atlantis' would arise off Bimini in '68 or '69; the coincidence that an underwater pattern of symmetrically-shaped stones was observed there in 1968 led to a flood of speculative literature, which in turn inspired the two expeditions to try to balance this with some facts. Below is a shortened version of John Steele's report on the latest that is known about the mysterious 'Road' of Bimini.

Archaeological report

One day early in September 1968 Bonefish Sam, a local Bahamian fishing guide, brought archaeologist Dr J. Manson Valentine to see a curious line of rectangular stones lying in seven metres of water about a kilometre north of Paradise Point. To men like Sam and his family it was a well-known underwater site, the turtle grass and other marine plants growing there making it a feeding ground for many kinds of fish.

To Manson Valentine, however, it was a revelation. Honorary curator of the Museum of Science in Miami, Florida, veteran of expeditions to Yucatan and the South Pacific, and an explorer who has spent 15 years in the Bahamas searching for remnants of lost civilizations, he wrote in his museum *News* that he was amazed to see two parallel lines of stones some 600 metres long. He described them as: 'An extensive pavement of regular and polygonal flat stones, obviously shaped and accurately aligned to form a convincingly artefactual pattern. These stones had evidently lain submerged over a long span of time, for the edges of the biggest ones had become rounded off, giving the blocks the domed appearance of giant loaves of bread or pillows of stone.'

Early doubts

Since then, the problem has been to discover just how 'convincingly artefactual' the stones are. The reason why people are still not sure, even after ten years' exploration, is that natural rock formations *nearly* like it exist close by. Thus the first report following Valentine's announcement had no reservations. John Hall, Professor of Archaeology at Miami University, wrote after diving to examine the stones in 1970: 'Our investigations revealed that these stones constitute a natural phenomenon called Pleistocene beachrock erosion and cracking... we found no evidence whatsoever of any work of human hand or any kind of engineering and therefore, alas for those who believe in the old legend, another Atlantis is dismissed.'

But since then doubts about the stones have persisted. John Gifford, a marine geologist and chief scientist on the same 1970 expedition, wrote a dissenting note ('none of the evidence conclusively disproves human intervention in their formation'), and although the following year he modified his views to bring them in line with those of John Hall, he is by no means the only one to think that 'in both their mode of origin and composition the blocks of Paradise Point remain something of a geological enigma.'

Man or nature

The difficulty is that the stones could be at the same time both natural in form, yet put in place by man. Fractured beachrock on Bimini certainly exists, as for instance on the west coast of South Bimini. What if this had been used to form the causeway off Paradise Point? There are many precedents for this type of megalithic construction, including the transport for unknown reasons of the blue stones at Stonehenge from the Prescelly Mountains in Wales 200 kilometres away.

The purpose of our 1975 expedition was to conduct the first full field survey of the Bimini Road, and three months on the site were spent mapping, measuring, and taking geological samples. For the most part the 'road' consists of huge stone blocks about 5 × 5 × 1 metres in size, extending more than 1000 metres distance on the seaward leg, which is aligned north-east. There is a pronounced arc at the southern end where the road doubles back on itself; the shoreward or inner leg of the 'J' so formed is

aligned 7° further to the east at N52°E. During the last week of the expedition I discovered that the inner leg, after apparently ending in a patch of turtle grass, continued on the other side of the grass for at least 750 metres beyond the northern extremity of the seaward leg.

Apart from four or five exceptions where there are two or more blocks resting vertically on top of each other, the structure consists of one layer of blocks. Although they are not of standard size throughout the structure, we derived through statistical analysis a theoretical building unit of 1.15 metres, based on a number of stones with dimensions clustering around 2.30 metres and 3.45 metres. Exact measurement on rounded stone blocks underwater is necessarily imprecise. The closest unit of measurement in the ancient world to the supposed Bimini unit would be a module of two Phoenician cubits, equal to 1.14 metres.

Geological queries

Dr David Zink, leader of the expedition, raised a number of queries concerning the proposal that they were naturally formed beachrock *in situ*, including the observation that the joints between stones on the top layer do not coincide with the joints in the bedrock beneath, as would be geologically expected. Additionally:
(1) No beachrock in the Bimini area was observed to run continuously in a straight line for much more than 50 metres (compared with the longest measured straight leg on the site of more than 600 metres). (2) Jointing in the bedrock averages about 28 cm in width, compared with 10–15 cm on the top layer. (3) Joints developed in natural formations tend to die out slowly; they do not usually stop against an unbroken block. In scores of cases, the joints of the top layer terminate abruptly against unbroken blocks. (4) The arc of the 'J' consists of stones which turn through a remarkably precise arc of 90° (the latter part of the arc is less distinct). In aerial photographs this feature is as striking as the long straight run of stones.

Dating

The sea level in the area rose steadily from the end of the Ice Age (*c.* 10,000 BC) and showed a more rapid rise around 5000 BC. The best estimates are that the upper layer of stones would have been above the surface of the ground by 10–12 metres in 6000 BC, and 2–3 metres below sea-level in 2000 BC. This gives us an approximation for its most recent human

Aerial photographs clearly reveal the symmetrical 'J' of the Bimini Road, mapped by John Steele beneath.

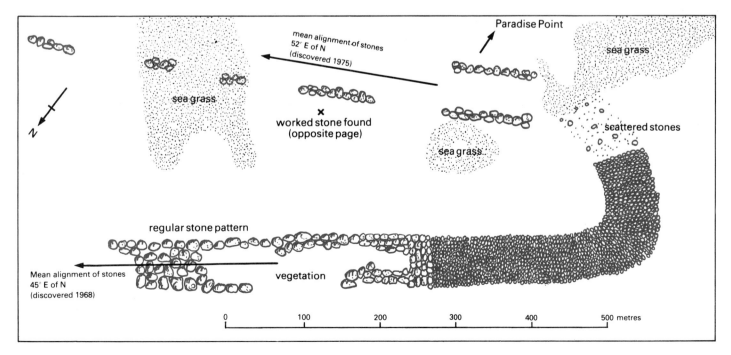

Explorer David Zink with tongue-and-groove masonry block at Bimini. Its origin has not yet been established.

occupancy, if it was so used. A sample of bedrock was dated as 15,000 years old by the thorium/uranium method (Th^{230}/U^{234}), which may give the earliest date for the road.

Artifacts

Conclusive proof of human habitation would come from the discovery of prehistoric artifacts, either from a known culture found in an unambiguous archaeological context (e.g. beneath a stone block of the top layer), or of an unquestionably unknown origin.
Neither has so far been found, although there are a few objects that may turn out to be significant.

The first is a most unusual fragment of worked stone found by David Zink lodged in the blocks of the Road. It is undoubtedly man-made, with a sophisticated tongue-and-groove jointing pattern; one edge is semi-cylindrical and the other is rectangular. Nothing like it has been found before in Bimini, nor in any other Bahamian island – indeed, no archaeologist or architect has been able to identify its origin conclusively. Although very hard, it has not been fired, and therefore cannot be dated by thermoluminescence.

Otherwise, it is Pino Turolla's discovery of marble beneath the sea that is potentially interesting. Marble is not native to the Bahamas, but several fluted marble columns have been found about four kilometres to the south of the Road. The marble has not been matched to any known quarry. The question is whether the marble and

the tongue-and-grooved stone may come from a lost civilization, or are ballast from wrecked ships. The expedition preferred the first explanation, and it is perhaps noteworthy that persistent enquiries in museums and archaeological departments throughout the world have not been rewarded with plausible alternatives; nobody, for instance, has been able to suggest a comparable example of marble columns being used as ballast.

On balance, therefore, we believe there are strong indications that the structure is archaeological, rather than geological, in origin. But its purpose must remain a matter for speculation. The only megalithic structures of comparable magnitude would be the great stone avenues of Carnac (page 59), the Avebury complex in southern Britain, and perhaps some of the pre-Incan constructions in Peru. Although described as a 'road', because of its resemblance to a large stone causeway, the sharp hairpin bend makes nonsense of it having been simply an avenue of economic transportation. Similarly its interpretation as a 'wall' or harbour jetty is inconsistent with its height, which in the main is only one layer of stones about one metre in depth. Basically it is the scale and geometry of the structure which is outstanding. On the assumption that the stones were deliberately placed, we cannot reconcile this with a mundane (as opposed to a religious ceremonial) purpose. The task of interpreting the structure is made particularly difficult because the cultural context of the site is completely unknown; nor is there a megalithic tradition in the Bahamas.

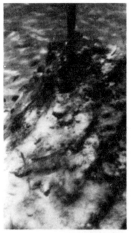

Blocks of marble pillars, of a type unknown elsewhere in the Bahamas, have been found in south Bimini.

The outer space confusion

Santa Barbara rock paintings
date unknown

Olmec sculptures
c.1500–800 BC

The Palenque 'astronaut'
683 AD

Ecuador tunnels
Date unknown

Nazca lines
c.300 BC – 900 AD

Tiahuanaco
c.800 AD

Easter Island statues
17th century AD

Piri Re'is map
1513 AD

Ezekiel's vision
592 BC

Great Pyramid
c.2500 BC

Elephantine

Tablets from Ur
c.2000 BC

Non-rusting pillar
5th century AD

Dates for the supposed arrival of space-men on Earth show large discrepancies in time. If they came at all, they must have been here often.

Erich von Däniken's success story is both a phenomenon and a mystery of our time. *Chariots of the Gods*, his first book, was published in 1967, and within five years was a best-seller in 26 languages, among them Bengali, Marathi, Canarese, Malayalam, Hebrew and Chinese. The five and a half million people who bought it were asked to go along with his fervent belief that (as summarized in the magazine *Encounter*'s learned analysis):

1 Alien beings from a distant galaxy visited the Earth about 10,000 years ago, possibly after an intergalactic battle;
2 These 'sons of the stars' created 'intelligent man by altering the genes of monkeys 'in their image';
3 The alien astronauts were 'worshipped as gods' by mankind because of their unfathomable technology;
4 Many hitherto unidentified archaeological finds may be relics of the astronauts' visit;
5 Myths, the Bible, and other 'sacred books' are really accounts of the sojourn on earth of 'gods'.

This Atlas is devoted to mysteries, and the basic idea that something special happened to nudge mankind along its evolutionary path is not in itself absurd. The sudden appearance of modern man from an unknown birthplace 35–30,000 years ago has been discussed in Section Two; early societies were often surprisingly advanced, contrary to what has generally been thought by archaeologists; the unexpectedly fast development of civilization around 3000 BC in

Mesopotamia and then Egypt needs to be explained. Unfortunately, Erich von Däniken's 'evidence' supporting this approach to prehistory is almost totally irrelevant – an insidious mixture of half-fact and half-truth that sometimes spills into complete falsehood.

His success has spawned a large number of books on the same theme (and given new life to some that were written in a similar vein before him); they largely agree among themselves about the way certain ancient events and artifacts should be interpreted – as examples of extra-terrestrial intervention. Thirteen of von Däniken's best-known 'proofs' are discussed below, in all of which it can be shown that he is wrong. In a sample of 13 related books, no less than nine of these proofs also occur as supposed evidence. The books are:

Jacques Bergier *Extra-Terrestrial Visitations from Prehistoric Times*
Joseph F. Blumrich *The Spaceships of Ezekiel*
Robert Charroux *The Mysterious Unkown*
Marc Dem *The Lost Tribes from Outer Space*
Raymond Drake *Gods and Spacemen in the Ancient West*
John Keel *Our Haunted Planet*
Peter Kolosimo *Not of This World*
Peter Kolosimo *Timeless Earth*
Alan and Sally Landsburg *In Search of Ancient Mysteries*
Alan and Sally Landsburg *The Outer Space Connection*
Brinsley le Poer Trench *Temple of the Stars*
Eric and Craig Umland *Mystery of the Ancients*
George Hunt Williamson *Road in the Sky*

The way that these books interpret the various artifacts or legendary happenings differs from von Däniken only in degree; on the whole, they are more cautious. Von Däniken himself has modified his views hardly at all since publication of *Chariots of the Gods*, from which most of the quotations below have been taken as best resenting his method of supposition and suggestion. The page numbers following some subjects refer to a part of this Atlas where they have been covered more fully; the number of mentions means the number of times the same topic occurs in the books sampled.

Olmec sculptures (three mentions)
'The sculptures of the Olmecs are incredible. With their beautifully helmeted giant skulls, they can only be admired on the sites where they were found, for they will never be on show in a museum. No bridge in the country could stand the weight of the colossi.'

An exaggeration of their size and weight, implying that they are too massive to be moved with modern equipment (also imputed to other ancient artifacts, e.g. pyramid blocks, Easter Island statues); in fact, three are on display in Mexico City, and another was transported to the Metropolitan Museum of Art in New York.

The Palenque astronaut (two mentions)
'There sits a human being, with the upper part of his body bent forward like a racing motor-cyclist; today any child would identify his vehicle as a rocket . . . The crouching being . . . is manipulating a number of indefinable controls and has the heel of his left foot on a kind of pedal . . . With our knowledge of similar pictures, we should be surprised if the complicated headgear were missing. And there it is with the usual indentations and tubes, and something like antennae on top . . . The astronaut's front seat is separated from the rear portion of the vehicle, in which symmetrically arranged boxes, circles, points and spirals can be seen.'

The astronaut is in fact the Mayan King Pacal, who died in 683 AD, buried beneath a stone slab on which all the carved motifs are usual in the context of Mayan art. The 'rocket' is basically a cross-shaped sacred maize tree, symbol of

rebirth, from which Pacal is about to pluck a fruit, not manipulate 'indefinable controls'. He is seated on a throne above the Lord of the Underworld, suspended between life and death.

The non-rusting pillar (no mentions)
'In the courtyard of a temple in Delhi there exists . . . a column made of welded iron parts that has been exposed to weathering for more than four thousand years without showing a trace of rust, for it contains neither sulphur nor phosphorus. Here we have an unknown alloy from antiquity staring us in the face.
Perhaps the column was cast by a group of far-sighted engineers who did not have the resources for colossal building, but wanted to bequeath to posterity a visible, time-defying monument to their culture?'

Four errors of fact are contained here. The pillar is not in Delhi, it is in nearby Mehauli. It is a single piece of iron, not 'a column made of welded parts'. It is rust-free because it is made of pure iron, not an 'unknown alloy'. Its origin is known precisely, since it was erected as a tribute to King Chandraguptra II in the Fifth Century AD. The caption to the photograph in *Chariots of the Gods* contradicts 'more than four

thousand years' by saying that 'it cannot be accurately dated, but is hundreds of years old'. Von Däniken says later he was misled about this artifact.

The Great Pyramid
(pages 65–69); (six mentions)
'Several hundred thousand workers pushed and pulled blocks weighing twelve tons up a ramp with (non-existent) ropes on (non-existent) rollers. This host of workers lives on

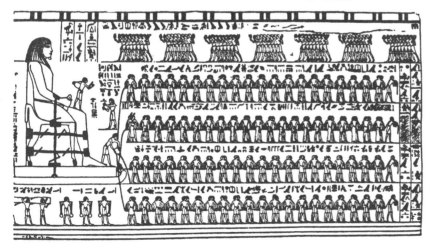

(non-existent) grain.' It took 664 years to build, and is 'visible testimony of a technique that has never been understood. Today, in the 20th Century, no architect could build a copy of the pyramid of Cheops, even if the technical resources of every continent were at his disposal.'

Remarkable though the Pyramid is, every statement above is simply wrong. The limestone blocks were one-and-a-half tons. Ropes existed, and are portrayed in the carving. So did rollers, although Egyptian engineers may well have used more sophisticated lifting devices. The 5th-century BC Greek traveller-historian Herodotus, who usually exaggerated, suggested a work-force of 100,000 for 22 years. Architects and engineers today could certainly build it with less people in less time, given enough money. And however many people were involved, the fertile Nile valley could comfortably have fed them.

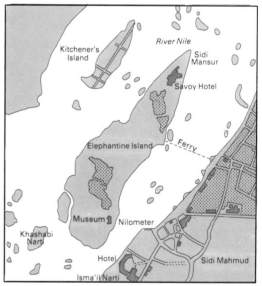

Elephantine Island (no mentions)
'Every tourist knows the island of Elephantine with the famous nilometer at Aswan. The island is called Elephantine, even in the oldest texts, because it was supposed to resemble an elephant. The texts were quite right. The island does look like an elephant. But how did they know that? Because the shape can only be recognized from an aeroplane. For there is no hill offering a view of the island that would prompt anyone to make the comparison.'

The island looks nothing like an elephant, and was named by the Greeks because of the ivory (in Greek, *elephantinos*) trade carried on there.

Piri Re'is map (page 117; four mentions)
'The coasts of North and South America and even the contours of the Antarctic were also precisely delineated on Piri Re'is's maps . . . Comparison with modern photographs of our

globe taken from satellites showed that the original of Piri Reis's maps must have been aerial photographs taken from a very great height. How can that be explained? A space-ship hovers high above Cairo and points its camera straight downwards . . . Whoever made them must have been able to fly and also to take photographs.' The maps were discovered in the 18th Century and were 'absolutely accurate'.

There is only one Piri Re'is map, found in 1929, a compilation of earlier maps. It demonstrates the ability of early navigators, but by no stretch of the imagination is it absolutely accurate. Only one small section of the map (the Caribbean) apparently uses a spherical projection based on Egypt.

mysterious world of Tiahuanaco has been archaeologically dated from bone and charcoal remains. It is assumed that the buildings originated around 600 BC. An ideal date! The prophet Ezekiel's encounter with a spaceship took place in 592 BC. Is it not conceivable that the extra-terrestrial spacemen set up a base at Tiahuanaco?'

There is a contradiction in the two dates that von Däniken states; neither is correct in orthodox archaeological terms, since radiocarbon dating consistently puts the construction of Tiahuanaco at around 800 AD.

The Nazca lines (pages 70–73; seven mentions) 'At some time in the past, unknown intelligences landed on the uninhabited plain near the present-day town of Nazca and built an improvised airfield for their spacecraft which were to operate in the vicinity of the Earth. They laid down two runways on the ideal terrain. Or did they mark the landing-strips with a material unknown to us?

Tiahuanaco (four mentions)
Chariots of the Gods: 'There is no plausible explanation for the beginning or the end of this culture. Of course this does not stop archaeologists from making the bold and self-confident assertion that the site of the ruins is 3000 years old. They date this age from a couple of little clay figures which cannot possibly have anything in common with the age of the monolith.' *In Search of Ancient Gods:* 'The

(left) **Global projection based on Cairo, compiled from NASA sources.**

As on other occasions, the cosmonauts carried out their mission and returned to their own planet.' The Nazcan Indians, he says, added further runways and other drawings to entice the space-gods to return.

What kind of a rocket is it that needs runways kilometres long? As archaeologist Maria Reiche remarked after investigating the lines for a quarter of a century, 'the ground is quite soft; I'm afraid the spacemen would have gotten stuck.' Von Däniken has subsequently said in interviews that they may not have been runways, but navigational aids. So how did the spacemen find their 'ideal terrain' in the first place?

Ezekiel's vision (five mentions)
The Old Testament records that while the prophet Ezekiel was by the River Chebar in Mesopotamia 'behold, a whirlwind came out of the north, a great cloud, and a fire unfolding itself, and a brightness was about it, and out of the midst thereof as the colour of amber, out of the midst of the fire. Also out of the midst thereof came the likeness of four living creatures. And

this was their appearance; they had the likeness of a man. And every one had four faces, and every one had four wings. And their feet were straight feet; and the sole of their feet was like the sole of a calf's foot and they sparkled like the colour of burnished brass.'

Von Däniken thinks this is a description of a spacecraft arriving with extra-terrestrial occupants. Ezekiel himself thought he was experiencing dream-like 'visions of God' in an ecstatic religious moment, and underlined what he meant by saying that 'the hand of the Lord was upon him' – a phrase consistently used in the Old Testament to denote a state of altered consciousness. Who then are we to believe – von Däniken or Ezekiel? Do spacemen have four faces and straight feet?

Tablets from Ur (no mentions)
'Cuneiform texts and tablets from Ur, the oldest books of mankind, tell without exception of 'gods' who rode in the heavens in ships, of 'gods' who came from the stars, possessed terrible weapons and returned to the stars.'

Nothing known from Sumerian literature would fit this interpretation of the tablets. Far from telling of the exploits of their gods 'without exception', tablets from Ur are mainly concerned with business and legal documents, and mundane messages and lists. At least 1700 of the tablets found are of this sort and are not religious texts. Sumerian gods did not 'come from the stars' – they *were* the stars, such as the sun and moon gods who rode in celestial boats like their equivalents in most Near Eastern mythologies.

Ezekiel's vision as depicted by the 19th Century scholar, Eliphas Levi.

Babylonian Moon-god in crescent boat

Babylonian Sun-god in boat

Santa Barbara Rock paintings (no mentions)
'So far no one has given a plausible explanation of these complicated rock paintings.' One of them

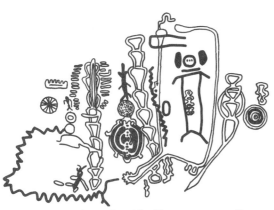

may be a complex scientific diagram, according to a Swiss electronics engineer whom von Däniken quotes – 'a blueprint for artificially inducing the elements of life.'

Quechan Indians, whose ancestors made the paintings, say they are simply symbolic marks left by hunters. They contain practical information on mundane matters such as the route to the nearest water-hole.

Easter Island statues
(three mentions)
'A small group of intelligent beings was stranded on Easter Island owing to a technical hitch. Life on the little island became boring and monotonous . . . Perhaps to leave the natives a lasting memory of their stay, but perhaps also as a sign to the friends who were looking for them, the strangers extracted a colossal statue from the

volcanic stone.' After being rescued, the spacemen left the island with a legacy of unfinished stone monuments whose completion defied the feeble technology of 'the carefree inhabitants who lived only for the day'.

In 1956 the writer Thor Heyerdahl arranged an archaeological experiment with the mayor of Easter Island and six islanders. Using traditional methods, they carved out the contours of a new statue in three days using stone tools and gourds of water to soften the volcanic rock.

Ecuador tunnels (no mentions)
In *Gold of the Gods* von Däniken said he had gone with the explorer Juan Moricz through a secret entrance to an extensive network of tunnels which contained a library written thousands of years ago on thin sheets of metal so as 'to remain legible in perpetuity'. During the expedition 'we switched on our torches and the lamps on our helmets, and there in front of us was the gaping hole which led down into the depths . . . We slid down a rope to the first platform.' Later he 'burst out laughing' and 'felt tremendously happy' and 'had the feeling of being constantly watched.'

Four months after the book was published, von Däniken admitted in an interview that he had never been to the part of Ecuador that he had described, having remained in the town of Cuenca 100 kilometres away. Moricz, on his part, said that von Däniken had never been down a cave with him: 'We could not enter this cave; it was blocked.'

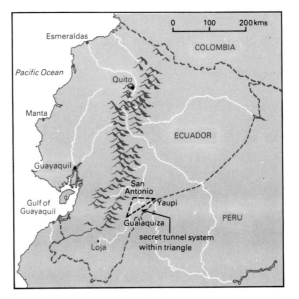

Amphibians from Sirius

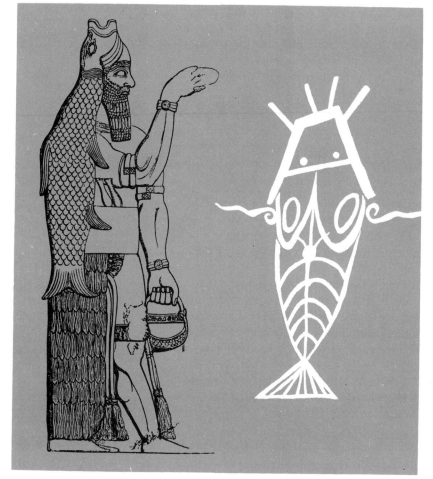

Oannes, the civilizing amphibian sea-god of ancient Babylonia, and the amphibian god Nommo of the Dogon African tribe, have many of the same characteristics. (below right) How the Dogon picture the arrival of the space creatures Nommos in their 'ark'.

Quite the most remarkable example of unexplained astronomical knowledge among primitive peoples (page 108) is that of the Dogon tribe of Africans living in Mali, south of the Sahara desert. They know accurate details about a small star, totally invisible to the human eye, that orbits Sirius, the brightest star in the sky. They know it is massively heavy, it has an elliptical orbit, and the position of Sirius within the orbit. Details apart, it is astonishing that they know about it all for they could not have been told about it by explorers; its existence was not suspected by Western astronomers until the middle of the 19th Century, and it was not photographed, so faint is it compared with Sirius, until 1970.

Yet this star (called Sirius B by modern astronomers) has formed the basis of the most sacred Dogon beliefs since antiquity. So how could they have learned so much about it? There seem only two conceivable possibilities: either they used some form of divination or distant viewing, as in psychic experiments being carried out today (page 82); or, as the Dogon themselves believe profoundly, visitors from a planet attached to Sirius B landed on Earth and passed on the knowledge themselves. This is the solution which the historian Robert Temple has explored in a remarkable book *The Sirius*

Mystery, in which he makes out a persuasive case for the Dogons being the last people on Earth to worship extra-terrestrial amphibians who landed in the Persian Gulf at the dawn of civilization, and whose presence can be detected in drawings and legends of the gods of ancient Babylonia, Egypt, and Greece.

Nommo's ark

He describes how the Dogon call the creatures *Nommos*, who have to live in water. They are said to have arrived in an ark, and drawings in the dust portray 'the spinning or whirling of the descent of the ark'. They describe the noise of thunder that it made, and a whirlwind of dust caused by the violence of its impact with the ground. Other legends tell of 'spurting blood' from the ark, which may refer to its rocket exhaust; the Dogon also seem to make a distinction between the ark that actually landed on earth, and a star-like object in the sky that may represent the main inter-stellar spaceship.

All this might just be science fiction curiosity were it not for the extraordinary scholarship that took Robert Temple back to the origins of the Dogon in Libya, and from there to the undoubted parallels between their Nommo and the amphibian god of Babylon, *Oannes*, a superior being who with his companions was said to have taught the Sumerians mathematics, astronomy, agriculture, social and political organization, and written language – in other words, according to Professor Carl Sagan of Cornell University, 'all the arts necessary for making the transition from a hunter-gatherer society to the first civilization'. Surviving fragments of the *Babylonian History* written in Greek by a priest named Berossus, describe

Oannes closely: 'The whole body of the animal was like that of a fish; and it had under a fish's head another head, and also feet below, similar to those of a man, subjoined to the fish's tail. His voice, too, and language, were articulate and human; and a representation of him is preserved even to this day . . . When the sun set, it was the custom of this Being to plunge again into the sea, and abide all night in the deep; for he was amphibious.'

Mystery religions

Having established the parallel between the two gods, Robert Temple makes a closely-argued case that Oannes and the Sirius connection is at the heart of the Classical 'mystery religions' that have so far defied explanation because they were deliberately recorded in coded form; initiates of the mysteries were forbidden to reveal the arcane knowledge they had been taught. But various clues were written down to indicate

Many Greek myths tell of amphibian beings, similar to those described by Dogon Africans today, who were 'civilizers' teaching writing and other arts.

1 Home of the Annedoti ('Repulsive Ones'), the fish-men who the Babylonians said brought them civilization. The first and most famous was called Oannes or Oe, who was thought to have come from 'a great egg'.
They were said to have appeared at the dawn of history, but as late as the 2nd Century AD Plutarch reported a mysterious 'man' who appeared from the Gulf once a year, spending 'the other days of his life with roving nymphs and demigods'.

2 The oldest city in Sumer, where kingship first 'descended from Heaven'. It was the city of Enki or Ea (= Oannes, Oe), god of wisdom and the patron of mankind. Ea was thought to live in the 'Apsu', a submarine palace, and there are traces of his worship (piles of fish-bones) at one of the earliest temples at Eridu, *c.* 3500 BC.

3 The Philistines worshipped two amphibian deities, Dagon (male) and Atargatis (female), who were represented with the tails of fishes and human bodies. Atargatis was also known as the 'Syrian Goddess' who was said to have been born from an 'egg' that dropped from heaven into the River Euphrates.

4 Home of the amphibian god Proteus ('First Man'), known as the 'Old Man of

the Sea'. He could change his shape and see into the future. He used to rest in a cave, among sea-lions, to 'shelter from the heat of the star Sirius'. Many of the Greek heroes consulted him as an oracle.

5 Home of the amphibian god Triton, who could foretell the future and possessed immense powers, including control over the sea. He assisted the Argonauts when the *Argo* became stuck in Lake Triton. (Temple identifies an important 'Sirius factor' in the myth of the fifty Argonauts.) 'Triton' became the common Greek word for 'merman'.

6 Home of Nereus, another 'Old Man of the Sea'; like Proteus and the Telchines, he could change his shape and give oracles. He had fifty daughters – the Nereids – who were represented in art, like him, with half a human body, and a fish's tail. Nereus was also thought to live in 'Eridanus', which connects him with the Sumerian god Enki/Ea of Eridu.

7 Haunt of the prophetic amphibian god Glaucus ('Grey-green'), who taught divination to Apollo, the Greek god of prophecy and the owner of the oracle at Delphi.

8 Where a pickled 'Triton' was exhibited in the Temple of Dionysus. The Greek traveller Pausanias (2nd Century AD) saw

it, and a similar one at Rome: 'Tritons are certainly a sight; the hair on their heads is like the frogs in stagnant water: not only in its froggy colour, but so sleek you could never separate one hair from the next: and the rest of their bodies are bristling with very fine scales like a rough-skinned shark. They have gills behind the ears and a human nose, but a very big mouth and the teeth of a wild beast. I thought the eyes were greenish-grey, and they have their hands and fingers and finger-nails crusted like sea-shells. From the breast and belly downwards they have a dolphin's tail instead of feet.'

9 Site of an ancient sanctuary described by Pausanias, where an image of Artemis (Goddess of Sirius according to Temple) was kept – the image was of a woman down to the waist, and below that of a fish. It was also known as 'Eurynome', one of the oldest of the Greek goddesses, who dwelt under the sea.

10 Home of the Telchines (see text), amphibian gods with magical powers who were both feared and respected. Zeus attempted to destroy them after they had interfered with the weather, and scattered them from Rhodes. They fled to Lycia, where they built a temple to Apollo, and some to Greece, where they became the fifty 'hounds of Actaeon'.

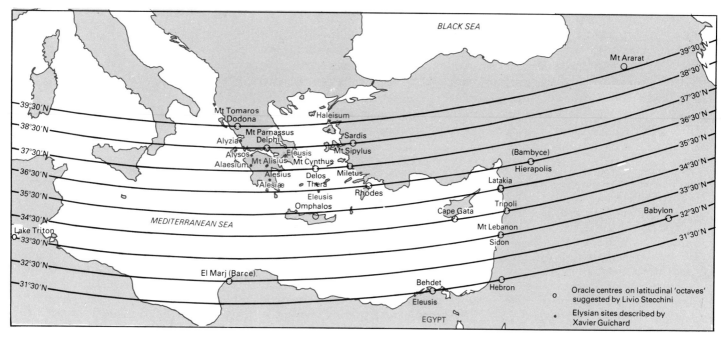

Oracle centres of the classical world seem to be spaced symmetrically, according to Robert Temple (see text). Overlaid are sites with 'Eleusis' names referred to on page 77 of this Atlas. (below) The geodetic map of ancient Egypt, with Behdet as the point from which all measurements were taken.

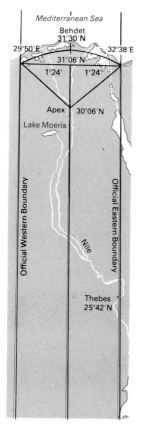

the link with Sirius – for instance, the repeating motif of 50 representing the orbital period of Sirius B, and a dog-headed deity or other dog-associations representing Sirius A, the 'Dog Star'.

Temple recounts many legends that back up his theme, and because these were originally intended to be elusive, it is not surprising that they have many other interpretations. But it is hard to disagree that a Sirius factor is present in many of them. Moreover, there is a rich fund of material in Greek myth that tends to support his theory, but is not included in his book. Some of these myths are included in the map on the preceding page, and a particularly compelling one concerns the islands of Rhodes and its legendary first inhabitants, the Telchines.

Demons of Rhodes
Diodorus Siculus, the Greek historian, wrote of them that they were the 'discoverers of certain arts and that they introduced other things which are useful for the life of mankind. They were also the first, men say, to fashion statues of the gods, and some of the ancient images of the gods have been named after them.'
This description of the Telchines as civilizers, already a close parallel to Oannes and the fish-people of the Persian gulf, is made even more precise by other descriptions of how they were wizards who could summon clouds and rain and hail at will, were 'submarine magic spirits', and 'demons of the depths of the sea'.
Robert Graves wrote that they had dogs' heads, and flippers instead of hands. Clearly the original myth of the amphibian gods spread far through the Mediterranean. There is also no doubt that, according to legend, the Telchines were forced to flee and their survivors became the 50 hounds

of Actaeon; this too is a link with a key part of the Sirius evidence that Robert Temple has compiled.

One other conclusion of Robert Temple's connects directly with various themes already touched on in this Atlas. He believes that the science of geodetics used by the ancient Egyptians (page 65), in which they marked out their country according to certain rules derived from the dimensions of the Earth, was given to them in the first place by the amphibians from Sirius, and was applied throughout the Classical world. He has traced the sacred oracle centres, each containing a large megalith called an *omphalos*, as lying on equally spaced bands that cover the entire Mediterranean and Near East. It is not too far-fetched to suggest that the system spread even further. The oracular secrets formed part of the Eleusinian mysteries. 'Eleusis' became 'Alaise' in Europe (page 77) and a 'ley' in Britain – near-identical words describing the alignments between ancient sites. The parallel is undeniably close, and although the record of exactly what was going on in those times was destroyed for ever in the fire of the Alexandrian Library, we can be sure that the lost science, which was the foundation of civilization and lasted for 3000 years or more, was based on an intense desire to understand earth patterns and forces whose existence is nowadays unhappily ignored.

Section seven
Myths and legends

Strictly speaking, history is only concerned with what is written down about our past. Anything else is prehistory, gleaned mostly from the archaeological record of what has been physically preserved over the years. This is necessarily incomplete, and those who sometimes complain that archaeologists spend too much time in the morbid pursuit of examining what happened in ancient graveyards are being somewhat unfair; tomb-robbing may not be a pleasant pursuit, but it provides a wealth of hard evidence about the life-styles of the people who were buried, and we would know only a fraction of what happened during our ancestry if experts were not prepared to dig among the bones.

However, there is a more vital form of testimony to the past: myth and legend. The problem here is that though most of them have now been written down and can be dissected and analysed as closely, as say, the decorative style of a funerary urn, the result is always ambiguous. If you are an extreme sceptic, you will say that a traditional story must be so confused and embroidered by the passage of time that it contains no valid historical truth whatsoever; on the other hand you can say that it is relatively easy, usually, to sort out the historical from the mythological, and by doing so you gain an insight into prehistory that you are otherwise denied.

Dorothy B. Vitaliano, whose ideas about the location of Atlantis were disputed in the previous section of the Atlas, summarized the two attitudes in her book *Legends of the Earth*: 'If we think in terms of our modern world, in which a piece of gossip may be relayed with substantial changes at every retelling until all semblance of truth is lost, it is difficult to believe that any resemblance to fact could long survive in oral tradition. But there is another modern analogy which might be more apposite. How often, parents, have you retold a bedtime

story to your offspring and found yourself corrected if you deviated by so much as a word from the first version the youngsters had heard? In the very same way, would it not be difficult to introduce variations into the tales told by professional storytellers to peoples whose cultures remained virtually unchanged for thousands of years . . . changes would creep in only with exceeding slowness.'

In all the myths and legends examined in this section of the Atlas, we incline towards the latter point of view. In *Old Testament Truths*, for instance, we say it is not at all difficult to find the point, at the end of Chapter XI of Genesis, where the Bible changes from myth to history; from then on it may biased, elusive, or even fallacious, but nonetheless it is unmistakably history.

This is not on the whole the orthodox view of myths; scholars usually become extremely nervous when gods appear in a legend intermingling in human affairs, assuming that this automatically dismisses any element of historical authenticity. R. G. Collingwood, in his standard work *The Idea of History*, says that myth 'is not concerned with human actions at all. The human element has been completely purged away and the characters of the story are simply gods . . . the divine actions that are recorded are not dated events in the past . . . the work of Homer is not research, it is legend.'

We think Homer lived not long after the events he described, and that the intervention of his heroic gods can be separated from his reported facts; after all, as the great amateur archaeologist of all time, Heinrich Schliemann, demonstrated, Homer's Troy was exactly as he described it. Legends, we say, have a historical basis, and it is impossible to imagine what inspired our forebears, and what happened at the crucial moments in our prehistory, without probing their cryptic message.

Patterns of life

The greatest labyrinth in the world no longer exists. Built by the Egyptian King Amenemhet III about 2000 BC beside his pyramid at Fayum on the southern end of Lake Moeris, it was monstrously large: Professor Flinders Petrie, who discovered its exact location in 1888, worked out from its plundered foundations that it must have been more than 1000 metres in circumference. The Greek historian Herodotus, who visited it in the middle of the Fifth Century BC, described with wonder how its construction had involved greater expense and labour than 'all the works and buildings of the Greeks put together'. It had, he said, 'twelve covered courts, with opposite doors, six courts on the north side and six on the south, all communicating with one another and with one wall surrounding them all.' Its 3000 rooms were divided equally above and below ground, the lower ones containing tombs of kings and of sacred crocodiles, which were strictly guarded from visitors. Four centuries later another great traveller of Classical times, Strabo, described its labyrinthine architecture and the many courtyards to be approached by 'long covered alleys with winding intercommunicating passages, so that a stranger could not find his way in or out unless with a guide'. In the First Century AD Pliny wrote that its 'laborious windings with their baffling intricacy' were mostly in total darkness. But what was its purpose? Like labyrinths the world over, its

Plan of temple labyrinth built for Amenemhet III *c.* 2000 BC, as drawn by the Italian archaeologist L. Canina in 1840, based on Classical descriptions.

origin and motive is shrouded deep within the human psyche. Some powerful unconscious drive must be at work since it is possible to find an identical maze pattern emerging in places as far separated in time and distance as, say, a rock in Tintagel, Cornwall, a coin design in Crete, and a symbol for the Earth Mother among the Hopi Indians of Arizona. Mazes are divided into two main sorts: those like Amenemhet's that are designed architecturally to baffle and confuse, and those that take a winding spiral shape back and forth. What each has in common is a convoluted journey to the heart of the maze, and then a return after achieving this goal.

Cretan labyrinth

The legend of Theseus and the Minotaur at Knossos in Crete enshrines the story. At the centre of the maze lived the fearsome Minotaur, half man, half bull, to whom the Athenians were bound to send for sacrifice seven young boys and seven maidens every nine years. The architect of the maze, Daedalus, had designed it with so many ingenious twists and turns and false exits that the victims, sent in one by one, invariably lost their way and were slaughtered by the Minotaur. Theseus, a young Athenian hero, offered himself as one of the fourteen, and on arrival in Crete fell in love with Ariadne, daughter of the King of Crete. On the advice of Daedalus, she gave him a thread with which he could re-trace his steps. He slew the Minotaur, and having accomplished this feat, led the rest of the group safely to the mouth of the labyrinth.

Whether or not a man-made Cretan labyrinth of this description ever existed is open to doubt. Its location has not been found, and although various Classical authors, including Pliny, assumed that its architecture was a copy of Amenemhet's, the first visual representation of the labyrinth on Cretan coins shows it as the second type of maze, with a clearly-defined spiral pathway to and from the centre. Symbolically, this is the most basic and most satisfying form, and how it emerged as the pattern for rituals in many places in the world. A famous Etruscan wine vase of about 600 BC (18 on map opposite) shows armed horsemen taking part in a warrior's ritual called the game of Troy. The word *Troya* is written backwards, as in a mirror, within the maze from which the horsemen seem to have emerged and is probably a cryptic reference to the defensive walls of the ancient city of Troy. In Britain, many similar mazes are known as *troys*, or are located at places called Troy; even today, elaborate processions and dances take place on some of them, a reminder of more regular occasions in the past. The early Christian Church

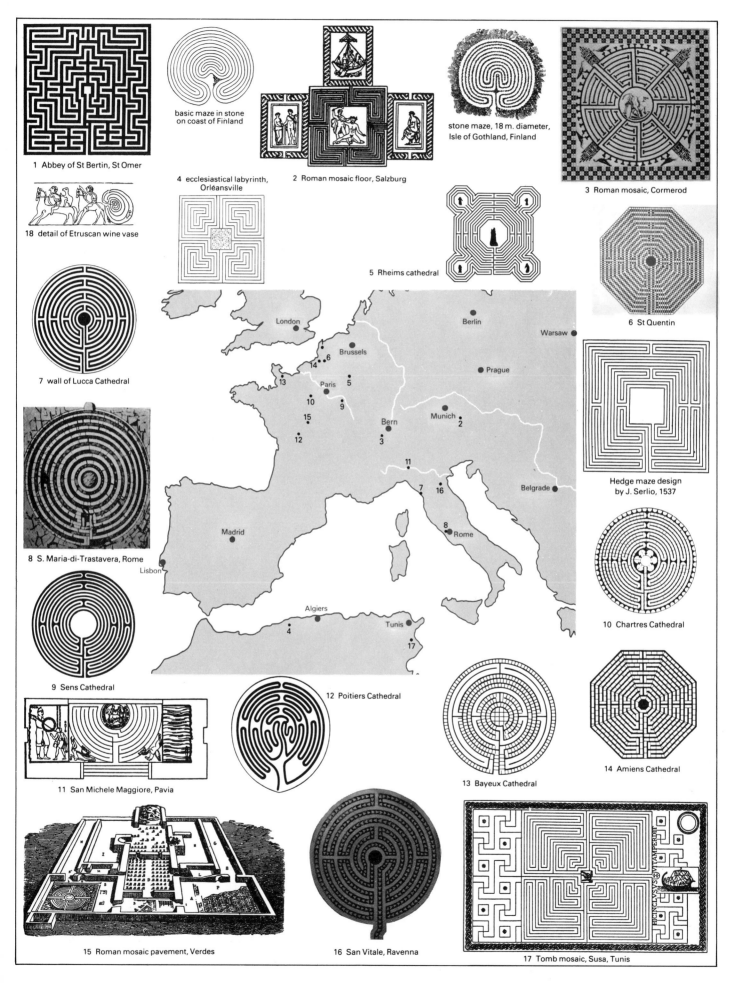

1 Abbey of St Bertin, St Omer

basic maze in stone
on coast of Finland

stone maze, 18 m. diameter,
Isle of Gothland, Finland

4 ecclesiastical labyrinth,
Orléansville

2 Roman mosaic floor, Salzburg

3 Roman mosaic, Cormerod

18 detail of Etruscan wine vase

5 Rheims cathedral

6 St Quentin

7 wall of Lucca Cathedral

Hedge maze design
by J. Serlio, 1537

London

Berlin

Warsaw

Brussels

Prague

Paris

Bern

Munich

Belgrade

Madrid

Rome

Lisbon

Algiers

Tunis

8 S. Maria-di-Trastavera, Rome

9 Sens Cathedral

10 Chartres Cathedral

11 San Michele Maggiore, Pavia

12 Poitiers Cathedral

13 Bayeux Cathedral

14 Amiens Cathedral

15 Roman mosaic pavement, Verdes

16 San Vitale, Ravenna

17 Tomb mosaic, Susa, Tunis

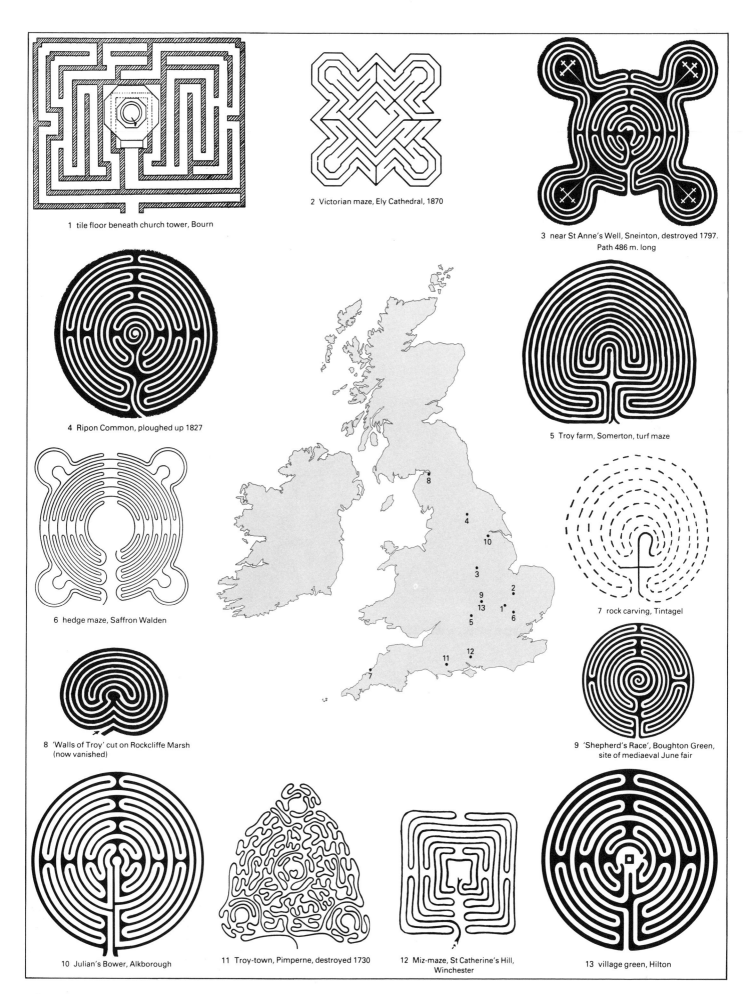

1 tile floor beneath church tower, Bourn

2 Victorian maze, Ely Cathedral, 1870

3 near St Anne's Well, Sneinton, destroyed 1797.
Path 486 m. long

4 Ripon Common, ploughed up 1827

5 Troy farm, Somerton, turf maze

6 hedge maze, Saffron Walden

7 rock carving, Tintagel

8 'Walls of Troy' cut on Rockcliffe Marsh
(now vanished)

9 'Shepherd's Race', Boughton Green,
site of mediaeval June fair

10 Julian's Bower, Alkborough

11 Troy-town, Pimperne, destroyed 1730

12 Miz-maze, St Catherine's Hill,
Winchester

13 village green, Hilton

enthusiastically took up the basic maze pattern. To begin with, it was a symbol of the Church itself, for instance as carved on the stonework of Lucca cathedral, or embroidered in the vestments of deceased bishops who were thus depicted as lying in the bosom of the Church. Then, when the Crusader period was drawing to a close and an actual pilgrimage to Jerusalem became impractical, faithful Christians would tread a maze as penance for not making the dangerous journey. The centre of the maze was known as *ciel* (sky) or Jerusalem, and a link with the pagan past was often maintained by the depiction there of a centaur or Minotaur; a metal plate with such an engraving was at the heart of the celebrated maze in the Chartres cathedral right up to the Napoleonic Wars, when it was taken to be melted down for cannon. By this time, church mazes were being used as a means of penance for sins of omission and commission in general, according to Edward Trollope, Archdeacon of Stow, writing in the *Archaeological Journal* in 1858. The penitents were 'ordered to follow out all the sinuous courses of these labyrinths upon their hands and knees, to repeat so many prayers at fixed stations, and others when they reached the central *ciel*, which in several cases took a whole hour to effect.'

Early mazes

Although all such rituals and dances are thousands of years removed from the beginnings of mazes, many writers feel that it is possible to speculate on what they originally meant by trying to find some common element fundamental to all mazes. The first of these may be that the path to the centre of a maze is never straight, nor easy. Even in a maze without false exits, you can find your way to the centre and out again only by treading every part of it. It is a reasonable guess that the earliest, naturally-formed mazes were the caves used by Cro-Magnon Man as long ago as 30,000 BC; in the depths of those, in claustrophobically tiny spaces, some of the most marvellous and perhaps most sacred cave paintings were executed (page 41) – a journey to the furthest point and out again. Caves too, at a later date, may have provided the origin of the Cretan labyrinth, for the underground rock faults and quarries in several places on the island make formidable natural mazes. Many 19th-century travellers took this view, including one who, having led a party down the caverns, using a piece of string like Theseus, wrote that the 'apparently endless number of galleries impressed me with a sense of horror and fascination I cannot describe. At every ten steps one was arrested, and had to turn to right or left,

sometimes to choose one of three or four roads. What if one should lose the clue!'

The next common element is the idea of a spiral, and especially a spiral with seven turns, playing a significant part in the attempt by early priesthoods to make use of certain earth energies, now mostly forgotten. Megalithic sites are said by dowsers to be placed over the crossing of labyrinthine underground streams, in order to amplify a force that emerges from the ground in a seven-coil spiral (page 97). The majority of carved patterns on megaliths are either spirals, or the so-called cup-and-ring markings that show up on the face of stones as a series of concentric rings interrupted by a snake-like course to the centre – conceivably the design of a primitive maze.

Three-dimensional spirals

A twin seven-coil spiral, drawn in three dimensions, forms the pattern of a basic maze. Geoffrey Russell, a retired businessman living in Ireland, believes he has discovered this on the undulating mounds that meander around Glastonbury Tor, one of the most important early Christian sites in southern Britain, and certainly a sacred pagan place for many centuries before the legendary arrival there of St Joseph of Arimathea bearing the Holy Grail (page 228). Backed by a Royal Air Force photographic survey, he can trace a twisting, seven-circuit path along which he imagines pilgrims and initiates trod, the way that some children in Europe today still play a game called 'Heaven and Hell', in which the object is to take a precisely-defined route, without short cuts, from the start (Hell) to the finish (Heaven).

Glastonbury Tor, an enigmatic sacred landmark, its rearing volcanic shape surrounded by man-made serpentine paths.

The basic maze

rock carving, Tintagel

coin design, Knossos

sacred symbol, Hopi Indians

Halebid temple, Mysore, India

Manas-Chakra, Rajasthan, India

Nazca, Peru

Isle of Weir, Finland

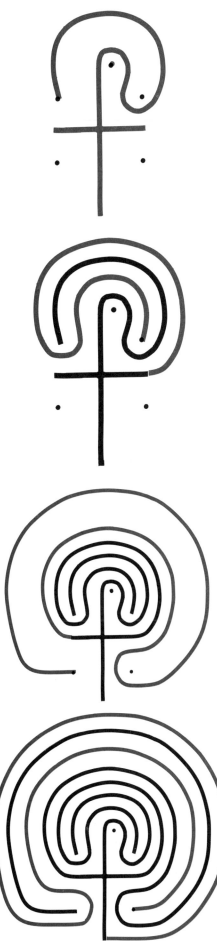

As if to confirm that man's universal fascination with a maze stems from a deeply mystical source, Geoffrey Russell's own interest in the subject came in 1944 as a result of dreaming so vividly of a pattern then unknown to him that he felt compelled, on waking, to draw its outline and keep it safely among his private papers. Not until 18 years later, casually looking at a magazine which had photographs of a newly-discovered rock carving at Tintagel in Cornwall (outline above left), and noting its similarity to a coin from Knossos in Crete, did he realize what he had drawn – a perfect basic maze. Since then he has found the pattern occurring in many countries; and everywhere, as the writer Jill Purce puts it in *The Mystic Spiral*, 'the labyrinth both creates and protects the centre, and allows entry only on the correct terms.'

Patterns of life

Patricia Villiers-Stuart, a geometrician and numerologist who has shown how the basic maze shape is usually created (left), has written that 'The Mexican Indians drawing mazes hold them to be an expression of the universal plan of creation, and they may well be very right. The geometry on which this form of maze is based implies a concept of number and space with which we seem to have lost touch. To explain the workings of this number geometry in its simplest terms would be to say that it is a way of integrating the seventh and eighth divisions of a circle upon squares. This entails a rhythmical approach to number and shape that can be applied at one extreme to atomic structure and at the other to the stars.'

In human terms, though, it is the concept of movement within the maze that is the important thing. Geoffrey Ashe wrote in *The Ancient Wisdom*: 'One plausible conjecture is that the rites enacted in the maze shrines had been enacted before, in simpler societies, by dancers circling round an image or tomb. Mazes may well mark the track of forgotten companies filing along in sinuous imitation of serpent gods, or spiralling in and reversing out, first towards a symbolic death and then towards a new life.'

What is a dragon?

Since the beginning of recorded history, dragons have turned up everywhere: in the earliest accounts of civilization in Assyria and Babylon, in Old Testament Jewish history, in ancient texts of China and Japan, in the mythology of Greeks, Romans and early Christians, in the symbols of early America, in the myths of Africa and India. As with the flood, it is hard to find a society that has not included a dragon in its legendary history. It is remarkable, too, how many subjects in this Atlas are incomplete without a connection to the dragons of ancient lore. Dinosaurs (page 10), sea monsters (page 198) and unknown beasts (page 202) raise the question of prehistoric survival. Venus theorists (page 26), meteor spotters (page 182) and UFOlogists (page 188) have all used dragons as evidence for their beliefs. The concept of earth energies believed in by ley-hunters (page 74), Chinese geomancers (page 99) and maze-walkers (page 152) is impossible to understand without knowing something of the dragon symbolism attached. Truly, the dragon is a versatile beast.

So perhaps the first question is whether it has a basis in physical reality. Most text-books say no – it is a fabulous creature that did not appear in art or literature until about 3000 BC, and is thus the product of relatively advanced civilizations. J. E. Cirlot in *A Dictionary of Symbols*, for instance, says it is 'a kind of amalgam of elements taken from various animals that are particularly aggressive and dangerous, such as serpents, crocodiles, lions as well as prehistoric animals . . . The dragon, in consequence, stands for "things animal" *par excellence*, and we have a first glimpse of its symbolic meaning, related to the Sumerian concept of the animal as the "adversary", a concept which later came to be attached to the devil.'

Real dragons?

However, this certainly doesn't apply to all dragons, notably the Chinese sort who were famed for their kindly deeds. The idea of an amalgam of fierce beasts also seems somewhat unfair. Compared with other fabulous hybrids such as centaurs or griffins, many dragons conform nicely to the laws of anatomy, if you

discount as exaggerations the way that some of them breathe fire, consume elephants, and wing their way from hill top to hill top. There is a startling resemblance between certain kinds of dinosaurs and certain dragons, and it is not totally impossible that up to a few thousand years BC, with at least 90 per cent of the Earth's surface uninhabited by man, a few of these creatures were living millions of years beyond their time.

Aristotle, Pliny, and other Classical writers insisted that dragons were based on observation of nature rather than imagination, and if so the best candidates are lizards. A number of species of small Indo-Malayan lizards, which swoop in the air on webbed wings, look so like dragons that they have been given the generic name *Draco*. The armoured lizard *Moloch horridus* strongly suggests some of the dragons pictured with spiky scales. The Indonesian lizard *Varanus komodoenis*, known locally as a dragon, can grow to more than three metres in length, and one of its extinct Australian cousins was more than twice that. Fervent believers in the reality of the dragon such as Charles Gould, who has written the definitive book about it, go so far as to construct an entire lost species of lizard, 'hibernating and carnivorous, with the power of constricting its snake-like body and tail', having *Draco*-like wings, mobility on its hind legs in emergency, and protected by armour and spikes. 'Probably it preferred sandy open country to forest land; its habitat was the highlands of Central Asia; and the time of its disappearance about that of the Biblical deluge.'

Unlikely though it is that a single species could have given rise to the multiplicity of dragon

(left) **Medieval dragon as generally depicted in Christian iconography.**

Flying lizards found in India and southeast Asia are so dragon-like that they have been given the zoological name *Draco*.

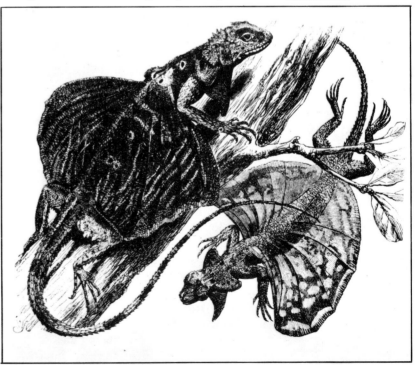

Chinese New Year card, the dragon and procession noisily warding off evil spirits.

with supposedly incalculable consequences for life on Earth.

According to this interpretation, the fire-breathing dragon originated in a fearsome celestial event or events, imprinted on humanity's unconscious. Many UFOlogists, for instance, say the event was an extra-terrestrial battle fought in the skies between warring spacecraft, as perhaps described in the Biblical *Apocalypse*: 'And there was war in Heaven: Michael and his angels fought against the dragon; and the dragon fought Michael and his angels, and prevailed not; neither was their place found any more in Heaven. And the great dragon was cast out, the old serpent, called the Devil, and Satan, which deceiveth the whole world; he was cast out into the Earth, and his angels were cast out with him.'

Comet dragons

More prosaically and more probably, natural events in the sky may have sparked off the dragon legend. Geoffrey of Monmouth's *History of the Kings of Britain* written in the 12th Century AD shows how readily an association with comets was made: 'There appeared a star of marvellous bigness, stretching forth on a ray whereon was a ball of fire, spreading forth in the likeness of a dragon, and from the mouth of the dragon issued forth two rays, whereof the one was of such length that it did seem to reach beyond the regions of Gaul, and the other toward the Irish Sea did end in seven lesser rays.' As late as 1892, when Swift's comet and Holmes' comet both appeared, they were described as 'flying serpents', and it is not surprising to find that Immanuel Velikovsky and his supporters, who believe that Venus once approached very close to Earth (page 26), relate this event to the origin of dragon-lore. Carter Sutherland imagined how the Venus/dragon might have looked: '. . . a writhing, bright elongated thing. It was irregular in outline; it was apparently on fire. This thing, the dragon, seemed to be driving off the terrible flaming globe and so to be benevolent as well as powerful.'

Although it is probably no more sensible to place the origin of the dragon within a single happening than within a single family of lizards, the Venus/comet interpretation at least comes to terms with one of the most puzzling of dragon characteristics – the way that it symbolizes so many different things, both good and bad, to different people. In the West, we are accustomed to thinking of the dragon as a symbol of evil, lying dead on the ground beneath one of the great dragon-killing saints; George of Cappadocia (and England), Margaret of Antioch, even Michael the Archangel. But this is a much over-simplified version of what a dragon meant

forms, there is still good reason to suppose that reptiles of one sort or another played their part in establishing the basic concept of the dragon; there is something so distinctively different about them, compared with mammals, as to make them peculiarly suitable as the basis for nightmarish awe or fear. Nevertheless the idea of them flying and breathing fire is, on the face of it, an odd development. Why should these specific attributes be attached to an earthbound lizard?

The answer probably lies in the veneration with which people in ancient times viewed the celestial bodies. Early man's preoccupation with the night-time sky is hard to imagine nowadays, especially in an urban society, but in those days, planets and stars were revered as deities that had an objective reality. Mars was not just a symbol for war, but a living God of War. Anything that interrupted the pre-ordained movement of the skies – a comet, an eclipse, the conjunction of two planets – was a moment of supreme importance

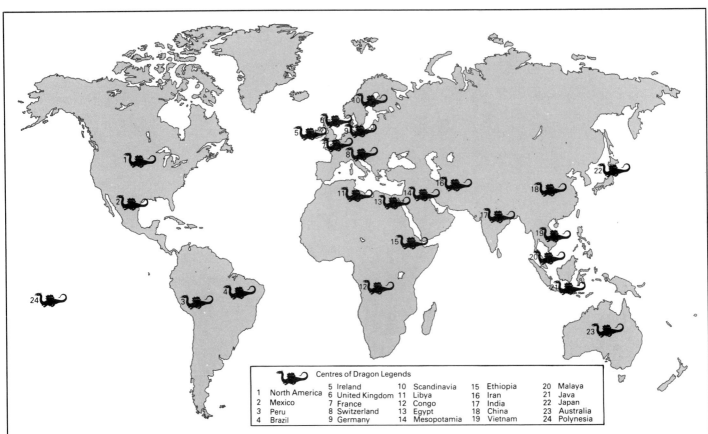

Centres of Dragon Legends

1 North America	5 Ireland	10 Scandinavia	15 Ethiopia	20 Malaya
2 Mexico	6 United Kingdom	11 Libya	16 Iran	21 Java
3 Peru	7 France	12 Congo	17 India	22 Japan
4 Brazil	8 Switzerland	13 Egypt	18 China	23 Australia
	9 Germany	14 Mesopotamia	19 Vietnam	24 Polynesia

1 Ohio earth mound, built in the form of a partly coiled serpent, 410 metres long. The body is 10 metres wide.

2 The god Quetzalcoatl was represented as a feathered snake; he was said to have taught man the arts of civilization and rode on a raft pulled by serpents.

3 A traveller describes 'a serpent of frightful magnitude and of the most deleterious nature. Some affirm it would swallow any beast whole.'

4 The serpent Liboya, 'the biggest of all serpents, some being 30 feet long and the thickness of a man in his middle.'

5 'The serpent is certainly a token or symbol of an ancient race celebrated for wisdom.' *Irish Druids and Legends*, James Bonwick.

6 Immortalized by Celts, e.g. 'While Cymr's dragon, from the Roman's hold, spread with calm wing o'er Carduel's domes of gold.'

7 Five winged dragons in the William Museum, Paris, described in the 18th Century as 'two legged with slender wings'.

8 In 1619, Prefect Scherer reported he had seen 'a fiery dragon' fly over a lake from out of a cave on Mount Pilatus.

9 The legend of Siegfried tells how he slew the dragon Fafnir and stole his gold. Siegfried ate the dragon's heart, but was doomed because the treasure was cursed.

10 In the legend of Hromind Greipson, the hero was let down into a cave by a rope to attack the dragon-king Thrain. In the struggle the dragon tripped on the bones of Hromind's dead horse, and Hromind then killed him.

11 'In Libya the serpents are very large. For some persons say as they sailed along the coasts they saw the bones of many oxen and it was evident to them that they had been devoured by serpents.' Aristotle, *History of Animals*, 4th Century BC.

12 The Harleian collection of travels, 1745, describes serpent-like beasts, and: 'certain other creatures which, being as big as rams, have wings like dragons and divers rows of teeth, feed upon raw flesh.'

13 'The story goes that with the spring the snakes come flying forth from Arabia towards Egypt and are met in the gorge by birds called ibises.' Arabian legend related by Herodotus, *c.* 450 BC.

14 In the 12th Century, Benjamin of Tudela described several dragons he had seen infesting the ruined palace of Nebuchadnezzar of Babylon.

15 The Roman writer Lucan addressed the Ethiopian dragon: 'You, also the dragon shining with golden brightness; you move the air on high and burst asunder great bulls.'

16 Iranian myths tell of dragon fights in primeval times. They usually have 'three heads, three jaws and six eyes'.

17 The dragon is: 'perpetually at war with the elephant, and it is itself of so enormous a size as to envelop the elephant within its folds, and encircle them in its coils.' Pliny, *Natural History*, 1st Century BC.

18 'The chief dragon has its abode in the sky, all clouds and vapours, winds and rains are under his control. All vegetable life is dependent on him.'

19 In 1965 Bezacier's *Arts Asiatique* described the Vietnamese *long-ma* as having a horn. The Vietnamese believed the dragon and the fish had a common origin, but different destinies.

20 In November 1880 the *Straits Times* reported a woman as having been attacked by a monstrous snake in Campong Batta. After a vicious battle, her husband killed the creature and exhibited its skin.

21 In *Voyage to the East Indies* (1708) Francis Leugat described a serpent 'at least fifty feet long'.

22 Screens decorating the Chi-on-in Monastery in Kiolo are decorated with many composite creatures, half-dragon and half-bird.

23 'It was conspicuous for its size, and especially for its great girth, swiftness and disgusting odour.' Giant serpent seen in 1860s by the traveller G. R. Moffat.

24 According to Polynesian legend, the serpent was the source of all wisdom: the coconut plant first appeared from an 'eel' which had magical qualities.

The legend of St George has inspired illustrators and painters for centuries. (above) from *The Dragon* by Charles Gould (below) Uccello's painting in the National Gallery, London.

in the rest of the world (indeed, the world over, in pre-Christian times). As the 1974 *Encyclopaedia Britannica* puts it; 'Christianity confused the ancient benevolent and malevolent serpent in a common condemnation.'

In the East, the dragon is a much more complex creature. In literature and art from the earliest times, it is noted for its ability to change its features and form at will, and thus assume the appearance of other creatures. Its influence on the weather was supposed crucial, because it could produce catastrophic storms, droughts, or gentle rains. Thus it became the yang/yin dragon which the Chinese geomancer's art of *feng-shui* tried to balance (page 99), embodying both negative and positive energies, capable of both harmful and benign effects. So important was the dragon to Chinese life that it became an emblem of the Emperor's power. He sat on a dragon throne, slept on a dragon bed, wore dragon clothes, and had the sole right to keep a five-clawed dragon among his ornaments (his officials' dragons having only four).

In Chinese philosophy, the dragon and serpent represent 'the most profound and all-embracing cosmic significance', according to the Chinese philosopher Chuang-Tzŭ, and are symbols for 'rhythmic life'. Unlike Western dragons, they are never conquered or slain, for they were essential intermediaries between the Earth and the sky; male and female, they lived in springs, rivers, lakes, and seas and in the rain clouds. If the dragon was insulted, the legend goes, it would hide in the water on Earth and go to sleep there, causing a drought. To awaken it a great noise and commotion had to be made; thus the traditional Chinese New Year festivals in which a great mock dragon is carried down the streets, twisting from left to right like a snake or serpent.

Dragon-slaying

In the West too, in earlier times, there was an ambivalence about the nature of a dragon. True, almost all ancient mythologies contain legends that feature the slaying of a dragon: the Sumerian god Ninurta destroyed the monster Asag, the Babylonian god Marduk fought with the she-dragon Tiamat, Perseus rescued Andromeda from a sea-dragon, and so on. But in all these instances it is not just a simple question of a supreme combat to overcome evil, but also of an attempt to harness and control cosmic forces within the dragon that have somehow got out of hand.

In Greek and Roman lore, dragons were given the task of guarding temples, because of their sharp eyesight, their strength, their wisdom, and their talent for prophecy. This association of dragons with knowledge/treasure is also widespread elsewhere in pre-Christian Europe. Siegfried's encounter with the dragon Fafnir was to release a hoard of dwarf gold on which the dragon lay. Beowulf, who died of a mortal wound after killing a dragon, was buried with the dragon's treasure heaped around his funeral pyre. Above this a huge mound of earth was heaped, forming a barrow like those found on megalithic sites in southern Britain; many of these have similar legends of treasure, and even sometimes the name Dragon Hill. A number of writers have followed the British antiquarian John Michell in noting ancient dragon sites on which the early Christian missionaries placed churches dedicated to a dragon-killing saint (page 75). The comparison with the Chinese concept of a dragon having control over the essential life force is compelling; in mediaeval alchemy, when dragons fought, psychic disintegration set in. Ultimately, the dragon is much more than a symbol of evil; the good/bad dragon of ancient history represents the age-old struggle of mankind to preserve a cosmic harmony.

The Deluge

Of all the world's myths, that of a universal deluge must surely be the most persistent and widespread. The idea that a great flood destroyed almost all mankind, or at least a substantial part of it, can be found in virtually every country, and in compiling a list of 83 floods for the map (page 165) it was apparent that most of them closely conformed to the pattern summarized by Ignatius Donnelly in *Atlantis*:

(a) The founder of the race is warned of coming disaster.

(b) Others disregard the warning.

(c) There is a cosmic disturbance, followed by a flood.

(d) The founder escapes with his family, either on a ship or by climbing a high mountain.

(e) If on a ship, he sends out birds or animals to see if the flood has subsided.

(f) He eventually reaches dry land, usually a mountain, where he finds other survivors.

(g) To perpetuate the race requires desperate expedience.

The question is whether these myths tell of a single, cataclysmic, real event, or merely a series of local ones. Was there once a world-wide catastrophe, or is it simply that most places at some time have suffered a disastrous spell of weather? Since the victory by 19th-century scientists over the fundamentalist dogma of the Church, the second view has been the orthodox one – indeed, belief in the Flood is as much anathema to geologists as the idea of Adam and Eve to biologists. Dorothy B. Vitaliano's *Legends of the Earth – their geologic origins* provides perhaps the best contemporary argument: 'The universality of flood traditions can be explained very easily without requiring a widespread flood of cosmic or any other origin, if we bear in mind that floods, plural, are a universal geologic phenomenon.' She reviews possible causes of local floods, such as *tsunamis* (popularly known as tidal waves set off by earthquakes), and concludes: 'From the purely geologic point of view we should *expect* independent flood traditions to have arisen almost anywhere in the world at almost any time, engendered by flood catastrophes stemming from perfectly natural causes, and of all the possible causes of floods, only *tsunamis* are capable of giving rise to flood legends in widely separated places at the same time.'

Cosmic disturbance

Vitaliano says that the various points arise naturally and logically when analysing Donnelly's Deluge legends. On point (d), for instance, 'when we come right down to it, there are only two basic ways in which people can survive a flood: by getting above it, or by riding it out on some floating object.'

Victorian depiction of the Deluge, from an illustrated Bible of 1860.

However, this logical analysis fails to take into account perhaps the most important element in the flood myth: the cosmic disturbance of point (c). In nearly all the legends, some event totally exceptional and not in the least like a normal flood is supposed to have caused the disaster – an enormous climatic change that involved the sun changing, or even being replaced, as in the Buddhist mythology that says 'when now a long period elapsed from the cessation of the rains, a second sun appeared.' At the same time a whole world order changed, all that had gone before having been destroyed and life having started again.

But if such a cosmic catastrophe really took place, what could its nature be? For Christian fundamentalists, who have by no means given up the struggle against scientific rationalism, the answer is straightforward: it was a deluge sent by God, exactly as described in the Bible. Their attitude is no different from the first 19th-century missionaries who were so delighted to find identical flood legends among primitive peoples to explain mountains of fossils: 'As proof that the deluge once overflowed the whole earth, they say that many shells, and relics of fishes, have been found far within the land where men could never have lived, yea that bones of whales have been found upon a high mountain.' Before the Flood, say the fundamentalists, dinosaurs, mammoths and men were all contemporary; the various strata of fossils, which orthodox geology teaches as being tens of millions of years apart, were laid down when the Flood subsided, the heavier animals (dinosaurs) sinking into the mud

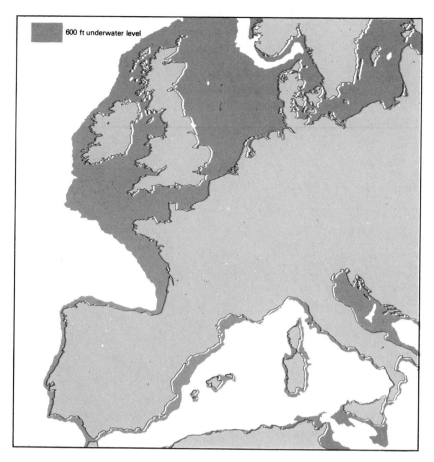

600 ft underwater level

Some theories say the Deluge myth arose because of a rapid rise in ocean levels around 10,000 BC, drastically altering the outline of continents.

first and forming the 'earlier' strata, followed in order of size by mammoths and human beings, which settled in 'later' strata.

This kind of argument is completely outside normal scientific analysis. If anybody points out that on meteorological grounds alone, it would be impossible to produce such a large quantity of water from the clouds, and equally impossible for it all to evaporate again, the response is that with Heavenly intervention all things are possible. So a rationalist has to look elsewhere for his catastrophic cause of the great flood; and easily the best bet is the ending of the most recent Ice Age around 10,000 BC.

Ice-age decimation

Nobody knows what triggered off the melting of the ice – as Cesare Emiliani, the eminent oceanographer and geologist, put it: 'Question: did the ice melt by surging under its own weight (mechanical collapse), and *therefore* temperature rose, or did temperature rise and *therefore* ice melted? If the latter, what produced the extremely rapid temperature rise?' Supporters of Velikovsky (page 26) argue that it must have been a catastrophe associated with the violent planetary changes that his model of the universe demands. Using as evidence a complex blend of myth and astrophysics, they suggest Saturn underwent a cosmic explosion that caused drastic changes in the weather and an upset of the Earth's orbit; Saturn may actually have provided

the waters of the Deluge itself, since it is known to be composed mainly of water.

Certainly something unusual happened (page 52). Mammals over three-fifths of the Earth's land surface were decimated; as many as 40 million died in North America alone, described vividly by Professor Frank C. Hibben in *The Lost Americans*: 'This is no ordinary extinction of a vague geological period which fizzled to an uncertain end. This death was catastrophic and all-inclusive . . . of such colossal proportions as to be staggering to contemplate.' In Alaska, it looks as though 'the whole world of living animals and plants was suddenly frozen in mid-motion in a grim charade.' In the Yukon valley 'the evidences of violence are as obvious as in the horror camps of Germany. Such piles of bodies of animals or men simply do not occur by any ordinary natural means.'

Indian legend

Chaotic circumstances like these, preceding the melting of the ice caps, fit perfectly into many flood legends, and it is perhaps highly significant that the Chippewa Indians from Ontario, whose ancestors experienced these events, have a legend that precisely attributes the flood to the melting of the snow. 'In the beginning of time, in the month of September, there was a great snow. A little mouse nibbled a hole in the leather bag which contained the sun's heat, and the heat poured out over the earth and melted all the snow in an instant. The meltwater rose to the tops of the highest pines and kept on rising until even the highest mountains were submerged.'

A connection between the ending of the Ice Age and the origin of the Flood has always been rejected by scientists in the past because, as Dorothy Vitaliano wrote: 'Not only are those changes far too slow to have provoked traditions of catastrophe, but in any case they fell far short of being the kind of deep flood envisioned in most of the traditions.' However, in 1975 there was a striking piece of research that seems to show she is wrong, and that the catastrophe perhaps caused by the mythical 'dying sun'/Saturn had a much faster effect on sea levels than had been thought. Cesare Emiliani described how analysis of deep-sea cores from the Gulf of Mexico showed a rapid rise about 9600 BC, the annual rate being some tens of metres. It must, he said 'have caused widespread flooding of low-lying areas many of which were inhabited by man . . . It was apparently a surge, which brought ice to lower latitudes and caused rapid melting . . . We submit that this event, in spite of its great antiquity in cultural terms, could be an explanation for the deluge stories common to many Eurasian, Australasian and American traditions.'

World Deluge myths

1 Angry with the giants, God flooded the world to destroy them, but commanded a man to build a large canoe. The man survived and, floating on the flood-waters, he threw an otter overboard. The otter returned with a clod of earth from which the man created a new world by floating it on the waters and blowing on it.

2 Originally the Sun was much larger in the sky than it is now and the Earth benefited from a warmer, more even climate. This 'golden age' was ended by a terrible flood which destroyed all life except for the hero Montezuma and the coyote that had warned him of the coming deluge. They built boats to survive the Flood, and afterwards helped the Great Spirit to restock the world with men and animals.

3 After the world had existed for 1716 years the Flood came: 'all mankind was lost and drowned, and found themselves changed to fish. In a single day all was lost.' Only Nata and his wife Nana were saved, having been warned by the god Titlacahuan to make a boat from a cypress tree.

4 Once the Sun and Moon turned red, yellow and blue, a rumbling was heard above and below the ground and wild beasts mingled freely with men. A month later there was a roar and the Earth was plunged into darkness and a downpour of heavy rain. The waters rose and destroyed everybody except for Uassu and his wife, whose descendants repopulated the world.

5 A man called Yaya killed his son Yayael ('Earth') and put his body in the skin of a calabash fruit. One day Yaya went to see his son's bones but found they had changed into a multitude of fishes. The four sons of Itaba-Yanuba tried to steal the fish and eat them, but were caught in the act by Yaya and dropped the calabash. It broke, and the contents flooded the world, forming the sea and its fishes.

6 The *Younger Norse Edda* tells how Odin, Wili and We, sons of Bor, slew the giant Ymir, father of the ice-giants. So much blood flowed from Ymir's wounds that all the race of giants were drowned, except for Bergelmir, who saved himself and his wife in a boat and fathered a new race of giants.

7 'A long time ago men fought a terrible war. Efé [a Pygmy hero] escaped by climbing a tree which had a big hole in the trunk. He hid in the hole while the battle raged on earth and in heaven. Then our chameleon man, our angel and saviour, came with his axe and cut the trunk of the tree. The flood gushed out of the trunk, turned into a mighty river and went all over the world. Efé came out with the flood but the water did not wet him. Efé thought he would be lonely, since he was the last man on earth. Then he met a beautiful woman . . . All men are their children.'

8 The hero Yima was warned by Ahuramazda (God) that the world was about to be destroyed by water. He was ordered to construct an enclosure and to store in it the seed of animals, plants and men. When the Flood came everything was annihilated except for Yima's garden, from which the world was restocked.

9 The hero Manu came across a tiny fish in his washing-water which announced that it would save him from a 'purification of the worlds' about to occur. Manu reared the fish, first in a jar, then in a pond, until it was fully grown. He then released it into the Ganges, and the fish rewarded Manu for his kindness by instructing him to prepare a ship and stores. When the Flood came everyone was destroyed except Manu and the seven Rishis he had taken with him. For many years the fish guided their boat until they reached a mountain-top, where it revealed itself as Prajapati Brahman, the supreme God. With his help Manu recreated all living beings.

10 There was once a great deluge from which only two people were saved – Pawpaw Nan-choung and his sister Chang-hko. They escaped in a large boat with nine cocks and nine needles, which they daily threw into the water to see if they were subsiding. On the ninth day the last cock crew and the last needle was heard to strike a rock. They took refuge in a cave with two elves, and Chang-hko eventually bore a child. The female elf, a witch, tore it to pieces at a nine-fold crossroads and curried parts of it. The unfortunate Chang-hko ate the curry, discovered the crime and invoked the Great Spirit to avenge her – he named her the mother of all nations and caused the races of the world to spring up from the nine roads.

11 Once all the waters of the world were swallowed by a gigantic frog, and all other animals deprived of drink. They decided the best way to release the waters was to make the frog laugh, but the ridiculous contortions of an eel made the frog laugh so much that the whole world was flooded. Many people were drowned, and mankind would have been completely destroyed had not the pelican gone about in his canoe picking up survivors.

12 Mankind once became so disrespectful of the great god Tane who had created them that there were only two prophets left who preached the truth. Insulted by men, they built a house on a large raft, stocked it with food and dogs, and brought down heavy rains by incantations to demonstrate the power of Tane. The waters rose and the prophets embarked with a few others. After six months the Flood began to subside and they settled on dry land, to discover that the whole world and its inhabitants had been destroyed.

Noah's ark

Noah the shipwright as depicted in the Nuremberg Chronicles of 1493.

As elsewhere in the world, the legend of a catastrophic deluge is powerfully enshrined in Near Eastern literature of ancient times. A cuneiform text called *The Epic of Gilgamesh*, transcribed in the Seventh Century BC, tells of a flood long ago that is identical except for detail with the Hebrew flood legend of Noah (in the Sumerian version, the preceding rains lasted only seven days and nights, compared with the

15th-century stained glass window of Noah by Hans Acker in Ulm Cathedral.

Biblical 40). The questions are: whether a flood of this size ever took place in the area, whether a Noah (or Utnapishtim) actually floated an ark, and whether this gave rise to the world-wide deluge mythology.

Disappointingly for fundamentalists who wish to prove every word of the Old Testament true, and archaeologists who wish to show that all flood legends have their origin in a local calamity, the probable answer is a triple no. On the first question, archaeologists have tried unavailingly since the 19th Century to establish, by excavation, that a stratum of flood-water deposit exists at key sites. Their search has been punctuated by false success. In 1928/1929, great excitement was raised by Sir Leonard Woolley's discovery of a layer of clay at the city of Ur. In parts, it was 3.7 metres thick, and he concluded: 'So vast a mass of silt laid at one time could only be the result of a very great flood.' It was dated at around 3500 BC.

No evidence of a similar flood has been found nearby, and Woolley himself admitted that there were many survivors of the flood, and that Ur, although suffering damage, survived – hardly a model for the annihilation suggested by the story of Noah. Later scholars, such as Sir Max Mallowan, formerly Director of the British School of Archaeology in Iraq, have suggested flood deposits at Kish as the historical prototype. But the same objections apply. At Kish the floods damaged some walls but left others intact, and civilization continued almost without a break. The street walls, he says, were 'sufficiently strong to protect the houses, wherein traces of flood debris were on that account less obtrusive, and moreover in several places the debris was presumed to have been cleared away by the occupants.' To use his own words, the flood was 'not altogether of Biblical dimensions'.

Local floods

Archaeological investigation of Mesopotamian cities has so far drawn a complete blank so far as the origin of the Babylonian and Hebrew deluge myths is concerned. Floods there were (and still are) in plenty. A 22nd-century BC prayer of Gudea of Lagash speaks of 'waters pouring out . . . destroying cities like the flood wave'. Two hundred years later a tablet records a deluge in Ur 'which obliterated the bounds of heaven and earth'. The climate today is little different, and Mallowan writes of Babylon itself that 'it is easy to imagine the streets of the city awash with the waters of the Euphrates during the spring festival.' So frequently did floods happen that you have a clear impression of a society that had come to terms with them, rather than regarding them as

something so special that they gave survivors the impression that they were the only beings left on earth.

Mount Ararat

This lack of archaeological evidence makes it all the less likely that Noah's ark (a) ever existed, or (b) that bits of it are still around. However, the unlikelihood has not deterred numerous expeditions, many of which have claimed success. Mount Ararat, the biblically named site, has been the goal (although the Babylonian legend sites it at Mount Nisir). Its unstable, snow-covered, boulder-strewn slopes make it a difficult climb, and at the summit of 5165 metres, oxygen starvation is a reality. However, Chaldean priests of the 5th Century BC are supposed to have climbed the mountain and scraped bituminous coating from the wood of the ark. It remained unclimbed afterwards until AD 1829, when the Russian Frederic Parrot reached the summit. He thought the large, smooth top was wide enough to have been used as a haven for the Ark.

Souvenir hunting started in 1876 when Lord Bryce brought back a piece of shaped wood found at 3900 metres; in 1893 the 'ark' was seen by the Nestorian Archbishop Nourri, who reported that it was 'made of dark-red beams of very thick wood'; in 1916 it was definitely seen on the edge of a frozen lake by a Russian aviator; an American oil worker said in 1953 he had taken six large, clear photographs (they disappeared after his death in 1962); the French industrialist Fernand Navarra came back with a spar of wood in 1955, and successfully guided another expedition to the site in 1969 when further wood samples, carbon-dated to 3000 BC, were found.

But were they from the ark? Was there ever an ark? Or are the pieces of wood from Mount Ararat remains of a ritual vessel or building commemorating the supposed landing-place of the ark? The archaeological excavations have not altered the view that the Universal Deluge happened long before civilizations were advanced enough to leave contemporary records. As John Bright, one of the leading Biblical scholars in the United States, put it in the *Bulletin* of the American School of Archaeology: 'We must regard it as a catastrophe taking place far back in the Stone Age.'

Mount Ararat, traditional but uncertain location for Noah's landing place; other mountains further north have also been suggested.

While most people reject the Bible story of Noah's Flood simply because 'all those animals couldn't have fitted into the Ark' some Biblical fundamentalists and 'arkaeologists' claim that calculations based on the figures given in the Bible demonstrate its feasibility. The fundamentalist magazine *Plain Truth* claims that 'Criticisms of the Bible usually flourish in the rich soil of misconception. Traditional images and popular literature picture the Ark scarcely larger than an ordinary fishing smack – sitting helpless before the slightest squall.'

They are certainly right in saying that the ark described in the Bible was a massive vessel by any standards. It was supposed to be 300 cubits long, 50 broad and 30 high. Even the smaller estimates of the cubit would put these figures at 450, 75 and 45 feet, the dimensions of a vessel of some 1.5 million cubic feet, displacing 43,000 tons, while the larger estimates put this last figure at 66,000 tons. The ark of Babylonian myth was even larger – it had seven storeys to Noah's three and would have displaced a staggering 228,000 tons. Even allowing that ancient navigational achievements were more advanced than is usually thought (page 113), it seems unlikely that a vessel of these dimensions could have been constructed in prehistoric times.

Passing over the problem of *how* Noah could have built it, the fundamentalists explain that Noah took on board two specimens of each 'kind' (species) of 'unclean' animal and seven of 'clean' animals, all creatures that had 'the breath of life in their nostrils'. Seventy per cent of land animals are insects, and allowing 16 cubic inches for a pair of every known modern species some 63,000 cubic feet of storage space would be required. Remaining land animals – mammals, birds and reptiles – are on average the size of a rhesus monkey, which can be safely kept in a cage of about 15 cubic feet. Estimates of the number of known species are around 18,000. Allowing for the fact that 'clean' animals (which are few) went in in sevens, perhaps there were 40,000 animals apart from insects, needing around 600,000 cubic feet.

So – if one chooses to believe the Biblical figures – the total amount of space required would have been around 663,000 cubic feet, only 45 per cent of the ark on low estimates for the cubit and just over 20 per cent on the larger estimates. As the fundamentalists would have it: '... the final question. What did Noah ever do with all that room?'

Old Testament truths

Exodus of the Israelites from Egypt, the most significant event in their history, was recognized as such by 19th-century Biblical scholars.

The grand sweep of the Old Testament is the finest record of ancient history existing in the world today, the most readable and the most secure in its description of long-buried events. The mythological beginning – the Creation, the Flood, the longevity of Noah's offspring – takes up only the first eleven chapters of Genesis; from then on, beginning with Abraham around 1900 BC, it consists of a superbly detailed account of Near Eastern history as seen through the pulsating fortunes of the Hebrews. There have been wildly varying estimates of when the version we read now was transcribed, current opinion putting it at around 500 BC. But however much allowance is made for errors and exaggerations in this transcription, and bias in putting the Israelite point of view, it remains a marvellous flesh-and-blood history, the only fully extant continuous account of the period that we have.

Compared with it, the records from Egypt and Babylon are fragmented and ambiguous. The main Egyptian source is a lost work written in the 3rd Century BC by an historian named Manetho. All that exists are summaries by later writers, and king-lists made dubious by the fact (noted in our commentary on the dating of Atlantis, page 133, and the origin of races, page 44) that he was probably in competition with the contemporary Babylonian historian Berossus to exaggerate the antiquity of their respective

nations. For the reign of each king there are hieroglyphic texts describing the famous victories and glorious events that occurred; the problem is to put the bewildering number of Pharaohs into the right order.

Given the disparity in the quality of evidence, it may seem puzzling that archaeologists, as a whole, have consistently denigrated the source material offered by the Bible. A 1977 BBC-TV series, *BC: The Archaeology of the Bible Lands*, whose presenter Magnus Magnusson faithfully represented orthodox archaeological opinion, down-graded some of the most spectacular Biblical events simply because, from the accepted chronology of the Pharaohs, there appears to be no mention of them in Egyptian records.

If this chronology is wrong – and an increasing number of people think it is – not only will huge chunks of text-books have to be re-written and the majority of Egyptian antiquities in museums re-ordered and re-labelled, but the Bible itself will be viewed in a profoundly different way. 'The Bible as history', in the words of the best-selling title, should read the Bible *is* history. The furthest that such books can go at the moment is to show that most of the places mentioned in the Bible existed in reality – there was a well at Gideon, there were walls round Jericho, and so on – but they add regretfully that the events described in the Bible probably didn't

happen there. All this would be changed if the revised chronology (or something close to it) charted on the next page turns out to be correct. The Bible would take on a new dimension and become the essential source of material.

Dating dogma

Before going into some solid evidence why this may be the case, it is important to analyse why archaeology has allied itself with the opposite camp, and is so reluctant to shift. As with so many other scientific disciplines, the orthodox attitude stemmed originally from the battle in the 19th Century between the Church and rationalism, convincingly won by the latter with the publication of Darwin's *Origin of Species*. The creation versus evolution and geology versus deluge arguments also seemed to have been settled for ever; and because the first eleven chapters of Genesis were historically discredited, doubt spilled over all the rest of the Old Testament.

Meanwhile, Egyptian hieroglyphics were at last deciphered, and scholars set upon the muddled king-lists with glee. By the turn of the century a 'scientific' method of dating was devised by Eduard Mayer and James Henry Breasted, based on a complex interpretation of supposed references to the rising of the star Sirius at several crucial points in Egyptian history. The basis of their system was never confirmed, and their evidence from the papyri has been recently debunked *in toto*; but at the time it had immense scientific appeal as it relied on data provided by astronomers. Although originally adopted only as a temporary measure until properly confirmed, it became the unchallenged 'astronomical dating system' of Egypt, and subsequently the whole ancient Near East, including Palestine, followed suit.

Unorthodox challenge

Once a basic assumption gets into the text-books, academic *immobilisme* tends to set in, and until recently it has been literally unthinkable to question an Egyptian date. The life work of a great many scholars would be in doubt if the orthodox chronology were successfully challenged – a difficult enough feat if attempted from within the ranks of archaeologists, and near-impossible when the person to mount the challenge, in 1952, was Immanuel Velikovsky. Two years before, his book *Worlds in Collision* had been published amid an unprecedented furore and an unmerited barrage of criticism (page 26). When *Ages in Chaos* came out – a typically provocative title – threatening to undermine the entire basis of Near Eastern dating, the general archaeological reaction was to suppose (a) that he had been exposed by astronomers as a crank with impossible theories, and (b) his ideas on ancient history could therefore safely be ignored.

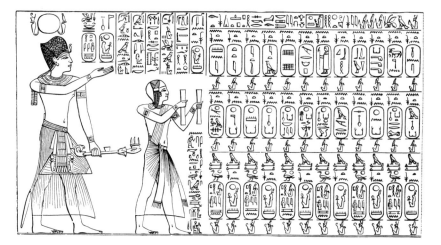

In fact it is probably his best argued book. He has always attracted a loyal band of supporters, and these are now on the increase. *Ages in Chaos* has been around for a quarter of a century, enough time for evaluation, and his major points seem well supported by recent evidence. Two episodes in particular are satisfyingly complete in his presentation, compared with the strained compromises and contradictions of the orthodox accounts: Exodus and its aftermath at Jericho; and the meeting between King Solomon and the Queen of Sheba.

Exodus to the Promised Land

The exodus of the Hebrew slaves from the bondage of Pharaoh is undoubtedly the seminal event in the history of the Jewish people. 'Let my people go,' Moses demanded – and the Pharaoh capitulated, allowing the 12 Tribes of Israel to 'borrow' clothes and jewellery, and to depart (according to the Bible) in huge numbers; the figure of 603,550 males of military age is so exact as to sound suspiciously like an exaggeration, but the general context of all that follows leaves no doubt that a large population of nomads wandered the desert for 40 years before reaching their Promised Land. Four complete books in the Bible cover the period: Exodus, Leviticus, Numbers and Deuteronomy. During that time Moses received the Laws, and the whole structure of Jewish culture was formulated. After a generation of wandering, the Israelites arrived in Canaan and conquered its key cities, including Jericho. The Bible is specific as to details: some cities were burnt, some spared with all their inhabitants, some captured and the inhabitants put to slaughter, others not captured at all. In the case of Jericho, the Israelites were helped by an earthquake.

Yet you look in vain in the conventional chronology for confirmation of this dramatic transfer of population and power. The date of Exodus is usually put during the reign of

One of the three primary Egyptian sources for the chronology of the Near East as taught in books today. The Table of Abydos shows King Seti I paying tribute to his predecessors. Unfortunately the list is incomplete (e.g. Tutankhamun and his immediate predecessors were deliberately omitted for political/religious reasons).

Chart comparing the conventional chronology, Velikovsky's revised version, and biblical history

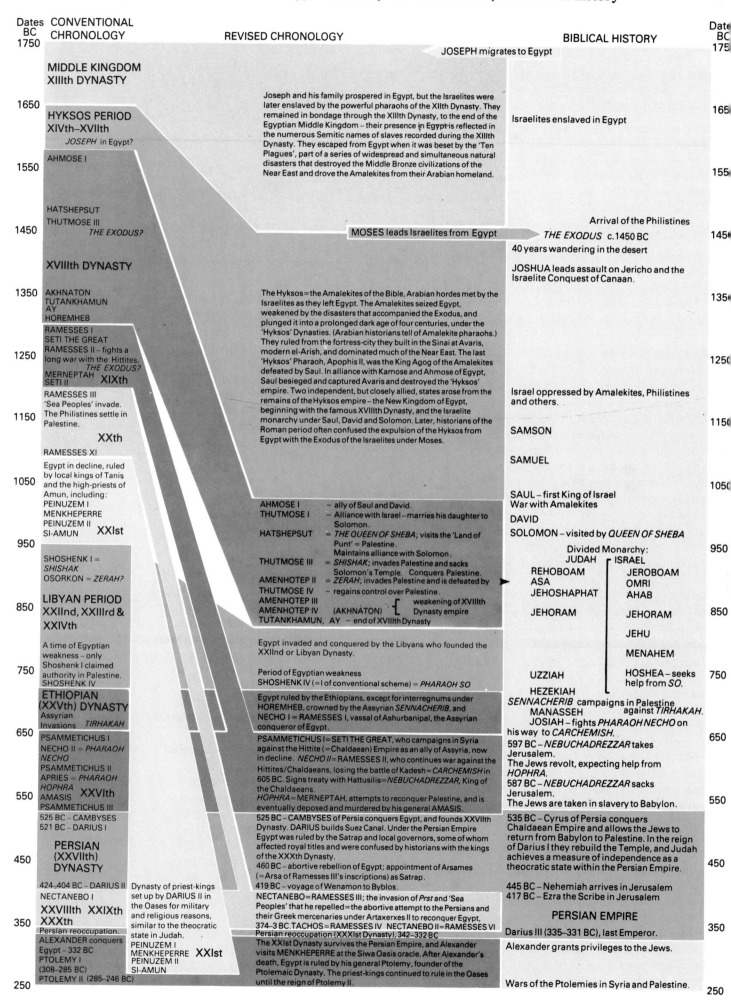

The text-book version of Egyptian history is based on the theory of 'Sothic dating' which claims that the Egyptians regulated their calendar by the rising of the star Sothis (Sirius). Once in every 1460 years this star rises with the Sun on the New Year's day of the ordinary solar calendar, the last but one occasion being in AD 139. A marginal jotting in a late Greek manuscript says that 1605 years had passed from 'Menophres' to the year AD 283. Since both of these calculations lead us back to 1321-2 BC, Egyptologists have assumed that a 'Sothic period' began at that date in the reign of a king called 'Menophres'. Identifying him with Ramesses I (also called Menpehtire) they fixed the beginning of the XIXth Dynasty at 1321 BC, using this 'firm astronomical basis' for dating the rest of the New Kingdom.

How sound is this 'Sothic dating system'? Regarding the Sirius-calendar it is based on, the Egyptologist H. E. Winlock pointed out in 1940 that: 'The ancient Egyptians, from the Old Kingdom to the Roman period have not left a single trace of such a fixed calendar . . .' Sir Alan Gardiner, probably the greatest Egyptologist this century, thought that 'Menophres' was not Ramesses I, but Seti I (Merneptah), and considered the link with a Sothic period as just a 'clever conjecture' that 'may or may not be right'. He declared in 1961: 'What is proudly advertised as Egyptian history is merely a collection of rags and tatters.'

Despite this, 'Sothic dating' still remains the basis for accepted Egyptian history. Velikovsky's dating system, by contrast, is based on 'synchronisms' (e.g. simultaneously recorded events and other links between chronologies) of which he found many between the histories of Egypt and Israel, but are conspicuously lacking in the conventional scheme.

For the period from the Middle Kingdom to the end of the XVIIIth Dynasty (c. 820 BC) his scheme is firmly based and has been supported by the work of numerous scholars of ancient Near Eastern history. However, while it seems that the dates of the later Dynasties must also be lowered considerably, Velikovsky's detailed model of this is disputed, and several alternative dating schemes for the XIXth Dynasty onwards have been suggested. For instance, it is doubtful that Velikovsky's identification of the XIXth Dynasty with the XXVIth is correct, and there is firm evidence that it should be dated to the 8th rather than the 7th Century BC. A speaker at a 1978 Congress on the subject in Glasgow, Scotland, summed up: 'The case for *a* revised chronology is conclusive; whether Velikovsky's is *the* revised chronology in every detail is less sure.'

Ramesses II (1290-1224 BC), a powerful and prosperous Pharaoh whom it is hard to imagine giving way to a rebel slave leader. In the hieroglyphic texts describing his rule, there is no mention of Moses, of the Plagues, of the Israelites fleeing or the Egyptians attempting to return them to Egypt, nor of the inevitable social upheavals that must have accompanied their departure. Alternatively, it is suggested the Exodus took place during the reign of his successor, Merneptah, in many ways an even more unlikely choice, since the stele commemorating his exploits tell of famous victories over the Israelites on their own territory – surely not the same Pharaoh who was defeated in the parting of the Red Sea trying to pursue the fleeing slaves.

Misinformed guides

The same improbability applies to the orthodox interpretation of the ruins of Jericho. Visitors there will be shown the great earthen banks with facings of plaster to make them especially hard to climb, with remains of walls on top. Archaeological evidence shows that before their

The route of the wandering Israelites in the years in the wilderness is uncertain; however there is no doubt they arrived in Canaan after the 40 years recounted in the Bible.

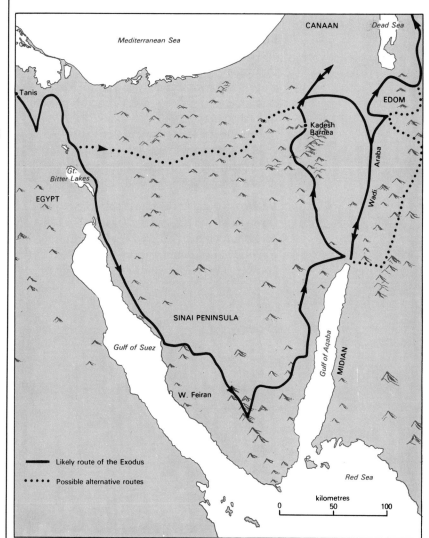

destruction there was an epidemic that caused high mortality among the inhabitants of Jericho, followed by an earthquake; scorching and ashes throughout the city prove, in the words of Dame Kathleen Kenyon who excavated the site during the 1950s, that 'the destruction of the walls was the work of enemies.'

This is precisely how Joshua's campaign is described in the Bible – a plague, an earthquake that broke down the city's walls, the inhabitants slaughtered and the whole city burned to the ground. *Yet visitors are also told that Joshua had nothing to do with the invasion.* The collapse of Jericho, it is said, happened at the end of the Middle Bronze Age, around 1550 BC, and Joshua did not arrive until the Late Bronze Age some 300 years later, when he found a city already abandoned and in ruins.

Degraded Israelites

In the conventional view, the Exodus and the conquest of Canaan is degraded to the activities of a few roving bands of labourers who haphazardly ended up in the Promised Land. Magnus Magnusson explained away the embarrassing lack of Egyptian records by saying that 'the Egyptian chroniclers were more interested in royal affairs than in social questions, and the activities of a small group of Semitic immigrants and their escape from the work-gangs would hardly engage their attention.' As for Jericho and the other conquests so nobly described in the Bible, they were either 'the result of a series of incursions by different groups at different times', or perhaps 'the occupation was not accomplished by military means at all, but by peaceful infiltration.'

Velikovsky will have none of this. Searching through ancient Egyptian literature, he came across a document called *The Admonitions of an Egyptian Sage*, commonly known as the Papyrus Ipuwer. This clearly told of a series of disasters

so close to those described in Exodus (see panel) that they must surely be referring to the same set of events. However the Papyrus comes not from the time of Ramesses II, but from a much earlier period at the end of the Middle Kingdom when Egypt was in a state of collapse, law and order breaking down, and royal power almost non-existent. As a basis for re-staging Jewish history, this makes a far more plausible scenario. Instead of the slaves revolting against a Pharaoh of commanding stature, there is a disintegrating empire in which a slave revolt is actually recorded. In Velikovsky's reconstruction, the Hyksos people who came storming down from Asia and are agreed by all historians to have conquered Egypt at the end of the Middle Bronze Age are the Amalekites mentioned in the Bible whom the Israelites defeated on their way northwards to the Promised Land. The walls of Jericho that came tumbling down in the face of Joshua's army are precisely those which, as tourists can see, once dominated the city.

Solomon and Sheba

It is a satisfyingly rounded model, made more complete by his interpretation of the encounter between Solomon and Sheba. Once again the Bible leaves us in no doubt about the size and scale of Solomon's empire. He 'exceeded all the kings of the earth for riches and wisdom'. He traded with spice merchants and kings of Arabia, importing gold, ivory, silver, precious stones, exotic flora and fauna. His Temple was a marvel of gold and brass, with immense carved statues on its ornate pillars. He was supported by a great navy, and an army consisting of 1400 chariots and 12,000 horsemen – truly, the golden age of Hebrew prosperity and power.

But once again, if you follow the conventional chronology, you will find absolutely no mention of this glorious empire. According to the Bible, Solomon married the daughter of a Pharaoh who was powerful enough to sack the Philistine city of

The siege of Jericho, one of the most dramatic and specifically described events in the Israelite conquest of Canaan.

Gezer and present it to Solomon as a dowry. Yet records of the ineffectual Pharaoh identified with the period of Solomon's reign according to conventional dating methods make no reference to Palestine whatsoever. After Solomon's death, his Temple was sacked by a Pharaoh called Shishak, and the amassed treasures described in minute detail in the Bible were carried off to Egypt. Shishak, in the orthodox view, is Shoshenk I, a minor king who left a list of Palestinian cities and little else – no mention of Jerusalem, or conquest, or the Temple, or even one item of treasure.

So archaeologists are again forced to rewrite the Bible to make it conform to their dating system. Magnusson says 'the Temple was a relatively small structure,' although he has absolutely no justification for saying so, since it has never been found. The lack of contemporary Egyptian references to David or Solomon he finds understandable because 'everything about Solomon in the Bible sounds wildly exaggerated – his wisdom, his wealth, his wives, his concubines . . . as far as archaeology is concerned,

it was a paper (or papyrus) empire only,' dreamed up by later scribes as an invented period of glory.

Velikovsky overcomes the problem in a way that is both more radical and more satisfactory. By putting the date of the powerful XVIIIth Dynasty in Egypt some 500 years later, it matches well with Solomon's Empire. One of the later rulers, Thutmose III, he identifies as the Pharaoh Shishak who sacked Solomon's Temple. The campaign of Thutmose III into Palestine is proudly described in hieroglyphic texts, and the stolen treasures vividly displayed (see illustration on page 175).

Queen of Sheba
Even more dramatically, this juggling of dates has allowed Velikovsky to offer the best solution yet to the identity of the mysterious Queen of Sheba, argued over by Egyptologists and Biblical scholars for centuries. The Bible offers a reasonable amount of information about her – she is at least the equal of Solomon in wealth and prestige: 'she came to Jerusalem with a very great train, with camels that bore spices, and very much gold, and precious stones.' The journey

The plagues of Egypt that preceded the Exodus are described in startlingly similar detail in the Bible and in a Middle Kingdom Egyptian document known as the Papyrus Ipuwer. This parallel was the starting point for Velikovsky's re-dating of Egyptian history.

Why really, the River is blood.	. . . and all the waters that were in the river were turned to blood. (Exodus 7:20)
If one drinks of it, one rejects [it] as human and thirsts for water. [Papyrus 2:10]	And the fish that were in the river died; and the river stank, and the Egyptians could not drink of the water of the river;
Plague is throughout the land. Blood is everywhere. [2:6]	and there was blood throughout all the land of Egypt. (7:21)
Why really, all animals, their hearts weep. Cattle moan because of the state of the land. [5:5]	. . . behold, the hand of the Lord is upon thy cattle which is in the field, upon the horses, upon the asses, upon the camels, upon the oxen, and upon the sheep: there shall be a very grievous murrain. (9:3)
Why really, gates, columns and walls are consumed by fire. [2:10]	. . . and the Lord sent thunder and hail, and the fire ran along upon the ground; and the Lord rained hail upon the land of Egypt. So there was hail, and fire mingled with the hail, very grievous . . . (9:23–24)
Why really, trees are destroyed. [4:14] Why really, that has perished which yesterday was seen, and the land is left over to its weakness like the cutting of the flax. [5:12–13]	. . . and the hail smote every herb of the field, and brake every tree of the field. (9:25)
No fruit nor herbs are found for the birds. [6:1] Why really, grain has perished on every side . . . Everybody says: 'There is nothing!' The storehouse is stripped bare. [6:3]	And the locusts went up all over the land of Egypt . . . very grievous were they; before them there were no such locusts as they, neither after them shall be such. For they covered the face of the whole earth, so that the land was darkened; and they did eat every herb of the land and all the fruit of the trees which the hail had left: and there remained not any green thing in the trees, or in the herbs of the field, through all the land of Egypt. (10:14–15)
. . . fear . . . Poor men . . . the land is not light because of it. [fragments, 9:11]	And Moses stretched forth his hand toward heaven; and there was a thick darkness in all the land of Egypt for three days. (10:22)
Why really, the children of princes are dashed against the walls. The [once] prayed-for children are [now] laid out on the high ground. [4:3]	And it came to pass, that at midnight the Lord smote all the firstborn in the land of Egypt, from the firstborn of Pharaoh that sat on his throne unto the firstborn of the captive that was in the dungeon. (12:29)
It is groaning that is throughout the land, mingled with lamentations. [3:14]	. . . and there was a great cry in Egypt;
He who places his brother in the land is everywhere. [2:13]	for there was not a house where there was not one dead. (12:30)
Behold now, the fire has mounted up on high. Its flame goes forth against the enemies of the land. [7:1]	And it came to pass, when Pharaoh had let the people go . . . the Lord went before them by day in a pillar of cloud, to lead them the way; and by night in a pillar of fire, to give them light. (13:17,21)

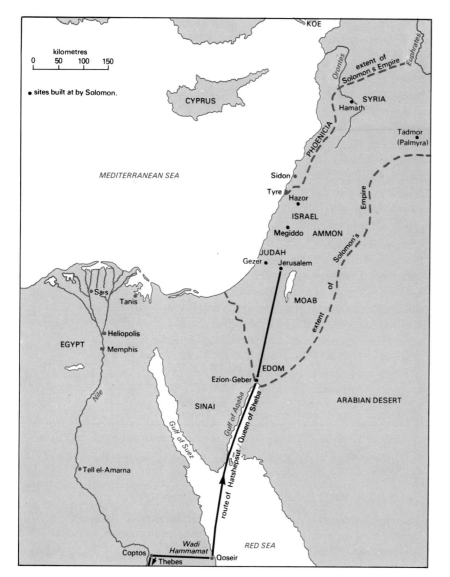

Was the Queen of Sheba really the Queen of Egypt? The shortest route of a state visit from Thebes to Jerusalem, the capital of Solomon's empire, is consistent with Jewish traditions that she came by sea and by land.

was an extremely important one to her, and she went away deeply impressed – 'thy wisdom and prosperity exceedeth the fame which I heard'.

But where was the land of Sheba to which she returned? The Authorized Version of the Bible places it both in Arabia (where most archaeologists today think it was) and in Ethiopia, where it was the name of the capital. But Josephus, who translated the Bible for a Graeco-Roman audience in the First Century AD, called her 'the Queen of Egypt and Ethiopia'. Velikovsky's revised chronology supports this, as the XVIIIth Dynasty ruled over Ethiopia as well as Egypt. There was probably a Nubian, black, strain in the royal family's blood; and to clinch the argument, it had a ruler who made a spectacular expedition whose details correspond harmoniously with the Biblical information – Queen Hatshepsut and her voyage to the legendary land of Punt (page 115).

Land of Punt

As with Sheba, the location of Punt has long been argued by scholars. According to the

inscriptions, it lay not far away from Egypt, and to the east. It was sometimes called 'God's Land', and held in some reverence; without doubt Queen Hatshepsut considered her Punt expedition the greatest achievement of her reign, and on her return she built a grand temple modelled on what she had seen. Her reliefs describe and depict in detail a land of peace and affluence, with 'terraces of myrrh', gardens, and a bewildering array of exotic plants and animals. Using these as their clues, botanists and zoologists were recruited by Egyptologists in their search for this fabulous land. No agreement was reached simply because of the unnatural richness of the fauna and flora displayed – some was African, some Arabian, some defied identification. Opinion is divided as to whether Punt was in Arabia or in Somaliland or encompassed them both.

But if Punt describes Palestine in Solomon's time, everything fits into place. The Bible tells repeatedly of Solomon's interest in exotic plants and animals; there are, too, frequent references to 'mountains of myrrh' and 'hills of frankincense'. The name Punt (which should be read *Pwene*) could simply be the Egyptian version of the name Phoenicia. Puntites, as depicted on Hatshepsut's reliefs, are Semites with pointed beards, fine aquiline noses and skins a shade paler than the Egyptians. She made her voyage to Punt by sea and then by land – presumably from Thebes up the Red Sea to the Gulf of Aqaba. There she found herself in a narrow strait, on both sides of which she pitched her tents, with date palms growing down to the beach – a perfect description of the head of the Gulf. When finally she returned, she lyricized about the enormous quantity of luxuries she had been given – 'the marvels of Punt'.

The parallel with the Queen of Sheba is so compelling that were it not for the straitjacket of conventional chronology, it would surely have been spotted long ago, and in fact archaeologists are increasingly ready to identify Punt with an area north of the Sinai. Dr Eva Danielus, a respected Egyptologist, has shown in the *Journal of Egyptian Archaeology* that the marine life depicted in Hatshepsut's reliefs was typical of Red Sea fauna; Dr Alessandra Nibbi, in the same journal, has proved that frankincense and myrrh were abundant in Palestine during the period in question, and has selected northern Sinai as the location for Punt. But one question still remains: if Hatshepsut was simply travelling to Sinai, why did she laud the expedition as the major achievement of her reign? Velikovsky's theory provides a satisfying and neat answer – she was visiting Solomon and reacted to him with just the amazement attributed in the Bible to the Queen

of Sheba; likewise the visit was memorable because it concerned the state visit of a ruling monarch of Egypt, and not the ruler of a tiny kingdom of Sheba in the far south of Arabia.

Gospel truth

How long will it be before Velikovsky's revised chronology is widely debated by mainstream archaeologists, let alone accepted by them? There is a powerful urge in museums throughout the world to let exhibits rest where they have been put, rather than undertake the far-reaching upheaval of a new scheme of ancient history. Velikovsky's cause is sometimes damaged, too, by a handful of over-eager supporters in the United States who seem to believe that every word he has ever written is, to use an appropriate phrase, the gospel truth. Some idea of the built-in resistance may be gathered from the reaction to the evidence in a study by Dr John Bimson of Cambridge University, published in the *Journal* of the Society for Inter-Disciplinary Studies. In this he showed that the Biblical description of the manner in which the various cities of Canaan were conquered – i.e. by burning, or depopulation, or left intact – agrees satisfactorily with the archaeological evidence. So striking were the similarities that the late Israeli archaeologist of distinction, Y. Aharoni, merely looked at the evidence from two of the cities and decided that existing text-books on the

period would have to be radically revised. Even so, Aharoni could not bring himself to believe that it was Joshua and the wandering tribes of Israel who had performed the conquest; because of the chronology, it must have been 'some other tribe' hundreds of years before, and the Hebrews had 'borrowed' their traditions and written them into Jewish history.

You do not have to accept every detail of what Velikovsky suggests, or what the Bible says, to see that in several major areas he has mounted a highly plausible challenge. One rule-of-thumb test is to imagine that at the end of the 19th Century, Egyptologists had settled on the dating model such as Velikovsky later invented, and that today this was the scheme of Near Eastern prehistory they were defending. How much credence would be given to some crackpot who came along suggesting that, actually, there never was an Exodus, and the Hebrews didn't conquer Canaan, and Solomon's Temple was insignificant and the Queen of Sheba was the head of some small unimportant state? Not much, one would suppose. Curiously enough, this very nearly happened. Isaac Newton devised a chronology for Egyptian and Jewish history based on Biblical sources that was regarded as plausible until the Sothic dating came in to confuse the picture. Broadly, it is just what Velikovsky is unsuccessfully suggesting today.

Queen Hatshepsut, most powerful female Pharaoh in Egypt's history. Was she the Biblical Queen of Sheba?

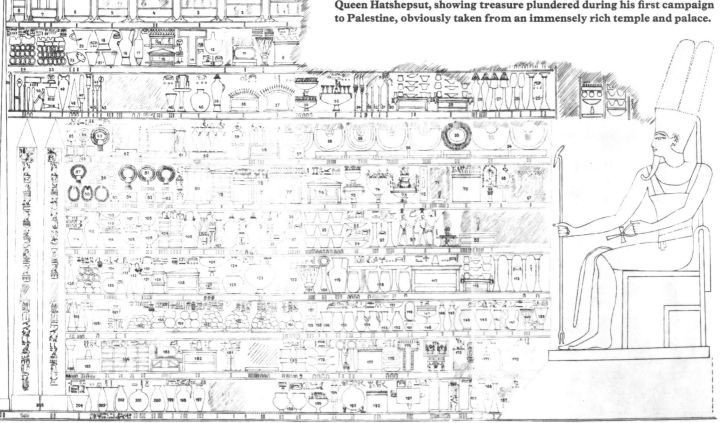

An Egyptian bas-relief of Thutmose III, nephew and successor of Queen Hatshepsut, showing treasure plundered during his first campaign to Palestine, obviously taken from an immensely rich temple and palace.

Who was Homer?

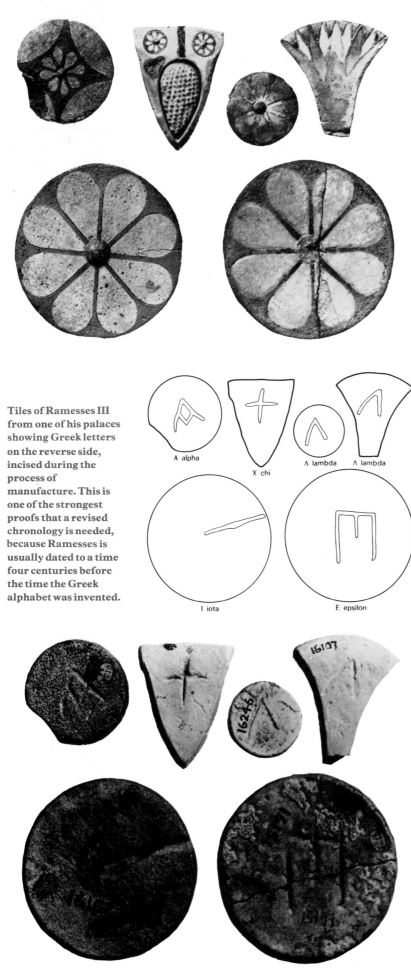

Tiles of Ramesses III from one of his palaces showing Greek letters on the reverse side, incised during the process of manufacture. This is one of the strongest proofs that a revised chronology is needed, because Ramesses is usually dated to a time four centuries before the time the Greek alphabet was invented.

A alpha
X chi
Λ lambda
Λ lambda
I iota
E epsilon

One of the most spectacular consequences of bringing forward the dates of Egyptian history by 500–700 years is the effect this has on the mystifying period of ancient Greek history known as the 'Dark Ages'; for if Velikovsky is right, the Dark Ages never happened – they are simply a colossal invention by archaeologists attempting to overcome the problems forced on them by a faulty chronology.

Although scholarly text-books on these supposed Dark Ages appear almost every year, none can hide the poverty of evidence.
The theory is that, probably through invasion from Asia, the flowering, heroic civilization of Mycenae vanished for half a millenium, only to spring to life again instantly as if nothing had happened at the end of that period.
V. R. d'A. Desborough wrote in *The Greek Dark Ages*: 'the changes that come about are little short of fantastic. The craftsmen and artists seem to vanish almost without trace: there is very little new stone construction of any sort, far less any massive edifices; the metal-worker's technique reverts to the primitive and the potter, except in the early stages, loses his purpose and inspiration; and the art of writing is forgotten.'

Common-sense alone suggests that something here is seriously wrong, and as the panel on the right shows, evidence at all major Aegean archaeological sites can be more easily explained without the Dark Ages than with them. And for everyone who enjoys the stirring stories of Homer's *Iliad* and *Odyssey*, there is another advantage – under the revised chronology he comes into his own right as a poet writing about the Trojan Wars within a generation or so of them happening, while people's memories were still fresh.

The Greeks themselves believed that he wrote soon after, and Isaac Newton deduced from genealogies of the Greek royal houses, notably the two lines of Spartan kings, that the date of the Trojan Wars was no earlier than 900 BC. However, cross-dating of pottery styles has led modern conventional archaeology to place it as contemporary with the XVIIIth and XIXth Dynasties in Egypt – say, 1250–1200 BC. Under Velikovsky's system, the date becomes *c.* 800 BC, which solves all number of problems: Homer, for instance, makes frequent mention of the Phoenicians, who were not a powerful trading people before the 9th Century BC. But above all, abolishing the Dark Ages should re-establish Homer's reputation as the world's first great chronicler-poet and dispel the currently held view that he was a collector of ancient tales, or perhaps even a collective name for a group of poets.

Some dating anomalies in the Greek 'Dark Ages'

1 In the late 19th Century two archaeologists excavated the Temple of Hera and dated it to the 13th or 12th Century BC on the basis of the Mycenaean pottery associated with it, but a bitter dispute arose over the meaning of the 8th-century Geometric ware found with it. One (Dörpfeld) proposed re-dating the Geometric Age to the second millennium to make it contemporary with the Mycenaean, the other (Fürtwängler) showed that the Geometric must be dated to the 8th and 7th Centuries. The conflict would not have taken place if they had placed less reliance on Egyptian chronology – both kinds of pottery date to the 8th Century according to Velikovsky.

2 Nestor, one of the kings who fought at Troy, had his capital city at Pylos, according to Homer, and an extensive Mycenaean palace has been excavated there. Its destruction by fire was dated to *c.*1200 BC by its Mycenaean pottery. Yet 7th-century pottery was found in several places, mixed up with the Mycenaean ware in the same level. The excavator (C. Blegen) assumed that the later ware 'must have somehow penetrated from above' through debris and other deposits that would have collected during the site's supposed 500 year abandonment.

3 The famous Lion Gate is dated to the 13th Century BC by Mycenaean pottery but its style clearly shows eastern influence, the closest parallel being Phrygian examples no earlier than the 8th Century, a date actually assigned to the Gate by earlier archaeologists. A trench dug near the Gate to determine the date of Mycenae's destruction (supposedly *c.* 1100 BC) revealed no pottery at all for the period 1100–700 BC, yet the level containing 12th-century pottery was thoroughly mixed with ware of the 7th Century.

4 At Tiryns, the Mycenaean palace was supposedly destroyed by fire *c.*1200 BC. But the 8th/7th-century temple that stands above it follows its ground-plan closely, and according to the excavators was built almost immediately after the palace perished in flames – this is quite impossible if Tiryns was abandoned for 500 years in a 'Dark Age'.

5 Archaeologists today associate the Trojan War with the destruction of Troy VI or VIIa, dated to *c.*1300 and *c.*1260 BC. Troy VIIb was supposed to have been abandoned in the 12th Century BC, despite the fact that a 9th-century sherd was found *underneath* one of its buildings, in an undisturbed context. Moreover the inhabitants of Troy VIII, founded by Greeks in 700 BC used pottery derived from that of Troy VIIa, after 400 years from which period there are no remains at all.

6 According to Homer the Phrygians helped defend Troy against the Greeks. Yet the earliest Phrygian remains are from around 800 BC, while archaeologists date the War to the 13th Century BC. Moreover, the gateway at Gordion, capital of the Phrygian king Midas, had 'its closest parallel', in the words of the excavator (R. Young), 'in the walls of the sixth city at Troy . . . separated in time by five hundred years.' The walls of Troy VI were supposedly buried by those of settlement VIIa *c.*1300 BC – if they are dated correctly, how could they serve as models for 8th-century walls at Gordion?

7 'In central Anatolia, up to now, neither Phrygian nor indeed any cultural remains of any people have come to light which might be dated to between 1200 and 800 BC.' (Ekrem Akurgal, leading Turkish archaeologist.)

8 The capital of the Hittites, supposedly destroyed around 1200 BC, was re-occupied by the Phrygians in the late 8th Century BC. Despite this 'long abandonment', 'the earliest constructions were undertaken at a time when the Hittite ruins still lay visible above the surface. On top of them there is no trace of a sterile stratum such as would have been formed by natural sedimentation.' (K. Bittel, excavator.)

9 The most important Hittite town in Syria during the Empire period – supposedly the 14th and 13th Centuries BC. Yet there are no strata from the Imperial period, and all the Imperial remains, including jewellery and sculpture, are found in 'neo-Hittite' contexts of the 10th Century onwards. The *only* Mycenaean pottery from the site was found on a 9th-century floor, along with monuments of the Empire.

10 An impressive gate with lions and a series of reliefs were found, dated by art experts to the Hittite Empire (13th Century BC) – but the excavations showed that they must have formed an integral part of, and been made for, a building complex of the 8th Century BC.

11 A rich Syrian city usually dated to the 14th Century BC. But its cuneiform tablets show that the Hebrew alphabet was known, and the Hebrew used was 'surprisingly akin' to that used in the Bible. Its poetry follows rules which 'are precisely those of Hebrew poetry, and even the language from some of our Ras Shamra texts is entirely Biblical.' But in the conventional chronology the Hebrews were still in Egypt in the 13th Century BC. Further, the tablets revealed Greek elements and a religion and epic literature that has many similarities with Homer. In the revised chronology Ugarit dates to the 9th Century, and all these problems are resolved.

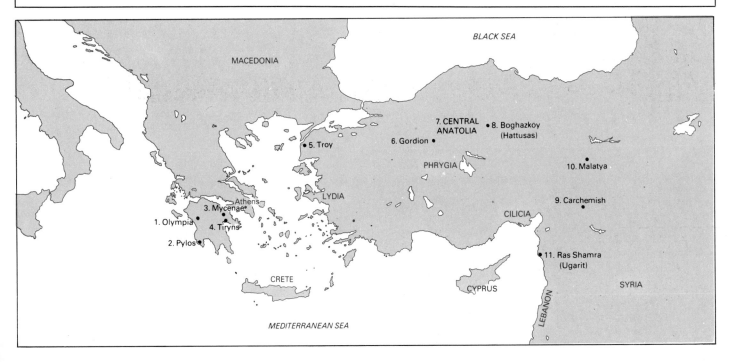

Sacred relics

Imprint on the Turin shroud. The process by which it was put on the fabric, whether biochemical or by some means so far undiscovered by science, is not known.

Everyone agrees there are far too many sacred relics in the world for them all to be genuine: there are *three* corpses all claimed to be of St Mary Magdalene lying in three separate French churches; thorns from the 'original' crown of thorns, along with Christ's robe and undergarments, are scattered throughout the churches of Europe; Mark Twain quipped that there were enough pieces of the 'true' cross to build a battleship (unfairly, as a typical cross used by Romans for execution has been estimated as having a volume of 178 million cubic millimetres, whereas the volume of attested pieces of the 'true' cross in existence at the end of the last century was less than 4 million cubic millimetres); against three or four nails used in the crucifixion, some 32 are preserved and venerated in various places.

To a cynic, this simply means that they are all probably worthless. However, without unduly straining credulity, it is possible to take a much more sympathetic view – certainly about venerated relics in general. In Buddhism, for instance, relic worship is well established and authenticated: tradition has it that the cremated remains of the Buddha were divided on his death in 483 BC equally among the eight Indian tribes.

Mohammedans, in spite of official disapproval, revere relics associated with the Prophet or the early saints in much the same way as many Christians of the Catholic faith.

Worship of the remains of the dead is probably as old as religion itself. Neanderthals (page 39) and possibly *Homo erectus* even earlier, practised ritual cannibalism, thus invoking a sympathetic magic through which a dead person's soul, powers and qualities could continue to work; the tradition developed that anyone who wore a relic, carried it, touched it or prayed to it, would benefit from its power.

Site of Golgotha

So deeply felt is this belief that there is a strong probability that the objects associated with Christ's crucifixion have been preserved and venerated locally. Jerusalem was razed to the ground by Titus and the Romans in AD 70, but within 100 years the Church was flourishing there again, according to the historian Eusebius, who describes pilgrims at that time coming to worship on the Mount of Olives. In AD 326 Constantine, the first Roman Emperor to recognize the Christian church, ordered a search for Golgotha, the site of the crucifixion and burial. 'I have nothing more at heart,' he wrote, 'than to adorn that holy place.'

Consequently Bishop Macarius of Jerusalem selected a site, and, after excavation, a number of rock tombs were found (not surprisingly, since the site was a cemetery), and one was selected as the sepulchre in which Christ had been buried. Accounts conflict about the discovery of the cross and the nails. In the Constantine version, they were found in a cistern 85 metres to the east of the sepulchre. The Catholic Church today prefers the version that Constantine's mother, the Empress St Helena, an inveterate relic-collector, learned the secret of their location from Cyriacus, a devout Hebrew, and established their authenticity by using the cross to work a miracle healing on a widow named Libania who was lying critically ill nearby. At all events, a church was built on the site of the sepulchre that is now called Golgotha, and Eusebius's *History of Constantine* states that after the sepulchre beneath was discovered, the distribution of relics began immediately.

Whether or not the relics were genuine, and how many of them may have survived nearly two millennia of nature's ravages, becomes a question of faith and educated guesswork. There is perhaps a good chance that relics existed in Jerusalem; whether, having been protected for three centuries, they were freely handed over to the Empress St Helena, and whether Bishop Macarius did anything more than choose a likely

burial ground, is much more doubtful.
The *Catholic Encyclopaedia* defines a relic as:
'... The body or whatever remains of a holy
person after death, as well as objects that had
actual contact with the saint's body during his
lifetime. Real (or first class) relics include the
skin and the bones, clothing, objects used for
penance, instruments of a martyr's imprisonment
or passion.' In the case of Christ, these are the
supposed relics:

The cross
After St Helena left Jerusalem with the
cross-piece (and other assorted relics), the
upright of the cross was divided into several
pieces – despite the opposition of many
Christians – and the main portions distributed
between Jerusalem, Rome, and Constantinople.
Today most main churches of the Catholic faith
claim to possess a fragment of the true cross.
As for the superscription on the cross (the piece
of wood bearing the charges against Christ),
accounts say this was also divided up, and that
St Helena took the part that was written in

Greek and Latin (now lost). A section written
in Hebrew, held in the Santa Croce in Jerusalem,
was authenticated in 1839, and held then as too
idiomatic to be a forgery.

The nails
Of the three or four nails used in the crucifixion,
Constantine is said to have used three of them to
ward off the enemies of Rome. The fourth was
allegedly bequeathed by St Helena to the city of
Trèves in southern France along with the holy
robe (page 180). Some 32 places now claim to
have the nails; in the 1935 'census' Venice had
three, Rome two, and Notre Dame in Paris one.
A possible explanation is that fragments of the
true nails were forged into replicas.

Crown of thorns
If the shroud of Turin is genuine (page 180), it
seems that the crown of thorns was never a ring
as depicted in virtually all Christian iconography,
but a bundle of thorns in the shape of a cap.
The 'true' crown is currently kept at Notre Dame
in Paris along with a piece of wood from the

**Distribution of
Christian relics
throughout Europe.
It is mathematically
possible, but highly
unlikely, that all of
them are genuine
fragments of the
originals.**

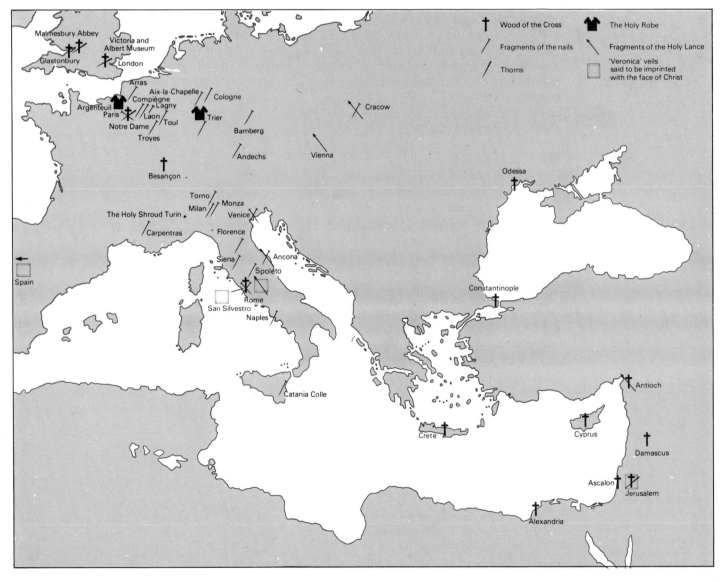

cross. It belongs in that group of relics removed from Calvary immediately after the crucifixion. The early Christians guarded it jealously, and during the 4th and 5th Centuries AD it was venerated in the Basilica of Sion, where it remained until 1063 when it was removed with the holy lance to Constantinople. Baldwin II, a ruler of the Roumanian Empire, tried to redeem his debts to the Venetians by offering them the crown, but St Louis of France (Louis IX) intervened and personally carried it to Paris in 1239, in which city it has remained ever since.

Christ's two robes

The long-standing theological dispute between the cathedral of Trèves and the Convent of Argenteuil for the honour of possessing 'the' genuine coat of Christ has now been settled amicably by a judgment that one possesses the Holy Robe, and the other the Holy Tunic. The Trèves garment is the most precious, not least because of two miracle healings seen to have occurred in 1844 after the people involved had touched it. There is an undisputed tradition that St Helena brought it to Trèves – her home city, and second only to Rome in the Christian hierarchy at the time. Unless she was given a false relic in Jerusalem, it is likely that the robe we see today is genuine; it was hidden from view from the 4th to the 11th Century, and handled with great care when subsequently exposed. It is certainly ancient, although no modern scientific tests on it have been carried out.

The Turin shroud

This is the most closely investigated and best-attested relic, and even sceptics no longer doubt that the fabric of the cloth portrays the image of *someone* who was crucified by the Romans in the 1st Century AD. What is more, with each new investigation it becomes increasingly probable that the imprint is genuinely that of Christ.

Understandably, the shroud has a controversial history. The Biblical account says that the shroud placed on Christ's body consisted of 'burial linens'. Apart from enigmatic accounts in the 4th Century AD, there is nothing known about it until 1157. From then on, it survived the sacking of Constantinople by the Crusaders, a fire at Besançon Cathedral in France, an attack on its authenticity in 1389 by Peter d'Arcis, Bishop of Troyes, a fire at the chapel in Chambery in 1532, and its final transfer to Turin in 1572. It has remained there ever since.

David Rolfe's film *The Silent Witness* from which this still is taken, is the best visual evidence yet of the shroud's authenticity.

In 1868 Secondo Pia photographed the shroud and discovered the negative imprint that clearly shows a face and the outline of a body previously mutilated in exactly the way that both the Bible and recent medical findings describe

the circumstances of Christ's death.

The argument that it was a mediaeval European forgery seems conclusively contradicted by several recent findings: nails are shown to have gone through Christ's wrists, which is archaeologically accurate, rather than the palms as shown in all mediaeval paintings; the image shows a naked body – blasphemous had it been painted as such; blood stains show a chemical separation that is medically correct but unknown until recently; flower pollen taken from the shroud contains eight species that could only have come from Palestine; the wounds from the thorns suggest a rough bunch unceremoniously crushed on the head, rather than the traditional ringed 'crown' – a unique and plausible punishment; the back shows some 125 strokes from a three-pronged whip as used by Roman soldiers in the 1st Century AD.

Some mysteries still remain, notably why blood seems to have continued to flow into the shroud after Christ was taken from the cross – as though he may still have been just alive. Even more puzzling is the nature of the imprint itself. Why was it not noticed by earlier scholars? Why is it a surface image which fails to penetrate the fabric in the way that blood and sweat should? How is it that the image can produce, when computer-enhanced, a three-dimensional image like a hologram? Christ's image it may be; but there are revelations yet to come.

Section eight
Aerial phenomena

When Desmond King-Hele, the noted British mathematician and space scientist, delivered the 1974 Halley Lecture in Oxford, he chose as his theme Truth and Heresy over Earth and Sky, and remarked that 'nothing is more misleading than an unchallenged false assumption.' In the last section we saw how, for the flimsiest of reasons originally, the chronology of the ancient Near East has been built up on misplaced foundations, and although now demonstrably fallacious, has become almost immovably entrenched in the system. The next section deals with the even more disputatious matter of strange things that happen in the sky, and as some of these, such as falls of frogs and other creatures, are of mind-stretching improbability, the warning about false assumptions is one to keep firmly in mind.

The history of how science in a particular period regarded phenomena in space is littered with dogma being replaced by other dogma; as Desmond King-Hele put it, 'where established ideas have been completely overturned, where former heresies are now respectable "truth", and old accepted truths are now despised'. A number of examples have already been noted in this Atlas – continental drift (page 14), ball lightning (page 24), and others. Here meteors provide another classic case, having been regarded as of extra-terrestrial origin in ancient times, as an insubstantial atmospheric effect from the time of Aristotle until the 19th Century, and now extra-terrestrial again, with gathering academic enthusiasm for ever-larger chunks of space debris bombarding us from the heavens.

The question is, what other aerial phenomena will in future come to be accepted? Space travel itself has gone through the same cycle of belief, disbelief and belief, and as recently as 1935 Dr F. R. Moulton, then one of the world's foremost authorities on celestial mechanics, was able to say confidently: 'In all fairness to those who by training are not prepared to evaluate the fundamental difficulties of going from one planet to another, or even from the Earth to the Moon, it must be stated that there is not the slightest possibility of such journeys.' Yet Chinese legends of flight go back to 2200 BC, Greek and Roman gods conquered space without difficulty, and the Dogon Africans of the Sahara (page 150) know with certainty that they were visited in the past by amphibian travellers from the star system Sirius.

Desmond King-Hele concluded: 'It is easy for us to laugh at all the mistakes of the past, but don't they leave you with rather an uneasy feeling about the present? How many of the heresies of today will become the truths of tomorrow? How many of the truths of today will be discredited? Academic learning is a marvellous edifice, permanent and satisfyingly interlinked, but even so, it may still be legitimate to define science as a thought-system that appeals to the scientists of a particular era, because it allows them to convince themselves that they are making some progress towards better understanding of natural phenomena. They programme their brains into a way of thinking, and then try to indoctrinate the innocent into the same mould, a process sometimes called education. Actions subversive of scientific orthodoxy are forcefully resisted, nowadays in the form of censorship, because scientific papers are sent to referees, good sound scientists who will veto anything revolutionary.'

Some strange things are described in this section and the next, many of them challenging the orthodox ways of perceiving the world. So far as UFOs are concerned, it is somewhat arrogant to imagine that the laws of science devised by us here on Earth apply to matters of time and space that may involve another dimension. Tibetan lamas (page 238) can create solid objects by a form of thought-projection, it is said. In gathering together some of the wonders that seem to originate in the skies, our attitude has been that if enough people see them, they have a reality of their own which more than justifies publishing a description of their behaviour.

Meteor bombardment

Meteor Crater in Arizona, the most spectacular example of aerial bombardment in the world, used by trainee lunar astronauts.

There are by now many millions of puzzled people who have seen a UFO at first hand, or have had a psychic experience so compelling that they do not for one moment doubt its reality. For any of them who are worried why scientists, as a whole, don't take their stories seriously, there may be some comfort in the following cautionary history of the scientific attitude towards meteors, those streaks of light in the night sky known as shooting stars which from time to time are large and robust enough to penetrate the Earth's atmosphere and fall violently to its surface. Something like 200 million of them enter the Earth's atmosphere daily, and of these about one million are as bright as a star of the first order of brightness. When they hit the ground, they can hurt.
Mrs E. Hulitt Hodges of Alabama was taken to hospital in 1954 after being struck by a meteorite.

Had she lived 200 years ago her story would have been ridiculed. The idea that meteors – or anything else – could come to Earth from outer space was dismissed as totally preposterous and unscientific. 'It is easier to believe that two Yankee Professors would lie, than that stones would fall from Heaven,' pronounced Thomas Jefferson, scientist and US President, when, in 1807, he heard of two Yale University Professors who had weighed 300 pounds of meteorites that had fallen at Weston, Connecticut, during December.

Before Aristotle, in a more inclusive era of science, meteorites were accepted gratefully as a contribution from Heaven, and even revered. The Hittite King Mursilis II was pleased to report in his *Annals* that a fireball had struck down his enemy the King of Apashash (Ephesus), and believed that the God Teshup (Jupiter) had ordered it. A meteorite 'as big as a cart' which fell at Aegospotamos in Thrace in 467 BC was venerated locally. The Ephesian meteorite was later carved into an image of the great Goddess Diana. Aztec shrines were built around them. The sacred stone at Mecca, to which Mohammedans even today turn to while praying, is almost certainly a meteorite.

Aristotle's mistake
However Aristotle (d. 322 BC) believed differently. He accepted the reality of shooting

stars/meteors, and identified the phenomena correctly as being atmospheric. But he could not accept the possibility of solid objects being the cause, classing meteors instead with rainbows, haloes and aurorae, which 'hung in the air'. If stones, even as big as a cart, were reported to have fallen from the sky, then they must have been carried off the ground by strong winds and later deposited.

Although the reports of meteorite falls inevitably continued after this judgment, and although there were a number of notable dissenters (e.g. the Roman historian Plutarch), the eminent British mathematician Desmond King-Hele has incisively summed up the established scientific attitude for the 2000 years after Aristotle: 'The general opinion among the learned in the West was that meteors were atmospheric, because Aristotle said so; and if meteorites did appear to fall from Heaven, that was an illusion, because earthy things could not fall from Heaven, which only contained heavenly things. Peasants privileged to see and hear meteorites no doubt thought differently, but they were written off as mere country yokels whose unwritten opinions died with them.'

Galactic debris

The orthodoxy was at its most stubborn in the 18th Century. The Académie Française, then the foremost scientific body in the world, was so convinced of the absurdity of stones falling from the sky that they actively encouraged several museums and collections to throw away long-treasured meteorites, with the result that very few pre-1790 examples exist today. Meteors were explained as lightning, or 'phlogistous gas catching fire in the upper atmosphere'. Halley's famous Comet, for which his calculations are now known to have been accurate, was dismissed as heresy; in King-Hele's words 'a cloud of dusty debris in space was a messy, unsatisfying hypothesis.'
On 24 July 1790 a meteorite shower fell in south-western France and more than 300 statements were sent to the Académie, together with samples of the rock. These were ridiculed by Academicians, who called the shower a 'physically impossible phenomenon'.

The capitulation of this attitude, during the next two decades, was fairly sudden. The weight of geological evidence – for instance, the amount of iron found in the fireballs – at last became too much to discount, and by 1820 (Thomas Jefferson notwithstanding) the idea that foreign bodies may come from outer space was generally accepted. Today this is absolutely accepted, and the main mystery is a technical one of what size of particle constitutes a meteor, and what a meteorite (the former supposedly connected with cometary debris and the latter being mini-asteroids or fragments of asteroids).

But even if this obscurantism about meteorites lies in the past, there may well be some contemporary lessons to be learned.

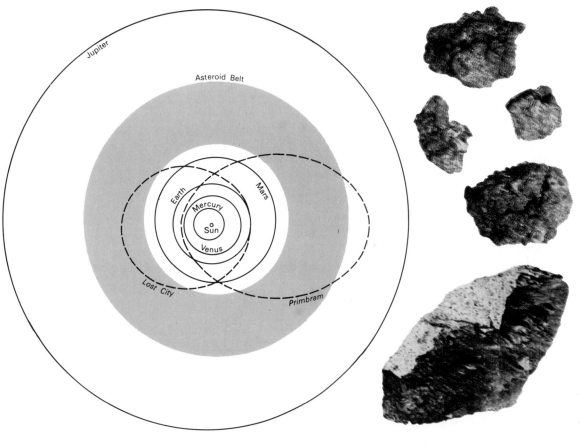

The orbits of two fallen meteorites, established by simultaneous photographic records, show they intersect with the asteroid belt, their probable point of origin.

As Charles P. Olivier, one of the world's leading authorities today on meteorites, commented on the attitude of the Académie Française: 'In the face of all this evidence, we have an example of stupidity and bigotry, exhibited by the foremost scientists of the day – men who doubtless considered themselves, and were so considered by others, the most advanced and "modern" of their time – which for all ages should stand as a warning to any man who feels that he can give a final verdict upon a matter outside his experience.'

Today's mistake?

What may be happening nowadays is that scientific orthodoxy is making a different sort of mistake. It has now become abundantly clear that the Earth's surface is thickly strewn with meteorites – in fact, so many thousand tons of dust and micro-meteorites arrive on the Earth each day that one scientist called our planet a 'cosmic dustbin'. At the same time, the 1970s have seen a revolution in meteorite study, with scientists suggesting ever-larger extra-terrestrial bodies that at one time or another have collided with Earth. The mistake may be that the implications of these very large meteorites have not yet penetrated scientific theory.

As with small meteorites, acceptance of these was slow to happen. René Gallant wrote in *Bombarded Earth* in 1964: 'It was believed that the size of meteorites was relatively slight and that their weight did not exceed a few hundred pounds. Nobody would have dared to think that meteorites, able to hollow huge craters, could strike our Earth. Consequently the study of meteorites was of interest only to astronomers, and it remained inconceivable that it could have any bearing on our planet's geological evolution.'

By 1939 a half-million dollar drilling operation finally established Meteor Crater in Arizona as being of genuinely meteoritic origin, and massive though it still is (two and a half kilometres in diameter, 175 metres deep), it is dwarfed by what have come to be known as astroblemes – 'star wounds', or fossil craters, which lack proper crater rims but show remains of a circular shape from the air. There are several spectacular Canadian examples, such as Deep Bay Crater (10 km) and Clearwater Lakes (16 km and 32 km), and even bigger areas such as the Gulf of St Lawrence Arc (380 km) and the Nastapoka Islands Arc of Hudson Bay (450 km) are being put forward as the result of astroblemes.

Still more recently, three geologists at Imperial College, London, have invented the word 'astrons' to describe even bigger astroblemes that they believe may have had an effect on continental drift (page 14), creating the curves of the west African coast, the Peruvian part of the Andes, and the Gulf of Mexico. Whether or not they are right, this steady scientific upgrading by scientists of the size of meteoritic impact on Earth has a bearing on the whole question of catastrophism – the unorthodox theory described

Astrons, said by some geologists to be Earth's oldest scars, are gigantic circular formations that can be photographed from space, and were originally caused by the impact of vast meteorites.

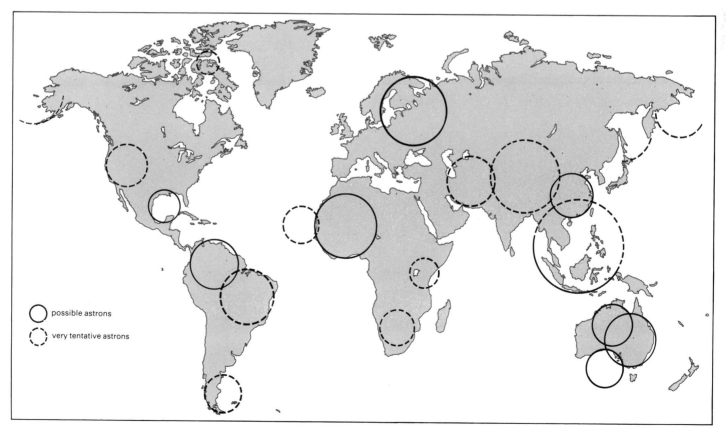

○ possible astrons

◌ very tentative astrons

in section one of this Atlas, whereby it is held that the Earth's evolution has been punctuated by disastrous events. The rock from outer space that created Meteor Crater, Arizona, calculated as travelling at around 50,000 kilometres per hour, probably destroyed all plant and animal life within a 100 kilometre radius. The impact of astroblemes and astrons would be greater in direct proportion to their size – enough, surely, to create catastrophes such as a tilt of the Earth's axis that have been as much derided by geologists was was the basic idea of 'stones from Heaven'. In 1958, L. La Paz calculated in *Advances in Geophysics* that the chances of anybody living in the 20th Century being hit directly by a meteorite (Mrs Hodges of Alabama was hit first bounce) was 'only' three in 10. But what if the meteorite happened to be the size of a small moon?

Tektites – the outer space dispute

Tektites are curious pieces of glass, most commonly pear-shaped and about the size of a walnut, scattered over the earth in quite well-defined groups. As long ago as 1897 a German scientist suggested they had been ejected from lunar volcanoes; since then the debate on whether they have a terrestrial or extra-terrestrial origin is instructive in the way that it shows (a) the growing readiness of geologists to accept the idea of missiles hitting Earth from outer space and (b) how ancient myths may be a more accurate guide to the past than most geologists admit.

Those who argue that they are terrestrial say that they were formed as the result of being thrown into space after the impact of a meteorite or larger body and acquired their shape and characteristics by being heated on their return journey through Earth's atmosphere. But while this theory seems justified for tektite deposits in Africa, Czechoslovakia and the United States, where known or supposed meteorite craters are close at hand, this does not apply to the vast fields in Australia and southeast Asia, where scientists have to suggest a hypothetical crater in Wilkes Land, for which there is no evidence at all.

Legend, on the other hand, has always suggested in these areas that tektites are objects that have fallen from the sky; Indians and Javanese call them 'tear-drops' of the Moon, and evidence from a sample brought back from the *Apollo 12* lunar flight suggests that this may be scientifically correct – although there are discrepancies in a few trace elements. One sample was reported to have 'a remarkable resemblance to tektites from Java'. To those who support Velikovsky's theories about the former near-collision between the Moon and Venus, this finding is of special significance: the tektites in question are not more than 5000 years old – and thus within the time scale needed for his catastrophist theories.

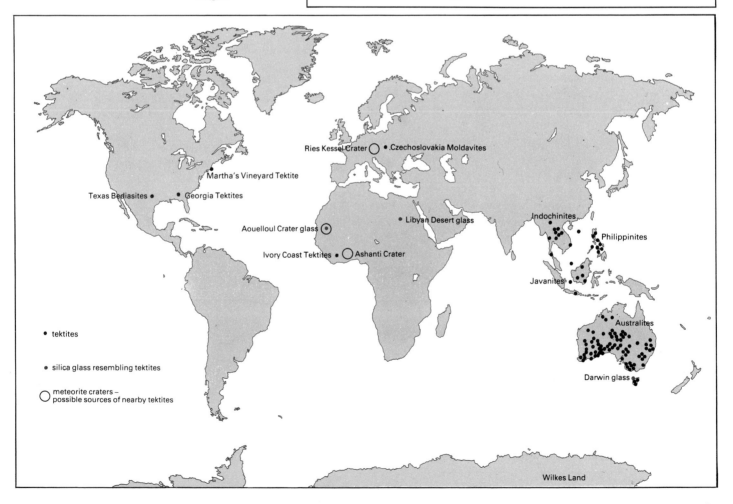

- • tektites
- • silica glass resembling tektites
- ◯ meteorite craters – possible sources of nearby tektites

Ries Kessel Crater ◯ • Czechoslovakia Moldavites

Martha's Vineyard Tektite

Texas Bediasites • • Georgia Tektites

Libyan Desert glass

Indochinites

Philippinites

Aouelloul Crater glass ◉

Ivory Coast Tektites • ◯ Ashanti Crater

Javanites

Australites

Darwin glass

Wilkes Land

Siberian space disaster

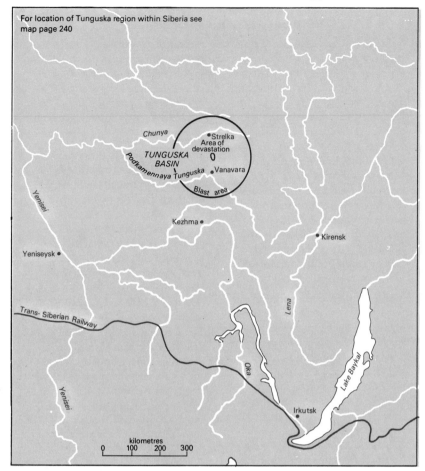

For location of Tunguska region within Siberia see map page 240

Maps made by Russian scientists in 1958 summarized the available data concerning the area affected by the Tunguska event.

At 7.17 a.m., local time, on 30 June 1908 a fireball of devastating proportions struck Earth in the valley of the Tunguska river, a remote part of northern Siberia. Its blazing heat laid waste an area the size of Leningrad, melting metal objects and incinerating herds of reindeer. Foliage was ripped from trees, the blast uprooting them like matchsticks. Nomads were lifted bodily from the ground and their tents flung away in the violent wind. A farmer sitting on his porch 60 kilometres away described it: 'There appeared a great flash of light. There was so much heat that I was no longer able to remain where I was – my shirt almost burned off my back. I saw a huge fireball that covered an enormous part of the sky. I only had a moment to note the size of it. Afterwards it became dark and at the same time I felt an explosion that threw me several feet from the porch. I lost consciousness for a few moments and when I came to I heard a noise that shook the whole house and nearly moved it off its foundations.'

The pre-revolutionary state of Russia at the time meant that this exceptional cosmic disaster, the largest in recorded history until Hiroshima, went uninvestigated until 1921 when a Soviet mineralogist, Leonid Kulik, heard of it by accident when investigating meteorite falls in general. Six years later he mounted an expedition, and when he arrived in the area

'the results of even a cursory examination exceeded all the tales of the eye-witnesses and my wildest expectations.' On this and subsequent expeditions during the following two years he searched for evidence to substantiate his belief that the devastation had been caused by a meteorite of similar scale to the one that carved out the Meteor Crater in Arizona (page 182). He never found it conclusively. A small amount of meteoritic dust has turned up, and a few small apparent craters, but nothing of the size needed to support his theory. There was no huge crater, and to the mystification and excitement of the world's newspapers, the centre of the explosion was marked by less damage than the oval-shaped area that had been destroyed around it.

Various theories

Whatever caused the Tunguska explosion, it wasn't a meteorite, it seems. Since Kulik's findings, the controversy about other possible causes has split investigators into those who believe that it was a comet (a kind of dirty cosmic snowball consisting of chunks of frozen gases with meteoritic material and dust mixed in), and those who prefer a more fanciful explanation (see below). The main point at issue is whether there was a significant rise in the level of radiation in the world after the Tunguska explosion, as there would be if the explosion were nuclear. Tests on two tree-rings in the United States show a one per cent jump at the critical time, although this has not been confirmed elsewhere. There are also reports of accelerated forest growth in the area, which may be the result of genetic mutation; but this, too, may be the result of more fertile soil following fire. Findings from many sources now strongly favour the comet, but the last word has certainly not been said. The alternative theories are in any case provocative and appealing enough to be worth considering.

Black holes

Although as yet unproved, there is strong theoretical support for the idea that after the big bang which created our universe, a number of 'black holes' were left; others may occur spontaneously even now. A black hole, according to the US physicist John B. Carlson, is 'a geometrical quirk in our Einsteinian four-dimensional space-time. If a massive object can collapse to a small enough radius, its gravitational field would be so high that light could not escape from it . . . it closes off a region of space-time around itself, in some sense separating itself from the universe.'

If the Sun were to become a black hole, it would have a radius of three kilometres. A good-sized asteroid of 100 kilometres radius would be about the size of an atom, and according to the

British physicists A. A. Jackson and M. P. Ryan in *Nature*, the effect of this hitting Siberia would be indistinguishable from the Tunguska event. As Carlson describes it: 'A massive atom-sized black hole entering the Earth's atmosphere at a typical collision velocity for an interplanetary body would create an atmospheric shock wave with enough force to level hundreds of square kilometres of Siberian forest, ionize air, produce flash-burning, and seismic effects. No major crater of meteoritic residue would result. The mini-black hole would then follow a rather straight path through the body of the Earth with very little interaction and emerge a few minutes later on the opposite side of the Earth.'

Since the theory was propounded, the objections have been made that there is no record of an unusual explosion on that day in the North Atlantic where it would have emerged from Earth and that a black hole would cause very severe subterranean shock waves, whereas the only recorded seismic effects were surface waves.

Anti-matter
Again, this only exists in theory – and as far as Tunguska is concerned, it seems an unlikely solution since 'anti-matter meteorites' are supposed to originate far beyond the Milky Way and would lose their explosive power by the time they reached our galaxy. Yet research into anti-matter is still in its infancy. It has been suggested as a solution for ball lightning (page 24), and several renowned scientists, including Nobel Laureate Willard Libby, prefer it as an explanation.

Extra-terrestrial nuclear explosion
This is often suggested to overcome the fact that the explosion happened with very little prior warning, such as would be expected with the prolonged approach of a comet (but see below). The idea was first put forward in a science fiction work in 1946 by the Russian, Alexander Kazantsev, who was convinced the Tunguska explosion was the result of a nuclear explosion in a space ship, which explained the radial scorching and the undamaged trees at the centre, the descriptions of a pillar of fire and billowing dust cloud consistent with the now-familiar mushroom cloud of an atomic explosion, why there was no crater, and why the object – whatever it was – appeared to slow down as it neared Earth. Other writers have suggested (in the absence of conclusive evidence about increased radiation) that it was a space ship powered by anti-matter that exploded after getting into trouble.

The comet hypothesis
This would seem to be the best explanation. Comets have been known to change direction and speed. The 1977 paper on the subject in *Nature*, by John Brown of Glasgow University and David Hughes of Sheffield University, calculated that although the temperature produced by the comet in the atmosphere would have been no more than a few million degrees, too low for a full-scale nuclear explosion, 'it is entirely fallacious to suppose that subnuclear temperatures cannot produce nuclear effects.' As to why the comet was not observed for a longer time, 'when the comet encountered the Earth it would be coming from a point in the dawn sky comparatively close to the Sun and would thus be most difficult to detect and observe. The orbital configuration is similar to Comet Mrkos which was only detected after having rounded the Sun and travelled beyond the Earth's orbit.'

Forests devastated by the explosion show relatively less damage at the centre of the disaster. A question-mark is also raised about the increased level of radioactivity that was recorded.

Hard-core UFOs

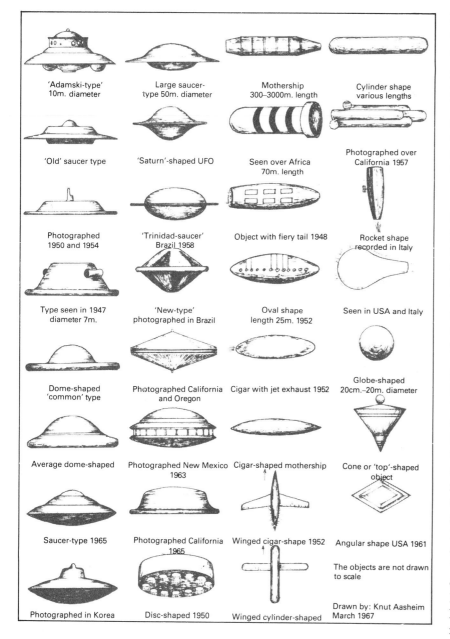

'Adamski-type'
10m. diameter

Large saucer-
type 50m. diameter

Mothership
300–3000m. length

Cylinder shape
various lengths

'Old' saucer type

'Saturn'-shaped UFO

Seen over Africa
70m. length

Photographed over
California 1957

Photographed
1950 and 1954

'Trinidad-saucer'
Brazil 1958

Object with fiery tail 1948

Rocket shape
recorded in Italy

Type seen in 1947
diameter 7m.

'New-type'
photographed in Brazil

Oval shape
length 25m. 1952

Seen in USA and Italy

Dome-shaped
'common' type

Photographed California
and Oregon

Cigar with jet exhaust 1952

Globe-shaped
20cm.–20m. diameter

Average dome-shaped

Photographed New Mexico
1963

Cigar-shaped mothership

Cone or 'top'-shaped
object

Saucer-type 1965

Photographed California
1965

Winged cigar-shape 1952

Angular shape USA 1961

The objects are not drawn
to scale

Photographed in Korea

Disc-shaped 1950

Winged cylinder-shaped

Drawn by: Knut Aasheim
March 1967

The variety of UFO shapes, according to *New Scientist*, is a 'testament to human imagination'. All shapes drawn by Knut Asheim in 1967 have been described in detail more than once.

The trouble with UFOs is that there are too many of them. J. Allen Hynek, the celebrated astronomer who was consultant to the somewhat discredited US Air Force investigation into UFOs, and who in dissociating himself from it coined the phrase *Close Encounters of the Third Kind*, asks his lecture audiences to raise their hands if they have seen one. Whether it is an audience representing a cross-section of the population (e.g. an entire University), or selective (e.g. those who pay to hear him), the figure stays steady at around 20 per cent. With specialist groups having a regular opportunity to observe the night-time sky – airline pilots, security guards – the proportion is generally higher. A 1974 Gallup poll put the US national figure at around 11 per cent (even so, perhaps 32 million people), but this may be an under-estimate because of reticence and embarrassment; another poll, by Opinion

Research Corporation, found that only 13 per cent of people who see a UFO report it.

When these sightings are translated into the number of UFOs that must be involved, the figures become incredible. Hynek's Center for UFO Research at Evanston, Illinois, receives an average of 100 reports a night. The US writer John Keel subscribed to a press cuttings service as part of his research and received up to 150 reported incidents a day; in his first year, 1966, he received more than 10,000 clippings (compared with 1060 reports supposedly received by the US Air Force investigation in the same period). Jacques Vallée, a French astrophysicist and computer scientist, has estimated that when non-reporting of incidents is taken into account, together with the fact that most sightings seem to take place at night when fewer people are around to watch them, as many as 3 million *landings* may have taken place in the last 25 years.

Daunting statistics
For those seeking a physical explanation of UFOs, this is absurd. While it is now widely accepted that there are many other star systems in the Universe capable of supporting life and while logically half of these might have a civilization in advance of ours, some by many million years, the implications of the finite speed of light are daunting. Philip J. Klass, senior avionics editor of *Aviation Week and Space Technology*, and author of two hard-line books debunking UFO reports, told *Playboy* magazine: 'It would require nearly 100 years for inhabitants of the nearest star system to ours that *could* have life, Alpha Centauri, to make a round trip to Earth – *if* their spacecraft could fly at 70 million miles per hour. And this is based on the optimistic assumption that there *is* a planet in orbit around Alpha Centauri, that there *is* intelligent life on it, and that it's so advanced technologically it can build spaceships capable of flying at that speed. So even if there *is* intelligent life relatively near to us, and if such creatures live to be 200 or even 400 years old, a 100-year trip is still not exactly inconsequential.'

Ian Ridpath, author of *Messages from the Stars*, put the problem another way in the *New Scientist*: 'Imagine, for a moment, that there are one million other civilisations in the Galaxy, all sending out starships. Since there must be something like 10 billion interesting places to visit (one tenth of all stars in the Galaxy), then each civilization must launch 10,000 spaceships annually for only one to reach here every year. If every civilization launches the more reasonable number of one starship annually, then we would expect to be visited once every 10,000 years.'

More than anything else it is this statistical improbability which divides investigators such as Philip Klass from UFO believers (although the latter now make up more than half the US population, according to one survey). He points to the total lack of physical evidence for UFOs. The *National Enquirer* in 1977 offered an open-ended award of one million dollars to anybody who could prove that UFOs come from outer space and are not natural phenomena.

Klass himself has laid several 10,000-dollar bets on the subject and offered to refund the purchase price of both his books to everybody who bought them if someone is able to produce 'one artifact, just one, that the National Academy of Sciences is willing to endorse as something that couldn't have been made on Earth . . . Human beings in general and Americans in particular are great souvenir collectors. Yet of all the dozens of people who claim to have been aboard a flying saucer, not one has bothered to pick up the equivalent of a paper clip or an ashtray or a book of matches.'

UFO quarrels

Ufologists themselves are divided between those who take a cautious, scientifically-based approach that inclines towards the physical reality of UFOs and those who invoke metaphysical or psychic explanations. A 1977 conference in Acapulco, Mexico gathered the most celebrated of them under one roof – the scientoids and the mystics, as they were dubbed by the magazine *New Realities*. Among the first group was J. Allen Hynek, one of six speakers to dissociate themselves from the more extreme mystics. He has long argued that UFOs should be treated with an open mind: 'Everyone seems to have adopted some particular viewpoint. I know too much about the history of science not to know how dangerous that is. I go so far as to

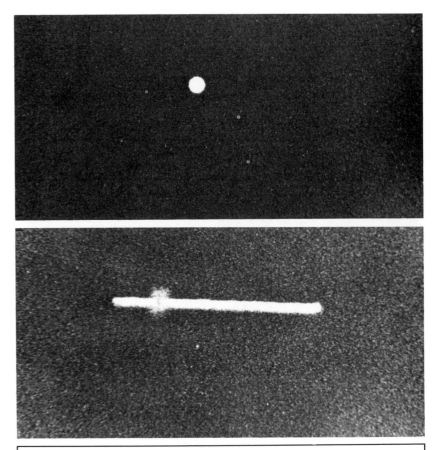

Project Starlight International is a UFO tracking centre 30 kilometres north-west of Austin, Texas equipped with a battery of scientific monitoring devices; the aim is to gather a broad range of data on UFOs and make this accessible to interested people, scientists or otherwise. The top picture is, according to PSI staff, a 'possible UFO photographed in a five-second exposure as an object hovered near the laboratory for nearly ten minutes beginning at 8.58 p.m. on 10 December 1975'. Film stock was Tri-X. The band of light in the picture below is the same object 'moving off to the left in an eight-second exposure. The strange burst-like effect was not seen by PSI staff. Time was approximately 9.09 p.m.' Below left is the team's laser device for measuring UFO distance; and a simulated display on a computer terminal designed to track UFOs over a colour topographic map.

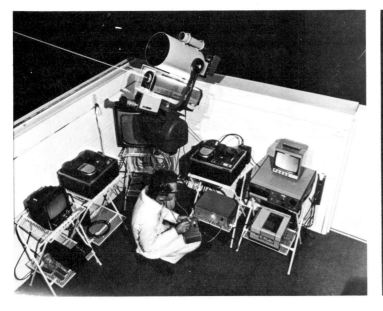

List of 19th-century UFO sightings

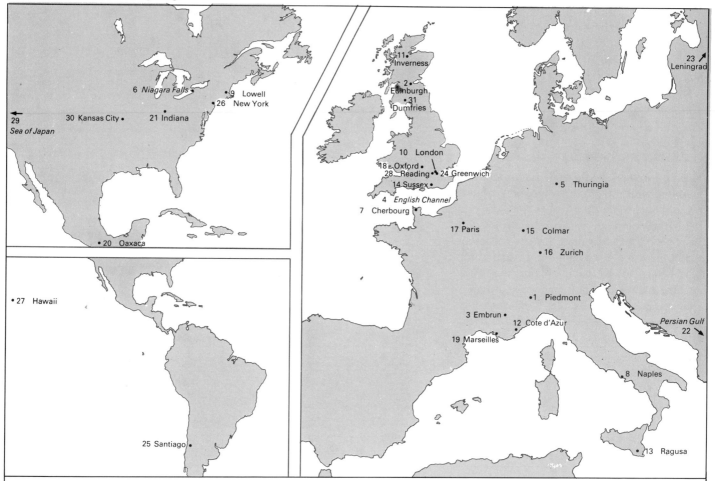

1 12 October 1808. Formation of 'luminous discs' observed.

2 October (?) 1816. Large, luminous crescent-shaped object seen over city by many people.

3 7 September 1820. Formation of flying objects crosses the town.
22 November 1821. Luminous disc observed from several ships.

4 1 April 1826. Grey, torpedo-shaped object seen in sky.

5 29 November 1831. Brilliant luminous disc seen in sky.

6 13 November 1833. Luminous flying object crosses city.

7 12 January 1836. Gleaming aerial vessel seen over city.

8 11 May 1845. Astronomer at local observatory reports number of luminous discs leaving trails.

9 26 October 1846. 'Luminous flying disc' reported over the area.

10 19 March 1847. 'Spherical craft' seen rising vertically through the clouds.

11 19 September 1848. Two large brilliant objects seen over town.

12 6 June 1850. Red sphere seen in sky.

13 26 October 1853. Brilliant disc seen moving from east to west during early hours of morning.

14 11 August 1855. Glowing circular objects 'with spokes like a wheel' crossed sky, visible for an hour.

15 6 April 1856. Dark 'aerial torpedo' seen in sky. One end round, the other pointed. Said to have emitted low-pitched sound.

16 27 April 1863. Zurich observatory reports 'aerial discs' emitting 'whining sound'.

17 10 October 1864. Noted French astronomer Leverrier reports appearance of luminous tubular object over city.

18 8 June 1868. Radcliffe Observatory reports four-minute appearance of luminous flying object.

19 1 August 1871. Large red disc hovers over city for almost ten minutes.

20 6 July 1874. Large conical object observed over the area.

21 7 September 1877. Dark objects seen crossing sky emitting flashes at four-second intervals.

22 15 May 1879. British warship reports two huge 'spinning aerial wheels' just above sea level.

23 30 July 1880. Large airborne spherical object accompanied by two lesser spheres.

24 17 November 1882. Vast green disc observed from Greenwich Observatory. Mottled appearance. Also reported in Europe.

25 5 November 1883. Pulsating disc-like object passes over city.

26 3 July 1884. Bright spherical craft with dark marking reported from many parts of State.

27 24 February 1885. Master of a freighter in the area reports fall of 'a huge fiery mass' into sea near ship

28 3 November 1888. Aerial vessel passes over county of Berkshire. Animals said to be affected by sound.

29 25 May 1893. Two British warships report formation of discs heading north and emitting smoke trails.

30 14 April 1897. Torpedo-shaped object observed with downward shining searchlight.

31 1 November 1899. Two circular black objects crossed sky during daylight. One said to be 'circling the other'.

say, "There is absolutely a UFO phenomenon. It is not all nonsense and misinterpretation." Then I simply say there are numerous hypotheses at present. It's a research problem.'

Another 'scientoid' at the conference was Ray Stanford, whose research project, Project Starlight International, is aimed primarily at using the best technical equipment – magnetometers, gravimeters, a laser, computer-enhanced photography – to establish that UFOs are more than the holographic thought projections that some ufologists have suggested. 'If we prove the existence of a G (gravity) wave, we'll contribute something fundamental to the understanding of the universe. Reports have indicated that UFOs during descent may somehow cause themselves to have an effective density just slightly more than the atmosphere.'

Disputed explanations

Research groups such as his agree that most UFOs are in fact IFOs – identifiable flying objects – while differing about the proportions involved. Of all sightings, perhaps only one or two per cent of the total can be regarded as genuinely inexplicable in terms of known technology; a group called Ground Saucer Watch, based in Phoenix, Arizona, has listed 109 objects able to move across the sky at night and be taken for UFOs, including fireflies, space satellites, and the planet Venus ('the all-time-champion-natural-type UFO' according to Professor Frank Salisbury of Utah State University, author of *The Utah UFO Display*). But a number of the remaining sightings resist even Klass's tenacious explanations. He has, for instance, many times claimed to have solved the case of the encounter 750 metres above Mansfield, Ohio in 1973 between the four-man crew of a helicopter piloted by Lawrence Coyne and a glowing object, apparently a grey metallic structure, which approached them at high speed, hovered above them for a few seconds, and then took off again; during the incident the helicopter, which had been falling rapidly to the ground to avoid collision, mysteriously rose to an altitude in excess of 1000 metres. Klass says that the only thing the men saw was a meteor fireball from the Orionid meteor shower that regularly takes place there during October. Hynek and others say this 'solution' is partial, and contradicts the witnesses' description, particularly the way the object remained stationary; meteorites simply do not behave like that.

UFO mischief

The most intriguing explanation so far put forward for UFOs and perhaps the most plausible for anybody who has studied the impishness and coincidence that surrounds so much of Fortean phenomena described in the following pages, is to suppose that the lack of UFO hardware is because the UFOs or their occupants have deliberately withheld it. Supporters of this view see UFOs as a modern manifestation of the devils, elementals and creatures of Hell that have plagued our unconscious since the beginning of mankind. People with psychic ability may be the most vulnerable and the confusion and ambiguity that invariably surrounds UFO reports is part of an intentional plan by somebody/something/Him to imprint doubt and uncertainty about what the intentions are.

The most lucid exponent of this is John Keel, whose objective research led him into an extraordinary series of personally-experienced events that have convinced him UFOs are insidiously dangerous, contacting and brainwashing susceptible people who, having had the memory erased from their conscious minds, are later able to describe what happened only under hypnosis. As for extra-terrestrial space-ships, 'a very small residue of them may be very real,' he wrote in *UFOs: Operation Trojan Horse*. The vast majority, because of their sheer number, have to be explained differently – '*someone* or *something* actually has the power to completely possess and control the human mind. Human beings can be manipulated through this power and used for both good and evil purposes. Suppose the plan is to process millions of people and then at some future date trigger all those minds at one time? Would we suddenly have a world of saints? Or would we have a world of armed maniacs shooting at one another?'

'Stars', by the Dutch surrealist painter M. C. Escher. His work is marked by a deliberate confusion of perspective and dimensions, and these elemental creatures half-imprisoned within geometrical time/space come near to the nightmare UFO vision of many SF writers.

Ice blocks from the sky

Returning home from work in the physics department of Manchester University on 2 April 1973, Dr R. S. Griffiths noted a single violent flash of lightning above him. Conscientiously – for he is an official lightning observer for the Electrical Research Association in Britain – he jotted down the relevant details: time, estimated position, height, weather conditions and so on. He had walked on for another nine minutes when a solid object crashed into the street only three metres away from him, smashing into several pieces. It had been a solid block of ice before it disintegrated, and as a scientist Dr Griffiths was quick to realize its significance. He picked up the largest piece and ran home to put it in his deep-freeze; as a result, it became the best-studied example yet of a phenomenon so far unexplained by science. How is it that large heavy objects, animate as well as inanimate, can fall from an apparently empty sky?

On analysis, Dr Griffiths' ice block turned out to be not especially big; the fragment weighed 612 grams and was probably about one-third of the original full-size block. But there are countless recorded examples much larger than that (the ones in the map on the opposite page being just a representative sample), all of them much larger than the heaviest hailstones, which rarely exceed 200 grams. These ice blocks, or 'ice-meteors' as they are sometimes known, have smashed through the roofs of houses and dented the metal of cars – on 9 November 1950 the London *Evening News* reported that a Devonshire farm had suffered a bombardment of ice blocks 'the size of dinner plates' and more, one of which weighed seven kilogrammes and was wedged in the ground beside the body of a decapitated sheep.

However, Griffiths' ice block was important for a number of reasons. His particular background as a physicist and meteorologist gave credence to the phenomenon, which until then had been regarded by scientists in much the same way as meteorites in the 19th Century (page 182) or ball lightning until the last few years (page 24) – that is to say, generally with disbelief. Griffiths showed that the structure of the block was in crucial respects different from any hailstone;

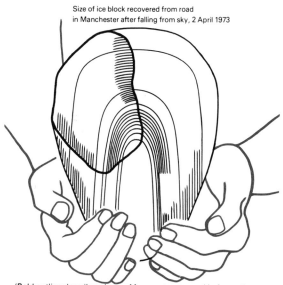

Size of ice block recovered from road in Manchester after falling from sky, 2 April 1973

(Bold outline describes shape of fragment preserved in freezer)

Life of Charles Fort

Robert J. M. Rickard, co-author of *Phenomena* and researcher for a number of topics in this Atlas, has long been a believer in the philosophy of Charles Fort, and is editor of *Fortean Times*, which continues Fort's work today. Here he outlines the man's life, which began when he was born into a wealthy New York family in 1874 and was brought up in a family ruled over with autocratic severity by his father, who frequently beat him with a horsewhip. Throughout the rest of his life he showed a contempt for established authority.

At 18 he ran away from home and spent more than three years travelling round the world, sleeping rough and working for his needs. He caught malaria on the way back to New York, married the girl who nursed him and settled down to a life of considerable poverty in the Bronx, relieved only by the meagre earnings of his journalism.

Prodigious research

In 1916, aged 42, he received an inheritance just large enough to free him from the need to earn a regular living. He worked prodigiously in the NY Public Library, collecting notes from papers, books and journals, on little scraps of paper (now held by that library). He reckons that he made the 'grand tour of the extant material at least three times, first accumulating 25,000 and then 40,000 notes,' destroying them each time and starting anew because they were 'not what I wanted'.

In the end, four books containing his research were published: *Book of the Damned* (1919), *New Lands* (1923), *Lo!* (1931) and *Wild Talents* (1931), all of them written in an outrageous, quirky and absolutely unmistakable style. After his mammoth achievement of sifting through the histories of the sciences, the journals, newspapers and other records, he had a huge collection of events and phenomena which either had no explanation acceptable to contemporary science, or which had been hastily and inadequately explained away.

Oddities and anomalies

A brief listing of his diverse and arcane topics would include: rains of blood, manna, stones or worms from the sky; people who turn up from nowhere, and their mysteriously disappearing counterparts; feral children and wildmen; invisible assassins and stigmatic wounds; teleportations of humans, objects and animals; artifacts and footprints found in 'pre-human' geological strata; coincidences of geophysical, astronomical and meteorological events; lightning curiosities; fire series; evidences for 'little people'; poltergeist phenomena.

Fort speculated on other life-forms and other worlds, suggesting (but not fully believing) that this Earth received visits by voyagers from space, and gave hundreds of accounts of lights and 'craft' in the sky; sometime before 1920, he coined the word 'teleportation' to describe the transport of people and objects through space (and even time).

Individual solutions

Fort was an individualist, both in his domestic life and in his championing the right of each of us to make up our own minds and to question science's self-proclaimed monopoly of the truth. He wanted people to think for themselves and refused to be drawn into explaining the mysteries he presented.

He thought his own interpretations of little consequence to anyone else; they were 'suggestions and groping and stimuli . . . but the data will be for anyone to form his own opinions on . . . I shall find out for myself, and anyone who cares to, may find out with me.'

Major Ice Block Falls (1801–1977) in North America, Britain, France and India

1 August 1801. Ice blocks in the shape of pencils.

2 May 1802. Ice blocks 1 × 1 × 0.7 m.

3 May 1811. Ice blocks 30 cm in circumference.

4 June 1811. Cuboidal mass of ice 15 cm in diameter.

5 July 1818. Sulphurous pieces of ice.

6 August 1828. Ice blocks 'about a cubic metre in volume'.

7 June 1829. Ice blocks weighing 2 kg.

8 June 1839. Exceptionally dark skies followed by ice falls.

9 July 1841. Half-melted pieces of ice containing frogs.

10 October 1844. Ice block weighing 5 kg.

11 August 1849. Ice block 7 m in diameter.

12 May 1851. Ice blocks 'the size of pumpkins'.

13 August 1851. Ice blocks weighing over 1 kg.

14 July 1853. Irregular ice blocks the size of a hand.

15 December 1854. Flat pieces of ice weighing several kilos.

16 August 1857. Ice blocks weighing 11 kg.

17 March 1860. Ice blocks 'the size of sheep'.

18 July 1864. Ice blocks about 50 cm in diameter.

19 June 1873. Heavy thunderstorms followed by fall of 'fish scales and very irregular hailstones'.

20 July 1874. Vegetable debris frozen on the surface of large hailstones.

21 May 1877. Ice blocks 50 cm in diameter.

22 June 1877. Ditto.

23 August 1879. Ice blocks 15 cm long.

24 June 1881. Mass of ice 50 cm in circumference.

25 June 1882. Hailstones and ice with frogs embedded inside.

26 August 1882. Piece of ice 20 cm long.

27 August 1882. Block of ice weighing 40 kg fell and preserved temporarily in sawdust.

28 July 1883. Ice block weighing 1 kg.

29 March 1887. Lumps of ice preceded by strange lights.

30 May 1888. Ice blocks weighing 750 g.

31 June 1894. 10-cm fragments of ice fell after a tornado.

32 November 1911. Exploding hailstones.

33 March 1968. 'Giant hailstone' weighing at least 1 kg.

34 August 1968. Ice blocks 15–30 cm thick.

35 February 1969. Roof shattered by 'ice bomb'.

36 August 1970. Ice block 'big enough to kill'.

37 June 1971. Ice block weighing 1 kg.

38 August 1971. Hailstones weighing over 1 kg, including one 'as big as a grapefruit'.

39 June 1972. Block of ice in excess of 1 × 1 metre.

40 April 1973. Lump of ice weighing nearly 2 kg.

41 June 1973. Ice block weighing 5 kg.

42 September 1973. 'Ball of ice' weighing 3 kg.

43 March 1974. 50-cm cube of ice.

44 June 1974. Ducks frozen in ice blocks.

45 June 1974. Ice block weighing 1 kg.

46 August 1974. 'Block of ice the size of a rugby ball.'

47 January 1975. 22-kg 'ice bomb'.

48 April 1975. 'Large ice block.'

49 December 1975. Circular block of ice 2 m in diameter.

50 March 1976. Ice block 'the size of a basket ball'.

51 May 1976. Lumps of cloudy ice.

52 January 1977. Ice block weighing about 50 kg.

Sources: *The Collected Books of Charles Fort,* and Fortean journals in US and UK (see *Bibliography* for page 193). Scarcity of information for the early part of this century due to gap between Fort's work and that of later researchers.

BY CHARLES FORT

Cover of *Lo!*, Charles Fort's third book out of four that chronicled the unexplained oddities recorded in newspapers and scientific journals.

moreover, the usual explanation that large blocks of ice 'must' have fallen from an aeroplane did not apply in this case, the various reasons given in his paper being borne out by the flight records of the only two aircraft in the vicinity. The only conclusion he reached about its origin was that 'it was composed of cloud water'.

Whether or not the lightning stroke nine minutes earlier was associated with it is another matter open to question. The British physicist Eric Crew believes so, and has constructed an ingenious theory about the way in which the theoretical properties of lightning may produce jets of hot air which are the basis for both ice-meteors and ball lightning. But reading through the list of cases, it seems on the face of it clear that, while some of them may have an electrical or meteorological or aeronautical basis, others are for the moment simply outside science. The writer Ronald J. Willis collected a number of qualified opinions from US Universities. Drexel Institute: 'The large chunks of ice which have fallen could not have been

Woodcut of fall of fishes published in *Historia de Gentibus*, by O. Magnus, in 1555.

meteorological in origin. Atmospheric processes cannot form or sustain the masses of ice which have been observed in such falls.' University of Colorado: 'Though some astronomers think that meteoritic material composed of ice exists, one doubts whether such chunks could survive the intense heating upon entering our atmosphere.' Virginia University: 'This is a very mysterious thing . . . It can be put in the class with the small percentage of UFOs which cannot be explained away.'

Forteana
Certainly, the general explanation of ice forming on the fuselage of an aeroplane, or being ejected as frozen waste, applies in only a few cases. Ice more than a few centimetres thick on an aeroplane wing would have disastrous effects on flying stability and all modern planes have automatic electrical de-icing equipment. In any case, there are many accounts of massive blocks of ice from pre-aircraft days. The classic 19th-century study *The Atmosphere* by C. Flammarion says that in the reign of Charlemagne a block fell measuring $5 \times 2 \times 3\frac{1}{2}$ metres. At Ord, Scotland, in 1849, a particularly well-described ice block had a circumference of more than six metres.

One useful function that these strange blocks perform is as a gentle introduction to the even stranger objects falling out of the sky that were assiduously noted over a period of 30 years by the American journalist Charles Fort (see panel on page 192) and nowadays classified as *forteana*. These include the vast catalogue of curiosities, anomalies, oddities and pecularities that happen in the world but are outside the accepted laws of science. Fort would have been delighted by the coincidence that the Manchester ice block fell at the feet of the one man in the whole city best qualified to observe it. To him, the universe was infinitely more wonderful and complex that that described by the neat mathematical laws of modern physics.

Time/space aberrations
Another good ice-fall example of the way that time and space fuse into 'coincidence' happened in Timberville, Virginia on 7 March 1976. At about 8.45 p.m. three people were watching television when a loud crash shook their house and a block of ice the size of a basketball smashed through the roof and a plasterboard ceiling to finish up in the living room. Two neighbours heard the event, one standing in his driveway, and another, a teenage girl, rushed out of her house to see what had happened. As if somebody up there was giving a repeat performance, *20 seconds later a near-identical ice-block crashed to the ground less than 50 metres away.*

Creature storms

World distribution of selected creature storms AD 200–1973

1 AD 200. A rain of frogs that swamped the inhabitants of Sardinia was reported by Athenaeus in the *Deipnosophists*.

2 1578. Contemporary reports describe a shower of yellow mice 'which swam ashore when they fell into the water'.

3 Easter 1666. A rain of sprats, smelts and whiting; some of the fish were sold publicly at Maidstone and Dartford.

4 May 1786. Observers reported a rain of black eggs; these eventually hatched into tadpoles.

5 August 1804. n a clear day a great cloud appeared. Bystanders saw several little toads fall from the cloud.

6 January 1806. Strange formations of larvae came down in a snowstorm.

7 December 1827. Large black insects came down with a heavy snowstorm.

8 February 1830. Various types of fish were found in the streets after torrential rain.

9 December 1830. Gnats and fleas came down in a heavy snowstorm.

10 May 1833. After torrential rain dead and dried up fish were found on the streets.

11 June 1833. M. Mauday, curator of Poitiers Natural History Museum, saw several little toads come down with heavy rain.

12 February 1841. John Lewis reported a rain of fish, some of which were later exhibited in Regents Park Zoo.

13 December 1857. After a thunderstorm some grey lizards were found on the streets.

14 February 1861. After an earthquake torrents of fish fell in the streets; villagers collected them in buckets.

15 July 1864. After a thunderstorm frogs were found embedded in hailstones.

16 February 1871. After a meteorite fall several dead fish were found near the site.

17 May 1879. Thousands of 'creek minnows' fell and the incident was reported to the Australian Museum.

18 January 1877. Thousands of snakes, 30–50 cm long, fell down with torrential rain in a localized area.

19 August 1880. Fall of long black flies of a species never seen before in the district.

20 May 1881. After a severe thunderstorm several periwinkles were found scattered around the locality. Some were still alive.

21 June 1882. During a snowstorm small blocks of ice fell; some of them contained tiny frogs.

22 January 1890. Observers reported falls of yellow and black larvae of a type unknown to the district.

23 June 1892. A fall of little frogs which were reported to be 'almost white' in colour.

24 August 1892. After torrential rain thousands of mussels were found in the streets.

25 July 1896. Many hundreds of dead birds fell on to the streets; there were wild ducks, cat-birds, and woodpeckers.

26 January 1911. After a storm snails – of a variety unknown to the district – were found scattered on the ground.

27 March 1922. During a shower numerous little insects like spiders, caterpillars and large ants fell on the mountain slopes.

28 October 1932. During a storm 'hundreds of small carp' were seen to fall on top of a hill.

29 November 1947. After torrential rain perch were found on the streets, but not on the roofs or in tanks.

30 June 1954. Bystanders witnessed hundreds of little frogs bouncing off people's heads and leaping about in crowded streets.

31 July 1959. After a storm fish about 10 cm long were found at Townsville airport. It was reported to the Australian Museum.

32 January 1969. Hundreds of dead ducks dropped on to the streets. Reports said the birds suffered injuries before they hit the ground.

33 April 1971. Numerous grunters (*Madigania unicolour*) about 8 cm long were found after heavy rain.

34 September 1973. 'Tens of thousands of small toads' fell from the sky in a freak storm.

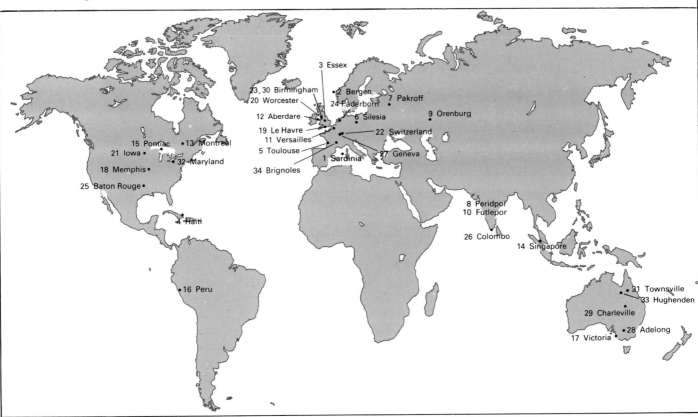

Plague of frogs, one of many to afflict Egypt before the Exodus of Israelite slaves. Like all the Biblical plagues, it seems to have been a sky-borne disaster.

Scientific analysis proved only that the ice was just like murky tap-water, and was 'explained' as being drinking water that had leaked from a plane's tank and built up on the fuselage, breaking off in 5–6 kilo pieces. In fact it was a clear night, there were no planes in the sky, and the aerial origin of the ice blocks must, logically, have been stationary for nine seconds; nevertheless, the official explanation still stands.

Fort would have scorned such a laboured approach. The phenomena that he noted often seem to be defying such physical laws as gravity, or even common-sense, with a hint of wilfulness. He described ice-blocks that floated rather than plummeted down from the sky. Why otherwise would the large ones not smash to pieces? Similarly many stones from the sky, attributed to meteorite falls, had the wrong characteristics. For instance, although they should all have been hot after their passage through the Earth's atmosphere, many were not, including the Dhurmsalla, India shower that fell covered with ice on 28 July 1860, described as 'so intensely cold as to benumb the fingers and hands'. Other reports were of stones falling slowly and gently; or of being associated with just one person around whom they fell profusely like rain without causing harm; or of appearing inside buildings without any sign of them having penetrated the structure.

Natural explanations also fail with many of the cases of creature falls that have occurred since the beginning of recorded history. Mice, rats, toads, frogs, larvae, manna, grain and even lumps of flesh have all reportedly landed on the Earth from nowhere, and the common solution is that a whirlwind sucked them up and deposited them elsewhere. But many ancient accounts do not tally with this. A Greek work, *The Deipnosophists*, of around AD 200, based on research in the Alexandrian Library, says that 'in the Chersonesus it once rained fish uninterruptedly for three days' – an impossibly long time for a whirlwind to last continuously. Another description in the same book says of a fall of frogs in Paeonia and Dardinia that 'so great has been the number of these frogs that the houses and the roads have been full with them'; at first the local people tried to deal with the plague by killing them and locking their doors against them, but without success: 'All their vessels were filled with them, and the frogs were found boiled up and roasted with everything they ate, and when besides this they could not make use of any water, nor put their feet on the ground for the heaps of frogs that were everywhere, and were annoyed also by the smell of those that died, they fled the country.'

Other objections to the whirlwind theory are that the falls are rarely accompanied by pond-debris or plants. Tadpoles hardly ever fall, nor full-grown frogs – they are usually thumb-nail sized, as described in 1977 by a London woman in a letter to *TV Times*: 'We first thought they were hailstones until we saw they were all tiny frogs and were jumping about. My son filled a sweet box to take home. The brim of my husband's hat was full of them while the storm lasted. They were everywhere.'

The problem of where such a quantity of airborne creatures come from is absolutely unresolved, by Charles Fort or anyone else. Sometimes the incidents involved worms – on one occasion on top of a 10-centimetre layer of snow near Sangerfield, New York, and described by *Scientific American* as 'inexplicable'. Other times it has been sticklebacks, or mussels, or sprats, or snakes, or lizards – each occasion showing the same curious selectivity, and the same baffling lack of an obvious place of origin, which Fort believed, perhaps half-jokingly, was 'somewhere aloft. Whether it's the planet Genesistrine, or the moon, or a vast amorphous region super-jacent to this earth, or an island in the Super-Sargasso Sea should perhaps be left to the researches of other super- or extra-geographers.' Fort died before space capsules orbited the Earth without discovering his Super-Sargasso Sea, and men set foot on the moon without finding organic life, so we can only guess today how he might have modified his views. The chances are, not at all. His probable retort would have been that the space travellers weren't looking in the right dimension and that sooner or later something would land at their feet that would prove his point for him. Certainly, since his death, mysterious ice-falls from the sky have continued unabated.

Section nine
Appearances and disappearances

Perhaps the most provocative and intriguing thought to emerge in the explanation of the puzzling aerial phenomena described in the last section, particularly with regard to UFOs and creature storms from the skies, is the idea that such phenomena have a built-in ambiguity. Has there never been a satisfactory photograph of a UFO because something about the substance of a UFO is impossible to capture on film? Can our repeated failure to obtain standard scientific proof be because they are essentially and deliberately elusive?

The word 'deliberately' here does not necessarily imply an intention by someone or something to prevent proof (although this is a perfectly valid hypothesis, believed by many people); rather, that it is the very nature of a phenomenon to teeter capriciously on the edge of what we call normal reality. In the words of the stage magician: now you see it, now you don't.

At any rate, it is a thought well worth bearing in mind when reading the strange stories of lake monsters and unknown beasts, of people who vanish into thin air and those who never seem to grow old, of disappearing ships and foundling children from the wild, of lost civilizations and materialized thought projections that make up the subject matter in the last two sections of this Atlas. As elsewhere, our frame of reference has been to try to explain each riddle and mystery within the accepted bounds of scientific probability before moving to more outrageous suggestions. But the more you research this kind of subject, the surer you become that something else is operating in addition to the model of the Universe to which we have become familiar.

Thus it is fairly easy, looking at it from a scientific viewpoint, to conclude that the likelihood of the world containing a few species of unknown large mammals or of large unidentified underwater creatures is pretty high. But which ones, out of all those reported, are actual living biological beasts that could be slaughtered with a gun or a harpoon? Tentatively, we conclude that this could probably happen with Bigfoot and not with the Yeti; probably with a variety of sea monsters, but only possibly with Nessie.

But even while coming to this fairly safe conclusion, personal investigation and research has strongly reinforced the idea of 'something else' being a crucial element in both cases. Preparing a film at Loch Ness, for instance, we interviewed at some length 20 or 30 people who had recently seen the monster. Anybody who does this, as opposed to sitting in a university and calculating that Nessie is impossible because insufficient salmon are being gobbled up in the loch, cannot fail to be impressed by the quality of testimony. A handful of the stories are concocted or embroidered and are easy enough to spot and weed out. The remainder represent an undeniable body of evidence. Why, then, is there no undisputed photograph or film? A nun and her colleague watched three monsters moving dolphin-like only 50 metres or so from the side of the loch for at least ten minutes. She took, as she thought, a complete roll of film. The camera jammed on the first exposure. Why?

Then there is the case of the Surrey puma, not mentioned in this section because of its biological and ecological incredibility, but a reality none the less for the dozens of witnesses who have seen it roaming in the commuter belt round London, the police who have chased it, and the RSPCA who have taken plaster casts of its paw marks and had them positively identified at London Zoo as those of a puma. Yet once again there is this ambiguity and elusiveness, to a degree that almost amounts to mischief. The paw marks are arguable. The photographs are fuzzy. And what does this colony of pumas eat? Once or twice a deer or a cow has been found with deep scratch marks on it as if made by a powerful beast but there is no evidence of the widespread disappearance of pets and farm animals that would be needed to provide the 140 kilos of meat needed each week by a single puma. Like the one unexplained footprint of an unknown beast found by Eric Shipton high in the Himalayas the puma leaves traces that confuse and perplex – as if deliberately to persuade us that there is another reality besides that in which we have become accustomed to live so comfortably.

Underwater monsters

There is an attitude among certain biologists that if you can't dissect something in a laboratory, it's not worth considering. The view came through strongly at the end of a BBC radio discussion on sea-serpents in February 1961, when a hard-line opponent of the possibility of an unknown air-breathing animal like a plesiosaur somehow living millions of years beyond its time noted the absence of a dead specimen. 'I think you really prove the crime when you've got the corpse.'

Exactly the same problem applies to the Loch Ness monster. In spite of intense and expensive efforts, nobody has yet succeeded in luring one into a position where it can be conclusively photographed, or trapped long enough for an examination to be made. After Dr Robert H. Rines of the Academy of Applied Science in Boston, Massachusetts, had secured the blurred 1975 underwater photographs from which, after computer enhancement, the British naturalist, Sir Peter Scott was able to paint a plausible reconstruction of the whole creature, the National Geographic Society mounted an expedition the following year in an attempt to verify its existence. An ingenious sonar bait was used, transmitting underwater the simulated sound pattern made by the movement of a wounded fish. Tested off the Florida coast, the device had been viciously attacked within minutes by shoals of sharks arriving from several miles away; Nessie obstinately refused, throughout an entire summer, to be tempted.

Obstinate paradoxes

So whatever the monster feeds on, it is unlikely to be the local salmon – and this is just the first of many paradoxes that surround the creature. Nobody can doubt that *something* has been seen and photographed with some success, many times. That every sighting is a hoax, or self-delusion, simply doesn't stand up to personal investigation. Researchers for a film in the US TV series *In Search of . . .* interviewed more than 20 witnesses who not only had strikingly vivid and consistent stories to tell, but who had no overt motive for inventing them – doctors, policemen, retired people who actively disliked the crowds Nessie brings; and these people represented only a tiny fraction of the hundreds, perhaps thousands, who had seen an unusual object in the Loch since the road alongside was opened in 1933 and made sightings much easier.

Lost photographs

But at the same time, whatever is there has much in common with UFOs (page 188) so long as 'hard' evidence remains defiantly elusive. Perhaps if it was renamed an unidentified moving object, or UMO, instead of being a monster (derived from the Latin *monstrum*, meaning marvel or omen), it would be more appropriate. No carcase has ever been found (perhaps because the nature of the cold, steep-sided loch causes them to sink to the bottom), and no obvious source of food is known; cameras and photographs have a strange habit of jamming or fogging at the crucial moment. Tim Dinsdale, who took the best cine film yet, says he missed a perfect opportunity when the creature's head and neck came through the surface of the water less than 200 metres away in 1971; after months of concentrated watching, he was temporarily paralysed and failed to activate any of the five telephoto cameras to hand. Doc Shiels, of Ponsanooth in Cornwall, who took the pictures on this page, tells of the 'cosmic trickster's game' that occurred:

'My original No. 1 colour slide went astray for days on end at the *Daily Record* offices in Glasgow. Other photographs from the same

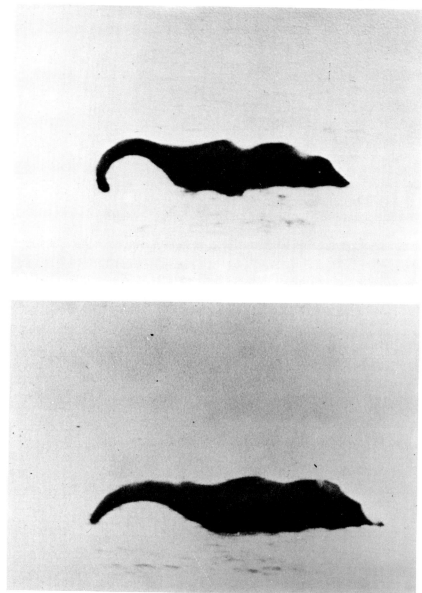

1977 photographs of object in Loch Ness, taken on high speed Ektachrome, and subject to many mishaps before appearing in newspapers (see text).

of film vanished entirely after being inspected by the picture editor, Martin Gilfeather. My original No. 2 slide somehow escaped from its carefully sealed envelope somewhere between Cornwall and Boston, Massachusetts. The only direct, negative, monochrome, glass copy-plate made from that slide (by David Benchley of Cornish Photonews) was accidentally dropped and broken (by me!). It's a disturbing fact that hardly any of the original negatives of the better known Loch Ness monster photographs taken since 1933 have survived. Nessie pix are supernaturally accident-prone!'

Statistical evidence

In the absence of 'concrete' evidence many scientists will understandably continue to reject the Monster idea *in toto*. However, there is another way – also scientific – of looking at the huge number of sightings of underwater monsters, pioneered by the great Belgian zoologist Bernard Heuvelmans: to see what picture can be drawn when the massive amount of cumulative reported detail is analysed statistically. His work on lake monsters has yet to be published, but will undoubtedly show that a variety of unlikely creatures exist in inland waters the world over, some, because of their size compared with the relatively small amounts of water in which they live, biologically even more doubtful than Nessie.

But in his classic work *In the Wake of the Sea Serpents* he has shown that it is totally unscientific to dismiss reports just because they do not coincide with the known catalogue of the world's sea-creatures. As with witnesses of the Loch Ness monster, he found it relatively easy to sort out the deliberate hoaxes and the mistakes from the 587 reports of monster-sightings that he examined, dating from 1639 to 1964. After eliminating these, and the ones too vague to be useful, he was still left with 358 there was no reason to doubt.

After computer enhancement techniques had been used on photographs taken by an expedition from Massachusetts Institute of Technology, the British naturalist, Peter Scott, created this image of what the Loch Ness monster may look like.

Long-necked (48 sightings)
Size: 5–15 metres or more.
Habitat: Widespread over globe, including steep-sided lakes.
Behaviour: Only amphibious sea-serpent, on land bounding like a sea-lion. Exceptional speed in water – 15–35 knots and upwards.

Merhorse (37 sightings)
Size: 10–30 metres or more.
Habitat: Almost anywhere except Polar seas and Indian ocean.
Behaviour: Mammal living mostly at 100 fathoms depth, fast enough to catch and eat squid.

Many-humped (33 sightings)
Size: 20–35 metres.
Habitat: Almost exclusively in warm waters of North Atlantic Gulf Stream.
Behaviour: Moves caterpillar-like very quickly – 20–40 knots. Humps may be air-filled sacs to allow prolonged diving.

Many-finned (20 sightings)
Size: 10–20 metres, sometimes larger.
Habitat: Tropical waters only.
Behaviour: Moves in vertical undulations at speeds up to 10 knots when chased. Main characteristic is breath seen coming from its nostrils.

Super-otter (13 sightings)
Size: 20–30 metres (approximate, because its wake confuses observers).
Habitat: Near surface of northerly seas.
Behaviour: Moves in undulation, propelled by webbed feet with toes. May be extinct.

Super-eel (12 sightings)
Size: Usually 10 metres or 30 metres, suggesting two or more species.
Habitat: Widespread in deep cold waters.
Behaviour: Has been observed fighting sperm-whales.

Marine saurian (4 sightings)
Size: Up to 20 metres – far bigger than any normal sea crocodile.
Habitat: Lives exclusively in tropical seas.
Behaviour: Moves horizontally at considerable speed.

Sea-serpent encounter

Consider for instance the evidence of two British soldiers, Captain John Ridgway and Sergeant Chay Blyth, who rowed across the Atlantic in 1966 and subsequently wrote a thoroughly sensible account of it in *A Fighting Chance*. Ridgway is rowing on a balmy night, 'lulled by the unending monotony'.

'I was shocked to full wakefulness by a swishing noise to starboard. I looked out over the water and suddenly saw the writhing, twisting shape of a great creature. It was outlined by the phosphorescence in the sea as if a string of neon lights were hanging from it. It was an enormous size, some 35 or more feet long, and it came towards me quite fast. I must have watched it for some ten seconds. It headed straight at me and disappeared right beneath me.

'I stopped rowing. I was frozen with terror at this apparition. I forced myself to turn my head to look over the port side. I saw nothing, but after a brief pause I heard a most tremendous splash . . . I am not an imaginative man, and I searched for a rational explanation . . . Chay and I had seen whales and sharks, dolphins and porpoises, flying fish – all sorts of sea creatures but this monster in the night was none of these. I reluctantly had to believe that there was only one thing it could have been – a sea serpent.'

Punch card analysis

As Heuvelmans says, such reports have an undeniable 'ring of truth', and from them he put on punch cards, prior to computer analysis, every detail that might throw light on the creatures: location of the sighting, general shape, length, relative size of head, neck, limbs, appearance of skin, method of propulsion, speed, behaviour, and many more characteristics were covered in his classification and coding. As a result, nine specific types of underwater monster emerged, of which the seven most important are illustrated on the left, together with the number of clear sightings that were analysed. He was somewhat surprised to find that some of them, superficially similar in description, turned out on analysis to be separate species; it was impossible, for instance, that 'the many-humped sea-serpent, chiefly seen in New England, could be the same as the Norwegian super-otter.' All of them satisfyingly filled 'quite distinct ecological niches', living in different levels of water and at different temperatures so that they 'cannot compete except where these habitats meet, which agrees perfectly with the laws of nature.'

Sea-serpents, however exaggerated some tales of the past, are a reality – and Nessie may yet turn out to be.

- • Merhorse
- ✗ Long-necked or Super-eel
- ✗ Long-necked
- • Super-eel

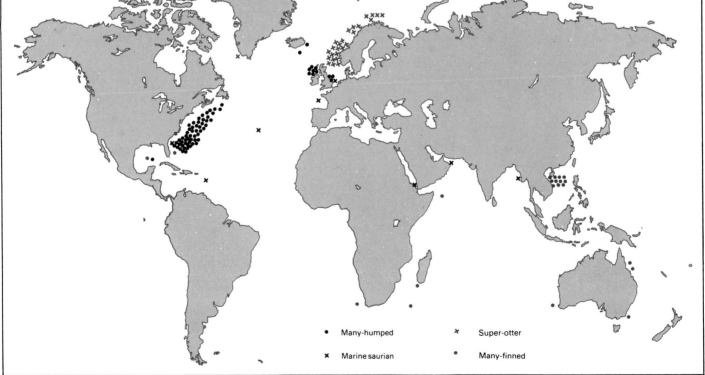

- • Many-humped
- ✗ Marine saurian
- ✗ Super-otter
- • Many-finned

The Belgian zoologist Bernard Heuvelmans' survey of sea-serpent sightings during the last 400 years has enabled him to classify a number of distinct types, many of which are located in specific areas.

Unknown beasts

The famous line of footprints was probably made by an animal no more monstrous than a mountain goat, the sun then enlarging the size of indentation made by the hoof. However, the hominid-type footprint below has never been explained. Taken by Eric Shipton in 1951, it is still the only piece of good evidence that Yetis really exist.

Contrary to the general view, this world is by no means fully explored. In spite of scientific scepticism, there is no good zoological reason why the equatorial rain forests of central Africa, the jungles of south-east Asia and south America, the forests of Siberia – indeed, any one of the dozen or so huge and inhospitable areas that leave ten per cent of the world's land surface unexplored – should not soon surprise us by revealing an unknown beast. As long ago as 1812 Baron Georges Cuvier, a great pioneering naturalist, said boldly that 'there is little hope of discovering a new species of large quadruped', only to be contradicted by the prompt appearance of a tapir and many other previously unclassified animals. Much the same attitude exists today concerning the widespread reports of hairy ape-men in different parts of the world; the reports are said to describe an 'impossible' or 'extinct' species and must therefore be fictitious. No doubt in many cases this is so, but at least with some such creatures we are now coming tantalizingly close to proof.

Abominable snowman

Unfortunately, the most appealing of these beasts, he is also the most elusive and most doubtful. One problem is that the reports do not form a consistent picture. Descriptions of the Yeti range from miniature hair-covered men of various colours to massive behemoths five metres and more tall; it is quite possible that more than one species is involved, the human-sized one being related to the surviving Neanderthals of central southern Russia (page 48). Bernard Heuvelmans in his survey *On the Track of Unknown Animals* says the reports suggest two other sorts – the *rimi*, up to three metres tall, living at a height of 3–4000 metres; and the *nyalmo*, 4–5 metres tall, living in the eternal snows above 4000 metres, carnivorous and even man-eating. The *nyalmo* as he describes it is surely the model of Western imagination: 'a huge creature, half man, half beast; it lives in caves high and inaccessible in the mountains. The skin of its face is white; the body is covered with a thick coat of dark hair. Its arms, like those on anthropoid apes, reach down to its knees, but its face looks rather more human. Its thick legs are bowed; its toes turn inward – some say they even turn backward. It is very muscular and can uproot trees and lift up boulders of remarkable size.'

However, it is much less easy even than with the lake monsters and sea-serpents (page 198) to back this picture with hard evidence, either of sightings or (with a solitary spectacular exception) of footprints. Colonel C. K. Howard-Bury, leader of the first Everest

Reconnaissance Expedition in 1921, the first to give publicity to the legend, was shown human-like tracks at 7000 metres but decided they were probably made by a loping wolf. In 1925 a scientist and photographer saw a figure at 5000 metres 'exactly like a human being, walking upright and stopping occasionally to uproot or pull at some dwarf rhododendron bushes'; from his description of the footprints, he is thought now to have seen a bear. The London *Daily Mail* expeditions of 1954 and 1957 photographed many footprints but none that could not be explained.

Sightings explained

Doubt surrounds the various reported sightings by Europeans and Sherpas alike. The snowman reported in *The Times* of 2 November 1921 and seen by the Englishman William Knight, 'almost stark naked in that bitter cold . . . a kind of pale yellow all over . . . a shock of matted hair on his head', was obviously one of the ascetic Hindu hermits known as *sadhu* who live at altitudes of up to 5000 metres; other bad-weather sightings of them, and of their footprints enlarged by the melting action of the sun, have become part of the general legend.

The existence of the langur monkey in the region must explain many of the accounts. They are large, have been seen above 4000 metres and are able to stand on two legs and hop for brief periods. The Wood/Kirkland/Maggs expedition of 1944, in its report of an 'abominable snowman' to *Country Life*, gave a perfect description of a langur, except for its size, which they said was about the same as a man. In 1970 Don Whillans, a mountaineer of high repute, photographed a series of mysterious footprints in Nepal at 4000 metres, and spotted by moonlight an 'ape-like creature' bounding on all fours along the crest of a ridge; although apes don't bound, langurs certainly do, and in all probability this is what Whillans saw.

Sherpa inventions

Sherpa evidence is unreliable for a number of reasons. Professor John Napier, formerly head of the primatology department at the Smithsonian Institute, has written in *Bigfoot* how their reports are suspect 'because Sherpas do not distinguish between the "reality" of the real world and the "reality" of their myth-ridden religious beliefs.' They have frequently attributed footprints to Yeti which European explorers identified as being those of a perfectly normal animal, and Napier also believes that 'it is a popular delusion to imagine that country folk are universally and automatically experts on the animals that live on their doorsteps.' Sherpas, for whom it is taboo to kill animals, 'never hunt leopards, bears, goats or

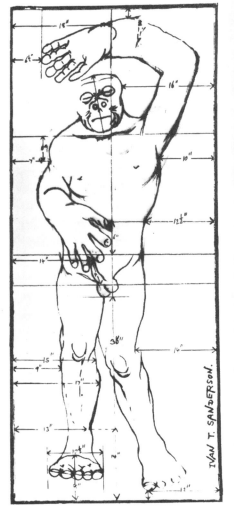

IVAN T. SANDERSON.

The Minnesota ice-man

Perhaps the most absurd monster story appeared in the *National Bulletin* on 30 June 1969 entitled 'I was raped by the Abominable Snowman.' In it, an American girl said that after having been (nearly) violated by a Bigfoot-type hominid in the woods of Minnesota, she escaped from its clutches by shooting it in its right eye. The creature in question was at the time on show as a touring exhibit in carnivals around the United States, safely enclosed in a block of ice, and hers was only one explanation in a series of perhaps intentionally baffling stories about where it had originated. Its 'owner' was Frank D. Hansen, a showman.

On various occasions Hansen said that (a) he had shot the beast himself (b) he had found it floating in a 6,000-pound block of natural ice in the Sea of Okhotsk, near Siberia (c) he substituted the original with another beast, a man-made model.

Today the biggest mystery is perhaps how two reputable zoologists, Ivan Sanderson and Bernard Heuvelmans, were sufficiently taken in by the 'monster' to have given it cautious scientific approval, Heuvelmans even going so far in the *Bulletin* of the Royal Institute of Natural Sciences of Belgium as to name it 'an unknown form of living hominid: *Homo pongoides*'. John Napier of Birkbeck College (see text), who has photographed and measured what the two men saw and has come to the conclusion that it was made basically of latex rubber and expanded polystyrene, thinks that it was a piece of top-rate showmanship performed on them. Sanderson and Heuvelmans were faced with a brilliantly executed model. Psychologically, anyone who had spent a lifetime in search of unknown animals as these two had was bound to be impressed by what he saw.

This 'giant-ape', in fact less than two metres in height, was shot by the Swiss geologist François de Loys in 1920. As the map shows, many sightings have been recorded of this and other creatures unknown to zoology in South America.

antelopes . . . the widely held view that the Sherpas would not mistake a bear, a monkey or anything else for a Yeti may be without foundation.'

Their confusion as to what they have truly seen and what they believe visitors want to find is reflected in the quality of the Yeti relics – various pelts and scalps, all of which when submitted to scientific analysis have been shown to come from local animals such as a bear or chamois goat. Indeed, considering the prolonged search for the Yeti that has taken place over the last half-century, it is remarkable that there is only one piece of genuinely unsolved hard evidence: the footprints photographed on Mount Everest at about 6500 metres by Eric Shipton and Michael Ward, accompanied by Sherpa Sen Tensing, on 8 November 1951.

After intensive study, Napier has concluded that 'as it stands, the footprint is not human; nor was it made by an ape or an ape-like creature known to science. What are the alternatives? No known creature anywhere in the world could leave such a spoor like this . . . without it I would have no hesitation in dismissing the Yeti as a red herring, or, at least, as a red bear. As it is, the issue must lie on the table unresolved.'

Giant apes

In the case of the giant apes of South America, the picture is much more disturbing to the orthodox zoological view. Apes, officially, do not exist in that continent – only many species of broad-nosed monkeys, none more than about a metre in height. However, there have been rumours of much larger creatures since the time of the first days of exploration. Sir Walter Raleigh reported at the end of the 16th Century that hairy men were supposed to live there: 'For my owne part I saw them not, but I am resolved that so many people did not all combine or forethinke to make the report.'

As in the Himalayas, there are accounts of improbable feats performed by these hairy men. Bernard Heuvelmans tells a friend's story of what happened in the 1950s, which has the kind of gruesome detail that puts it more into the category of Forteana (page 194): 'In an *estancia* about a hundred cattle were found dead without any wounds except that the tongue was torn out and gone. This went on for nearly eight months. Everything returned to normal, then, suddenly, two or three years later, the same events recurred in the same area but in a different *estancia*: another hundred cattle suffered the same fate.' Another story of dead cattle with their tongues wrenched out by the roots relates the incident to 'roars coming from the depths of the virgin

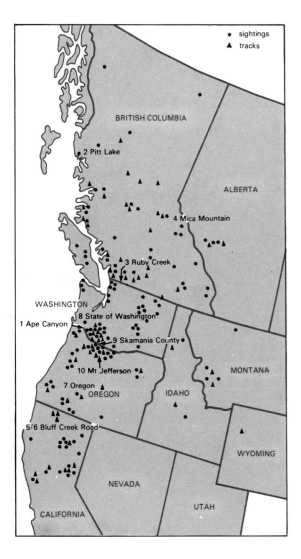

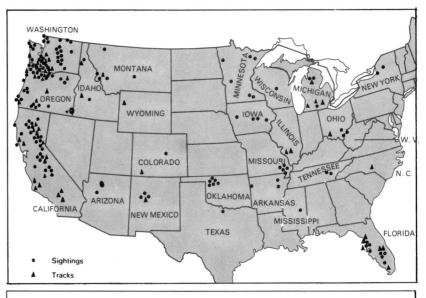

forest', and 'footprints in soft sand, which resembled those of man, but were 21 inches long'.

Human-like faces

The bulk of reports would be reasonable if they did not conflict with the list of known primates in South America but they are at least consistent on human-looking apes about 1.65 metres tall, which go about in pairs and usually become highly excitable when confronted by humans. They have been seen many times, and their cry is said to sound strangely like a human call. One of them has almost certainly been photographed – the specimen on the opposite page.

The picture was taken in 1920 when François de Loys, a Swiss geologist, was returning with an exhausted expedition after three years on the borders of Colombia and Venezuela. Not far from the river, says Heuvelmans, they suddenly met 'two tall monkeys which advanced towards them, walking upright and holding on to the bushes. They seemed besides themselves with rage, screaming, waving, and tearing off branches and brandishing them like weapons. At last they reached such a pitch of fury that they

The best sightings of Bigfoot

1 1924. Battle between prospectors and large ape-like creatures after one had been shot. Lawyers and reporters saw hundreds of enormous footprints, and damage to cabin.

2 1933. Two men having lunch at 4500 metres saw an animal with a 'human-like face on a fur-clad body' eating berries 400 metres below; its footprints were unlike a bear's.

3 1940. Mother and daughter in Chapman family saw 2.4 metre tall male hairy monster approach their farm. It followed them to a river and drank after overturning a barrel of salted fish.

4 1955. Man observed female Bigfoot feeding 20 metres away. It placed branches of bushes in its mouth and stripped off the leaves, afterwards excreting and examining its stool.

5 1958. Construction worker in a tool shack woken by noise, opened the door and saw an enormous hairy creature which accepted a chocolate bar from him and ran off.

6 1963. An unknown creature of

vast strength rampaged in a construction site, overturning concrete blocks and a truck. Fresh footprints seen.

7 1967. Two adults and a juvenile creature with rounded shoulders and shaggy bodies seen methodically moving piles of rock to discover a nest of hibernating or sleeping rats, which they ate 'like a banana'.

8 1969. Numerous sightings and footprints. Two involved dustbins being raided. A total of 1089 footprints were counted at a garbage dump near Bossburg. John Napier (see text) believes that evidence of a club-footed Bigfoot argues against fraud.

9 1970. Professional Bigfoot hunter saw red reflection of its eyes in the dark; found footprints and the fresh carcase of a dead elk which had been eaten.

10 1972. Two anglers on a rubber raft saw apes on the shore, 1.8 and 1.2 metres tall, which disappeared after staring at them; described as 'graceful and not at all fierce looking'.

defecated into their hands and hurled their excrement at their intruders,' at which point the expedition opened fire and the female was killed. The corpse was propped up against a packing case and photographed; the face is undoubtedly human-like, and no tail is visible (although suggestions have been made that this might have been propped up behind her). The recorded height of 1 metre 57 centimetres agrees with the probable height of the packing case, and

Enlarged section of a still from Roger Patterson's film of Bigfoot, taken at Bluff Creek, California. Sceptics, probably now a minority among experts, say the creature is a large actor dressed up in an animal skin.

Algonquin Indians called Bigfoot *windigo*, whose characteristics, according to a French Canadian priest in the 1930s, were that he 'wore no clothes. Summer and winter he went naked and never suffered cold. His skin was black like that of a negro. He used to rub himself, like the animals, against fir, spruce and other resinous trees. When he was thus covered with gum or resin, he would go and roll in the sand, so that one would have thought that, after many operations of this kind, he was made of stone.'

Several hundred more recent eyewitness reports are now known to exist, and from these John Napier made a personal sample of the best documented 72 to build up a composite picture. It walks 'just like man does' and is covered in reddish-brown or auburn hair, some 15 centimetres long on the head. Many reports speak of its broad shoulders and deep chest, and of a hunched appearance due to the apparent absence of a neck. The face has a backward-sloping forehead and there is little or no neck. Estimated heights range from two to over three metres, the commonest being around 2.3 metres – well over the average height of man. The size of its footprints varies accordingly, the most usual being around 40 centimetres.

Remaining enigmas

Odd though it may seem, the coniferous mountain forests of the north American continent are largely unexplored, and there is no compelling reason why a quite large population of unknown beasts should not exist there, surviving on a frugal and mostly vegetarian diet. Hunting is generally not good, and the roadmakers and loggers rarely have reason to stray far from the tracks they carve out.

Even so, why is it always footprints that are found and never a body, a skeleton, or even a single bone? Why is it that the camera imp is at work in Bigfoot territory just as he is at Loch Ness? The best movie taken, by Roger Patterson, has convinced a number of experts of its authenticity; but for John Napier it is invalidated because Patterson cannot remember whether the speed was set at 16 or 24 frames per second – and, if the latter, the Bigfoot figure is compatible with a large actor skilfully dressed up. Until the Bigfoot has been observed more closely, the sceptics will remain unconvinced.

there is little reason today to doubt that this is a unique photograph – a genuine picture of an unknown beast.

Bigfoot reality

As for the Yeti's American cousin Bigfoot, the evidence is now overwhelming that something strange is living in remoter woods of northern parts of the continent. The usual allowance has to be made for travellers' tales and a wide variation in the size of the reported creatures, and as ever the photographs are arguable. But sightings have continued since long before the United States was colonized.

Wild children

Perhaps because of an unconscious desire to re-discover our primal roots, we have always shown a curiously intense interest in people who manage to bridge the apparently insuperable gulf between man and beast. The wolf who suckled Romulus and Remus may have been mythological, but since then there have been many reported examples more factual than legendary. Lucien Malson's *Les Enfants Sauvages* listed 53 wild children who had been found in different countries since AD 1344, and several more authenticated cases have come to light since then: two gazelle boys in North Africa, a seven-year-old ape boy in the Central Republic of Burundi, another ape boy in Sri Lanka.

Almost without exception, the life-stories are unhappy ones. Children thrust back into civilization from natural surroundings do not on the whole respond well to the experience. They usually die after a relatively short period and few are able to learn more than a handful of words. The indignities suffered by some during their period of re-education were almost intolerably painful. The wolf child of Hesse, discovered in 1344 having lived naked in the forest for four years, eating his food raw and protected by wolves who had dug a hole for him, had become so used to moving on all fours that boards had to be strapped to his legs to make him stand upright and walk as a normal human. The Songi girl, aged about nine or ten, found in the Champagne district of France, so well adapted to forest living that she had developed extra large thumbs with which to swing from tree to tree, became a nun and was painstakingly taught to say: 'Why should God have searched for me and saved me from the power of wild animals, and made me a Christian? Should this have happened in order to leave me and make me die from hunger? This is not possible. I know only him; he is my father and the Virgin Mary is my mother; they will take care of me.'

Human experiment

The urge to experiment on such children in order to make them 'normal' has been universal, according to the French anthropologist Jean Claude Armen, who said in 1970 that he was offered facilities by an American professor to study a child to be given away by its mother and placed under the guardianship of wolves in the Siberian steppes. One of the more beneficient examples of re-training was the case of the wild boy of Aveyron, who was pulled out of a tree by hunters in 1799. About 12 years old, he had apparently become lost when wandering into the woods as a young child and survived living on nuts and berries. He escaped, was re-captured

The wild boy of Aveyron in central France, found naked in the countryside in 1799, running on all fours and vigorously at home in his environment, became after his capture a text-book case of education for the retarded.

and subsequently classified by the leading psychologist in France as an incurable idiot. He was then fortunate in coming under the care of Jean-Marc Itard, a teacher in a deaf-and-dumb school that practised surprisingly well-advanced remedial treatment and the progress of Victor, as he became named, has become a text-book example of what can be achieved with someone mentally sub-normal if he is helped with patience. Victor lived to be about 40, learned a few words, and became an agreeable and appealing character.

Academic denial

It is currently fashionable among psychologists to deny that children have been reared by animals, or have survived long periods living wild. Bruno Bettelheim, US author of the classic study of autism, *Empty Fortress*, writes: 'Belief in the truth of occasional reports of children having been reared by wolves and behaving like animals may in part be accounted for by a narcissistic unwillingness to acknowledge the human nature of the so-called feral children.' He believes that wolf children show identical symptoms to autistic children,

Boy found in the jungles of Sri Lanka in 1973, apparently brought up by monkeys.

Route taken by the French anthropologist Jean Claude Armen to discover his gazelle-boy.
To discourage hunters, he has never disclosed exact details of central section.

Exact route taken by Armen ——

Imprecise route across area where Gazelle Boy was found ·······

R. M. Zingg, at Denver University, analysed all the known cases of extreme isolation known until 1940, and analysed their most important characteristics for the *American Journal of Psychology*.

for instance urinating/defecating without knowing it; showing a desire to run about naked; being unable to speak and making screaming/howling noises; eating only raw food; biting humans severely.

Unique habits

However, this somewhat distant academic analysis does not take account of a number of physical characteristics that seem unique to wild children. Autistic children, although often resistant to extremes of heat and cold, do not have the fine and velvety skin noted on the two wolf children of Midnapore (illustration opposite) and on Victor, who squatted naked in cold, driving rain without showing any discomfort and could handle burning coals in a fire or take hot potatoes out of boiling water.

Autism does not explain why wild children move about like the animals whose life they share. Jean Claude Armen described the gazelle boy he discovered in the Sahara as having 'lively, dark, almond-shaped eyes and a pleasant open expression (not sullen like the children reared by carnivorous animals). He appeared to be ten years old; his ankles were disproportionately thick and obviously powerful.'

Examining the footprints of the herd as it moved away, he found traces of 'tiny and obviously human feet, several metres apart, the weight resting on the front part of the feet and hardly making any impression on the sand, revealing a rare suppleness, the human prints blending with the rhythm of the bounding prints of the gazelles.'

After some days of patient observation, calmly playing his flute near the herd and trying with varying success to attract the boy's attention, Armen was nuzzled by the senior gazelle with the end of its black, wet nose. Then: 'the boy comes up to me and sniffs my toes, still showing a few furtive traces of fear despite his great boldness and fitfully screwing up his nose, after the manner of his adoptive mentors.' The boy started licking him in a gazelle-like fashion, to which Armen responded and throughout the encounter the boy conformed to the behaviour pattern of gazelles – leaping and jumping about, sniffing various bits of thorn bush, flowers, berries, balls of dung, and so on. Armen also noticed the child's habit of twitching his ears and scalp at the slightest unusual or suspicious noise.

Armen's detailed observation of this case has led him to believe the anthropologist Claude Lévi-Strauss to be absolutely mistaken when he summarized the orthodox view as: 'The majority of wild children are congenitally abnormal children who have been deliberately abandoned.' On the contrary, says Armen, the chance of survival in the wild for a severely abnormal or subnormal child would be almost zero. The Saharan gazelle boy was almost completely integrated with the herd, joining in their sign language and participating in their games.

	Sex	Years old when rescued	Four-footed motion	Taught to walk	Dumb	Made animal-like sounds	Associate animal	Food	Ate or drank like an animal	Fond of company of animals	Insensitive to heat & cold	Degree of recovery
Lithuanian bear-boy of 1661	male	12	●	●	●	●	bear	cabbage, grass, meat				little
Hessian wolf-boy of 1344	male	7 to 12	●	●	?		wolf	no data				little
Irish sheep-boy of 1672	male	16			●	bleat	sheep	grass, hay			●	no data
Bamberger cattle-boy	male		●		●		cattle	no data				great
Wild Peter of Hanover 1724	male	12	●		●			bark, grass				little
The Pyrenees boys 1719	males		●					herbs, leaves				
The girl of Cranenburg 1717	female	18			●			frogs, fish				great
Girl of Songi 1731	female				●			greens, roots				great
Jean of Liége	male	21										no data
Second wolf-boy, Wetterau	male					●	wolf	no data				considerable
Second Lithuanian bear-boy 1694	male	10	●	●	●	●	bear	bread				slight
Third Lithuanian bear-boy	male	12	●		●	●	bear	raw meat				no data
Sleeman's first wolf-child	male		●	no data	●	●	wolf	raw meat	?		●	
Sleeman's second wolf-child	male		●	no data	●	no data	wolf		lapped like a dog	dogs		
Sleeman's third wolf-child	male				●	●	wolf	raw meat				
Sleeman's fourth wolf-child	male		●	●			wolf	no data				
Sleeman's fifth wolf-child	male		●	no data	●		wolf	bread, meat				
Sleeman's sixth wolf-child	male		●		●		wolf	raw meat		wolf		
Wolf-child of Sultanpur	male	4	●			●	wolf	raw meat				became policeman
Wolf-child of Shahjehanjur	male	6	●		●	●	wolf	raw meat			●	none
Dina Sanichar	male	6	●		●	●	wolf	raw meat	sharpened teeth on bones			none
Second Sikandra wolf-child	male	10	●		●	●	wolf	raw meat				little
Second Overdyke wolf-child	male							birds' eggs				
Clemens of Overdyke	male		●		unintelligible		pig	greens		pigs		
Swine-girl of Salzburg	female		crippled		●	pig-like	pig					none
Wild-boy of Kronstadt	male	23			?			grass, roots, meat				little
Wild-boy of Aveyron	male				●			nuts, roots			●	little
Half-wild boy of Zips, Hungary	male				●			roots, raw meat		horses		much
Kaspar Hauser	male	17	●		●			bread & water		animals		very great
Amala, younger Midnapore girl	female	2	●	●	●	●	wolf	raw meat	lapped milk	animals	●	some
Kamala, elder Midnapore girl	female	8	●	●	●	●	wolf	raw meat	gnawed bones on the floor	animals	●	some
Leopard-boy of India	male	5	●				leopard	raw meat				

As for the problem of diet, anthropologists such as Armen can only suppose that the human body is a great deal more adaptable than most Westerners credit it to be. The gazelle boy was seen throwing himself with gusto on roots of dhanoun – the survival food of the desert – that had been unearthed by the herd: '. . . teeth first, he peels them with clicks of his tongue, then cuts them up frantically with his incisors.' Later, when Armen was able to make a closer examination, he noted that the boy's teeth were level, like those of herviborous animals.

Lost opportunity

The pity is that the one fairly recent opportunity to observe the eating habits of children brought up by carnivorous animals was spoiled through a combination of mishap and missionary zeal. In 1920, in Midnapore during one of his evangelical trips, the Reverend J. A. L. Singh heard of two malevolent *manush-baghas* – small ghostly creatures with blazing eyes, neither human nor animal – that haunted villagers from the forests near Denganalia and were accompanied by a female wolf. Their lair was located in an abandoned ant-heap. Singh decided after two fleeting glimpses that the ghosts were human children running on all fours and 'hideous-looking'.

He arranged for a party of local tribesmen to dig the lair out and on 17 October the ant-heap was surrounded by beaters and diggers. Two wolves ran out as soon as digging started and broke through the cordon. A third wolf, a female, then appeared, and according to Charles Maclean's 1977 reconstruction of the event in *The Wolf Children* 'instead of running off like the others she made for the Lodha diggers, scattering them to all sides before diving back into the hole. She came out again and raced round, growling furiously and pawing the ground. Lowering her head with bared teeth and ears flattened against her neck, her tail whipping threateningly from side to side, she refused to leave the spot. The wolf made a second charge at the diggers, only this time the bowmen were standing by at close range. Before the Reverend Singh could stop them they loosed off their arrows and pierced her through, killing her instantly.'

The ant-heap was opened and the two children found huddled in a ball with two wolf cubs. After a fierce struggle, they were separated. Tribesmen sold the wolf cubs and the two children were taken to Midnapore Orphanage. The younger, aged about 18 months, died within a year. The elder, about eight years old, lived for nine years, eventually learning to stand upright, to eat by hand and to speak some 30 words of English. Alas, Singh's account of the way they were captured has been disputed ever since he made it and he himself at a later stage denied that he took part in the expedition. Had the mother wolf been captured alive, anthropology might have added a new dimension.

Kamala, eldest of two children found in a wolf's lair by the Reverend J. A. L. Singh in 1920, took three years to learn to stand. To begin with, she would eat only on all fours, but was later persuaded to take food from her adopted brother. She eventually spoke about 30 words before dying in her late teens. (below) Location of Midnapore, where she was brought up in Singh's orphanage.

Kaspar Hauser

For five and a half years before his violent and enigmatic death in 1833, the extraordinary story of Kaspar Hauser, the boy from nowhere, dominated gossip in Europe. An illiterate waif of 16 or 17 who arrived in the charming mediaeval city of Nuremberg on 26 May 1828 with bleeding feet claiming to have been locked in a tiny darkened cell for the greater part of his life, he soon developed remarkable intellectual and artistic powers, and gained access to the highest social circles. His contemporaries were polarized between those who thought he was the nobly-born victim of a plot to keep him from his rightful inheritance, and those who said he was simply a liar who wanted nothing more than the fame which his bizarre story brought him. The matter was fiercely debated but never resolved. Today, a century and a half later, there are hundreds of contemporary accounts from which to form a modern judgment, and although they all show a bias one way or another, the basic facts of the *scandale* are more or less agreed.

They begin with his arrival on a Whit-monday, when the cobbled streets of Nuremberg were the scene of the annual *Ausflug*, a public holiday when everyone took to the open air. It is not clear at what time Kaspar Hauser made his appearance, but the descriptions of him are consistent: his clothes, some with silk lining, had once been good but were now as tattered as a scarecrow's; he hobbled with an uncomfortable stiff-legged lurch, for the boots he wore did not fit and were reinforced with horseshoes and nails, his toes stuck out, bleeding. A local cobbler was the first person to spot him as he stood in Unschlitt Square, barely able to keep himself upright, his knees slightly sagging, his eyes staring and bewildered, which with his protruding jaw gave him a slightly animal-like look.

Apparently almost incapable of speech, he showed the cobbler a letter addressed 'to the Captain of the 4th Squadron, 6th Cavalry Regiment', where he was duly sent via the military guard house. Waiting for the arrival of the captain, he exhibited the first of the incongruous reactions to his surroundings that were to convince many people he had indeed been isolated from the world for most of his life. He tried to pick up the flame of a candle, and screamed when he was burned. The smell of cooking nauseated him, and the ham and beer he was offered nearly made him faint. However, he consumed bread and water voraciously. His only words in answer to questions were 'Don't know'. He seemed to regard the grandfather clock as being alive and refused to go near it.

Horse fixation

He perked up seeing the captain, whose uniform and scabbard he admired and stroked. A few more stumbled words came out: 'Want to be a soldier like my father', and 'Horse, horse'. The captain could make nothing of him. The two letters, which turned out to be blatant forgeries, made a confused request to the captain to turn the boy into a cavalry soldier, and 'if you will not keep him, you must strike him dead or hang him.' The captain decided he was 'either a primitive savage or an imbecile', and delivered him to the local police station as a foundling.

Here the next crucial elements in the story emerged. Given a pencil and asked to write his name and address, he firmly wrote KASPAR HAUSER; otherwise, he replied 'don't know' to everything. Stripped and searched by the station sergeant, he was found to be sturdy and healthy, with a good complexion. The soles of his feet were as soft as the palms of his hands, badly cut and blistered; because of the pain, he cried a good deal. He seemed somewhat relieved to be locked in a cell, where his jailer reported significantly: 'He can sit for hours without moving a limb. He does not pace the floor, nor does he try to sleep. He sits rigidly without growing in the least uncomfortable. Also, he prefers darkness to light, and can move about in it like a cat.' Two days

Nuremberg in the early 19th Century, a secluded provincial German city which greatly enjoyed its new-found notoriety.

later he was examined by the court doctor to establish whether he was feigning sickness. The doctor was convinced of his innocence: 'This man is neither insane nor dull-witted, but has apparently been forcibly prevented in the most disastrous way from attaining any personal or social development.' He called particular attention to a unique malformation in both knees; when the boy sat on level ground he could stretch his legs out directly in front of him – a peculiarity originating from sitting in this posture when he was very young and his bones were more flexible.

The boy was an instant public celebrity. Visitors in hundreds flocked to see him swallow his bread and defecate in his cell without embarrassment. The clamour from these people did not disturb him, for he played, deeply absorbed, with a toy horse that one of the police officers brought him. The smell of meat or wine still made him ill, and he continued to have difficulty in differentiating between animate and inanimate objects. A ticking watch gave him hours of enjoyment. When he ate, he fed his toy horse too. With his limited vocabulary, men and women were all 'boy', and animals all 'horse'.

Instant learning

Now began an astonishingly rapid learning process, as if to confirm the court doctor's view that his mental development had been actively retarded. Within six weeks he was speaking fluently and could read and write nearly as well as an average boy of his age. He no longer found difficulty in handling the utensils of civilized life – knives, forks, matches, lanterns and so on. On 7 July 1828 he compiled his first full statement about his early life, issued in the form of a bulletin signed by Burgomaster Binder of Nuremberg (who had helped him put it together) and members of the Town Council. He never afterwards deviated from this first account, nor indeed added much to it, even in his autobiography that appeared a year later.

In essence, the story was simple. From the time of his earliest memory, he had been imprisoned

in a darkened dungeon so small that he could not stand up in it. His entire life was spent sleeping full length on a straw mattress, or sitting bolt upright against a wall. There was absolutely no variation in his environment – no sounds, no change of temperature or light. When he woke, he always found a jug of water and a loaf of dark bread spiced with fennel, caraway or coriander.

Portrait of Kaspar Hauser holding his letter of introduction drawn some time after his mysterious arrival, and showing him to be remarkably well fed for a boy who has lived only on bread and water.

1 Medical examination His healthy complexion would have been impossible on a diet of bread and water and a dark room. Had he truly never stood for 13 years he would have been a cripple unable to walk. His only abnormalities were cut and blistered feet, and the ability to sit motionless in an unusual position, both of which could be intentional.

2 Education The speed with which he learned to talk, read and write is unreasonably fast for someone with a background such as he described. However it is entirely consistent with someone pretending to be illiterate.

3 Biography His account of imprisonment bears all the marks of an invention concocted to be tantalizing and at the same time impossible to disprove. It was never elaborated in enough detail to allow his jailers to be recognized, and indeed his supposed jail was never found.

4 Investigation Nuremberg city officials were delighted by the fame and trade he brought them, and were over-credulous in accepting his story.

5 Attacks The first attack was suspiciously incompetent for someone supposedly hired to kill Hauser. After the incident that led to his death, two out of three doctors said the wounds could have been self-inflicted, and there was only one set of footprints at the site. Dr Meyer was convinced Hauser was a fraud and said so publicly.

The fraud hypothesis

So extraordinary is the story of Kaspar Hauser that most scientists today would probably investigate it with the attitude that is taken to psychical research (page 85): unless the possibility of fraud has been eliminated, then the events should be disbelieved. Or putting it the other way round, the more improbable the story, the better must be the proof.

Looked at in this way, Kaspar Hauser does not stand up to ruthless examination. Almost all the incidents in his life can be seen as those of a man bent on pursuing fame, gain or amusement.

Occasionally the water would have a bitter taste, sending him into a deep sleep. Afterwards, he always found that he had been washed and tidied, his hair cut, his clothes and bedding changed. The unvaried routine meant that he had not, for many years, set eyes on another human being. His only companions were two toy horses, with ribbons that he tied to them. Knowing nothing else, he was neither happy nor unhappy, nor even lonely.

Towards the end of this imprisonment (having no sense of time, he was unable to suggest how recently), a man came into his cell, and patiently taught him to hold a pencil and write the words KASPAR HAUSER. The few phrases which he had used in the first few days in Nuremberg – 'don't know', 'want to be a soldier like my father', 'horse' – were also taught him by the man.

Forgotten route

Then, after one of his drug-induced sleeps, he found himself in boots and clothes. Led into the open air, the shock of all the new sensations almost overcame him, and he was unable to give details of the route he took into Nuremberg, nor even a good description of the man, except that he had been 'big and strong', and had promised him 'a big live horse after you become a soldier'.

Overnight, the bulletin turned Kaspar Hauser from a local curiosity into a national sensation. Police were set to find his place of imprisonment (they never did). Visitors from all over Europe travelled to Nuremberg to catch a glimpse of him, and those who could not go there speculated in their drawing rooms as to just who he might be, and into which important family he had been born (for surely, they argued, the family must have been important to have been able to incarcerate the boy for so long and so secretly, only to release him when the original shame, or scandal, or intrigue, had been buried with time).

Nuremberg officials released Hauser from prison to be educated by a local teacher and philosopher of some note, Professor George Friedrich Daumer, under whom he made remarkable progress. For about a year the gossip and tittle-tattle continued unabated, while Hauser himself seemed pleased by the amount of attention he was receiving. In August 1829, his autobiography, presumably much aided by Daumer, received a less than enthusiastic welcome; the story, perhaps, had been told too

---

The conspiracy theory

In anthroposophy, a form of spiritual enlightenment, belief in Kaspar Hauser is fundamental. His story of imprisonment is held to be true in detail, and happened as the result of a dynastic plot to prevent him inheriting the throne of Baden. It was not just kind-heartedness that led his captors to keep him alive; a deep knowledge of the occult among the conspirators made them realize that if they killed him, his reincarnated soul could do them much harm. They stifled the boy's development during his formative years, so he would be corrupted and discredited as a fraud by the world outside. In spite of the boy's almost supernatural talents, his captors largely succeeded. Now, however, the plot can be seen as follows:

1 Medical examination
The evidence of the doctor and the jailer is proof of Hauser's story. His subsistence on bread and water alone is well attested. The human body fed on this diet can make remarkable adjustments.

2 Education Hauser was put in the care of a remarkable teacher, Daumer, who was a homeopathic doctor and one of the last Rosicrucians. But Daumer could not have succeeded if the boy himself had not been totally exceptional, being gifted as the result of his experience with amazing sensitivity, an unsullied mind capable of photographic memory, and a near-psychic gift like dowsers (page 82) for perceiving hidden metal.

3 Biography What he described is a classic, even symbolic, case of sense-deprivation.

4 Investigation Daumer was only one of many who, at first sceptical, became convinced. Another was Anselm von Feuerbach, his guardian, who died in suspicious circumstances while attempting to clear Hauser's name.

5 Attacks The first attack was not meant to kill Hauser, but to create doubt and suspicion. Stanhope was involved to tempt Hauser from Nuremberg and put him in the charge of two other conspirators, Meyer and the police chief, who investigated his death. The single footprint evidence is unsupported.

Portrait of Kaspar Hauser in the latter part of his life, by this time plump and affecting a crop of curly hair.

often and with too many second-hand elaborations for this somewhat turgid piece of writing to satisfy speculation. But almost immediately, another sensation happened: on 7 October 1829 Hauser was found unconscious on the floor of Daumer's cellar, bleeding from a wound in his forehead. Relatively minor though the injury was, Hauser believed it to be an attack on his life, and described his assailant as wearing dark clothes, leather gloves and a silken mask.

It was from this moment that doubts about Hauser began to grow. While there were still many who said that the incident was a bungled attempt at murder by the same high-born people who had imprisoned him in the first place, a number were more sceptical: the wounds, they said, were self-inflicted. In any case Hauser was placed under close protection, and surrounded by people who had no doubt of his honesty.

During the next four years, the Nuremberg authorities became increasingly embarrassed by criticism that they were squandering public funds through their support of Hauser; half-way through the period, in 1831, they welcomed with relief the appearance on the scene of the eccentric English Lord Stanhope, who expressed an interest in the boy's education, and from time to time over the next two years toured with him round various European courts and principalities. It was apparently a stormy relationship, with increasing quarrels, law-suits from a number of Bavarian families denying a blood relationship with Hauser, and even a duel. However in 1833 Lord Stanhope suggested taking over the boy's upkeep and moving him to the smaller town of Ansbach nearby, to which the Nuremberg town council eventually agreed. Here he began his education anew under the tutelage of the local teacher Dr Meyer; he was said to have disliked intensely both Latin and history, and the manner in which he was taught. He was confirmed in the Protestant Church. Stanhope himself seems quickly to have lost interest in him, and by all accounts Hauser became unhappy and introspective, particularly after the unexpected death of his guardian, the esteemed Bavarian lawyer Anselm von Feuerbach. Then, as mysteriously and as suddenly as Hauser had appeared in Nuremberg, his end came in Ansbach. He staggered into Meyer's house on 14 December 1833 with severe stab wounds in his lungs and liver. A stranger, he said, had lured him to the town's park, promising news of the whereabouts of his mother. The stranger, 'tall, with dark whiskers, wearing a black coat', asked: 'Are you Kaspar Hauser?' Hauser nodded and was given a wallet. As he went to open it, he was stabbed. With blood soaking through his coat, Hauser's words to Meyer are supposed to have been: 'Man stabbed! Knife! Park! Gave wallet! Go quickly!' Police searched for, and duly found, the wallet. But the note inside it was as strange as everything else in Kaspar Hauser's life. It was in mirror-writing, to be read backwards from right to left: 'Hauser will be able to tell you how I look, whence I came from and who I am. To spare him the task I will tell you myself. I am from . . . on the Bavarian border . . . on the river . . . my name is MLO.' Police also found only one set of footprints – presumably Hauser's – leading in the snow to the scene of the alleged attack.

Both Meyer and the police chief responsible for Hauser's safety, Captain Hickel, were openly convinced from the beginning that Hauser had invented the attack. Meyer said the boy had tried to 'hurt himself a little', and that the dagger had inadvertently gone a little too deep. Hickel, with an increasingly hostile group of investigators round Hauser's death-bed, tried hard to persuade him to confess. He failed. Three days later, on 17 December, Kaspar Hauser died. His last recorded words were: 'I didn't do it myself.'

Nowadays, which version you believe is perhaps as good a test of personal credulity as could be devised, and the arguments for and against are summed up in the panels. Even if Kaspar Hauser exaggerated the story of his upbringing, and luxuriated in his brief notoriety, his life was special and significant. Like many psychics and sensitives, he may sometimes have cheated to draw attention to himself (in his case, perhaps fatally). But undeniably he had extraordinary gifts, and nobody can become both a legend and a symbol of uncorrupted youth without adding something to life itself.

Drawings by Kaspar Hauser have been perhaps unfairly used as evidence of his story being fraudulent, as they are considered too proficient for someone without training. But there are many other examples throughout art history of 'instant' or 'automatic' drawing at least as good as his.

Count St Germain

Count St Germain – or 'so-called Count St Germain' as he was known by friends and enemies alike during his phenomenal career in 18th-century Europe – was the kind of person who aroused suspicion, hostility, or disbelief because his talents out-stripped contemporary thought. The English writer Horace Walpole dismissed him as an eccentric (see panel opposite) but the great French writer Voltaire judged otherwise, describing him as a man who 'never dies and who knows everything'.

Like Kaspar Hauser (page 210) he arrived from nowhere on the European scene and throughout his life was surrounded by intrigue and hints of magic powers. Talking to Madame de Pompadour, mistress of Louis XV of France, he summed up the yearning of the time: 'Ah, madame, all the women want the Elixir of Youth and all the men want the Philosophers' Stone, the one eternal beauty, the other eternal wealth.' Count St Germain's achievement was that most people who met him believed he had discovered the secret of both – and put them to active use in his own life.

Today, a substantial cult has grown up around him, regarding him as the supreme 18th-century occultist, genuinely possessing strange powers related to, or deriving from, the ancient wisdom that is still being sought (page 236). Opponents of this view, both then and now, see him as no more than a quick-witted and fluent adventurer who was able to deceive a gullible nobility unable to distinguish between trickery and true achievement.

A careful analysis of his life is inclined to support the first attitude, and at the very least he was an extraordinary man. There is the question of his longevity: taking the reports at their face value, he was perhaps 45 or 50 years old in 1710, and a meeting between him and his friend Mme d'Adhémar was noted in her diary in 1820. On this reckoning, he lived to be at least 150. If the first and last dates are eliminated because they are uncorroborated, or because they are the mistaken memories of old ladies, there is still unequivocal evidence that he was a full-grown man in 1723, and active in the French Revolution in 1789 – a life-span of at least 90 years. Nearly all reports during this period said that he had the appearance of a man in his forties.

There is the question, too, of his undoubted achievements. Not only was he consistently described as being rich beyond even the highest standards of the time but as being a superb linguist (European, Arabic, Oriental and Classical), an accomplished pianist and violinist, a pioneering inventor of new chemical techniques that transformed the process of dyeing cloth and curing leather, and above all as a brilliant conversationalist – 'the most singular man that I ever saw in my life', said the Graf Karl Cobenzl.

This picture of him puts into perspective the other, and perhaps most important, aspect of his career: his tireless travelling in search of lost knowledge and his prestige in occult Societies and Lodges, all of which seem to have made him welcome. Although living very simply (he was a vegetarian and teetotaller and always ate on his own), his wealth undoubtedly stemmed from his collection of diamonds; he claimed to have the secret of the Philosophers' Stone, to be able to improve and enlarge diamonds. He had travelled in the Himalayas and found the men 'who knew everything', he said, adding that 'one needs to have studied in the pyramids as I have studied.' Three of the greatest occultists of the 18th Century, St Martin, Mesmer and Cagliostro, were his pupils rather than his teachers. He claimed to have achieved astral travel (as in what are now called out-of-body-experiences or remote viewing, page 82) – 'for quite a long time I rolled through space. I saw globes revolve around me and earths gravitate at my feet,' and on another occasion he 'passed the time while he lay unconscious in far-off lands'. If there is indeed an ancient wisdom, as research in many parts of this Atlas has suggested, then Count St Germain must surely have been one of the few who inherited or re-discovered it. Alas, the only surviving manuscript by him, *La Très Sainte Trinosophie* in the library at Troyes, France, is so cryptic that its symbolism has never been interpreted, and his life-story remains more a tantalizing hint than a satisfactory solution.

Court of Louis XVI of France, who was warned by Count St Germain of the coming dangers of the French Revolution.

1710 Seen by composer Jean-Philippe Rameau and the young Countess von Georgy, and said to look around 45–50 years old. Little is known of his life in the next two decades except he was a confidant of Madame de Pompadour and had great prestige in Masonic and other secret societies.

1737–1742 At the court of the Shah of Persia, where he may have acquired his extensive knowledge of diamonds and precious stones.

1743 Famed at the Court of Louis XV for his great wealth and alchemical skills. A diary says 'the rumour spread that a stranger, enormously rich to judge by the magnificence of his jewellery, had just arrived at Versailles. Whence did he come from? That is what no one has ever been able to learn.' He appeared to be between 40 and 45 years old.

1744–1745 In England, where he was arrested for spying and described by the writer Horace Walpole: 'He sings and plays on the violin wonderfully, composes, is mad, and not very sensible.' Released after questioning.

1745–1746 In the Viennese court was 'witty and brilliant'; lived as a prince.

1747–1756 Paid at least two visits to India, and wrote in an enigmatic letter that while there he gained his knowledge of melting jewels – a 'wonderful secret' that made all his previous attempts in Vienna, Paris and London 'worthless as experiments; the great work was interrupted at the time I have mentioned.'

1757–1760 Height of fame at the Court of Louis XV, who became completely entranced by his manner and his reputed powers of improving and enlarging diamonds; St Germain was given a laboratory for his experiments in physics and chemistry. Seen again by the Countess von Georgy, then in her seventies, who was astonished to find him looking as youthful as at their first encounter half a century earlier.

1760–1762 Mysterious mission to England as envoy/spy of Louis XV seems to have ended with him in disfavour, followed by a temporary retirement to Holland to continue his studies.

1762–1773 Reports of his activities, political and scientific, from many parts of Europe. 'A most singular man' who could transmute 'iron into a metal as beautiful as gold, and at least as good for all goldsmith's work.' He had a factory in Venice employing 100 workers using a process to make flax look like silk. Celebrated for 'the vastness of his political and philosophical knowledge'.

1774–1784 Following the death of Louis XV, he fruitlessly warned Louis XVI and Marie Antoinette of a 'gigantic conspiracy' which would completely overthrow the order of things. He then lived mostly in Germany. In 1777 he was said by one witness to be between 60 and 70 years old. He was actively engaged in Masonic, Rosicrucian, and Templar activities with his disciple and protector Prince Karl von Hesse-Kassel. The two

men worked on experiments together 'which were in all cases to be of use to the human race'.

1784–1820 His supposed death on 27 February 1784, and burial on 2 March 1784, recorded in the church register at Eckenförde, was followed by his well-witnessed appearance at Wilhelmsbad in 1785, where a conference was held between various groups of occultists – Rosicrucians, Illuminati, Necromantists and Humanitarians – to resolve their differences. He was accompanied by Cagliostro, Mesmer and St Martin. In 1788 he was again active in France, giving ominous warning to the nobility on the eve of the Revolution. Marie Antoinette, in her diaries, regretted not taking his earlier advice. In 1789 he departed for Sweden to try to prevent ill befalling King Gustavus III, and told his friend and diarist Mme d'Adhémar (who thought he still looked about 45) that he would see her five times more. There is only her word for it that this happened, 'always to my unspeakable surprise', the last occasion being on the eve of the murder of the Duc de Berri in 1820.

1821–present day Some occultists believe St Germain never died. In January 1972 a Parisian named Richard Chanfray appeared on French television claiming to be him; as 'proof' he achieved an apparently successful transmutation of lead into gold using a camping stove in front of the TV cameras.

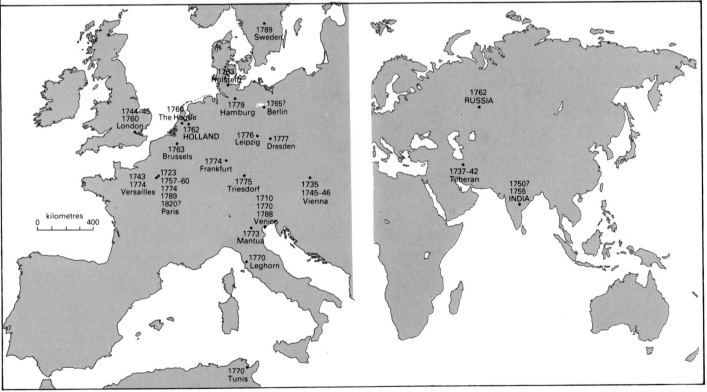

Mary Celeste

The facts of the most famous sea mystery are that two cargo-carrying brigantines set sail from New York in November 1872. Captain Briggs commanded the *Mary Celeste*, heading for Genoa; his friend Captain Moorhouse sailed for Gibraltar on the *Dei Gratia* a week later. Briggs was a profoundly religious man who read a chapter of the Bible daily and carried a harmonium on board on which to play hymns; he took his wife and two-year-old daughter on the voyage. There was a crew of eight, said by Briggs in a letter to have given him the impression of reliability.

A month later, on 7 November, Captain Moorhouse sighted the *Mary Celeste* in the Azores some 950 kilometres west of Gibraltar. Her sails were set, but she was sailing with the wind so erratically that he sent a boarding party to investigate.

The ship was completely deserted. The only lifeboat was missing, apparently having been launched rather than washed away in one of the storms that had obviously hit the ship during the voyage (the binnacle was knocked out of place and the glass on the compass was shattered). The deck cabins were tightly battened down with planks but rainwater had come through to soak bedding and floors. Even so, the ship was highly seaworthy. There was about a metre of water in

the hold – not enough to be dangerous – and evidence that the pumps had been recently checked. The cargo of 1,700 barrels of commercial alcohol was intact, there were six months' provisions in the stores, and an adequate supply of fresh water. Also left behind, in good order, were the crew's boots, oilskins, coats, and even their pipes and tobacco. Toys were on the captain's bed, as if his child had been playing there before being interrupted. Oliver Deveau, leader of the boarding party, told the enquiry later: 'There seemed to be everything left behind in the cabins as if left in a great hurry, but everything in its place.'

To this day, the mystery of the *Mary Celeste* is why she was abandoned, presumably by lifeboat, without the crew taking the basic necessities for survival. Only the navigation instruments and the ship's papers were missing; the ship's log remained, the last entry indicating a position eleven days earlier, 950 kilometres to the west. The only other clues of anything possibly untoward was that a forehatch was found open; two mysterious grooves, each about two metres long, were found on the sides of the bows, just above the waterline; there was a mark, apparently made by an axe, on the ship's rail; and some brownish stains, at first thought to be blood, were found on the deck and on the captain's sword in his cabin.

Even before her unsolved abandonment, the Mary Celeste was known as a jinx ship suffering misfortunes on every voyage she made.

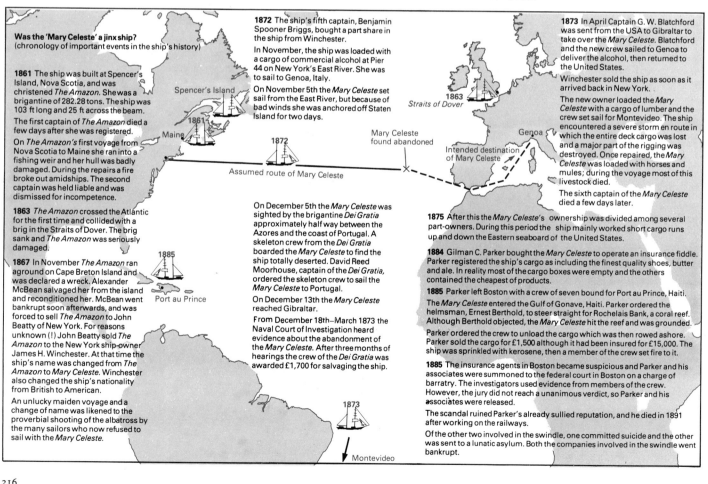

Was the 'Mary Celeste' a jinx ship?
(chronology of important events in the ship's history)

1861 The ship was built at Spencer's Island, Nova Scotia, and was christened *The Amazon*. She was a brigantine of 282.28 tons. The ship was 103 ft long and 25 ft across the beam.

The first captain of *The Amazon* died a few days after she was registered.

On *The Amazon's* first voyage from Nova Scotia to Maine she ran into a fishing weir and her hull was badly damaged. During the repairs a fire broke out amidships. The second captain was held liable and was dismissed for incompetence.

1863 *The Amazon* crossed the Atlantic for the first time and collided with a brig in the Straits of Dover. The brig sank and *The Amazon* was seriously damaged.

1867 In November *The Amazon* ran aground on Cape Breton Island and was declared a wreck. Alexander McBean salvaged her from the island and reconditioned her. McBean went bankrupt soon afterwards, and was forced to sell *The Amazon* to John Beatty of New York. For reasons unknown (!) John Beatty sold *The Amazon* to the New York ship-owner James H. Winchester. At that time the ship's name was changed from *The Amazon* to *Mary Celeste*. Winchester also changed the ship's nationality from British to American.

An unlucky maiden voyage and a change of name was likened to the proverbial shooting of the albatross by the many sailors who now refused to sail with the *Mary Celeste*.

1872 The ship's fifth captain, Benjamin Spooner Briggs, bought a part share in the ship from Winchester.

In November, the ship was loaded with a cargo of commercial alcohol at Pier 44 on New York's East River. She was to sail to Genoa, Italy.

On November 5th the *Mary Celeste* set sail from the East River, but because of bad winds she was anchored off Staten Island for two days.

On December 5th the *Mary Celeste* was sighted by the brigantine *Dei Gratia* approximately half way between the Azores and the coast of Portugal. A skeleton crew from the *Dei Gratia* boarded the *Mary Celeste* to find the ship totally deserted. David Reed Moorhouse, captain of the *Dei Gratia*, ordered the skeleton crew to sail the *Mary Celeste* to Portugal.

On December 13th the *Mary Celeste* reached Gibraltar.

From December 18th–March 1873 the Naval Court of Investigation heard evidence about the abandonment of the *Mary Celeste*. After three months of hearings the crew of the *Dei Gratia* was awarded £1,700 for salvaging the ship.

Spencer's Island

1861

Maine

1872

Assumed route of Mary Celeste

Mary Celeste found abandoned

1863
Straits of Dover

1885

Port au Prince

1873

Montevideo

Genoa

Intended destination of Mary Celeste

1873 In April Captain G. W. Blatchford was sent from the USA to Gibraltar to take over the *Mary Celeste*. Blatchford and the new crew sailed to Genoa to deliver the alcohol, then returned to the United States.

Winchester sold the ship as soon as it arrived back in New York.

The new owner loaded the *Mary Celeste* with a cargo of lumber and the crew set sail for Montevideo. The ship encountered a severe storm en route in which the entire deck cargo was lost and a major part of the rigging was destroyed. Once repaired, the *Mary Celeste* was loaded with horses and mules; during the voyage most of this livestock died.

The sixth captain of the *Mary Celeste* died a few days later.

1875 After this the *Mary Celeste*'s ownership was divided among several part-owners. During this period the ship mainly worked short cargo runs up and down the Eastern seaboard of the United States.

1884 Gilman C. Parker bought the *Mary Celeste* to operate an insurance fiddle. Parker registered the ship's cargo as including the finest quality shoes, butter and ale. In reality most of the cargo boxes were empty and the others contained the cheapest of products.

1885 Parker left Boston with a crew of seven bound for Port au Prince, Haiti. The *Mary Celeste* entered the Gulf of Gonave, Haiti. Parker ordered the helmsman, Ernest Berthold, to steer straight for Rochelais Bank, a coral reef. Although Berthold objected, the *Mary Celeste* hit the reef and was grounded. Parker ordered the crew to unload the cargo which was then rowed ashore. Parker sold the cargo for £1,500 although it had been insured for £15,000. The ship was sprinkled with kerosene, then a member of the crew set fire to it.

1885 The insurance agents in Boston became suspicious and Parker and his associates were summoned to the federal court in Boston on a charge of barratry. The investigators used evidence from members of the crew. However, the jury did not reach a unanimous verdict, so Parker and his associates were released.

The scandal ruined Parker's already sullied reputation, and he died in 1891 after working on the railways.

Of the other two involved in the swindle, one committed suicide and the other was sent to a lunatic asylum. Both the companies involved in the swindle went bankrupt.

Invented myths

So much for the facts. Some myths have emerged as well. *On the cabin table was a freshly-cooked breakfast of three cups of tea – lukewarm – oatmeal, coffee, bacon and eggs.* Deveau's testimony contradicts this: 'There was nothing to eat or drink on the cabin table.' *A terrific struggle took place in the captain's cabin, which was boarded up against a mutinous crew.* Chemical analysis showed no evidence of bloodstains; the boarding was protection against the weather. *The ship was called 'Marie Celeste' on the stern and 'Mary Sellars' on the bow, on account of a lazy and half-deaf sign-painter.* Pure fiction; Conan Doyle re-spelled the name 'Marie-Celeste'. *Neither the ship nor the cargo were insured.* Totally untrue since documents were produced at the inquiry showing a cargo insurance of £7000 and a separate ship insurance. *Within 24 hours of its discovery abandoned, someone on board signalled 'all's well' to the passing s.s. 'Highlander'.* Probably invented. It was used in newspaper

---

Violence/piracy

1 The crew drank the alcohol The first 'official' explanation, put forward by US Secretary of the Treasury William A. Richard in an open letter published in the *New York Times* of 25 March 1873: 'The circumstances of the case tend to arouse grave suspicion that the master, his wife and child, and perhaps the chief mate, were murdered in the fury of drunkenness by the crew, who had evidently obtained access to the alcohol with which the vessel was in part laden.'

Comment It was commercial alcohol, and totally undrinkable. Anybody unlucky enough to drink some would have suffered severe stomach ache.

2 Mr Trigg's explanation Another 'sole survivor' story that alleges wickedness on the part of all other members of the crew. In this version, the crew encountered a derelict ship containing treasure. They decided to stay aboard, changed the ship's name, and sailed away, leaving the *Mary Celeste* abandoned. Disgusted by this dishonesty, Trigg fled to safety in the lifeboat.

Comment A ring of personal authenticity, and a solution that neatly accounts for all the missing papers, contrived abandonment, etc. But what happened to the lifeboat and the derelict ship?

3 Mutiny by the Lorenzen brothers Two German crew members, unknown to their colleagues, were hardened criminals whose sole motive for joining the *Mary Celeste* was to escape to Europe with the proceeds of a big robbery. This scheme was somehow discovered by other members of the crew who tossed the Lorenzen brothers overboard after an affray. The captain intervened, but he too was thrown overboard. The sailors who remained fought it out for possession of the loot. Eventually only one sailor was left and when he realized he might be hanged for multiple murder he jumped into the sea.

Comment Where's the loot?

4 The crew of the *Dei Gratia* hi-jacked the *Mary Celeste* and killed its crew The chief investigator for the inquiry, Solly Flood, believed almost obsessionally that this was what happened. The motive, he thought, was a mistaken belief by the *Dei Gratia* crew that the *Mary Celeste* was secretly carrying a valuable cargo. So they boarded the ship and fought with the crew, as evidenced by the axe-mark on the ship's rail and the brownish stains on the deck. The sword in the captain's cabin also seemed suspicious to Flood, who supposed that, when the crew found nothing of worth on board, they decided to tow the ship to Gibraltar for salvage.

Comment The inquiry dismissed the idea, after rigorously cross-examining the crew. US Consul Sprague said there was no evidence whatsoever for a fight, and concluded: 'I have examined the sword. It was found on the floor of the captain's cabin by the Marshall of the court. By direction of the court, the marks which appeared on the sword, as well as on some of the woodwork, have undergone an analysis which is considered to negative anything like blood existing thereon.' The friendship of Moorhouse for Briggs should also be considered: it is unlikely he would have committed murder for the sake of 17 barrels of commercial alcohol.

5 The two captains concocted a plot for the ship's abandonment Another 'last survivor', Mr Pemberton, told the liveliest and, to some people, most convincing story of all. As cook on the voyage, he had witnessed horrific killings, nightmare storms, insane delusions of the captain's wife, and other dramas all stemming from a pact between Moorhouse and Briggs in a New York bar. As Pemberton recounted to the London *Evening Standard* of 6 May 1929, the two men became steadily more intoxicated and agreed to abandon the *Mary Celeste* in the Atlantic, splitting the salvage money between them. The voyage begun, events became a nightmare. Pemberton described how:

- what Mrs Briggs registered on the passenger list as a 'baby' was in fact a piano to which she screeched as she played.
- First Mate Holding, incensed by this continuous noise, threatened to break up the piano.
- during a severe storm, the piano slid across the room and crushed Mrs Briggs to death.
- after this, Captain Briggs lost his senses and refused to bury his wife at sea.
- Holding and the crew refused to work so long as the corpse was on board.
- a fight between Briggs and Holding ended with Briggs unconscious.
- the crew threw the corpse of Mrs Briggs overboard.
- Briggs regained consciousness and jumped in after her.
- mortal fights on board reduced the crew to five, of whom Pemberton was one survivor, and Holding another. The *Mary Celeste* was now nearly 200 kilometres off course, and Holding suggested Pemberton join him in rowing the lifeboat to Africa. Pemberton refused and was shortly picked up on the ship by Moorhouse and the crew of the *Dei Gratia*, which had coincidentally drifted off course in the same direction. Moorhouse towed the *Mary Celeste* in for salvage as planned, and Pemberton bided his time before exposing the whole story.

Comment A colourful tale.

correspondence to disprove a particular speculation, but was never considered as a fact by the official enquiry.

The explanations

The trouble with trying to solve the mystery is that so many suggestions are, as logicians say, incapable of disproof. You cannot say *definitely* that the crew was not captured by alien spacemen, which a number of Bermuda Triangle addicts believe; nor is it absolutely impossible

that Captain Briggs went berserk in a fit of religious fervour and slaughtered everybody before jumping overboard himself; or that a whirlwind or a giant sea-serpent sucked the crew off the deck. In general, the possible solutions seem to break down into three categories: crisis at sea; violence or piracy; illness or insanity. In the panel, we have arranged each category in what we guess is an order of probability, with the first 'crisis' explanation probably the most plausible of them all.

Illness/insanity

1 Ergot in the bread drove the crew insane The fungus ergot, which has a particular affinity to rye (such as in bread) is highly poisonous; according to the *Encyclopaedia Britannica* it creates 'fearful delusions, suicidal tendencies, and death'. Its effects are said to be much like a dose of LSD-25, and enough to drive people to throw themselves overboard, or to attempt an insane escape in a lifeboat.

Comment If the *Mary Celeste* had become the home of eight tripped-out sailors, it is hardly likely that everything would have been 'in its place'.

2 The cook poisoned the entire crew and threw himself overboard from the lifeboat in terror of his due punishment A variation of the above, and as imaginative.

3 A submarine explosion surrounded the ship with poisonous gas The gas gave off a rare vapour which drove the crew insane and made them jump *en masse* from the ship.

Comment As a theory to prove irrational behaviour by the crew, it ranks low in probability.

4 A rare fungus developed in the ship's wood and poisoned the crew and passengers Historically, this is known to have occurred on other ships.

Comment But why was the salvage crew not affected?

5 The captain had a spiritual frenzy This caused him to develop an 'Isaac complex' and slaughter the whole crew as a sacrifice. Having performed his mission, he commended himself to God and jumped into the sea.

Comment Incredible.

Crisis at sea

1 The ship was abandoned in a mad panic in the mistaken belief she was going to sink There are a number of precedents for incorrect reading of instruments leading to unnecessary abandonment – e.g. the *Marion G. Douglas* in 1919. Oliver Deveau suggested this at the inquiry: 'My idea is that the crew got alarmed, and, by the sounding rod not being found alongside the pumps, that they had sounded the pumps and found perhaps a quantity of water in the pumps at the moment, and thinking she might go down, abandoned her.' Additionally, if water between decks was finding its way into the hold, a sailor might have thought the ship was leaking badly and spread the alarm.

Comment Briggs was too experienced to allow this to happen, so you have to assume he was ill or dead. Reportedly, the *Mary Celeste* was in much better condition than several other ships crossing the Atlantic at the time.

2 In danger of being wrecked on Santa Maria island, the crew abandoned ship abruptly. A sudden breeze separated them from the *Mary Celeste* and swamped the lifeboat The idea of the lifeboat drifting helplessly away from the mother ship is a common explanation. The problem is that nobody knows the exact day when the ship was abandoned – the log may not have been up to date.

Comment The Santa Maria solution demands that an unsteered *Mary Celeste* held her course unaided for probably ten days – unlikely.

3 Captain Briggs became worried about the safety of the ship's cargo after there was a small explosion on board It is a fact that one of the casks of alcohol was damaged. The change of climate from wintry New York to the warmer temperature of the Azores could easily cause the barrels to leak and give off vapour. The front hatch cover was off; either a cask explosion caused this, or Briggs decided to open it to let the fumes out.

Comment A solution favoured by some of the most thorough investigators. But the inquiry dismissed it, because there was no physical trace of an explosion. Also, it assumes an ignorant and naïve crew.

4 Abel Fosdyk's story Several long-lost sailors whose names had unaccountably been omitted from the crew-list turned up in the years after the *Mary Celeste* became famous. Abel Fosdyk was one such. He described how everybody was crowded on a platform constructed on the ship's bows (explaining the strange grooves in the ship's woodwork) in order to get a better view of a race round the ship between the captain and a crew member. The structure collapsed and the occupants fell helplessly into the sea. The captain and his competitor were both eaten by sharks.

Comment And what happened to the lifeboat?

5 The crew saw an uncharted island and decided to investigate French scientists believe that many islands in the Azores are unstable because of a great river that flows under the Sahara Desert and empties itself upwards through the floor of the Atlantic. Sometimes the weight of sand that it displaces rises to the surface to form islands which later settle and sink.

Comment Intriguing, even if not yet geologically proved. But why would *everybody* leave the *Mary Celeste*, wife and child included?

Bermuda Triangle

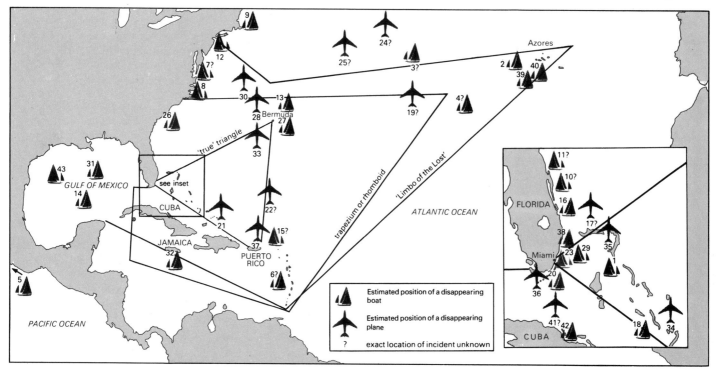

Estimated position of a disappearing boat

Estimated position of a disappearing plane

? exact location of incident unknown

M ost people date the beginning of the Bermuda Triangle legend to an article by Vincent Gaddis in the adventure magazine *Argosy* in 1964. A confirmed follower of Fortean philosophy (page 192), he then incorporated it into a book, *Invisible Horizons*, with the wider theme of mysterious disappearances in general – vanishing islands, lost crews, ghost ships – and put forward as a tentative solution a supposed 'Philadelphia Experiment' involving invisible effects created by eliminating the Earth's magnetic field (which the US Navy and the Office of Naval Research denies ever took place). The myth that he began, with consequences that he could surely have not imagined, is enshrined in his statement that 'this relatively limited area is the scene of disappearances that total far beyond the laws of chance . . . despite swift wings and the voice of radio, we still have a world large enough for men and their machines and ships to disappear without a trace. A mile is still a mile, and the miles can add up to a vast unknown – the same misty limbo of the lost feared by our forefathers.'

Perhaps it was the incantatory effect of the word 'triangle' that caused the explosion of interest, but an avalanche of books on the subject has followed, all using much the same examples and showing much the same lack of concern for statistical reality. For the fact is that the triangle is an illusion; many, perhaps most, of the tragedies cited happened outside the area delineated at its corners by Florida, Puerto Rico and Bermuda, which led a later writer, Richard Winer to say that the 'true' triangle was in fact a trapezium some four times larger, and another

Cases most often cited in the Triangle legend were re-examined by Lawrence Kusche, a research librarian at Arizona State University, and a natural explanation found for nearly all of them. In the summary below, an asterisk indicates cases where his explanation is disputed by later researchers (see text).

1 Rosalie (abandoned ship) 1800. *Ran aground, crew rescued.**

2 Mary Celeste (abandoned ship) 1872. *Still a mystery.*

3 Atalanta (vanished ship) 1880. *Severe weather.**

4 Ellen Austin (derelict ship) 1881. *Source of story not available.*

5 Freya (deserted ship) 1902. *Sank in Pacific seaquake.*

6 Joshua Slocum (vanished seaman) 1909. *Ill health or capsize.**

7 Cyclops (Navy cargo ship) 1918. *Bad weather.*

8 Carroll A. Deering (abandoned ship) 1921. *Still a mystery.*

9 Raifuku Maru (missing freighter) 1925. *Bad weather.*

10 Cotopaxi (freighter) 1925. *Phenomenal storm.*

11 Suduffco (freighter supposedly swallowed by sea monster) 1926. *Storms.*

12 John and Mary (abandoned schooner) 1932. *Engine explosion.*

13 La Dahana ('ghost ship' from the deep) 1935. *Waterlogged derelict.*

14 Gloria Colita (abandoned schooner) 1940. *Storms.*

15 Proteus, Nereus (sister ships of 9 above) 1941. *Torpedoed.*

16 Rubicon (abandoned cargo ship, dog on board) 1944. *Hurricanes.*

17 Flight 19 (five missing bombers) 1945. *Human navigational error.**

18 City Belle (abandoned schooner) 1946. *Bad weather.**

19 Star Tiger (vanished airliner) 1948. *A modern mystery of the air.*

20 Al Snider (vanished jockey, amateur fisherman) 1948. *Record gale.*

21 DC-3 (missing aeroplane) 1948. *Navigational error.*

22 Star Ariel (vanished airliner, sister of 19 above) 1949. *Unsolved.*

23 Sandra (missing freighter) 1950. *Storms.*

24 York Transport (troop aeroplane) 1953. *Bad weather.*

25 Super Constellation (US Navy) plane 1954. *Unsolved.*

26 Southern Districts (Navy cargo ship) 1954. *Storms.*

27 Connemara IV (abandoned yacht) 1955. *Hurricane.*

**28 Naval patrol bomber, 1956. *Explosion.*

29 Revonoc (vanished yacht) 1958. *Storms.**

30 KB-50 (vanished Air Force plane) 1962. *Unsolved.*

31. *Marine Sulphur Queen* (cargo ship) 1963. *Multiple natural causes.**

32 Sno' Boy (missing fishing boat) 1963. *Bad weather, overloaded.*

33 Two KC-135's (Air Force strato-tankers) 1963. *Mid-air collision.**

34 C-119 Flying Boxcar (Air Force plane). *Engineering failure.*

35 Chase YC .122 (cargo plane) 1967. *Structural failure.*

36 Beechcraft Bonanza (light aeroplane) 1967. *Engine failure.**

37 Piper Apache (light aeroplane) 1967. *Bad weather or engine failure.*

38 Witchcraft (cabin cruiser) 1967. *Storm.**

39 Scorpion (nuclear submarine) 1968. *Structural failure.*

40 Teignmouth Electron (abandoned round-the-world yacht) 1969. *Suicide.*

41 Piper Comanche (light aeroplane) 1970. *Pilot error engine failure.**

42 El Caribe (missing freighter) 1971. *Possible hi-jacking.*

43 V. A. Fogg (missing tanker) 1972. *Explosion.**

Magnetic aberrations reported in the Bermuda Triangle

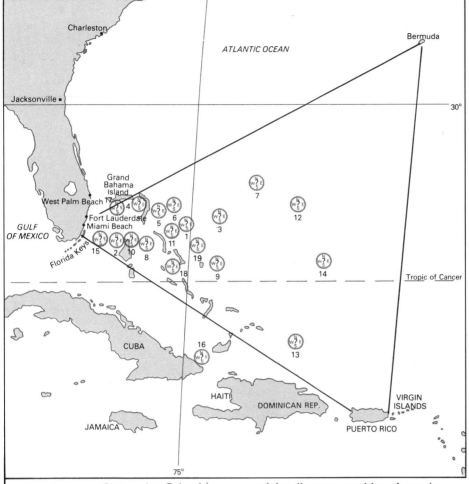

1 October 1492. Christopher Columbus and some of crew on *Santa Maria* saw a great 'flame of fire' flash across the sky, following severe compass disturbances and the appearance of a mysterious light.

2 February 1928. Charles Lindberg noted magnetic disturbances while flying over area in the *Spirit of St Louis*. Both compasses malfunctioned and the liquid compass card rotated freely.

3 July 1928. A tri-motor wooden-wing Fokker on route testing was misdirected by a 50 per cent compass variation and subsequently crashed; the pilot and crew also reported radio interference.

4 November 1943. Lieutenant Robert Ulmer noticed serious instrument anomalies when flying a B–24 over the Bahamas in good weather. Then the plane went suddenly out of control and the crew bailed out.

5 March 1945. Commander Billson, flying a Navy PBM over the Bahamas, noticed both the radio and magnetic compass going round in circles, while the radio went dead.

6 December 1945. All members of the doomed Flight 19 were dogged by instrument problems. The gyro-compasses were reported as 'going crazy',

and the pilots were unable to determine their position.

7 July 1955. W. J. Morris, a veteran seaman aboard the *Atlantic City*, saw the automatic steering device take on 'a mind of its own', directing the ship in a complete circle. Simultaneously there was an incident of ball lightning. A proportion of the navigation and electrical equipment was irreparably damaged.

8 November 1964. Pilot Chuck Wakely noted a mysterious glow, a 'localized fuzzy light', spread across his plane, accompanied by compass and radio failure.

9 July 1966. Don Henry, captain of salvage tug *Good News*, went on deck to look for the cause of engine and compass failure. The barge he was towing had disappeared, although the tow line was still taut; as he watched, the barge slowly re-materialized. Weather was clear. All batteries on the tug were drained of power.

10 February 1968. Pilot Jim Blocker noted radio failure, spinning compasses, and failure of high frequency direction finder.

11 December 1970. Pilot Bruce Gernon Jnr investigated massive 'doughnut-shaped' cloud reaching down to sea level. Flying through it, magnetic

and electronic instruments ceased to work and he lost contact with radar control. On reaching his destination he found he had 'lost' 30 minutes compared with normal flight time for the trip.

12 March 1971. Captain of USS *Richard E. Byrd* logged instrument malfunction and disorientation among crew. Journey took four days longer than usual.

13 March 1974. Crew of USS *Vogelgaing* reported electrical and mechanical failure, including engine room boiler, 'as if there was an invisible force field attempting to tear the ship apart.'

14 April 1974. Passengers aboard the *Queen Elizabeth 2* had to transfer to another ship when a mysterious power failure caused the entire lighting and heating system to fail.

15 August 1974. Crew of US Coast Guard cutter *Hollyhock* saw large land mass appear on radar in an area of empty sea; repeated checks of the radar revealed no faults. Simultaneously local radio communications ceased, but two-way messages could be exchanged with California.

16 December 1974. Pilot Mike Roxby in a Cessna 172 suffered instrument and radio failure twice in one day, the second time fatally. A surviving passenger said the event coincided with 'a cloud appearing from nowhere'.

17 December 1974. Pilot Jack Strehle was alarmed to see a flashing blue light above the wing of his plane, accompanied by a wildly spinning compass on his instrument panel.

18 July 1975. On a photographic trip, Dr Jim Thorne intended to take film of an electromagnetic storm. One photograph of lightning on the horizon also showed an old-fashioned square-rigged sailing ship, although there were no other ships in the area at the time. This 'apparition' on the negative has not yet been satisfactorily explained.

19 December 1975. The Coast Guard cutter *Diligence* suffered a total failure in radio transmission and navigation equipment while following up a report of a burning freighter. At the same time mysterious green lights repeatedly 'fell out of the sky'. Later investigation established that these could not have been rescue flares, and a thorough check on the instruments of the *Diligence* showed no obvious reason for their malfunction.

author to suggest a 'limbo of the lost' even bigger. Gaddis himself had suggested a further killer sea: 'Over all the seas of the earth, there is only one other localized area where mysterious disappearances have repeatedly occurred. This is the grim, but far more remote "Devil's Sea" region in the Pacific south of Japan and east of the Bonin Islands. Here, too, in a limited area, the usual dangers that menace planes and ships fail to explain why it is seldom that wreckage or bodies are found.' And this in turn led Ivan Sanderson to note that both places lay on roughly the same latitude – 36° north of the Equator – and to speculate that others existed in a symmetrical pattern round the globe. His twelve 'vile vortices' are directly related to Russian attempts to put a crystalline grid on the face of the Earth (page 56).

Chance fatalities

By no rational process can it be suggested that any of these areas receive more than their fair share of disasters, given that some are busier and meteorologically more extreme. The US Coastguard service has said that with some 150,000 boats and 10,000 calls a year for help in the area of the Bermuda Triangle, they are pleased so few vessels disappear. Their reports show that in 1975, 21 vessels were lost without trace off the US coast, 4 of which were in the triangle; in 1976, the figures were 28 and 6.

Lawrence Kusche, a librarian at Arizona State University, has also shown conclusively that almost all of the most important Triangle mysteries are only mysterious because of misquotation, or distortion and suppression of evidence. As he summarizes the legendary version of the schooner *Gloria Colita*, for instance, it 'was found mysteriously abandoned 200 miles south of Mobile in the Gulf of Mexico. There was no apparent reason for the desertion as the seas were calm and everything was in order.' Looking back on newspaper reports of the incident, in February 1940, he found that severe storms had hit the area at the time in question; 'the rigging was in shreds and her rudder and steering apparatus shattered . . . the hold was nearly filled with water.' In virtually every case, climatic conditions, human error, or structural failure was the realistic answer to the so-called mystery.

Magnetic anomalies

However, he has not quite drawn a final line under the story. A team working for Los Angeles film producer Alan Landsburg re-examined all the cases looked at by Kusche and came to a somewhat modified view, summarized in his book *Bermuda Triangle Secrets*. Totalling the incidents already reported in the literature plus some new cases uncovered by their investigation, the team found that Kusche had only dealt with about one third; they listed 54 sailing vessels, 48 motor vessels, 18 military planes, 19 light aircraft, 4 commercial airliners and 4 miscellaneous disasters – a total of 147, out of which they felt there were about half in which factors other than those listed by Kusche played a part. Secondly, they found some cases of unexplained magnetic aberrations completely convincing; if only half the cases listed by them and included in the panel on the opposite page are true, then there is still something to be explained in the Bermuda Triangle, and perhaps elsewhere. For although the theory of magnetism is supposedly well understood by scientists, the Earth's magnetism still remains unexplained (page 17), and the wildly spinning compasses that have come to light as the result of an extraordinary and instinctive popular interest in the Triangle may be an indication of energy not yet harnessed by man.

Ghost ship stories similar to those experienced in the Bermuda Triangle were common at the turn of the century; this illustration appeared in *Scribner's Magazine*.

Vanishing people

Six devilish phenomena portrayed in the frontispiece to Joseph Glanville's *Saducismus Triumphatus* include the teleportation of the Somerset witch Julian Cox (middle left).

Scept
cism about people who vanish mysteriously from sight, sometimes permanently and sometimes to re-appear as if by magic in a different part of the globe, goes back a long way. In 1655 the Inquisition put on trial a man who, minding his business in Goa, was unwittingly whisked into the air and a few moments later found himself back in his native country, Portugal. He was found guilty of a crime against the Godly order of things and burnt at the stake.

The Church took an equally quizzical view of claims made by the young Sister Mary in a convent at Agreda; between 1620 and 1631 she persisted in telling her superiors about her 'flights' to central America where she set about converting the Jumano Indians to Christianity. She was strongly criticized for what were felt to be hysterical tales, particularly as she described seeing the world as being round and revolving on its poles – then a heretical theory.

But in the 1630s her story was conclusively confirmed – indeed, it is one of the strongest pieces of historical evidence for the phenomenon that we have. The official task of converting the Mexican Indians had been given to Father Alonzo de Benavides and in 1622 he wrote to

the Pope and to Philip IV of Spain complaining that his work had been pre-empted. A mysterious nun, called by the Indians the 'lady in blue', had been there before him distributing crosses, rosaries and a chalice with which they celebrated Mass. Who was she?

No such person was known, but on his return to Spain in 1630 Father Benavides heard of Sister Mary's extraordinary claims. Over a period of time he interviewed her minutely, discovering that she gave details of Indian lore and custom and of the villages where they lived, known only to a handful of travellers, none of whom she had ever met. He also obtained signed statements from her superiors that she had never left the convent. Even more astonishingly, they recognized the chalice used by the Indians as having come from their own convent.

James A. Carrico's authorized *Life of the Venerable Mary of Agreda* concludes that she made some 500 missionary visits: 'That Mary really visited America many times is attested to by the logs of the Spanish conquistadors, the French explorers, the identical accounts by different tribes of Indians a thousand miles apart. Every authentic history of the Southwest of the United States records this mystic phenomenon unparalleled in the entire history of the world.'

Untenable theories

A number of theories have been put forward to explain why and where such events take place: the leys that supposedly link ancient sacred sites (page 74) are said by some to provide, under ideal circumstances, access to another dimension or level of consciousness; Ivan Sanderson conceived the notion of 'vile vortices' (page 57) or gravitational whirlpools that achieve the same effect. But for the moment these are hypotheses incapable of either proof or disproof, and so random and unexpected do the cases of vanishment and teleportation seem that it is best, perhaps, just to classify them as Forteana (those well-observed oddities like falls of fish from the sky described on page 196, which just happen but cannot be explained).

In every case some kind of a time/space aberration is involved and one of the things that encourages belief that occasionally they genuinely happen is how prosaic they often seem to the people concerned. The English writer Colin Wilson tells the story of two friends, Arthur and Mary Guirdham, from Bath in southern England, 'who simply recounted it as something odd that had once happened to them.' On holiday in Yorkshire, they visited a town 15 miles away and at the end of the day started to

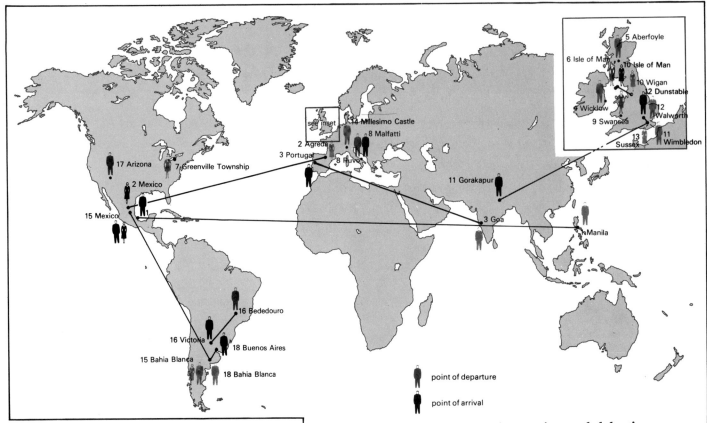

World distribution of supposed teleportations and abductions
(based on historical incidents published in Fortean journals)

drive back. 'It was a warm pleasant evening, and they drove slowly. They had only been driving for five minutes when Guirdham noticed a signpost that indicated they were only three miles from their destination. This was clearly impossible unless they had been driving at more than a hundred miles an hour. They stopped to consult a map to see if they had taken a short cut or mistaken the distance. They had not. If the signposts were right, then, they had covered 12 miles in less than five minutes. And the signpost was right. A few miles further on, the Guirdhams entered the town where their hotel was situated.'

Time-slip
In this case, he concluded, there was no question of lost time; it was only the distance that had apparently been telescoped. A time-slip seems to have been involved in the case of the Vaughans from Gloucester, in the west of England, investigated by another writer, Harold Wilkins. In 1906 a ten-year-old boy and his two younger sisters, aged eight and seven, went into a field near home and disappeared. For the next three days an intensive search was carried out by hundreds of police and neighbours; on the fourth day all three children were found asleep in a ditch in the same field from which they had vanished, and in a spot which had been walked over by many of the searchers. They had no idea where they had been, nor that three days had passed. They were not especially hungry. Abduction or kidnapping seems ruled out from

1 October 1593. A man was teleported from Manilla to Mexico City, but was unable to remember the experience.

2 c. 1620. Venerable Mary of Agreda was officially estimated to have made over 500 journeys by teleportation.

3 1655. A man was tried by the Spanish Inquisition for witchcraft after being teleported from Goa to Portugal.

4 1678. Dr Alan Moore was abducted by fairies in front of two witnesses.

5 1691. Reverend Robert Kirk said he was abducted by fairies.

6 1845. A Manx woman said her babies had been abducted and levitated by fairies. One baby was exchanged for another child.

7 March 1883. Jesse Miller's daughter was teleported several times from a locked house to the front garden.

8 January 1901. The Pansini boys were teleported from Ruvo to Malfatti. They appeared to be hypnotized.

9 December 1904. A woman was teleported from the Reverend David Phillips' house to a nearby brook. The house was plagued by poltergeists at the time.

10 January 1905. Alice Hilton, aged 66, disappeared from Wigan. She was

found semi-conscious on the shore at the Isle of Man.

11 1910. A Hindu magician confessed to having transported a boy from London to India.

12 September 1920. Leonard Wadham was teleported from Walworth to Dunstable.

13 December 1926. Agatha Christie disappeared from her home in Sussex. She re-appeared some days later unable to remember anything about her disappearance.

14 July 1928. Marquis Carlo Scotto was teleported from a sealed and locked room in his palace to a locked stable nearby.

15 May 1968. Dr Geraldo Vidal and his wife were teleported from Bahia Blanca to Mexico.

16 May 1969. Jose Antoniada Silva was teleported from Bebedouro to Victoria. He said he had been abducted by extra-terrestrials.

17 November 1975. Friends of Travis Walton said he had been abducted after he had run towards a UFO. He re-appeared five days later and confirmed the story.

18 January 1975. Carlos Diaz said he had been abducted from Bahia Blanca and was left near Buenos Aires.

Great Britain

1. Leeds Mr and Mrs Thomas Cumpston said they felt a tremendous wind and that the floor of their room 'opened before them'. *The Times,* 11 December 1873.

2. St Boswells Marian Scott reported that a man dressed as a clergyman disappeared in front of her. *Journal of the Society for Psychical Research,* November 1873.

3 Ballycastle Professor George Simcox, Senior Fellow of Queens College, disappeared; a search party found no trace of him. *The Times,* 4 September 1905.

4 Belfast Eight girls, all aged under twelve years old, disappeared from Newtownards Road in the space of a week. *Daily Mirror,* 5 August 1920.

5 Liverpool Socialist MP Victor Grayson stepped on a train and was never heard of again – despite the efforts of a search party in October and November 1920. *Sunday Mercury,* 8 December 1974.

6 Chester Flying Officer Brian Holding took off on a short flight and disappeared without trace. *Daily Chronicle,* 30 March 1922.

7 Southend Kathleen Munn disappeared with her two small children. *Evening Star,* 2 November 1926.

8 Lydd Airport Glenn Miller disappeared before or during a flight to Paris for a Christmas concert in 1944. Recent article in *Daily Mirror,* 14 December 1974.

9 Gorton Pauline Reade disappeared on her way to a party in July 1963. *Observer Magazine,* 29 October 1972.

10 Longsight Keith Bennett disappeared during a 400 metre journey to his grandmother's house in June 1964. *Observer Magazine,* 29 October 1972.

11 Fakenham Stephen Paul disappeared from outside his home in September 1969. *Sunday Mirror,* 18 August 1974.

12 Wallasey David McCraig disappeared during a one km. cycle ride to school. *Observer Magazine,* 29 October 1972.

13 Scunthorpe Christine Markham disappeared near her parents' home in May 1973. *Sunday Mirror,* 25 August 1974.

14 Manchester Heifers, sheep and pigs disappeared from two farms. *Manchester Evening News,* 19 April 1974.

15 Christchurch Florence Newitt disappeared from her home leaving signs of a sudden departure. *Daily Express,* 5 May 1974.

16 East Croydon William Nicholson arrived at the station to visit relatives, then disappeared. *Sunday Express,* 30 March 1975.

17 Newcastle Taxi-driver Anna Saint disappeared, leaving her taxi with her money and a coat in it. *Daily Mirror* 11 December 1974.

United States

1 New York The *Mary Celeste* left East River Harbour in November 1872. The entire crew vanished during the voyage. *The Times,* 29 January 1885.

2 New York James Conant, editor of *Harper's Weekly* disappeared without trace. *New York Times,* 29 January 1885.

3 Salem Isaac Martin, a young farmer, went to work in the fields then disappeared. *New York Sun,* 23 April 1885.

4 Connecticut Six people appeared in the streets, suffering from concussion, and unable to say how they got there. *St Louis Globe-Democrat,* 5 January 1888.

5 Augusta Mills Sherman Church ran into a cotton mill and vanished. A thorough search of the mill and its surroundings revealed nothing. *Chicago Tribune,* 5 June 1900.

6 New York Dorothy Arnold walked through Central Park, then vanished without a trace. *New York Sun,* 13 December 1910.

7 Long Island Albert Jewell left on a short flight to Staten Island, and was 'completely lost as if he had vanished into thin air'. *New York Times,* 14 October 1913.

8 Mexico Ambrose Bierce left New York to join Pancho Villa but no trace was found of him again. *New York Times,* 3 April 1915.

9 Toronto Ambrose Small left his office in the Opera House and disappeared. A long search campaign found nothing. *Toronto Globe and Mail,* 4 December 1919.

10 Lakes Erie and Michigan Otis Redding and others were lost on a flight from Cleveland to Madison. Jay Gourley *The Great Lakes Triangle* (Fawcett Books 1977) p67.

---

lack of motive. Years later the boy was re-interviewed and told exactly the same story.

It may be that he and his sisters were lucky, for there are many cases on record where people have been seen to vanish and never come back. On 29th November 1809, Benjamin Bathurst, a courier for the British Foreign Office involved in the war against Napoleon, was outside an inn near Berlin, preparing to climb into his carriage. He told his valet to wait at the carriage door while he inspected the horses. According to Sabine Baring-Gould in *Historical Oddities*: 'He stepped round to the heads of the horses – and was never seen again.' Another classic case is that of Owen Parfitt, a cripple who vanished from Somerset in the west of England in 1769. Formerly a pirate, he was immobilized by a stroke and was left sitting in a chair outside his cottage while a relative went briefly into the house; she came out moments later to find him gone, but the chair and the rug in which he was wrapped still there.

The circumstantial detail around the best modern account is compelling. Although the evidence is unsupported, it comes from the widely-respected US broadcaster L. J. Knebel, who describes himself as 'one of the most sceptical men in the business', and the account he gives in *The Way Out World* is supported by tape-recordings. He was watching his friend, the magician Dr William Neff, at the Paramount Theatre in New York at a matinée that drew a near-empty house. As he watched, in medium-bright stage lighting, 'it seemed that Neff's body was becoming minutely translucent,' and gradually – he was unable to estimate the time precisely, so astonished was he – 'you could see the traveller curtain clearly behind this transparent figure.'

Gradual materialization

What made the experience all the more uncanny was that Neff continued to speak normally, as if he didn't himself realize what was happening. Knebel described what happened when Neff began to re-appear: 'Gradually a rather faint outline, like a very fine pencil sketch of Neff, appeared again.'

Magician though he was, it was not an act William Neff could create at will. He went on record as saying that it had only twice happened at other times in his life: on the stage in Chicago; and to her terror, in front of his wife at home. Yet on none of the three occasions did he himself realize he was invisible, nor feel any physiological change. Like a pilot going through the sound barrier, the journey to another dimension may be smoother than we might imagine.

Section ten
Searches

One unique quality of mankind is that we are never satisfied. Classical Darwinian theory says that when a species reaches a level necessary for survival, it stays there subject to a continuing process that weeds out the weak ones unable to cope. But we don't follow this pattern; alone among living creatures, our brains have achieved a sophistication that gives us the power to control (subject to catastrophe) our destiny and, however ineptly, that is what we try to do.

Throughout this Atlas, the search for what mysterious energies make the Universe function and the methods we may use to control them has been an underlying theme. Each age has had its own thoughts about them. Nowadays physicists believe there are basically four such energies or 'forces': electromagnetism, gravity and the strong and weak forces that explain the behaviour of nuclear particles. But even cursory reading of the unending debate in scientific literature leaves no doubt that many aspects of the relationship between one force and another cannot at the moment be reconciled; they do not add up and there is no unified field theory such as Einstein yearned for and was disappointed not to find.

In earlier times, societies preferred other solutions. The megalith builders, if we can read the enigmatic message of their monument placing correctly (page 74 and generally through sections three and four), seem to have believed there are life-giving energies that involve synchronizing the rhythms of the Earth with the rhythms of the Universe. At the same time in history, a similar striving for a cosmic harmony may have been the motive of the priesthood which designed the Great Pyramid and placed it with infinite care precisely where it was thought that these energies

could best be studied and perhaps harnessed. Later came the Pythagorean and Platonic schools that are supposed to have codified these secrets and passed them on to a small number of enclosed societies whose initiates became adepts in the ancient wisdom.

At the heart of all these movements is a quest for something which is beyond normal perception: forces which people cannot see and rarely feel, but which they know instinctively are there. The impulse that made so many people want to know more about disappearances in the Bermuda Triangle, or about extra-terrestrial intervention in the history of man, is not to be derided just because the evidence so far brought forward is mainly spurious. The introduction of the Atlas suggested that there was still much for 21st-century science to find out (or 22nd-century, or 30th-century, for that matter) and mankind's unique propensity to search for new explanations assures us that this will happen.

In at least three of the quests chosen for this last section, it is notable that they have been searches for spiritual enlightenment rather than material riches. The Holy Grail provides fascinating glimpses of pre-Christian religious knowledge; from Shangri-la comes an Eastern wisdom which some people think penetrated the early civilizations of the Near East; even the search for El Dorado, during this century, has ceased being solely for gold, becoming instead an almost mystical quest for lost cities and lost civilizations whose discovery would add to our knowledge of a hidden past. This is surely an encouraging and healthy trend; a readiness to learn about past achievements is at the same time a step towards future science.

King Solomon's mines

If the Bible is right and conventional archaeological dating methods are wrong (page 168), King Solomon was without doubt phenomenally rich. I Kings tells how 'the weight of gold that came to Solomon in one year was six hundred three score and six talents of gold . . .' Descriptions of various precious metals and stones, together with other luxuries and exotica, clearly indicate that Solomon imported them, apparently from far-distant countries. An Egyptian bas-relief (page 175) illustrates the rich treasures looted from Solomon's Temple and palace by the Egyptian Pharaoh Thutmose III, successor to the Queen of Sheba.

Much of this treasure, it is now thought, was made of copper or brass, as described in the lists of Temple furnishings and decorations given in Kings and Chronicles. Copper was mined extensively in the Negev desert and recently an Egyptian cartouche of Thutmose III has been found there, confirming that copper was being mined actively at the correct time (according to Velikovsky's revised chronology).

However, mystery and argument still shroud the location of the fabled mines. The Bible gives clues that are tantalizing but formidably difficult to solve; they centre on the two place-names Ophir and Tarshish (or Tharshish). Ophir was the land where the gold came from, and Tarshish was connected with the navy that went to collect it. Thus I Kings: 'And they came to Ophir, and fetched from thence gold, four hundred and twenty talents, and brought it to King Solomon.' The navy that brought gold from Ophir is mentioned again during the visit of the Queen of Sheba as also bringing in 'from Ophir great plenty of almug trees and precious stones'.

So the Bible gives no help as to where Ophir was – only that it existed. The Tarshish texts are only marginally more helpful for some tell of ships that went *to* Tarshish, and others of ships *of* Tarshish. From I Kings we learn that Solomon undertook expeditions in collaboration with the Phoenicians, a great sea-going race under their leader Hiram I, King of Tyre. Their navy left from the port of Ezion-Geber on the Red Sea.

Solomon is described as having at sea 'a navy of Tharshish with the navy of Hiram: once in three years came the navy of Tharshish, bringing gold, and silver, ivory, and apes, and peacocks.'

But where was Tarshish? Ezekiel wrote that the Phoenicians traded there in silver, iron, tin and lead. About 100 years after Solomon's time, when the Israelite fortunes had been much reduced, King Jehoshaphat of Judah made an attempt to reach Tarshish from Ezion-Geber, but a storm wrecked the ships and they never left port. The only other useful reference is that Jonah was trying to escape there when he had his famous accident. But confusingly, he paid his fare for the trip at a different port, Joppa, which is on the Mediterranean.

So a number of possibilities arise. (1) There were a number of places called Tarshish (which can also be translated as a 'smeltery'), all referring to locations where Solomon obtained minerals, and perhaps also referring to the type of cargo ships used. (2) Josephus, the Jewish historian who made a translation of the Old Testament in the First Century AD, identified the word with Tarsus, a famous port in Roman times. His version of the Solomon passage reads: 'for the king had many ships which lay upon the Sea of Tarsus, these he commanded to carry out all sorts of merchandise from the remotest nations.' This can be reconciled with theory (1) by suggesting that Solomon had a navy *of* Tarshish (Tarsus) to go *to* Tarshish (various smelteries).

However, since Solomon was definitely linked with the sea-trading Phoenicians, theory (3) looks at independent accounts of their history and identifies Tarshish with Tartessos, an ancient kingdom near Cadiz in what is now Spain, described glowingly by the Greeks as a rich source of silver. The Phoenicians are known to have traded with and colonized Spain, which makes it plausible as the source for some of Solomon's minerals.

However, none of these three theories is completely satisfactory. Tarsus could well have been an outlet for the ores of the Black Sea coast and Tartessos could have supplied its own silver. But what about the apes, ivory, peacocks and negroes? The apes of Gibraltar apart, neither

Facsimile of a Phoenician text carved on stone describing a transatlantic sea voyage in the 6th Century BC. Most experts consider it a fraud, but cannot prove it to be so.

We are the sons of Canaan from Sidon, from the city where a merchant has been made king. He dispatched
us to this distant island, a land of mountains. We sacrificed a youth to the celestial gods and goddesses in the nineteenth year of Hiram, our King. *Abra!*
We sailed from Ezion–Geber into the Red Sea and voyaged with ten ships.
We were at sea together for two years around Africa. Then we got separated
by the hand of Baal and we were no longer with our companions. So we have come here, twelve
men and three women, into one island unpopulated because ten died. *Abra!*
May the celestial gods and goddesses favour us!

Spain nor Tarsus is a feasible source for all these goods. And why should Solomon's ships have taken three years to do a round trip to either place?

The meaning of the word Tarshish is unclear and if it is a place, perhaps it lies further afield, perhaps in more than one place. Excavations at Mahd adh Dhabab in Saudi Arabia have uncovered a gigantic gold mine active in Solomon's time; perhaps this was the Ophir to which he went with King Hiram and also the Tarshish which Jehoshaphat tried unsuccessfully to reach from the same Red Sea port of Ezion–Geber.

As for the exotica, perhaps Tartessos was the starting-point for a much more adventurous series of sea voyages that encompassed Africa and, conceivably, America. The account by the Greek historian Herodotus of how the Phoenicians, leaving the Red Sea around 600 BC and sailing southwards, were able to make a round trip of Africa and return through the Mediterranean to the northern coast of Egypt (map, page 114), is fully accepted by ancient historians. On the way, they passed through the Straits of Gibraltar and very near Tartessos. Similar voyages may have taken place in Solomon's time on which the apes, ivory, peacocks and negroes were collected, together with silver from Tartessos itself, which lent its name to the voyages as a whole and to the type of ships that took part in them.

Alternatively – or additionally – voyages to the New World during the same period now seem more likely than not and the starting point for these may have been in the reverse direction, from the Mediterranean through the Pillars of Hercules to the Atlantic. Cyrus Gordon, Head of the Department of Mediterranean Studies at Brandeis University, Massachusetts, says that a text mentioning 'gold of Ophir' found at Tell Qasile on the Mediterranean Coast of Israel, suggests that Ophir could be reached via Gibraltar.

According to his interpretation, the Phoenicians certainly knew Brazil, which they called the 'Island of Iron' (still the country's main resource). The Paraiba text on the opposite page, if his translation is correct, shows how one group of sailors in the 19th year of the reign of King Hiram III became separated from the rest of the fleet and finished up in Brazil, where the inscription was found in 1872. He thinks Tarshish refers to Mexico, rich in silver and other metal ores, 'though other Atlantic areas are not ruled out'.

As for the 19th-century explorers' tales that supposedly identified the mines with central Africa, and refused to accept that the massive stone fortress known as the ruins of Zimbabwe, and situated in that country, could have been built by native black Africans, these must be regarded as romantic (or racist) fiction. Zimbabwe is AD, not BC, and almost certainly the work of a powerful indigenous African empire.

Many places have been suggested as the location of Solomon's fabled mines. New respect for the seagoing abilities of early navigators makes central or southern America a strong possibility.

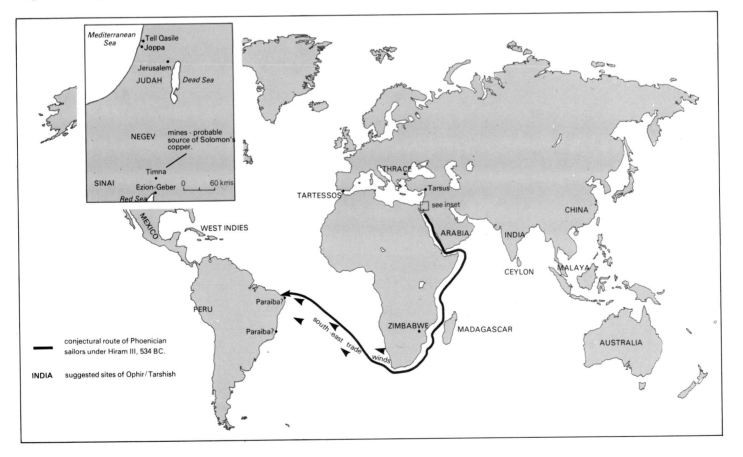

conjectural route of Phoenician sailors under Hiram III, 534 BC.

INDIA   suggested sites of Ophir / Tarshish

The Holy Grail

The quest for the Holy Grail is one of the most haunting themes in Christian history. By legend, the Grail is the cup used by Christ at the Last Supper, rescued from Pontius Pilate by Christ's uncle, Joseph of Arimathea and brought to Britain as a sacred talisman for the early Church. Buried or lost somewhere near Glastonbury, the earliest Christian centre in Britain, it became the object of a search that lasted many centuries. King Arthur's knights mysteriously found the Grail, by which time it was regarded not only as a Christian relic but also as a magical vessel that also contained hints of an early and secret wisdom. As obscurely as it was found, the Grail disappeared again and has been sought by scholars ever since.

It is this blend of occult with religious legend that sets the Grail apart from other Christian relics (page 178) and makes it an essential part of a wider search for lost knowledge. The first question is how much truth there is in the physical reality of the Grail and its supposed journey to Britain. Initially, the circumstantial evidence is fairly encouraging. There is the hard historical fact, recorded in the Gospels, that Joseph and Nicodemus received the body of Christ and buried it. The suggestion that Joseph was Christ's uncle (not recorded in the Bible) is made somewhat plausible by the fact that Pilate was willing to give him the body at all; since Christ had been condemned as a criminal, he would have been buried as such in the place reserved, unless under Roman or Jewish law a relative came to claim the body and dispose of it.

Cornish tin-trading

St Matthew tells us that Joseph was rich and there is no reason to doubt this; if he could afford to provide Christ with a tomb, he must have been quite wealthy. By tradition, he made his money in the tin trade and the legendary route that he took with the Grail to Britain, illustrated in the map below, agrees remarkably well with the trade route for tin described by the Greek writer Diodorus Siculus shortly before the birth of Christ. Tin, he wrote, was transported at low tide to the island of Ictis (thought to be St Michael's Mount in a bay

Accounts of Joseph of Arimathea's journeys from the Holy Land through Europe to Britain form the basis of the legend that the Holy Grail has a physical reality.

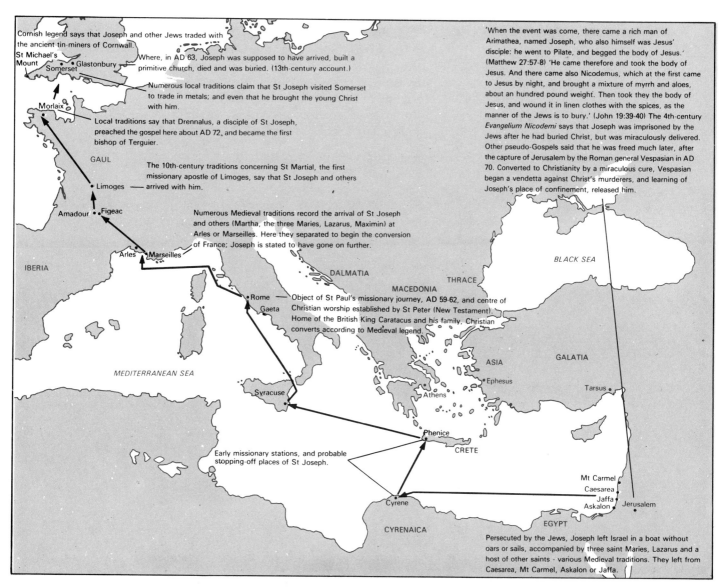

Cornish legend says that Joseph and other Jews traded with the ancient tin-miners of Cornwall.

Where, in AD 63, Joseph was supposed to have arrived, built a primitive church, died and was buried. (13th-century account.)

Numerous local traditions claim that St Joseph visited Somerset to trade in metals; and even that he brought the young Christ with him.

Local traditions say that Drennalus, a disciple of St Joseph, preached the gospel here about AD 72, and became the first bishop of Terguier.

The 10th-century traditions concerning St Martial, the first missionary apostle of Limoges, say that St Joseph and others arrived with him.

Numerous Medieval traditions record the arrival of St Joseph and others (Martha, the three Maries, Lazarus, Maximin) at Arles or Marseilles. Here they separated to begin the conversion of France; Joseph is stated to have gone on further.

Object of St Paul's missionary journey, AD 59-62, and centre of Christian worship established by St Peter (New Testament). Home of the British King Caratacus and his family, Christian converts according to Medieval legend.

Early missionary stations, and probable stopping-off places of St Joseph.

'When the event was come, there came a rich man of Arimathea, named Joseph, who also himself was Jesus' disciple: he went to Pilate, and begged the body of Jesus.' (Matthew 27:57-8) 'He came therefore and took the body of Jesus. And there came also Nicodemus, which at the first came to Jesus by night, and brought a mixture of myrrh and aloes, about an hundred pound weight. Then took they the body of Jesus, and wound it in linen clothes with the spices, as the manner of the Jews is to bury.' (John 19:39-40) The 4th-century *Evangelium Nicodemi* says that Joseph was imprisoned by the Jews after he had buried Christ, but was miraculously delivered. Other pseudo-Gospels said that he was freed much later, after the capture of Jerusalem by the Roman general Vespasian in AD 70. Converted to Christianity by a miraculous cure, Vespasian began a vendetta against Christ's murderers, and learning of Joseph's place of confinement, released him.

Persecuted by the Jews, Joseph left Israel in a boat without oars or sails, accompanied by three saint Maries, Lazarus and a host of other saints - various Medieval traditions. They left from Caesarea, Mt Carmel, Askalon or Jaffa.

St Michael's Mount · Glastonbury · Somerset · Morlaix

GAUL · Limoges · Amadour · Figeac · Arles · Marseilles

IBERIA · Rome · Gaeta · DALMATIA · MACEDONIA · THRACE · BLACK SEA

MEDITERRANEAN SEA · Syracuse · ASIA · GALATIA · Ephesus · Athens · Tarsus · Phenice · CRETE · Mt Carmel · Caesarea · Jaffa · Askalon · Jerusalem

Cyrene · CYRENAICA · EGYPT

off southern Cornwall). 'Hence the merchants transport the tin they buy of the inhabitants to Gaul and for thirty days' journey they carry it in sacks upon horses' backs through Gaul to the mouth of the river Rhône.'

Independent traditions in northern France, western Ireland, Gloucester, north London and the Cornish tin-mining region all tell of Joseph's involvement in the tin trade; the Cornish ones are particularly specific. A foreman tinsmith in the region was recorded early this century as saying: 'We workers in metal are a very old fraternity, and like other handicrafts we have our traditions among us. One of these, the memory of which is preserved in this invocation, is that Joseph . . . made voyages to Cornwall in his own ships, and that on one occasion he brought with him the Child Christ and his Mother and landed them at St Michael's Mount.'

Travels of Christ

A visit to Britain by the young Jesus with Joseph is historically feasible and backed up by a certain amount of local legend. Nothing is known of Jesus's life between the ages of 12 and 30 (the start of His ministry), and He is widely believed to have travelled abroad. There is a 'Jesus Well' at the mouth of the River Camel in Cornwall, en route to Glastonbury. At the little village of Priddy, eight miles to the north of Glastonbury, there is an exceptionally strong legend (linked somehow with the story of a strange energy said to emanate from a cave beneath the church) that Christ was once there as a boy; a commonly used local saying, even today, is: 'as sure as our Lord was at Priddy.' In Galilee, the tradition that Jesus was a carpenter is accompanied by the story that he visited Britain as a shipwright on a trading vessel from Tyre and was storm-bound on the shores of western Britain for an entire winter.

So there are encouraging hints of an early link between the Holy Lands and Britain, supported by both historical and archaeological evidence that the Christian religion was practised in Britain almost immediately after Christ's death. The 6th-century writer Gildas said that it began in the last year of the reign of Tiberius, which was only four years after the crucifixion. A metal drinking vessel of the 1st Century AD found at Hadrian's Wall bears an unmistakable early Christian symbol. Glastonbury, under its ancient name Glastonia, is specifically mentioned in religious texts as having had a church *before* missionaries of the Catholic Church arrived in the 6th Century AD.

Finally, there is the fact that Joseph himself is a curiously insignificant figure to become the centre of such an important legend, were there not some substance at the back of it. As the writer Geoffrey Ashe has put it, 'St Joseph's presence on British soil is too odd, under the circumstances, to have quite the air of pure invention.' But was Joseph more than a rich merchant who happened to be a Christian? Or if he was indeed Christ's uncle and made a journey with Him during Jesus's youth, did he return after the crucifixion? Did he, in fact, ever bring the Holy Grail?

Mediaeval legends

Here we are on much less firm ground, the chief cause for uncertainty being that Joseph does not appear in the local saint cults assiduously propagated by the Catholic Church through Britain. The biography of St Dunstan, written about AD 1000 and William of Malmesbury's *de Antiquitate*, c. AD 1125 both mention the traditions concerning Glastonbury as an early Christian site, but make no mention of Joseph – a striking omission, if he had founded the church there as later stories said. Significantly, a much later edition of Malmesbury's book, printed after the Arthurian Grail legends had become popular

French depiction of the Grail drawn in 1325 shows it as a ciborium, a lance and a sword on a bier.

a Tale Chronicled for One of the Truest and One of the Holiest that is in the World.'

Occult Symbols

Malory's exact French source is not known, but it is unlikely to have been very ancient; the earliest extant work is by the Burgundian, Robert de Boron. This book is a key source in unravelling the mystery of the Grail. In it, the legend is told in a way that leaves no doubt that a cryptic and occult meaning lies behind the romantic Christian legend: the original Grail was a pre-Christian Celtic symbol, disguised and kept alive in the trappings of Christianity. The real Grail-bearer, the book hints, was not Joseph, but a powerful pagan god called Bran, who in ancient Celtic myth was the possessor of a magical cauldron capable of bringing people back to life.

In Robert de Boron's book, Bran is disguised as Bron, Joseph's brother-in-law. This character, who also appears in all later books about the Grail, has no historical basis in the Bible, and must have been invented for a good reason – a reason which becomes clear towards the end of the story when Bron, also described as the Rich Fisher, takes over guardianship of the Grail from Joseph, and becomes a much more important character than Joseph. The Grail then remains in the hands of the Rich Fisher's descendants until King Arthur's quest was finally successful. The similarities between Bron (the Rich Fisher) and Bran (the Celtic God) have been traced by the scholar Roger Sherman Loomis and are so obvious that they can only be referring to the same being. According to various sources, the Rich Fisher was wounded through the thighs or the legs with a javelin in battle, just as Bran was when he invaded Ireland. Both entertained their guests lavishly, both led their followers westwards to a place where many idyllic years were spent unaware of the passage of time. Even the title 'Rich Fisher' may be explained by the fact that Bran was once a sea-god.

Magical vessels

The Grail itself is also mysterious. In early Christian documents it was generally conceived as a large dish containing the Host for some unnamed person. It was thought to contain mystical secrets and Arthur's young knight Sir Percival underwent many spiritual trials in order to penetrate them. Only later (and still before Joseph was mentioned) did it supposedly become the dish used by Christ to perform the rites at the Last Supper.

In its early, magical form, it has much more in common with the vessels and cups of Celtic myth. Bran (again) temporarily had possession of one of which it was said: 'the virtue of the cauldron is this: a man slain today cast him into the cauldron, and by tomorrow he will be as well as he was at best, save that he will not have the power of

in France, has a reference to Joseph added to the text, making it even more likely that Joseph's involvement was a recent invention.

In England, it was not until the 15th Century that the story of the Grail became embedded in folk-lore, when Thomas Malory's version of the Arthurian legends was published. He himself worked from French sources, entitling his version of the Quest of the Holy Grail as 'The Tale of the Sangkreal: Briefly Drawn Out of French, Which is

speech.' The same cauldron was credited with the power of distinguishing the weak from the brave: 'if meat for a coward were put in it to boil, it would never boil; but if meat for a brave man were put in it, it would boil quickly.' Other Celtic dishes included one belonging to the king of Rhydderch on which 'whatever food one wished was instantly obtained'. A similar fable attached to 'the horn of Bran the Niggard from the North', and 'the Crock and Dish of Rhygenydd the Cleric'. In all these Celtic stories there is an exact comparison with Malory's description of the knights watching the entrance of the Grail at Arthur's court, after which 'every knight had such meats and drinks as he best loved in this world.'

It seems certain that the Grail legends as we know them were concocted in the 12th and 13th Centuries by roving clerics and *conteurs* (or bards) using Celtic source material and disguising it in a Christian framework. The next question is: what was it that they wanted to preserve, and why the disguise? Robert Graves has shown in *The White Goddess* that there was a Druidic revival in Wales at the very time when the Grail romances were being developed – a resuscitation of a pagan religion that had defied attempts first by Caesar and then by the early Christian missionaries to suppress it. Bran, the magical cauldron, and the story of a miraculous child who possessed a secret doctrine were all part of this revival.

Another development that took place in Europe during the time when the Grail romances were being published was the rise of a powerful, occult organization certainly connected with the Grail: the Templars. *Parzifal*, a German version of the Grail romance, composed between 1200 and 1220, specifically refers to a movement like that of the Templars as the guardians of the Grail, and is one of the most mystical of the Grail stories. *Parzifal* openly describes a spiritual quest to provide a key to enlightenment. The chaste order of Knights that is depicted, residing in the *Munsalvaesche* (Grail Castle) is sustained 'by virtue of a stone most pure . . . Never is a man so ill but that, if he sees the Grail on any day, he is immune from death during the week that follows. Besides, his looks never change; he retains the same appearance as on the day he saw the stone. Whether it be maid or man, even if he beholds the stone two hundred years he keeps the appearance of his prime, except that his hair turns grey . . . The stone is also called the Grail.'

The Templars were founded in 1118 or 1119 as a kind of military police to protect the pilgrim routes to Jerusalem, newly freed from the infidel Turks. The knights took the same vows as monks – poverty, chastity, obedience – and were thus a religious as well as military order, calling

themselves 'poor knights of Christ' who adopted as a symbol two knights riding on one horse.

But there was always something enigmatically independent about them. Although in theory subject to the Pope, he exerted nowhere near the influence he had over, for instance, the Jesuits, and in real terms the Templars were led by their Grand Master, acting on the advice of the Grand Chapter. The Templar movement grew with amazing rapidity, recruiting not only the nobility but 'rogues and impious men, robbers and committers of sacrilege, murderers, perjurers and adulterers' (providing these sinners had repented). Two centuries later, by which time the Turks had once again captured Jerusalem, the Templars were immensely rich, owning 9000 manors in France alone.

They were also bitterly resented and had outlived their usefulness. With the agreement of Pope Clement II, a massive coup to arrest them was organized in 1307 by Philip IV of France. For the next 17 years he tried to destroy their wealth and influence and seized most of the leaders, who, under torture, admitted to a number of heretical practices.

Skull worship

So far as the Grail is concerned, one of these heresies is particularly noteworthy: the worship of an idol named Baphomet, usually described as a

Crusader siege of Jerusalem, from a manuscript in the British Museum.

A thorn tree still grows in the grounds of Glastonbury Abbey, supposedly a descendant of the one that grew miraculously from a thorn brought by Joseph of Arimathea.

skull, a human head, or three heads. This worship is deeply enshrined in precisely the Celtic religion which was being revived elsewhere in Europe, and it now seems highly likely that the Templars, while ostensibly serving the Pope, were secretly protecting a different form of religion.

Since the essence of esoteric practices is that they remain secret, the nature of this religion cannot be discovered precisely. But we can guess that it came in a straight line from megalithic times through the Druidic Celts discovered by Julius Caesar and was never entirely suppressed when Christianity came. The Templars may, in other words, have been protecting or propagating a banned element in true Catholicism – as Geoffrey Ashe describes it, 'a Something Else unknown or forgotten even in Rome'. During the Middle Ages, he points out, there were no clear boundaries separating 'white' magic from witchcraft, witchcraft from pre-Christian cults, or the cults themselves from the

darker Christian heresies. 'Italians frankly called witchcraft the Old Religion. Thus the Grail passed through curious transitions with remarkable ease.'

Meaning of the Grail

An interpretation on these lines fits best with what can be gleaned from the mystic and misty symbolism of the Grail romances. For the Celtic bards who cloaked the hidden message as they spread their embroidered stories round the courts of Europe, the Grail represented a magical power of agelessness and renewed life, such as had been known, they thought, to the ancient Gods and their priests whose monuments still stood on the hillsides of western Europe untouched by the new religion. It may be more than a coincidence that the line of the May Day sunrise stretching across southern Britain (page 75), believed by many today to have been consciously marked in prehistoric times, starts at the point where Christ is supposed to have entered Britain at St Michael's Mount and goes directly to the indisputably ancient sacred centre of Glastonbury. In this legend, as in the Grail, echoes of a long past can still be heard.

The legends of Glastonbury today are a different matter. That a thorn bush supposedly grew, putting out branches, budding and bursting into blossom within minutes, when Joseph thrust his staff into the ground, was first popularized by an 18th-century innkeeper. The one there today, said to be its descendant, is the freak variety of hawthorn *Cratageus oxycantha*, which is propagated by budding; it bears no fruit but blossoms in May and occasionally in January, at around the time of Christmas according to the Julian calendar. No grave of Joseph exists, despite many attempts to find one. The Chalice Well, another local legend, is probably a Victorian invention.

But the Grail itself is Holy indeed – and Holy from a time long before Christ.

El Dorado

The Age of Discovery started fitfully. For more than ten years after his round trip to the Bahamas in 1492, Columbus refused to admit that he had discovered a New World – in fact, not until Amerigo Vespucci's return from Brazil in 1504. By then 'America', as it was now dubbed by a German map-maker, had become of surprisingly little interest to most Europeans. The spices that Columbus had hoped for, together with the gold, rubies and silver 'more abundant than in King Solomon's mines' had failed to materialize. Spain and Portugal divided up the New World between them, forbidding anyone else to trade or explore there, and a number of cautious settlements were made in the West Indies and Brazil.

In 1520 the mood changed dramatically. It was the year Magellan first sailed past Cape Horn, but more importantly for the myth of a golden city it was the year Hernan Cortes arrived back in Spain after his journey to the rich city of Tenochtitlan in Mexico, whose powerful ruler Montezuma had made him gifts of treasure almost beyond value: 'A disc in the shape of the sun, as big as a cartwheel and made of a very fine gold . . . another large disc of brightly shining silver in the shape of the moon . . . twenty golden ducks of fine workmanship, some ornaments in the shape of their native dogs, many others in the shapes of tigers, lions, and monkeys . . .' – the inventory dazzled Europeans who knew nothing of the New World except that its inhabitants were barbarians. The germ of El Dorado had arrived.

Banking collateral

Even so, it was another ten years before the fever took a proper hold. As surety for a loan, King Charles I of Spain offered his German bankers the governorship of Venezuela and various associated benefits. The bankers despatched to the post a young and rich adventurer, Ambrosius Dalfinger, and he formally took it up on 24 February 1529. Almost immediately, he set off with 180 men on a trip to the interior to find out just what this country was that he now more or less owned. In September he reached his goal – the great lake of Maracaibo that had first been reached by river during Vespucci's voyages 30 years earlier. And here he found gold and legends of gold. The local Indians had abundant ornaments made of it – earrings, bracelets and so on. It came, they said, from a people further in the interior with whom they traded. So rich were these people that their leader was even painted gold – *el hombre dorado*, El Dorado, the gilded man.

In April 1530 Dalfinger and survivors of his expedition arrived back at their starting point emaciated and fever-stricken. In the autumn, while he recuperated in the West Indies, his

deputy Nicolaus Federmann made a less adventurous trip, returning in March 1531 with further tales of gold and jewels from a part of the vast regions of central southern America that still remained unexplored. Three months later, Dalfinger set off again with 170 soldiers on an expedition that was to last two years and three months. Only 35 returned. Dalfinger himself died of curare poisoning. But they had gained an additional clue to the location of El Dorado.

(left) Hundreds of golden figurines such as this, discovered by early explorers to central and southern America, inspired legends of entire cities made of gold.
(below) Ritual Indian practices included one in which a man was painted gold.

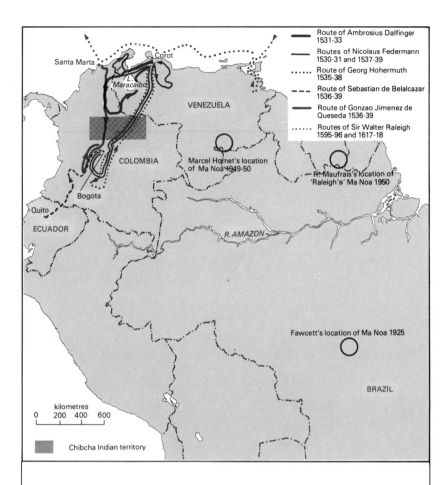

Route of Ambrosius Dalfinger 1531-33
Routes of Nicolaus Federmann 1530-31 and 1537-39
Route of Georg Hohermuth 1535-38
Route of Sebastian de Belalcazar 1536-39
Route of Gonzao Jimenez de Queseda 1536-39
Routes of Sir Walter Raleigh 1595-96 and 1617-18

Chibcha Indian territory

Ambrosius Dalfinger was appointed the first governor of Venezuela on behalf of the Welser banking family. Born in Ulm, Germany in 1500, Dalfinger founded the capital of Venezuela. Together with Esteban Martin he led the first expedition to Lake Maraciabo. Almost dead with exhaustion after this, Dalfinger remained intrigued by the 'Golden City', but his next expedition was a disaster. Dalfinger, having been shot by a poisoned arrow, died in 1533 of a sickness 'that is only curable by gold'.

Nicolaus Federmann was born in Ulm in 1506 and was sent to Corot to work for the Welsers. Born into a mill-owning family, he was an entrepeneur cum explorer. Federmann's first expedition escalated the rumours of a 'hidden kingdom' of gold. On his second expedition Federmann met Queseda and Belalcazar – with them he divided up the Chibcha Indians' territory. On his return to Europe, he was arrested in Ghent and charged with defrauding the Welsers.

Georg Hohermuth, born in Speyer-am-Rhein in 1518, succeeded Dalfinger as the Welsers' ambassador. An able administrator, Hohermuth reorganized the government of Corot, then set off with historian Phillip von Hutten to 'find El Hombre Dorado'. This fateful expedition lost 300 men for a handful of gold. On return to Corot in 1538 Hohermuth was taken in delirium to Santo Domingo.

Sebastian de Belalcazar, the formidable conquistador, was born in 1499 and joined Cortes on the early explorations. He was ruthless in his mission – 'disembowelling

Incas with considerable delight'. Belalcazar's elegantly dressed forces met up with Queseda and Hohermuth to divide up the Chibcha's territory in 1539. On his return to Spain Belalcazar was imprisoned for fraud, and died there in 1551.

Gonzalo Jimenez de Queseda, born in 1499 was trained as a lawyer. With the decline of the Spanish hidalgo class, Queseda lost his position in Spain and when the talk of El Dorado gained credence Queseda took his opportunity. First he joined Pedro de Lugo's expedition and soon became dedicated to the quest – 'Those who set out for wars and conquest put themselves in close touch with death . . . it would be ignoble to return with nothing.' Still not satisfied after co-founding a town in Chibcha territory and amassing a hoard of gold, Queseda led a final expedition in 1569. He was forced to return ignominiously to Bogota and died there in 1579.

Walter Raleigh, born in Devon in 1552, was inaccurately credited with introducing potatoes and tobacco to Europe. After an unpopular marriage, Raleigh was exiled from court and thus was free to search South America for Ma-Noa – the capital of El Dorado. To regain the Queen's favour Raleigh intended to ally with the people of El Dorado to defeat the Spanish. Two unsuccessful expeditions gained him little but public contempt. In 1603 James I was convinced Raleigh was plotting against him with Spanish aid. Raleigh was imprisoned until 1617 when he set off for his last and fateful expedition.

Indians had told them 'where the salt comes from, comes gold'.

Dalfinger's successor, Georg Hohermuth, took up the challenge. In June 1535 he set out with a force of 409 men to find a route to the uplands where he believed, from Dalfinger's information, the salt was located. The appallingly difficult expedition took exactly three years, and returned to base having lost three hundred men without having found gold or salt in worthwhile quantities. In fact, they had passed within 100 kilometres of their goal without knowing it and in April 1536 the final, and this time successful, Venezuela-based expedition took place under Gonzalo Jimenez de Queseda. In March the following year they reached the southern border of lands dominated by the Chibcha Indians, where salt could be found in profusion. By now the original force of 800 men was down to less than 200, but strong enough to conquer a succession of villages whose inhabitants were tortured to reveal the source of their emeralds, which they traded for the gold that gradually grew in quantity as the expedition proceeded. In June, Queseda was encamped less than 20 kilometres away from the 2800-metre high village of Hunsa when an Indian revealed that this was the 'place of gold'. With only 50 men Queseda stormed and took it. The neat, right-angled streets had houses made of wood or wicker work, nearly all of them hung with thin golden plates. Many families kept emeralds and gold dust in cloth bags. The men were adorned with gold rings through their nose and ears and wore bangles round their arms. The chief, whose imposing house was lined with massive sheets of beaten gold, sat on a throne decorated with gold plate and emeralds.

All these riches had been acquired through trading – mostly salt – and war, and it is astonishing that Queseda and his tiny band of men could frighten several thousand Indians into letting them take away their entire fortune; Queseda himself called it 'God's will'. Its contemporary value, incalculable today, was more than 150,000 pesos of gold, plus 230 emeralds. There was even a real El Dorado, the gilded man, for the Chibcha had a coronation ceremony in which their new king was anointed with the sap from a tree and then covered with gold dust so that he became literally a golden man; he was pushed out into the centre of Lake Guatavita and then immersed, staying there until the gold dust had washed off as an offering to the earth god.

Other El Dorados

Queseda's success did nothing to stem the search for El Dorado and he himself never believed he had found it, mounting two more expeditions and spending his declining years before his death in 1579 writing about his (as he imagined) fruitless

those of Egypt – exist in the far interior of the Matto Grosso.' And again: 'Whether we get through and come out again, or whether we shall leave our bones to rot inside, one thing is certain: the answer to the riddle of South America – and perhaps of the entire prehistoric world – may be found when the site of those ancient cities is fixed and made accessible to scientific exploration. This much I know: the cities exist . . . I have not a moment's doubt on that score. How could I have? I myself have seen a part of them . . . The remains appeared to be the outposts of greater cities.'

Percy Fawcett (left) about to leave on the expedition planned to last two years, from which he never returned.

quest. Even at the time of his first expedition, a paradise called Ma-Noa was supposed to exist elsewhere in South America, so richly described in travellers' tales that by comparison the Chibcha village of Hunsa was poor: 'Ma-Noa is on an island in a great salt lake. All the service dishes of the palace for the dining table and the kitchen are of pure gold and silver and even the most insignificant things are made of silver and copper. In the middle of the island stands a temple dedicated to the Sun. Around the building there are statues of gold which represent giants. There are also trees made of gold and silver on the island. And the statue of a prince entirely covered with gold dust.'

The thought of such wealth has entranced explorers ever since. Sir Walter Raleigh made two expeditions, in 1595 and 1616, the failure of the second one being the excuse for his long-delayed execution for an earlier political offence. Two or three times a century since then quests for the unknown city have been launched, most recently those connected with Colonel Percy Fawcett, last seen alive in 1925, and a worthy successor to the adventurous dreamers of 400 years before. Fawcett's hope was probably as unrealistic and as unlikely to succeed as any of those early treasure-hunters: he had convinced himself, in a time when a lot less was known about the date of early man and the growth of civilizations than it is today, that somewhere in the Brazilian jungle lay the first cities built by man.

'It is certain,' he wrote, 'that amazing ruins of ancient cities – ruins incomparably older than

Powers of endurance

Tantalizing statements such as these brought him enormous popularity. One of the explorers who later went looking for evidence of whether he was alive or dead, Peter Fleming, wrote that 'he was a rare combination of the mystic and the man of

Jungle country such as this was what Fawcett faced; his trail was soon obliterated.

A black stone idol made of basalt (thought by Fawcett to come from one of the lost cities) which he took with him on his last journey.

The pyramid of Teotihuacán in Mexico, a 'Temple of the Sun' like that which Fawcett went to discover.

Inset A   Area of the search routes for El Dorado and Ma Noa

Inset B   Area of Colonel Fawcett's expedition and the subsequent searches

action. As a subaltern in the Royal Artillery in India he became deeply interested in Buddhism and spent all his available leave and money on a fruitless search, carried out with the aid of a cryptic map, for the buried treasure of the Kandyan Kings. He was a Founder's Medallist of the Royal Geographic Society, and from 1906 to 1909 he was lent to the Bolivian Government, for whom he surveyed a long and excessively unhealthy sector of the Brazilian–Bolivian frontier . . . He was a man of indomitable courage, and his powers of endurance were extraordinary. Insects, fever and privation had no effect on him.'

It was doubtless these two charismatic qualities of story-telling and superhuman survival, that led to the extraordinary number of later attempts to rescue him. Learning from experience, both his own and that of the disastrously cumbersome Spanish expeditions of the 16th Century, he was accompanied by only two people: his school friend Raleigh Rimell and his eldest son Jack, 'big, very powerful physically, and absolutely virgin in mind and body. He neither smokes nor drinks. Neither do I.' His last despatch came from Dead Horse Camp, so-called because it was where his horse had died on the 1921 expedition: it said that Rimell's foot was poisoned and that some of his bearers were deserting because they were afraid of the local Indians. However, Fawcett had insisted he would be away for at least two years and, on the insistence of his wife, who remained sure for many years that Fawcett was alive somewhere in the jungle, the first search party did not leave until February 1927, when his trail was long obscured.

Fawcett's fate

Today the mystery surrounding Fawcett's fate is not so much the manner in which he died, for there are a dozen natural ways in which this might have happened, but whether his lost city – or indeed any lost city – existed other than in his mind. So much of what he said reads now like fanciful theorizing that it is easy to be cynical about it: the lost city, for instance, was supposed to possess a means of lighting based 'on some use of the ultra violet ray', because he had found the ancient dwellings devoid of lamp smoke. Also, the range of mountains in which the city was supposed to lie has proved non-existent by modern cartography and aerial photography.

And yet the Matto Grosso is still the largest area unexplored by modern man; tribes of white Indians are known to live there, just as he said; the 18th-century Portuguese document describing the mountain-top city, on which he placed so much reliance, is still as valid as it ever was and still contains circumstantial detail and hieroglyphic inscriptions beyond the range of a normal travellers' tale. It may not be El Dorado, nor Fawcett's birthplace of civilization, but it would be surprising if the remains of a mythical city lying buried in the tentacles of the Brazilian jungle did not one day come to light.

1 Cuyaba – Colonel Fawcett's point of departure.

2 30 May 1925. Fawcett reported his position in a cable to the North American Newspaper Alliance: Longitude 54° 35′ West. Latitude 11° 43′ South. This was the last report Fawcett made.

3 Territory inhabited by the Anauqua Indians.

4 Territory inhabited by the Kalapalos Indians.

5 May 1928. Commander Georg Dyott led a search expedition for Fawcett. Dyot claimed he traced Fawcett's route up the River Kuliseu to an Anauqua Indian village where the chief's son had a metal plate hung round his neck. Dyott said the plate came from one of Fawcett's trunks; he estimated Fawcett died about five days after he crossed the River Kuluene (see the area indicated on the map).

6 March 1932. Stephen Rattin told Arthur Abbot, the British Consul General in São Paulo, he had seen Fawcett 'with a long white beard, clad in skins and living in an Indian village.' Rattin reported the location of the village as: Longitude 57° West. Latitude 9° 30′ South.

7 June 1932. The Baceriri Indians reported Fawcett had passed the point marked. They found his compass and gave it to Colonel Aniceto Botelho.

8 November 1932. Leonard Letgers, a Presbyterian missionary, travelled to Simon Lopex. He continued north into the jungle until he came to a village. There, the children were playing with English beads and English trunks. Letgers claimed he had irrefutable evidence that Fawcett was dead.

9 November 1932. Estimate of position where Letgers said Fawcett was killed.

10 November 1933. Some Dominican friars reported Fawcett was living with his son and Rimell in an Indian camp in between River das Mortes and River Kuluene.

11 October 1937. Dr Willy Aurelli was told by a Salosian monk that Fawcett was now living with Indians in an area near River das Mortes.

12 April 1938. General Neanidido Rondon claimed Fawcett was killed by the Anauqua Indians soon after entering the jungle between River Kuluene and River das Mortes. Rondon said the chief of the Baceriri Indians told him Fawcett and his party were killed because they stole some canoes. This claim was contradicted by Fawcett's sister-in-law, Evelyn Isacke, who said Fawcett always built his own boats for the expeditions.

13 August 1946. Señor Orlando Vilas Boas tape recorded a confession from the chief of the Kalapalos Indians, who said he murdered Fawcett. On hearing of this, General Rondon changed his mind and suggested a new search for Fawcett's grave.

14 August 1951. Rondon's party found a skeleton in Kalapalos territory that was claimed as Fawcett's. They were told by the tribal chief Izaviri: 'The old man was killed and the other two were thrown in the river.' The skeleton was brought to London by millionaire Assis Chateaubriand and it was examined by Miriam Tildesley who reported: 'They don't seem to be Fawcett's bones at all. He had two teeth missing from his upper jaw, which were knocked out in a football match. This jaw still possesses these teeth and I would say this skeleton is at least 100 years old.'

15 June 1952. The medium and automatic writer, Estelle Gibbes, published her telepathic communications with Fawcett. He told her he died near the source of the Roosevelt River in 1935. He said he passed away peacefully and that his remains would never be found.

Rumours and travellers' tales about the route(s) taken by Percy Fawcett on his final expedition were still being told long after his presumed death.

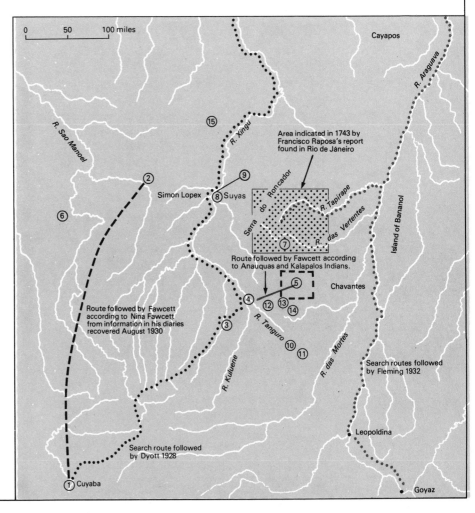

Shangri-La

Monasteries such as this abound beneath the Himalayan peaks; to Buddhists in them, Shambhala represents another level of consciousness.

James Hilton's story of two pilots lost in the Himalayas and finding a community cut off from the world was published as an adventure novel called *Lost Horizon* in 1933. The subject matter instantly captured the public imagination, perhaps to a greater and more lasting degree than any fictional book this century, describing a society locked in a place where remoteness had made time stand still and where life was run according to the collected wisdom of ancient arts and sciences. Its adepts lived in peace and harmony, one of them explaining: 'We have no rigidities, no inexorable rules. We do as we think fit, guided a little by the past, but still more by our present wisdom, and by our clairvoyance of the future.'

Although Hilton was not the first to write about an ideal community isolated from the corruption of modern civilization, his Shangri-La made a longed-for connection between the dissatisfaction of the materialist West and the mystical wisdom of the East. Many believed, and still do, that he based his novel on Far Eastern traditions that somewhere there is an actual place like the one he described, a hidden paradise lying in Tibet or Mongolia.

According to legend, this place is called *Chang Shambhala*, 'a northern place of quietude', and early Buddhist writings describe it as the source of a system of esoteric wisdom called *Kalachakra*. Several parallel traditions in India, China, Russia and Tibet have been summed up in Andrew Tomas's book *Shambhala*: 'In the Far East there is an ancient and widely spread belief in a galaxy of illumined minds living in seclusion in inaccessible parts of Asia. The historians and philosophers of

antique Greece and Rome also mention this tradition in their writings. The great Pythagoras was reputed to have travelled to Hindustan.'

In China, for instance, a desolate region of central Asia is dominated by the Kun Lun mountains where Nu and Kua, the Eastern equivalents of Adam and Eve, were born; the mountains are at the centre of several myths in Chinese history about a valley of immortals who live in peace and harmony. In 17th-century Russia, persecuted believers in an old religion told stories of an eastern paradise called Belovodye, a lost valley nestling among the peaks near the Altai mountains. Some Indian sects believe there is a region north of the Himalayas called *Kalapa* where 'perfect men' reside. *Shambhala* itself is supposed to be in or just north of Tibet, where many travellers have heard of the tradition from holy men: 'In the midst of high mountains there are unsuspected enclosed valleys. Many hot springs nourish the rich vegetation. Many rare plants and medicinal herbs are able to flourish on this unusual volcanic soil. Perhaps you have noticed hot geyers on the uplands . . . who may know the labyrinths of these mountains?'

Nomadic culture

Clearly, something of great spiritual importance exists in these vast regions, dating back to very early times; the difficulty is to find out whether it is an actual place or a mythical one, a real life Shangri-la or a parallel to the Garden of Eden. Tibet and Mongolia are both inaccessible countries which have generated nomadic and spiritually oriented civilizations. Tibet, particularly, is like an island in Asia, larger than France, Germany, Britain, Spain and Italy

combined, its wild, cold, dry, treeless plains ringed by ominous ranges of mountains. Until the union with China, Tibetans lived alone, cut off from the outside world. The testing climate made them nomadic – hardy, non-materialistic, always prepared to move to more fertile land. Several theologians have pointed to the fact that many of the world's religions were spawned under spartan conditions. Charles Bell wrote in *The Religion of Tibet*: 'Judaism, Christianity and Islam all trace their vigorous development to the life of the desert. Buddhism, of the type that has been formed in Tibet and Mongolia, flourishes characteristically in their great expanses, which although not absolute desert, come near to being so. The dry, cold, pure air stimulates the intellect, but isolation from the cities of men and from other nations deprives the Tibetan of subjects on which to feed his brain. So his mind turns inwards and spends itself on religious contemplation, helped still further by the monotony of the life and the awe-inspiring scale on which Nature works.'

Mind over body

Spurred by this climate, there is no doubt that lamas and mystics achieve extraordinary control over their bodies. Several expeditions to find the Abominable Snowman (page 202) have found ascetics high above the snow line wearing nothing more than a thin sheet of cloth. Stories of levitation (page 104) are widespread, and the ability of the *lung-gom-pas* runners may owe something to a mastery of the gravitational force. *Lung-gom* is a form of training involving a mystical concentration that allows its adepts to lighten their bodies and cover long distances in an astonishingly short space of time – 12 miles in 20 minutes is one feat recorded by a Western traveller.

Another occasion was observed by Alexandra David-Neel, an explorer who spent 14 years in Tibet in the early part of this century, learning to write and speak all the local dialects, becoming a Buddhist, and gaining the confidence of the most senior lamas. At the same time, according to her Professor at the Collége de France in Paris, she 'nevertheless remained a Westerner, a disciple of Descartes . . . practising the philosophic scepticism which should be the constant ally of the scientific observer'. Her account of the phenomenon tells of how she noticed, 'far away in front of us, a moving black spot which my field-glasses showed to be a man'. He was moving with extraordinary swiftness, and as he continued to advance towards her, 'his curious speed became more and more evident.' Although she was anxious to question and photograph him, a Tibetan companion prevented her: 'You must not stop the lama, nor speak to him. This would certainly kill him. These lamas when travelling must not break their meditation. The god who is

in them escapes if they cease to repeat the *ngags* (magical incantations), and when thus leaving them before the proper time, he shakes them so hard that they die.'

However, she was able to watch at close quarters as he bounded by. 'I could clearly see his perfectly calm impassive face and wide-open eyes with their gaze fixed on some invisible distant object situated somewhere high up in space. The man did not run. He seemed to lift himself from the ground, proceeding by leaps. It looked as if he had been endowed with the elasticity of a ball, and rebounded each time his feet touched the ground. His steps had the regularity of a pendulum.'

Alexandra David-Neel's book *With Mystics and Magicians in Tibet* is probably the best of two first-hand accounts of lamas and their beliefs published this century, the other being Nicholas Roerich's *Shambhala*, published in 1930. Both explorers were members of the Theosophical Society, founded in 1875 by the extraordinary medium, Madame Helena Petrovna Blavatsky (HPB, as she was universally known). The society is dedicated to her belief that mankind has existed in various racial forms in a number of now lost

Tibetan banner shows Shambhala as an oasis surrounded by snow-capped hills.

Legends of Shambhala's location

1 *Gobi Desert* – the location favoured by Theosophists, notably Helena Blavatsky. The Indian text, *Kurma Purana*, maintained there was an island in the northern sea called Sweta-dvipa; this island was said to be the home of the great yogis, and the sea referred to was thought to be a mass of water over the Gobi Desert.

2 *Syr Daria* – the Hungarian philologist, Csoma de Körös gave Shambhala's geographical bearings as Latitude 45°–50° North, beyond the river Syr Daria.

3 *Belovodye* – the Russian 'White Waters', an Eastern paradise, was the subject of speculation for centuries; in 1923 a party made an expedition to find Belovodye. Allegedly their projected route was 'over the Kokushi Mountains, through Bogogorshi, and over Ergor, to a snowy lake'. The expedition never returned.

4 *Kun Lun* – Chinese mythology describes the garden of humanity as located in the ice-covered Kun Lun Mountains.

5 *Tebu Land* – Taoist mythology speaks of the most beautiful country in the world as Tebu land; it was said to be hidden somewhere between Szechwan and Tibet.

6 *River Tarim* – the Italiam Tibetologist, Giuseppe Tucci 'located' Shambhala near the River Tarim which flows from the Altyn Tagh Ridge.

7 *Tashi Lhumpo Monastery* – the Shambhala legend has close connections with this monastery which was founded near Shigatse in AD 1447 and is also the headquarters of the Kalachakra wisdom.

8 *Altai Mountains* – summing up the legends about Shambhala Geoffrey Ashe

commented: 'Shambhala is best located in the same broadly Altaic country indicated by clues from Middle Eastern and Greek sources . . . if we want a literal mountain as Meru, Belukha is a good candidate.'

9 *Mongolia* – in the *Red Path to Shambhala*, a Tibetan abbot describes the route to Shambhala using cryptic directions. He locates the entrance in Mongolia.

10 *The Sign of Shambhala* – whilst camping in the Kuknor district near the Humboldt Chain, Roerich recorded seeing a mysterious flying object – 'We all saw, in a direction from north to south, something big and shiny reflecting the sun, like a huge oval moving at great speed.'

Other suggested locations

Lhasa – where Pocala, the old citadel of the Dalai Lama was situated. Allegedly there were tunnels leading from here to Shambhala.

Turkestan and Turfan – two more locations where there are supposed to be tunnels leading to Shambhala.

Mount Everest – British mountaineer, Frank Smythe saw two unidentified flying objects from his vantage point at 9000 metres.

Himalayas – the setting for James Hilton's Shangri-La in the fictional work *Lost Horizon*.

Darjeeling/Ghum – on the road between these two towns Nicholas Roerich saw a mysterious lama and was told by the Ghum monks that the lama was from Shambhala.

Tunguska – site of the great explosion in Siberia.

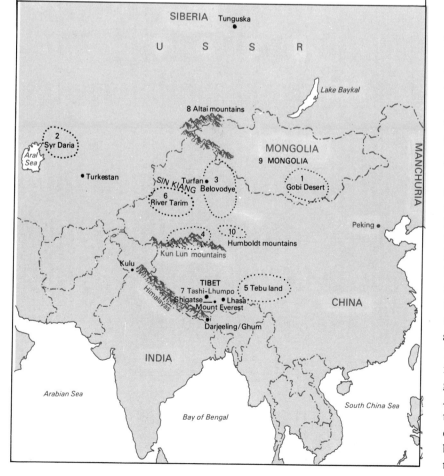

continents, including Atlantis and Lemuria, and whose history is preserved by religion and mythology. It grew highly influential in the late 19th Century as a non-Christian antidote to Darwinism, and although many of its basic premises seem insane in the light of modern scientific findings, its message that there is an etern Wisdom waiting to be discovered remains appealin

Ancient wisdom

As Geoffrey Ashe describes it in *The Ancient Wisdom*, this knowledge is 'a vast system of truths about cosmic law, the nature of man, reincarnation, and other matters. In the past few millennia it has gone through a phase of disintegration and perversion. But all religions and mythologies are based on it, and transmit pieces of it. Hinduism and Buddhism, one gathers, are closest to it, and India and Tibet are the countries with most to teach.'

Theosophists are convinced that Shambhala is the origin of this knowledge, but has no tangible material form, being rather a community of the spirit. 'Like Heaven, it exists in this world, but on another dimension,' it has been put. In 1928, on one of his many visits to Tibet, Nicholas Roerich asked a Tibetan lama about the reality of Shambhala and received the reply: 'Great Shambhala is far beyond the ocean. It is the mighty heavenly domain. It has nothing to do with our earth. How and why do you earthly people take interest in it? Only in some places, in the Far North, can you discern the resplendent rays of Shambhala.' To Alice Bailey, who edited the Theosophical Society's journal, Shambhala was 'the vital centre in the planetary consciousness'. Alexandra David-Neel called it 'the Holy Place where the earthly world links with the highest states of consciousness.'

Even those who incline towards thinking that there is an actual location for Shambhala (whether or not the masters of wisdom still live there) agree that the place has a mystical aspect which is more important than its geographical accuracy. Geoffrey Ashe, who tentatively suggests the Altaic Mountains in Russia as being the place described by most Tibetan literature on the subject, says that supposedly even travellers with a map of how to find it could not do so unless they had been spiritually prepared for the journey. 'A Tibetan abbot describes the route after a fashion in a book, *The Red Path to Shambhala*, locating the entrance in Mongol country. However, no one can simply go there, even with the aid of the abbot's itinerary. A would-be pilgrim has first to be called. If he tries without being called, he perishes. Given enough holiness or mental powers, the route can be short-circuited. One Tashi Lama was transported there in an ecstasy.'

Mystical importance

Today, when Shambhala's location is as elusive as ever, and likely to remain so given the nature of the regimes in power at any likely site, it is surely the nature of a lama's training, and the seemingly supernatural effects that it produces, which has contemporary meaning. Many of the mysteries touched on in this Atlas – underground energies, remote viewing, teleportation, telepathy, dowsing, UFOs as thought-projections, to name a few – did not appear to the lamas as mysteries at all, but as occurrences that could be produced by an effort of will.

According to Alexandra David-Neel, 'the secret of the psychic training, as Tibetans conceive it, consists in developing a power of concentration of mind greatly surpassing even that of men who are, by nature, the most gifted in this respect. Mystic masters affirm that by the means of such concentration of mind, waves of energy are produced which can be used in different ways. The term "wave" is mine. I use it for clearness' sake and also because, as the reader will see, Tibetan mystics really *mean* some ''currents'' or ''waves'' of force. However, they merely say *shugs* or *tsal*; that is to say, "energy". That energy, they believe, is produced every time that a physical or mental action takes place . . . The production of psychic phenomena depends upon the strength of that energy and the direction in which it is pointed.'

A concentrated use of this energy causes many marvels to happen. Objects can be made invisible; alternatively, phantoms can be made to appear – men, deities, animals, inanimate objects, even whole landscapes. These apparitions are known as *tulpas*, and in a totally compelling passage, Alexandra David-Neel tells how, being sceptical of these claims, she successfully experimented to produce one personally. 'In order to avoid being influenced by the forms of the lamaist deities, which I saw daily around me in paintings and images, I chose for my experiment a most insignificant character: a monk, short and fat, of an innocent and jolly type.'

Having been instructed in the various rites necessary to achieve the right level of concentration, 'after a few months the phantom monk was formed. His form grew gradually *fixed* and life-like looking. He became a kind of guest, living in my apartment.' Then she left on an expedition. 'The monk included himself in the party. Though I lived in the open, riding on horseback for miles each day, the illusion persisted . . . he walked, stopped, looked around him. The illusion was mostly visual, but sometimes I felt as if a robe was lightly rubbing against me and once a hand seemed to touch my shoulder.'

As an isolated incident, this might seem no more

than a personal hallucination. But the point about *tulpas* is that everybody sees them, not just their creator; they have a reality of their own, just as do UFOs, creatures falling from the sky, and other phenomena which are outside scientific explanation. The introduction of this Atlas expresses the hope that such wonders will be included in the embrace of 21st-century science, and suggests that this may be as much a process of re-discovery as of discovery. There would be few better places to start looking for clues than at Shambhala, in its literature, and at its hints of a wisdom that existed before modern civilization began.

(left) Nicholas Roerich (1874–1947) with Pandit Nehru; Roerich's accounts to the Theosophical Society did much to explain Shambhala.

A symbolic painting by Roerich titled *Pearl of Searching* shows an initiate being instructed in the ancient wisdom.

Sources and select bibliography

Sources are listed as far as possible in the order in which they have been incorporated or directly quoted in the text of the Atlas.
● indicates a source recommended for introductory reading.
● indicates an important but more technical source.
Additional sources have not been directly used in the Atlas text but are recommended for background reading.

General introduction

● Ronald Duncan and Miranda Weston-Smith (ed): *The Encyclopaedia of Ignorance* Pergamon Press 1977)

Section one Introduction: The unstable universe

George Grinnell: 'The origins of modern geological theory', KRONOS I:4 (1976) pp.68–76
Kenneth J. Hsü *et al.*: 'History of the Mediterranean salinity crisis', *Nature* 267 (1977) p.399

Additional source:
● Glyn Daniel: *The Idea of Prehistory* (Harmondsworth 1964) Chapters I and II

Death of the dinosaurs

● Adrian J. Desmond: *The Hot-Blooded Dinosaurs* (Futura Publications 1977) pp.211, 66, 224
● Robert T. Bakker: 'The superiority of dinosaurs', *Discovery* 3:2 (1968) pp. 11–22
Edwin H. Colbert *et al.*: 'Temperature tolerances in the American alligator', *Bulletin* of the American Museum of Natural History 86 (1946) pp.331–73
Norman D. Newell: 'Crises in the history of life', *Scientific American*, February 1963, pp.77–92
● Dale Russell: 'The disappearance of the dinosaurs', *Canadian Geographical Journal* 83 (1971) pp.204–15
● Dale Russell: 'Supernovae and the extinction of the dinosaurs', *Nature* 229 (1971) pp.553–4

Additional source:
● Robert T. Bakker: 'Dinosaur renaissance', *Scientific American*, April 1975, pp. 58–78

Continents on the move

● Ursula B. Marvin: *Continental Drift* (Smithsonian Institution, Washington 1973) Introduction
● Walter Sullivan: *Continents in Motion* (McGraw-Hill 1974) Chapter I
Alfred Wegener: *The Origin of Continents and Oceans* (Dover 1966)
N. A. Pupke: 'Continental drift before 1900', Nature 227 (1970) pp.349–50
Henry N. Pollack and David S. Chapman: 'The flow of heat from the Earth's interior', *Scientific American*, August 1977, pp.60–76
Peter J. Smith: 'Evidence for earth expansion', *Nature* 268 (1977) p. 200; see also *Nature* 271 (1978) p.316
● Robert S. Dietz and John C. Holden: 'The breakup of Pangaea', *Scientific American*, October 1970, pp.102–13
Amos Nur and Zvi Ben-Avraham: 'Lost Pacifica continent', *Nature* 270 (1977) pp.41–3.
C. J. Ransom: *The Age of Velikovsky* (Kronos Press 1977) pp.196–201.
Nigel Calder: *Restless Earth* (BBC Publications 1972) pp.45–6

Additional source:
D. H. and M. P. Tarling: *Continental Drift* (Harmondsworth 1973)

Magnetism and life

Allan Cox, G. Brent Dalrymple and Richard R. Doell: 'Reversals of the Earth's magnetic field', *Scientific American*, February 1967, pp.44–54; 'Geomagnetic polarity epochs and Pleistocene geochronometry', *Nature* 198 (1963) pp.1049–51; 'Reversals of the Earth's magnetic field', *Science* 144 (1964) pp. 1537–43
● Walter Sullivan: *Continents in Motion* (McGraw-Hill 1974)
E. Irving: *Palaeomagnetism and its Application to Geological and Geophysical Problems* (John Wiley and Sons Inc. 1964)
C. J. Ransom: 'Magnetism and archaeology', *Nature* 242 (1973) pp.518–9
● M. W. McElhinny: *Palaeomagnetism and Plate Tectonics* (Cambridge University Press 1973)
Editorial: 'Reversed geomagnetic events in the Brunhes Epoch', *Nature* 239 (1972) pp.305–6
Michael Barbetti and Michael McElhinny: 'Evidence of a geomagnetic excursion 30,000 years BP', *Nature* 239 (1972) pp.322–30
Mark Noël and D. H. Tarling: 'The Laschamp geomagnetic event', *Nature* 253 (1975) pp.705–6
J. P. Kennet and N. D. Watkins: 'Geomagnetic polarity change, volcanic maxima and faunal extinction in the South Pacific', *Nature* 229 (1970) pp.930–4
R. J. Uffen: 'Influence of the Earth's core on the origin and evolution of life', *Nature* 198 (1963) pp.143–4
C. G. A. Harrison and J. M. Prospero: 'Reversals of the Earth's magnetic field and climatic changes', *Nature* 250 (1974) pp.563–4
● Ian K. Crain: 'Possible direct causal relation between geomagnetic reversals and biological extinctions', *Bulletin* Geol. Soc. Am. 82 (1971) pp.2603–6
● Francis Hitching: *Pendulum: The Psi Connection* (Fontana Books 1977) Chapters 5 and 6; in United States *Dowsing: The Psi Connection* (Anchor/Doubleday 1978)

Spontaneous human combustion

Larry E. Arnold: 'The flaming fate of Dr John Irving Bentley', *Pursuit*, SITU, Columbia, NJ, Fall 1976
● Michael Harrison: *Fire From Heaven* (Pan Books 1977)
Vincent Gaddis: *Mysterious Fires and Lights* (Dell Paperbacks 1968)
Eric Frank Russell: *Great World Mysteries* (Dobson Books 1957)
Ivan Sanderson: *Investigating the Unexplained* (Prentice-Hall 1972)
S. Smith and W. G. H. Cook: *Taylor's Principles and Practice of Medical Jurisprudence* (Churchill 1957) pp.500–5
● Charles Fort: *Complete Books* (Dover 1976)
Robert J. M. Rickard: *Fortean Times* 16 (June 1976)
Livingston Gearhart: *Pursuit* 8:2 (April 1975)

Balls of fire

R. C. Jennison: 'Ball Lightning and after-images', *Nature* 230 (1971) p.576
Neil Charman: 'The enigma of ball lightning', *New Scientist* 14 December 1972, pp.632–5
C. Maxwell Cade and Delphine Davis: *The Taming of the Thunderbolts* (Abelard Schumann 1969)
Stanley Singer: *The Nature of Ball Lightning* (Plenum 1971)

Mark Stenhoff: 'Ball lightning', *Nature* 260 (1976) pp.596–7
P. C. W. Davies: 'Ball lightning', loc. cit., p. 573
I. Ginsburgh and W. L. Bulkley: 'Ball lightning', *Nature* 263 (1976) p.187
D. E. T. F. Ashby and C. Whitehead: 'Is ball lightning caused by anti-matter meteorites?', *Nature* 230 (1971) pp.180–2
E. W. Crew: 'Lightning in astronomy', *Nature* 252 (1974) pp.539–42

The Venus effect

● Immanuel Velikovsky: *Worlds in Collision* (New York/London 1950); *Earth in Upheaval* (London/New York 1955); for other works see references for Old Testament Truths in Section Seven.
Alfred de Grazia (ed): *The Velikovsky Affair* (Sidgwick and Jackson 1966)
Horace M. Kallen: 'Shapley, Velikovsky, and the scientific spirit', *Pensée: Immanuel Velikovsky Reconsidered* I (1972) pp.36–40
Carl Sagan, quoted in *Pensée* VII (1974), p.37
William T. Plummer: 'Venus clouds: test for hydrocarbons', *Science* 163 (1969) pp.1191–2
I. Velikovsky: 'Venus and hydrocarbons', *Pensée* VI (1973–74) pp.21–3; Albert W. Burgstahler: 'The Nature of the Cytherean atmosphere', loc. cit., pp.24–30; I. Velikovsky: 'Venus' atmosphere', loc. cit., pp.31–7

Additional sources:
● C. J. Ransom: *The Age of Velikovsky* (Kronos Press 1977) *SISR (Journal* of the Society for Interdisciplinary Studies) I:3 (1976) pp.31–2
● S. Talbott (ed): *Velikovsky Reconsidered* (Sidgwick & Jackson 1977) contains many papers from the now defunct *Pensée*. Back numbers of *Pensée* and *SISR* are obtainable from: Ralph Amelan, Hon. Sec., Society for Interdisciplinary Studies, 6 Jersey House, Manchester 20.

Velikovsky's predictions

I. Velikovsky: 'H. H. Hess and my memoranda', *Pensée* II (1972) pp. 22–9
● Thomas Ferté: 'A record of success', *Pensée* I (1972) pp. 11–15
● Robert W. Bass: 'Did worlds collide? "Proofs" of the stability of the solar system', *Pensée* VIII (1974) pp. 8–20, 21–6
Lynn E. Rose and Raymond C. Vaughan: 'The orbits of Mars, Earth and Venus', *Pensée* I (1972) p. 43
C. J. Ransom and L. H. Hoffee: 'The orbits of Venus', *Pensée* III (1973) pp. 22–5
Ralph E. Juergens: 'Velikovsky and the heat of Venus', KRONOS I:4 (1976) pp. 86–92
I. Velikovsky: 'Are the Moon's scars only three thousand years old?', *Pensée* I (1972);
Derek York: 'Lunar rocks and Velikovsky's claim', loc. cit.; I. Velikovsky: 'When was the lunar surface last molten?', loc. cit.; Robert C. Wright: 'Effects of volatility on rubidium-strontium dating'; Robert Treash: 'Magnetic remanence in lunar rocks', loc. cit.
Claude Schaeffer: *Stratigraphée Comparée et Chronologie de l'Asie Occidentale* (Paris 1948)
Carl Sagan: 'An analysis of *Worlds in Collision*', *The Humanist*, November/December 1977, p.12
Further references, supporting statements, and discussion are obtainable from the Society for Interdisciplinary Studies, 6 Jersey House, Manchester 20.

Section two Introduction: The emergence of man

● Desmond Collins: *Human Revolution: From Ape to Artist* (Phaidon 1976) p.74. [Lothagam jaw]
Stuart Fleming: 'Man emerging: (i) The first 33 million years', *New Scientist* (1 July 1976) pp.6–8
M. L. Keith and G. M. Anderson: 'Radiocarbon dating: fictitious results with mollusk shells', *Science* 141 (1963) pp.634–6
John G. Funkhouser and John J. Naughton: 'Radiogenic helium and argon in ultramafic inclusions from Hawaii', *Journal* of Geophysical Research 73 (1968) pp.4601–7

Additional source:

● Roy MacKinnon: 'The inexact science of radiometric dating', *Society for Interdisciplinary Studies Review* 1:5 (1977) pp.8–15

The missing links

● John E. Pfeiffer: *The Emergence of Man* (Harper and Row 1973)
Ralph L. Holloway: 'The casts of fossil hominid brains', *Scientific American*, July 1974, pp.106–15
Anthony Smith: *The Human Pedigree* (London 1975), pp.23–4
● Loren Eiseley: 'The real secret of Piltdown' in *The Immense Journey* (Vintage Books 1959) pp.79–94, 74–5
● Norman Macbeth: *Darwin Retried* (Garnstone Press 1974)
G. Herberer: 'Man and his ancestors' in Grzimek's *Encyclopaedia of Evolution* (Van Nostrand Reinhold 1976) pp.489–505
Elwyn L. Simons: 'Ramapithecus', *Scientific American*, May 1977
Björn Kurten: *Not From The Apes* (Victor Gollancz 1972)
Editorial: 'The discovery by L.S.B. Leakey of *Zinjanthropus boisei*', *Current Anthropology*, January 1960, pp.76–7
R. E. F. Leakey and Alan C. Walker: '*Australopithecus*, *Homo erectus* and the single species hypothesis', *Nature* 261 (1976) pp. 572–4; R. E. F. Leakey: 'New hominid fossils from the Koobi Fera formation in Northern Kenya', loc. cit. pp.574–6
William W. Howells: '*Homo erectus*', *Scientific American*, November 1966, pp.46–53

Additional sources:

● Solomon H. Katz (ed): *Biological Anthropology: Readings from Scientific American* (W. H. Freeman and Co. 1975)
● J. Jelinek: *The Evolution of Man* (Hamlyn 1975)

Neanderthal inheritance

J. S. Weiner: *Man's Natural History* (London 1971) pp.99–100
● Ralph S. Solecki: *Shanidar: The Humanity of Neanderthal Man* (Harmondsworth 1971) pp.8, 180, 191
George Constable: *The Neanderthals* (Time/Life 1973)
● Carleton Coon: *The Origin of Races* (London 1963) p.520
Grahame Clark and Stuart Piggott: *Prehistoric Societies* (Harmondsworth 1970)
● R. Solecki: 'Shanidar IV, a Neanderthal flower burial in northern Iraq', *Science* 190 (1975) pp.880–1
● Desmond Collins: *Human Revolution: From Ape to Artist* (Phaidon 1976)
François Bordes, cited in John E. Pfeiffer: *The Emergence of Man* (London 1973) p.281
Peter J. Ucko and Andrée Rosenfeld: *Palaeolithic Cave Art* (World University Library 1967)
Stan Gooch: *The Neanderthal Question* (London 1977)

Additional sources:
See previous entry The Missing Links.

The racial question

● Carleton Coon: *The Origin of Races* (London 1963); with Edward E. Hunt *The Living Races of Man* (New York 1965)
● William Howells: 'The distribution of man', *Scientific American*, September 1960
Theodosius Dobzhansky: '*The Origin of Races* by Carleton S. Coon' [review] *Scientific American*, February 1963
Solomon H. Katz: *Biological Anthropology: Readings from Scientific American* (W. H. Freeman & Co. 1975) p.230
● Edward Babun: *The Varieties of Man* (Collier–Macmillan 1969) p.6

Hominid survival

Yuri Zerchaninov: 'Is Neanderthal man extinct?', *Moscow News*, February 22 1964 [Topilsky's account]
● Boris F. Porshnev: 'The Troglodytidae and the Hominidae in the taxonomy and evolution of higher primates', *Current Anthropology* 15 (1974) pp.449–50; comments by E. A. de Enriquez, B. Blumenberg, S. H. Malik, Frank E. Poirier, B. E. Raemsch, loc. cit. pp.450–2; reply by Dmitri Bayanov and Igor Bourtsev, loc. cit. pp.452–6
Gordon Strasenburgh: 'On *Paranthropus* and "relic hominoids"', *Current Anthropology* 14 (1975) pp.486–7
Dmitri Bayanov and Igor Bourtsev: 'On Neanderthal v. *Paranthropus*', *Current Anthropology* 17 (1976) pp.312–18
Emanuel Vlcek: 'Old literary evidence for the existence of the "Snow Man" in Tibet and Mongolia', *Man*, August 1959, pp.133–4
Odette Tchernine: *The Yeti* (Neville Spearman 1970) [Kofman's work]
● John Napier: *Bigfoot* (Jonathan Cape 1972) p.153

The vanished mammoths

Norman D. Newell: 'Crises in the history of life', *Scientific American* February 1963, pp.77–92
'Siberian baby mammoth', *New Scientist*, 8 September 1977, p.591
Joseph August: *A Book of Mammoths* (London 1963)
● William R. Farrand: 'Frozen mammoths and modern geology', *Science* 133 (1961) pp.729–35; Harold E. Lippman: 'Frozen mammoths' [letter] *Science* 137 (1962) pp. 449–50; Farrand's response, pp.450–52
● Dwardu Cardona: 'The Problem of the Frozen Mammoths', KRONOS 1:4 (1976) pp.77–85
● Ivan Sanderson: 'Frozen mammoths' in *More Things* (New York 1969) pp.103–16
Immanuel Velikovsky: *Worlds in Collision* (London/New York 1950) Chapter II: 'The Mammoths'; *Earth in Upheaval* (Victor Gollancz/Sidgwick & Jackson 1955) Chapter I: 'The Ivory Islands'
Charles Hapgood: *The Path of the Pole* (Chilton Book Co. 1970) pp.249–79

Section three Introduction: Earth patterns

Colin Renfrew: *Before Civilization* (Jonathan Cape 1973) See also Section Five of this Atlas (Lost Achievements) and its references.

Crystalline planet

Plato: *Phaedo* 109A–110D
Nikolai Goncharov, Vyacheslav Morozov and Valery Makarov: *Khimiya i Zhiza* (1973) translated by Christopher Bird and published in *New Age Journal*.
Ivan T. Sanderson: *More 'Things'* (Pyramid Books 1965) pp.116–25

Megalithic engineering

Leslie V. Grinsell: *Folklore of Prehistoric Sites in Britain* (David and Charles 1976)
● John Michell: *The Old Stones of Lands End* (Garnstone Press 1974)
● Francis Hitching: *Earth Magic* (Picador 1977)
J. Michell: *Astro-Archaeology* (Thames and Hudson 1977) pp.5–6, 27, 47
J. Norman Lockyer: *Stonehenge and Other British Monuments Astronomically Considered* (Macmillan 1906)
H. Boyle Somerville: 'Instances of orientation in prehistoric monuments in the British Isles', *Archaeologia* 73 (1923)
● Alexander Thom: *Megalithic Sites in Britain* (Oxford University Press 1967) and *Megalithic Lunar Observatories* (Oxford University Press 1971); various offprints from the *Journal for the History of Astronomy* 1971; Carnac alignments in *JHA* 6 (1972) pp. 11–26 and 151–64. Obtainable from Science History Publications, c/o Dr M. A. Hoskin, Churchill College, Cambridge CB3 0DS.
Fred Hoyle: 'Speculations on Stonehenge', *Antiquity* XL (1966) p.262
Gerald Hawkins: *Stonehenge Decoded* (Souvenir Press 1966)
C. A. Newham: *The Astronomical Significance of Stonehenge* (John Blackburn 1972)
Richard Atkinson: 'Moonshine on Stonehenge', *Antiquity* 60 (1966) pp.212–16; *Journal for the History of Astronomy* 6 (1975) p.51
● Euan W. MacKie: *Science and Society in Prehistoric Britain* (London 1977); *The Megalith Builders* (Phaidon 1977); 'Archaeological tests on supposed prehistoric astronomical sites in Scotland', *Philosophical Transactions of the Royal Society of London*, Sec. A, 276 (1974) pp.169–94; 'Megalithic astronomy and catastrophism', *Pensée* 10 (Winter 1974–75) pp.5–20

Additional sources:

● Elizabeth Chesley Baity: 'Archaeoastronomy and ethnoastronomy so far', *Current Anthropology* 14:4 (1973) pp.389–449, contains by far the most comprehensive list of references on the subject.
Aubrey Burl: *The Stone Circles of the British Isles* (Yale 1976)
Peter Lancaster Brown: *Megaliths, Myths and Men* (Blandford 1976)

Pyramid placing

Charles Piazzi Smyth: *Our Inheritance in the Great Pyramid* (London 1864) Parts I, II and V
● I. E. S. Edwards: *The Pyramids of Egypt* (Harmondsworth 1961)
● Peter Tompkins: *The Secrets of the Great Pyramid* (Allen Lane 1971) Introduction p.xiv
Kurt Mendelssohn: *The Riddle of the Pyramids*

(Thames and Hudson 1974)
L. Sprague de Camp: *Citadels of Mystery* (London 1965) pp.27–42
Peter White: *The Past is Human* (Angus and Robertson 1974)

Additional sources:
J. R. Harris (ed): *The Legacy of Egypt* (Oxford 1971) Chapters I, IV and VI

Patterns in Peru

● Maria Reiche: *Mystery on the Desert* (Maria Reiche, Nazca, Peru S/A, 1976)
Loren McIntyre: 'Mystery of the ancient Nazca lines', *National Geographic Magazine*, May 1975, pp.716–28
Gerald Hawkins: *Beyond Stonehenge* (Hutchinson 1973) pp.91–154
● Jim Woodman: *Journey to the Sun: Nazca* (Pocket Books 1977)

Alignments and connections

R. J. C. Atkinson: 'Neolithic engineering', *Antiquity* 35 (1961) pp.292–9
J. Norman Lockyer: *Stonehenge etc . . .* (Macmillan 1906)
Alfred Watkins: *The Old Straight Track* (Garnstone Press 1971)
John Coles: *Field Archaeology in Britain* (Methuen 1972) Introduction
● Francis Hitching: *Earth Magic* (Picador 1977)
● John Michell: *The View Over Atlantis* (Garnstone Press 1969)
John Michell: *Astro-Archaeology* (Thames and Hudson 1977) pp.58–65
Xavier Guichard: *Eleusis Alesia* (F. Paillart, Abbeville 1936)

Additional sources:
John Michell: *The Old Stones of Lands End* (Garnstone Press 1974)
The bi-monthly periodical *The Ley Hunter* is obtainable from PO Box 152, London N10 1EP. *Stonehenge Viewpoint*, another bi-monthly which covers the subject and offers discount books, is obtainable from PO Box 30887, Santa Barbara, California 93105. A number of relevant books are published by RILKO (Research Into Lost Knowledge Association) c/o Mrs Janette Jackson, 36 College Court, Hammersmith, London w6.

Section four **Introduction: Unknown energies**

Norma Lee Browning: *The World of Peter Hurkos* (Doubleday 1970)
Allan Angoff and Diana Barth (ed): *Parapsychology and Anthropology*: Proceedings of an International Conference in London 1973 (Parapsychology Foundation, New York 1974)
G. E. W. Wolstenholme and E. C. P. Millar (ed): 'Psychical phenomena among primitive peoples', *Ciba Foundation Symposium on Extrasensory Perception* (London 1956)

Remote viewing

● Russell Targ and Harold E. Puthoff: *Mind-Reach* (Delacorte Press 1977)
Harold E. Puthoff and Russell Targ: 'Information transfer under conditions of sensory shielding', *Nature* 252 (1974) pp.602–7; 'A perceptual
● channel for information transfer over kilometer distances: historical perspective and recent research', *Proceedings of the IEEE* 64 (1976) pp.329–54; 'Physics, entropy and psychokinesis', *Proc. Conf. Quantum Physics and Parapsychology* (Geneva), (Parapsychology Foundation, New York 1975)
Ingo Swann: *To Kiss Earth Goodbye* (Laurel

Books 1977)
● Francis Hitching: *Pendulum: The Psi Connection* (Fontana 1977); In United States *Dowsing: The Psi Connection* (Anchor/Doubleday 1978)

The migration instinct

● Mathieu Ricard: *The Mystery of Migration* (Constable, London 1969) p.192
J. D. Carthy: *Animal Migration* (Unwin Books 1956)
● W. B. Yapp: *The Life and Organisation of Birds* (Edward Arnold, London 1970) Chapter VII
Georges Blond: *Great Migrations* (Hutchinson 1958)
William T. Keeton: 'The mystery of pigeon homing' *Scientific American* (December 1974) pp.96–107
Rudiger Wehner: 'Polarised light navigation by insects' *Scientific American* (July 1970) pp.106–14
E. G. F. Sauer: 'Celestial navigation by birds' *Scientific American* (August 1958)
● Klaus Schmidt Koenig: *Migration and Homing in Animals* (Springer Verlag 1973)
● Patrizia Krachmalnicoff: *The Magic of the Animals* (Arlington Books 1974)

Additional sources:
G. V. T. Matthews: *Bird Navigation* (Cambridge University Press 1955)
David Andrews: 'Science and the homing pigeon' *Racing Pigeon Pictorial* (Coo Press, London 1974)
Jeremy Cherfas: 'How birds follow invisible maps' *New Scientist* (4 August 1977) pp.292–97
J. G. Llavrado (ed) *et al.*, *Biological and Clinical Effects of Low-frequency Magnetic and Electric Fields* (Charles Thomas, Illinois 1974) Chapter XI

Underground streams

Loren Eiseley: *The Immense Journey* (Vintage Books 1959) p.16
David A. Ross: *Introduction to Oceanography* (Prentice-Hall 1977) pp.18–19
● Cuchulaine A. M. King: *Introduction to Marine Geology and Geomorphology* (London 1975) pp.253–9
Ferren MacIntyre: 'Why the sea is salt' *Scientific American*, November 1970, pp.104–15
● Christopher Bird: 'The dowsers', *New Age Journal*, July 1977, pp.26–37, 76–81
Herbert Douglas: 'Dowsing and arthritis', *American Dowser*, November 1971, November 1973 and February 1977; reprinted in *Journal of the British Society of Dowsers* 157 (September 1972); and 164 (June 1974)
Francis Hitching: *Pendulum/Dowsing* See entry in Chapter VI
Georgi Piccardi: *The Chemical Basis of Medical Climatology* (Charles C. Thomas 1963)
S. V. O. Somander: 'Wild elephants as water diviners', *Loris*, December 1962, pp.244–6
James A. Gordon: 'Elephants do think', *African Wild Life* 20 (1966) pp.75–8
C. H. Stockley: 'Drinking habits of wild animals', *Scottish Zoo and Wildlife* 14 (1949)
● Francis Hitching: *Pendulum Dowsing* See entry in Remote Viewing above
● Guy Underwood: *The Pattern of the Past* (Abacus 1972)

Feng-shui

● E. J. Eitel: *Feng-shui, The Rudiments of Natural Science in China* (Trubner and Co. 1873, Cokaygne 1973)
Steve Moore: 'Leys and feng-shui', *The Ley Hunter* 72, pp.11–13

● John Michell: *The Earth Spirit* (Avon Books 1975) pp.12–16

Section five **Introduction: Lost achievements**

C. C. Lamberg-Karlovsky (Introductions): *Old World Archaeology: Foundations of Civilization* Readings from *Scientific American* (W. H. Freeman and Co. 1952–72)
Gordon R. Willey and Jeremy A. Sabloff: *A History of American Archaeology* (Thames and Hudson 1974)

The gravity enigma

Nandor Fodor: *Encyclopaedia of Psychic Science* (Citadel Press 1974) entry under 'Levitation'
● Herbert Thurston: *The Physical Phenomena of Mysticism* (Burns Oates 1952) Chapters I–III
P. T. Plunkett, in *Illustrated London News*, 6 June 1936, pp.19ff.
Alexandra David-Neel: *With Mystics and Magicians in Tibet* (Bodley head 1931) Chapters VI and VIII
[?] 'Weightless Stones' in *Scientific American*, July 1880
Mme Dunglas Hume: *Life of D. D. Hume* (Turner & Co. 1888)
● R. J. M. Rickard: 'Walking on air', *Fortean Times* 21 (1977) pp.16–24
Carlos Casteneda: *Conversations with Don Juan* (Harmondsworth 1974)
W. von Braun and F. I. Ordway: *History of Rocketry and Space Travel* (New York 1966)
B. Laufer: *Prehistory of Aviation* (Chicago 1928)

Early astronomers

● Arthur Koestler: *The Sleepwalkers* (Harmondsworth 1968) pp.374–5
Jean Pierre Hallet: *Pygmy Kitabu* (Souvenir Press 1974) pp.285 and 291
Robert Temple: *The Sirius Mystery* (Sidgwick & Jackson 1976) pp.20–8
Elsdon Best: *The Astronomical Knowledge of the Maori* (Dominion Museum Monograph, No. 3, Wellington, 1922) pp.27, 35, 36, 41 and 64
Alfred de Grazia: 'Ancient knowledge of Jupiter's bands and Saturn's rings', KRONOS II:I (1976) pp.65–9
Journal of the British Astronomical Association 87, 5 (1977) pp. 523–4

Gulliver's moons

Jonathan Swift: *Gulliver's Travels*, Part III, Chapter iii
Immanuel Velikovsky: *Worlds in Collision* (London and New York 1950) Part II, Chapter v: 'The steeds of Mars'
Erich von Däniken: *Chariots of the Gods* (Corgi Books 1971) pp.152–3
Carl Sagan: *The Cosmic Connection* (New York 1971) pp. 104–5
● Ronald Story: *The Space Gods Revealed* (New English Library 1976)

Early navigators

Grahame Clarke and Stuart Piggott: *Prehistoric Societies* (Hardmondsworth 1970) pp.98 and 103
Paul Johnstone: 'Stern first in the Stone Age', *International Journal of Nautical Archaeology and Underwater Explorations* 21 (1973) pp.3–11
Alice B. Kehoe: 'Small boats upon the North Atlantic' in Carroll Riley, J. Charles Kelley, Campbell N. Pennington and Robert L. Rands (eds): *Man Across the Sea: Problems of Pre-Columbian Contacts* (University of Texas

Press 1971) pp.275–92
●George F. Bass (ed): *A History of Seafaring* (Thames & Hudson 1972) pp.12–15
Santiago Genoves: 'Papyrus rafts across the Atlantic', *Current Anthropology* 14:3 (1973) pp.266–7; reply by H. K. J. Cowan, 15–3 (1974) pp.332–3
Alessandra Nibbi: *The Sea Peoples and Egypt* (Noyes Press 1975)
A. Crichton Mitchell: 'Chapters in the history of terrestrial magnetism', *Terrestrial Magnetism and Atmospheric Electricity* (London 1932)
Rüdiger Wehner: 'Polarized-light navigation by insects', *Scientific American* 235, 1 (1976) p.106
Keith Oatley: 'Mental maps for navigation', *New Scientist* (19 December 1974) pp.863–6

Early cartographers

Charles Hapgood: *Maps of the Ancient Sea Kings* (Chilton Book Co. 1966); *The Path of the Pole* (Chilton Book Co. 1970), pp.106, 122
Peter White: *The Past is Human* (Angus & Robertson, 1976) pp.91–7
For background to ancient seafaring see references to previous entry on Early Navigators.

Who discovered America?

Gordon R. Willey and Jeremy A. Sabloff: *A History of American Archaeology* (Thames & Hudson 1968) p.190
Glyn Daniel: *The Idea of Prehistory* (Harmondsworth 1964) p.99; *The First Civilisations* (Thames & Hudson 1968) p.190; cited in Report of Symposium on Sir Grafton Elliot Smith, Zoological Society of London/Anatomical Society of Great Britain and Ireland, p.420
● Robert A. Kennedy: 'A transatlantic stimulus hypothesis for MesoAmerica and the Caribbean circa 3500 to 2000 BC', in Riley *et al.* (eds): *Man Across the Sea* p.266 (See entry Early Navigators)
● Alice B. Kehoe: 'Small boats upon the North Atlantic' (See entry Early Navigators)
Betty J. Meggers and Clifford Evans: 'A transPacific contact in 3000 BC', *Scientific American*, January 1966
R. von Heine-Geldern: 'The problem of transPacific influences in MesoAmerica' in R. Wauchope *et al.* (eds): *Handbook of Middle American Indians* (Austin 1966) pp. 277–96
Frank Waters: *The Book of the Hopi* (Viking Press 1972) p. 25
Francis Hitching: *Earth Magic* (Pocketbooks 1978) pp.91–8.
● Geoffrey Ashe: *Land to the West* (Collins 1962) pp.195–220.
Santiago Genoves: 'Papyrus rafts across the Atlantic' (See entry Early Navigators)
Thor Heyerdahl: *Early Man and the Ocean* (George Allen & Unwin 1978)
R. A. Jaurazbhoy: *Ancient Egyptians and Chinese in America* (London 1974)
Alexander von Wuthenau: *Unexpected Faces in Ancient America, 1500 BC–AD 1500: The Historical Testimony of Pre-Columbian Artists* (New York 1975)
● Cyrus Gordon: *Before Columbus* (Turnstone Press 1972)

Ancient anomalies

Marija Gimbutas: 'Varna: a sensationally rich cemetery of the Karanovo civilisation about 4500 BC', *Expedition* (Pennsylvania University) 19, 4 (1977) pp.139–47
Beno Rothenberg: 'Archaeometallurgy is

exploring mining's ancient history', *Engineering and Mining Journal*, December 1977, pp.68–73
Adrian Boshier and Peter Beaumont: 'Mining in South Africa and the emergence of modern man', *Optima*, March 1972
Walter Winton: 'Baghdad Batteries BC', *Sumer* XVIII (1962) pp.87–9
Albert Al-Haik: 'The Rabbou'a galvanic cell', *Sumer* XX (1964) pp. 103–4 *Popular Electronics*, July 1964
Ronald J. Willis: 'Ancient technology', INFO III, 1 (Autumn 1972) pp.1–7
American Antiquarian 16 (1894) pp.501 [lightning-rods] *The Times* (London) 18 May 1972 [Saqqara glider]
Derek de Solla Price: 'Gears from the Greeks: the Antikythera mechanism–a computer-calendar from 80 BC', *Transactions of the American Philosophical Society*, New Series 64, 7 (1964)

Undeciphered writing

Adolf Reith: *Archaeological Fakes* (London 1970) pp.92–107
Alexander Marshack: *Roots of Civilization* (New York 1971)
E. Garrod: 'Recollections of Glozel', *Antiquity* XLII (1968) pp. 172–7; Editorial, *Antiquity* XLVIII (1974) pp.261–4; Hugh McKerrell, Vagn Mejdahl, Henri François and G. Portal: 'Thermoluminescence and Glozel', loc. cit., pp.265–71; R. J. Atkinson (Editorial), *Antiquity* XLIX (1975), pp.84–5; C. Renfrew: 'Glozel and the two cultures', loc. cit., pp.222–3; Martin Aitken and Jean Huxtable: 'Thermoluminescence and Glozel: a plea for caution', loc. cit., pp.223–6, McKerrell *et al.*: 'Thermoluminescence and Glozel: a plea for patience', loc. cit., pp. 267–72; Editorial, *Antiquity* XLI (1977) pp.89–91
McKerrell *et al.*: 'Études sur Glozel', *Revue Archéologique du Centre* 57–8, pp. 3–41
M. S. F. Hood: 'The Tartaria tablets', *Antiquity* XLI (1967) pp. 99–113
M.S.F. Hood: 'The Tartaria tablets', *Scientific American*, May 1968
Evzen Neustupny: 'The Tartaria tablets: a chronological issue', *Antiquity* XLII (1968) pp.32–5.
Colin Renfrew: *Before Civilization* (Harmondsworth 1976) pp.73–4, 193–4

Section six Introduction: Before civilization

I. Velikovsky: 'The catastrophic worlds of Immanuel Velikovsky' [interview] *Science and Mechanics*, 7 July 1968, p. 103
● William R. Corliss: *The Sourcebook Project*: a series of titles, e.g. *Strange Phenomena, Strange Planet*, obtainable from Glen Arm, Maryland 21057

Atlantis solved?

Plato: *Timaeus and Critias*, Desmond Lee (translator) (Harmondsworth 1965) pp.34–8, 129–43
Aristotle: cited by Strabo: *Geography* XIII, i, 36
Derek Ager, letter to *Catastrophist Geology* I:1 (1976) p.5
● L. Sprague de Camp: *Lost Continents* (Dover Publications 1970) p. 232
Plutarch: Solon, 26, 31, 32 in Ian Scott Kilvert (translator): *The Rise and Fall of Athens* (Harmondsworth 1960) pp. 69, 75–6
T. H. Martin: *Études sur le Timée de Platon* (Paris 1841) cited in de Camp, op. cit., p.80

Ignatius Donnelly: *Atlantis, the Antediluvian World* (new and revised edition, Egerton Sykes, Sidgwick & Jackson 1970) *Ragnarok, the Age of Fire and Gravel* (Steinerbooks 1971)
Spyridon Marinatos: *Antiquity* (1939) pp.425–39; 'On the legend of Atlantis', *Cretica Chronica* IV (1950) Reprinted as Appendix A in Martin Ebon: *Atlantis: The New Evidence* (New York 1977)
Immanuel Velikovsky: *Worlds in Collision* (New York/London 1950) Part I, Chapter VII: 'Atlantis'
● A. G. Galanopoulos and E. Bacon: *Atlantis: The Truth Behind the Legend* (Nelson 1969)
J. V. Luce: *The End of Atlantis* (Paladin 1970)
James W. Mavor: *Voyage to Atlantic* (Collins 1969)
Dorothy B. Vitaliano: *Legends of the Earth* (Indiana University Press 1973) Chapters VIII–X
Hans Pichler and Wolfgang Schiering: 'The Thera eruption and late Minoan I-b destructions on Crete', *Nature* 267 (1977) pp. 819–22
Israel Isaacson: 'Some preliminary remarks about Thera and Atlantis', KRONOS I:2 (1975) pp.93–7
Marcellus, cited by Proclus: *Commentary on the Timaeus of Plato*, Section 148, Thomas Taylor (translator) (London 1820)
Geoffrey Ashe: *Land to the West* (Collins 1962) pp.190–2
Lewis Spence: *The Problem of Atlantis* (New York 1924); *The Occult Sciences in Atlantis* (Rider 1943)
E. MacKie: *The Megalith Builders* (Phaidon 1977) p.174

Bimini revealed

J. Manson Valentine: 'Archaeological enigmas of Florida and the western Bahamas', *Muse News* I (Museum of Science, Miami, Florida, June 1969)
Hans W. Hannau and Bernd H. Mock (eds): *Beneath the seas of the West Indies: Caribbean; Bahamas; Florida; Bermuda* contains article by John Hall: 'Marine archaeology in the West Indies'
John A. Gifford: unpublished ms., 25 February 1971
David Zink: 'Poseidia '75: A progress report', *The A.R.E. Journal* XI:3 (May 1976) pp.102–5
John Steele: 'The Bimini Road', *The Ley Hunter* 76 (1977) pp.3–5

The outer space confusion

Erich von Däniken: *Chariots of the Gods?* (Souvenir Press 1969); *Return to the Stars* (Souvenir Press 1970); *The Gold of the Gods* (Souvenir Press 1973); *In Search of Ancient Gods* (Souvenir Press 1974); *According to the Evidence* (Souvenir Press 1977)
Editorial: 'Anatomy of a world best-seller', *Encounter* XLI: 2 (August 1973) pp.8–18
Publishers of books sampled (see page 144); Bergier: (*Mysteries of the Earth*, Futura 1975); Blumrich: Corgi 1974; Charroux: Neville Spearman 1972; Dem: Corgi 1977; Drake: Sphere Books 1974; Keel: Futura 1975; Kolosimo: Souvenir Press 1970, Garnstone Press 1973; Landsburg: Bantam 1974, Corgi 1975; Trench: Fontana 1973; Umland: Panther 1976; Williamson: Futura 1975
E. W. Castle and B. B. Thiering (eds): *Some Trust in Chariots* (Bailey Brothers and Swinfen 1973)
● Ronald Story: *The Space Gods Revealed* (New English Library 1976)
Peter White: *The Past Is Human* (Angus and Robertson 1974)
Von Däniken's quotes as follows, taken from

Sources and select bibliography

Corgi paperback editions: Olmec sculptures, *COTG* p.117; Palenque 'astronaut', *COTG* p.123; non-rusting pillar, *COTG* p.94; Great Pyramid, *COTG* pp.97, 101; Elephantine Island, *COTG* p.91; Piri Re'is map, *COTG* p.29; Tiahuanaco, *COTG* p.37, *ISOAG* p.101; Nazca lines, *RTTS* p.105; Tablets from Ur, *COTG* p. 40; Rock paintings, *RTTS* p.68; Easter Island statues, *RTTS* p.115; Ecuador tunnels *COTG* p.6ff. Interview in *Encounter*, loc. cit.

Amphibians from Sirius

Robert Temple: *The Sirius Mystery* (Sidgwick and Jackson 1976)

Livio Stecchini: *Appendix* to Peter Tompkins: *Secrets of the Great Pyramid* (Allen Lane 1971)

Carl Sagan: *The Cosmic Connection* (Anchor Press/Doubleday 1973) pp.204–5; with I. S. Shklovskii: *Intelligent Life in the Universe* (Picador 1977) pp.454–64

Diodorus Siculus: *The Library of History* V: 55, 2

Robert Graves: *The Greek Myths* (Harmondsworth 1960) Vol. I, pp. 188, 278, 305

Homer: *Odyssey* IV, 77–592

Apollonius of Rhodes: *Argonautica* IV, 1550ff.

Hesiod: *Theogony*, vv.233ff.

Pausanias: *Guide to Greece* Peter Levi (translator) (Harmondsworth 1971) IX, 20:4–21:1

Section seven Introduction: Myths and legends

Dorothy B. Vitaliano: *Legends of the Earth* (Indiana University Press 1973) Chapter I

R. G. Collingwood: *The Idea of History* (Oxford University Press 1956) p.15

Patterns of life

Herodotus: *Histories* ii, 148–9

Strabo: *Geography of the World* XVII, i, 37

Pliny: *Natural History* xxxvi, 19

W. H. Matthews: *Mazes and Labyrinths* (Longmans Green 1920: republished Dover 1970)

Edward Trollope: 'Ancient and mediaeval labyrinths', *Archaeological Journal* XV (1858) pp.216–35

C. R. Cockerell: *Travels in Southern Europe 1810–17* (London 1903)

Jill Purce: *The Mystic Spiral* (Thames and Hudson 1974)

Keith Critchlow and Graham Challifour (ed): *Earth Mysteries: A Study in Patterns* (RILKO 1977)

Geoffrey Russell: 'The secret of the Grail' in Mary Williams (ed): *Glastonbury: A Study in Patterns* (RILKO 1969) pp.16–19

Patricia Villiers-Stuart: 'How to make a maze', *New Life Magazine* (Journal of the Festival for Mind and Body, London 1977) p.4; 'Bend me a maze' in Anthony Roberts (ed) *Glastonbury* (Zodiac House 1976)

Geoffrey Ashe: *The Ancient Wisdom* (Macmillan 1977) p.90

Additional sources:

Janet Bord: *Mazes and Labyrinths of the World* (Latimer New Dimensions 1975)

Keith Critchlow, Jane Carroll, Llewylyn Vaughan Lee: *Chartres Maze: a model of the universe?* (RILKO 1975)

What is a dragon?

Charles Gould: *The Dragon* (Wildwood House 1977) pp.99–100

Heinz Mode: *Fabulous Beasts and Demons* (New York 1973) pp.116–54

J. E. Cirlot : *A Dictionary of Symbolism* (Routledge and Kegan Paul 1962) entries under 'Dragon' and 'Serpent'

E. T. C. Werner: *Myths and Legends of China* (London 1921)

Sheila Savill: *Pears Encyclopaedia of Myths and Legends: the Orient* (Pelham Books 1977) pp.86–7, 98–9, 226–7

Peter Tompkins: *Mysteries of the Mexican Pyramids* (Harper and Row 1976)

John Michell: *View Over Atlantis* (Abacus 1971)

Immanuel Velikovsky: *Worlds in Collision* (London and New York 1950) Part I, Chapter iii

E. J. Eitel: *Feng-shui* (London 1873)

Dwardu Cardona: 'Tektites and China's dragon', KRONOS, I:4 (1975) pp.35–42

Carter Sutherland: 'China's dragon', *Pensée*, Vol. 4, No. 1, pp.47–50

Additional sources:

F. W. Holiday: *The Dragon and the Disc* (Sidgwick and Jackson 1973)

Rev. Sabine Baring-Gould: *Historical Oddities and Strange Events* (Methuen 1889)

M. W. de Visser: *The Dragon in China and Japan* (Amsterdam 1913)

The Deluge

Ignatius Donnelly: *Atlantis: The Antediluvian World* (edited and revised by Egerton Sykes) (Sidgwick & Jackson 1970) p.95

Theodor Gaster: *Myth, Legend and Custom in the Old Testament* (Harper and Row 1975) pp.82–131 [deluge legends]

Dorothy B. Vitaliano: *Legends of the Earth* (Indiana University Press 1973) pp.144, 150, 169–70

J. C. Whitcomb and H. M. Morris: *The Genesis Flood* (Presbyterian & Reformed Pub. Co. 1961)

Reginald Daly: *Earth's Most Challenging Mysteries* (Craig Press 1972)

Donald Patten: *The Biblical Flood and the Ice Epoch* (Pacific Meridian Pub. Co. 1966)

Cesare Emiliani: 'Paleoclimatological analysis of late quaternary cores from the northeastern Gulf of Mexico', *Science* 189 (1975) pp.1083–8

William Mullen: 'A reading of the pyramid texts', *Pensée* III (1973) pp.10ff.

Harold Tresman and B. O. Gheoghan: 'The primordial light?', *Society for Interdisciplinary Studies Review* II:2 (1977) pp.35–40

Frank C. Hibben: *The Lost Americans* (New York 1946) pp.168, 170, 291

Noah's ark

A. Heidel: *The Gilgamesh Epic and Old Testament Parallels* (University of Chicago Press 1949) Chapter IV: 'The Story of the Flood'

Leonard Woolley: *Ur Excavations* IV, Appendix VID: 'The flood deposit', pp. 165–6

M. E. L. Mallowan: 'Noah's Flood Reconsidered', *Iraq* XXVI (1964) pp.62–82

Dorothy B. Vitaliano: *Legends of the Earth* (Indiana University Press 1973) pp.153–6

Fernand Navarra: *Noah's Ark: I Touched It* (Logos International 1974)

John Bright: 'Has archaeology found evidence of the Flood?', *Bulletin* of the American School of Archaeology V, 4 (1942) pp.55–62

For additional references see previous entry, The Deluge.

Old Testament truths

Magnus Magnusson: *BC: The Archaeology of the Bible Lands* (The Bodley Head/BBC 1977) Chapters III–VIII, pp.148, 155–6

Immanuel Velikosvky: *Theses for the Reconstruction of Ancient History* (Scripta Academica Hierosolymitana, No. 2, 1945); *Ages in Chaos* (Sidgwick & Jackson 1952); *Peoples of the Sea* (Sidgwick & Jackson 1977)

Donovan Courville: *The Exodus Problem and its Ramifications* (Crest Challenge Books 1971), 2 vols

Kathleen Kenyon: *Digging Up Jericho* (London 1957) p.186

Geoffrey Gammon: 'The walls of Jericho', *Society for Interdisciplinary Studies Review* (SISR) I:3 (1976) pp.4–5

Eva Danelius: 'The identification of the Biblical "Queen of Sheba" with Hatshepsut, "Queen of Egypt and Ethiopia" in the light of new archaeological discoveries', KRONOS I:3 (1976) pp.3–19 and I:4 (1976) pp.8–24; with H. Steinitz: 'The fishes and other aquatic animals on the Punt reliefs at Deir el-Bahari', *Journal of Egyptian Archaeology* 47 (1961), pp.19–23

Alessandra Nibbi: 'Remarks on the two stelae from the Wadi Gasus', *Journal of Egyptian Archaeology* 62 (1976)

John Bimson: 'The conquest of Canaan and the revised chronology', *SISR* I:3 (1976) pp.2–7

Y. Aharoni: 'Nothing early and nothing late: re-writing Israel's conquest', *Biblical Archaeologist* 39 (1976) pp.55–76

Frank E. Manuel: *Isaac Newton: Historian* (Cambridge University Press 1963)

Additional sources:

Peter J. James (ed): 'From Exodus to Akhnaton' (Special Issue, *SISR* II:3, 1977/8); A free pamphlet, 'A revised chronology for the ancient Near East' and *Ages in Chaos? (How valid are Velikovsky's views on Ancient History?)* Proceedings of the April 1978 conference organized by Glasgow University, obtainable from S.I.S. 6 Jersey House, Manchester 20.

Who was Homer?

V. R. d'A. Desborough: *The Greek Dark Ages* (London 1972) p. 18

Immanuel Velikovsky: 'Olympia', KRONOS I:4 (1976) pp.3–7

Carl Blegen and M. Rawson: *The Palace of Nestor at Pylos in Western Messenia* I (Princeton 1966) p.294

Israel M. Isaacson: 'Carbon 14 dates and Velikovsky's revision of ancient history', *Pensée* IV (1973) pp. 26–32

Immanuel Velikovsky: 'The Lion Gate at Mycenae'; Lewis Greenberg: 'The Lion Gate at Mycenae', *Pensée* III (1973) pp.26–30

Immanuel Velikovsky: 'Tiryns', *Pensée* VI (1974) pp.45–6

Israel M. Isaacson: 'Applying the Revised Chronology' *Pensée* IX (1974) pp.5–20

R. Young: 'Gordion: preliminary report 1953', *American Journal of Archaeology* 59 (1955) p.13

Ekrem Akurgal: *Phrygische Kunst* (Ankara 1955) p.12

Kurt Bittel: *Hattusha: The Capital of the Hittites* (Oxford University Press 1970) p.137

Peter J. James: 'Velikovsky's revised chronology and the archaeology of the Hittites', in *Ages in Chaos?* See *Additional Sources* for Old Testament Truths above.

Sacred relics

H. M. Gillet: *Relics of the Passion* (Basil Blackwell, Oxford 1935)

J. Charles Wall: *Relics of the Passion* (London 1910)

Rev. William J. McDonald (ed in chief): *New Catholic Encyclopedia* (McGraw-Hill 1967) Vol. XII, pp.235–40

J. D. Hastings (ed): *Encyclopaedia of Religion and Ethics* (T. and T. Clark, London 1918) Vol. X, pp.650–61

John Walsh: *The Shroud* (W. H. Allen 1964)

Ian Wilson: *The Turin Shroud* (Gollancz 1978) Father H. David Sox: 'The Shroud', *New Realities* Vol. I No. 4, pp. 42–6

Additional source:
Robert K. Wilcox: *The Shroud* (Macmillan 1977)

Section eight Introduction: Aerial phenomena

Desmond G. King-Hele: 'Truth and heresy over earth and sky', *The Observatory* 95 (February 1975) pp. 1–12

Meteor bombardment

Frank W. Lane: *The Elements Rage* (David and Charles 1966)

A. A. Moss: *Meteorites: A Concise Account* (Natural History Museum, London 1975)

Peter J. James: 'Diana at Ephesus', *Society for Interdisciplinary Studies Review* I:2, p. 13

D. G. King-Hele: 'Truth and heresy over earth and sky' [See reference in Section Introduction above] pp.3,4

Charles P. Olivier, cited in Lane: op. cit., p.138

Keith Hindley: 'Fallen stones by the tonne', *New Scientist* (7 July 1977) pp.20–22

René Gallant: *Bombarded Earth* (John Barker 1964) p.42

Keith Hindley: 'Meteoritics at Cambridge', *New Scientist* (11 August 1977) p.353

John Norman, Neville Price and Muo Chukwu-Ike: 'Astrons, the Earth's oldest scars?', *New Scientist* (24 March 1977) pp.689–92

L. LaPaz in: *Advances in Geophysics* 4 (1958) p.228

Virgil E. Barnes: 'Tektites', *Scientific American* (November 1961) pp.58–65

J. A. O'Keefe: 'Tektite Glass in Apollo 12 Sample', *Science* 168 (1970) p.209

Dwardu Cardona: 'Tektites and China's Dragon', KRONOS I:2 (1975) pp. 35–42

George Baker: 'Tektites', in *Memoirs of the National Museum of Victoria, Melbourne* 23 (1959); E. D. Gill: 'Age of australite fall', *Journal of Geophysical Research* 75 (1970) pp.996–1002

Siberian space disaster

L. A. Kolik: 'The problem of the impact area of the Tunguska meteorite of 1908', *Doklady Akad SSSR (A)* No. 23 (1927) pp.399–402

John C. Brown and David W. Hughes: 'Tunguska's comet and non-thermal C production in the atmosphere', *Nature* Vol. 268 (1977) pp.512–14

Ian Ridpath: 'Tunguska – the final answer', *New Scientist* (11 August 1977) pp. 346–7

Rupert Furneaux: *The Tungus Event* (Panther 1977)

John Baxter and Thomas Atkins: *The Fire Came By* (Macdonald and Jane's, London 1976)

Jack Stonely: *Tunguska – Cauldron of Hell*, (Star Books, London 1977)

John G. Taylor: *Black Holes – The End of the Universe?* (Random House 1977)

A. A. Jackson and M. P. Ryan: 'Was the Tungus event due to a black hole', *Nature* Vol. 245 (1973) pp.88–9

H. Crannel: 'Experiments to measure the antimatter content of the Tunguska meteorite', *Nature* Vol. 248 (1975) pp.396–8

G. L. Wick and J. D. Isaacs: 'Tunguska event revisited', *Nature* Vol. 247 (1974) p.139

Hard-core UFOs

J. Allen Hynek: *The UFO Experience* (Ballantine 1972)

Hayden C. Hewes: 'UFOs after 30 years', *New Realities* I:3 (1977) pp.34–41

J. Allen interviewed in 'Playboy Panel: UFOs', *Playboy Magazine*, January 1978, pp. 67–98, 128

John A. Keel: *UFOs: Operation Trojan Horse* (Abacus 1973) pp. 18ff., 290

Jacques Vallée: *Playboy*, loc. cit., p.68

Philip J. Klass: *Playboy*, loc. cit., pp.92, 75

Ian Ridpath: 'Flying saucers thirty years on', *New Scientist* (14 July 1977) pp.77–9

Don Strachan and James Karnstedt: 'Scientoids and saucerites', *New Realities* I:3 (1977) pp.57–60

John W. Macvey: *Interstellar Travel* (Stein and Day 1977) pp. 235–9

Additional sources:
Charles Bowen (ed): *Flying Saucer Review*, obtainable from Compendium Books, 281 Camden High St, London NW1

Jacques Vallée: *Invisible College* (Dutton 1976)

John G. Fuller: *Incident at Exeter* (G. P. Putnam's Sons 1966); *The Interrupted Journey* (Dial Press 1966)

Philip J. Klass: *UFOs – Identified* (Random House 1968)

Brad Steiger (ed): *Project Blue Book* (Ballantine 1976)

Ice blocks from the sky

G. T. Meaden: 'The giant ice meteor mystery', pp.137–41; E. W. Crew: 'Fall of a large ice lump after a violent stroke of lightning', pp.142–7; Robert J. M. Rickard: 'The timberville multiple ice fall', pp.148–9; all the above in *The Journal of Meteorology*, Vol. 2, No. 17 (March 1977)

R. F. Griffiths: 'Observation and analysis of an ice hydrometer of extraordinary size', *The Meteorological Magazine*, Vol. 104 (1975) pp.253–60

Charles Fort: *The Collected Works of Charles Fort* (New York 1941) pp.183 ff., 285, 301, 760

John Michell and Robert J. M. Rickard: *Phenomena* (Thames and Hudson 1977)

Ronald J. Willis: 'Ice Falls', *INFO Journal*, Vol. II No. 3 (Spring 1968), pp.12–23

Robert J. M. Rickard (ed): 'Ice Falls' *Fortean Times*, Nos 3, 6, 15, 23

Creature storms

William R. Corliss: *Strange Phenomena* (Glen Arm, Maryland 1975) pp.33–48

Dr D. P. Thompson: *Introduction to Meteorology* (London 1849) p.103

Charles Fort: *The Complete Books of Charles Fort* (New York 1941), pp.48, 81ff., 95, 183, 184, 190, 302, 525, 544

Gilbert Whitley: 'Rains of fishes in Australia' *Australian Natural History* (March 1972)

John Michell and Robert J. M. Rickard: *Phenomena* (Thames and Hudson 1977) pp.12–16

Untitled Articles: 'Fish falls', *INFO Journal*, Vol. II No. 4 (Winter/Spring 1972); Vol. III No. 2 (Spring 1973); Vol. IV No. 2 (Winter 1974)

R. J. M. Rickard (ed): 'Fish falls', *Fortean Times*, Nos 6, 22, 24

Section nine Introduction: Appearances and disappearances

John Mitchell and Robert J. M. Rickard: *Phenomena: A Book of Wonders* (Thames and Hudson 1977) pp.124–5

R. J. M. Rickard: *Fortean Times* Nos 6 and 9

Underwater monsters

Bernard Heuvelmans: *In the Wake of Sea Serpents* (New York 1968) p.535

Lt. Com. R. T. Gould: *The Case for the Sea Serpent* (London 1930)

Peter Costello: *In Search of Lake Monsters* (London 1974)

Nicholas Witchell: *The Loch Ness Story* (Terence Dalton 1976)

Peter Scott: 'The Loch Ness Monster – fact or fancy', *The Sunday Times* (14 August 1960)

Maurice Burton: 'Verdict on Nessie', *New Scientist* (23 January 1969)

Tim Dinsdale: *Loch Ness Monster* (Routledge Kegan Paul 1976)

Additional Sources:
Willy Ley: *Exotic Zoology* (Capricorn Books, New York 1966)

John Keel: *Strange Creatures from Time and Space* (Greenwich, Connecticut 1970)

Unknown beasts

Bernard Heuvelmans: *On the Track of Unknown Animals* (Hill and Wang) Chapter VI, pp.204–5; 'Note préliminaire sur un specimen conservé dans la glace, d'une forme encore inconnue d'hominide vivant: *Homo pongoides*', *Bulletin Inst. r. Sci. nat. Belg.* 45, 4 (1969)

M. Grumley: *There are Giants in the Earth* (Panther 1976)

Odette Tchernine: *The Yeti* (Neville Spearman 1970)

John Napier: *Bigfoot* (Abacus 1976) pp.54, 92, 169, 177–8

W. Tschernezky: 'A reconstruction of the foot of the abominable snowman', *Nature* 186 (1960) pp.496–7

Ivan T. Sanderson: 'Wandering Woodpersons', in *More 'Things'* (New York 1969) pp.65–79

Loren E. Coleman and Mark A. Haill: 'Some Bigfoot traditions of the North American tribes', in Jacques Bergier and the Editors of INFO (eds): *Extraterrestrial Intervention: The Evidence* (Chicago 1974) pp.85–96

Ivan T. Sanderson: 'Preliminary description of the external morphology of what appeared to be the fresh corpse of a hitherto unknown form of a living hominid', *Pursuit* 8, 2 (April 1975) pp.41–7, and 8, 3 (July 1975) pp.62–7

Sources and select bibliography

Wild children

- Lucien Malson: *Les Enfants Sauvages* (Paris 1964)
- R. M. Zingg: 'Feral man and extreme cases of isolation', *American Journal of Sociology* No. 53 (1949)
- Jean-Claude Armen: *Gazelle Boy* (Bodley Head 1974) pp.34, 35, 27
  Bruno Bettelheim: *The Empty Fortress* (New York 1967)
  Harlan Lane: *The Wild Boy of Aveyron* (Allen and Unwin 1977)
- Charles Maclean: *The Wolf Children* (Macmillan 1977), p.65

Additional sources:
W. Dennis: 'The significance of feral man', *American Journal of Psychology*, No. 54 (1941)
W. N. Kellog: 'More about the wolf children of India', *American Journal of Psychology*, No. 43 (1931); 'A further note on the wolf children of India', *American Journal of Psychology*, No. 46 (1934)
W. F. Ogburn: 'The wolf boy of Agra', *American Journal of Psychology*, No. 53 (1940)
Basil Copper: *The Werewolf* (New York 1977)

Kaspar Hauser

- P. J. A. Feuerbach: *Caspar Hauser* (London 1834)
- Jacob Wasserman: *Caspar Hauser – The Enigma of a Century* (Rudolph Steiner Publications, New York 1973)
  Carlo Pietzner: *Kaspar Hauser – the Child of Europe* (Rudolph Steiner Library, London 1965)
  Peter Tradowsky: 'Caspar Hauser and his enemies', *The Golden Blade* (Rudolph Steiner Press, London, 1977)
  Eric Russell: *Great World Mysteries* (Dobson Books, London, 1957)
  John Godwin: *This Baffling World* (Bantam Books 1973)

Count St Germain

- Isabel Cooper Oakley: *The Count of Saint Germain* (Steinerbooks 1970)
  Horace Walpole: *Letters of Horace Walpole, Earl of Oxford, to Sir Horace Mann* (London 1833) ii, pp.108–9
  Eliphas Levi: *The History of Magic* (Rider 1913) pp.295–300

Mary Celeste

Lloyd's of London (Insurance) Library: file on *Mary Celeste*
Vincent Gaddis: *Invisible Horizons* (Ace Books, New York 1965)
Lt. Com. R. T. Gould: *The Stargazer Talks* (London 1943)
John Godwin: *This Baffling World* (Bantam Books 1973)
Eric Russell: *Great World Mysteries* (Dobson Books, London 1957)

Additional sources:
- MacDonald Hastings: *The Mary Celeste* (Michael Joseph 1972)

Bermuda triangle

- Vincent Gaddis: *Invisible Horizons* (Ace Books, New York 1965) p.190
  Richard Winer: *The Devil's Triangle* (Bantam Books, 1975)

John Wallace Spencer: *Limbo of the Lost* (Bantam Books 1975)
Lawrence Kusche: *The Bermuda Triangle – Solved* (Warner Books 1975)
Alan Landsburg: *The Bermuda Triangle Secrets* (Warner Books 1978)
Theodore Maher: 'The Devil's Triangle', *FAA World* (October 1975) pp.4–8
Don Bedwell: 'They doubt the Devil is in the Triangle', *The Miami Herald* (7 November 1975)

Additional sources:
- Martin Ebon (ed): *The Riddle of the Bermuda Triangle* (New American Library 1975)
  Ivan T. Sanderson: *Invisible Residents* (World Publishing Company, New York 1970) Chapters VIII and IX

Vanishing people

T. D. Kendrick: *Mary of Agreda – Life and Legend of a Spanish Nun* (Routledge and Kegan Paul 1967)
L. J. Rebel: *The Wayout World* (Lancer, New York 1962)
Colin Wilson (ed): *Enigmas and Mysteries* (Aldus Books 1976) p.29
Harold Wilkins: *Mysteries Solved and Unsolved* (London 1949)
- Sabine Barine-Gould: *Historical Oddities and Strange Events* (Methuen 1889)
  Eric Russell: *Great World Mysteries* (Dobson Books, London 1957)
- Charles Fort: *The Complete Books of Charles Fort* (New York 1941) pp.521ff., 600, 681ff., 691ff., 695ff., 844ff., 953ff., 986
  John Michell and Robert J. M. Rickard: *Phenomena* (Thames and Hudson 1977)
  Ronald J. Willis: 'Lost Ships and Crews', *INFO Journal* Vol. II, No. 1 (Autumn 1969) pp.4–8
  Robert J. M. Rickard (ed): 'Disappearances' *Fortean Times*, Nos. 9, 18

Section ten **Introduction: Searches**

- Fritjof Capra: *The Tao of Physics* (Fontana 1976)

King Solomon's mines

I Kings 9:26–38; I Kings 10:11; II Chronicles 20:35–37; Ezekiel 27:12; Jonah 1:2–3
Josephus: *Antiquities of the Jews*, VIII, vii, 2
Kathleen Kenyon: *Archaeology in the Holy Land* (London 1970) pp.258, 346
Eva Danelius: 'The identification of the Biblical "Queen of Sheba" with Hatshepsut, "Queen of Egypt and Ethiopia"', KRONOS 1:3 (1975), pp.3–19, 1:4 (1976) pp.9–24
Cyrus Gordon: *Before Columbus* (Turnstone Press 1972) pp.113ff.; *Riddles in History* (Arthur Barker 1974) pp.71–92
L. Sprague and Catherine de Camp: *Citadels of Mystery* (Souvenir Press 1965) Chapter VI: 'Zimbabwe and King Solomon's Mines'

The Holy Grail

- Roger Sherman Loomis: *The Grail: From Celtic Myth to Christian Symbol* (University of Wales Press 1963)
  John W. Taylor: *The Coming of the Saints* (Methuen & Co. 1911)
  Diodorus Siculus: *The Library of History*, v, ii
  Lionel Smithett Lewis: *St Joseph of Arimathea at Glastonbury* (James Clarke & Co. 1922)
- Geoffrey Ashe: *King Arthur's Avalon* (Collins 1957) p.190

Robert Graves: *The White Goddess* (Faber & Faber 1961)
Jessie L. Weston: *From Ritual to Romance* (London 1920)
Pierre Morizot: *The Templars* (Anthroposophical Publishing House 1960)
Eliphas Levi: *History of Magic* (Rider 1913) p.208
Pennethorne Hughes: *Witchcraft* (Harmondsworth 1965) pp.170ff.
Idries Shah: *The Sufis* (W. H. Allen & Co. 1964) pp.225–7

El Dorado

- Victor W. von Hagen: *The Golden Man* (Saxon House, London 1974)
  Marcel Homet: *Sons of the Sun* (Neville Spearman 1963) Book 2 Chapters I, II, VIII, IX and XII
  Marcel Homet: *On the Trail of the Sun Gods* (Neville Spearman 1965)

Additional sources:
John Augustine Zahn: *The Quest of El Dorado* (New York 1917)
Sir Walter Raleigh: *The Discovery of the Empire of Guiana* (London 1848)
F. M. A. Voltaire: *Candide* (Oxford University Press 1968)
John Milton: *Paradise Lost* (Cambridge University Press 1975) Books I–XII

Fawcett's lost world

Peter Fleming: *Brazilian Adventure* (Jonathan Cape 1966) pp.23–4
Geraldine Cummins: *The Fate of Colonel Fawcett* (The Aquarius Press, London, 1955)
- Col. Percy Fawcett (ed John Kennet): *Expedition Fawcett* (Blackie 1953)
  Adrian Cowell: 'The grave of Colonel Fawcett', *The Sunday Times*, 7 September 1958, 14 September 1958, 21 September 1958

Shangri La

James Hilton: *Lost Horizon* (London 1935)
Andrew Tomas: *Shambhala* (Sphere Books 1977) p.15
Charles Bell: *The Religion of Tibet* (Oxford University Press 1931) p.6
- Alexandra David-Neel: *With Mystics and Magicians in Tibet* (Bodley Head 1931) pp.201–2, 293, 314–15
- Geoffrey Ashe: *The Ancient Wisdom* (Macmillan 1977) pp.25, 160
  Nicholas Roerich: *Shambhala* (Frederick A. Stokes, New York, 1930)

Additional sources:
Nicholas Roerich: *Altai – Himalaya* (Jarrolds 1930)
Nicholas Roerich: *Himalayas – Abode of Light* (David Marlowe 1947)

Index

Index

Illustration acknowledgements

All maps and line drawings by Kenneth Smith copyright©
Francis Hitching 1978: pages 10, 11, 12, 13, 15, 16, 17, 19,
21, 22, 23, 27, 29, 30, 31, 34, 35, 36, 40, 41, 43, 45, 46,
47, 48, 49, 50, 51, 52, 53, 54, 56, 57, 58, 59, 60, 61, 62,
63, 65, 66, 68, 69, 70, 72, 74, 75, 76, 77, 78, 79, 80, 82,
87, 89, 90, 92, 93, 94, 95, 96, 97, 103, 108, 110, 113, 114,
117, 118, 120, 123, 124, 125, 130, 133, 134, 135, 139, 140,
141, 142, 144, 149, 151, 152, 153, 156, 158, 161, 164, 165,
171, 174, 177, 179, 183, 184, 185, 186, 187, 190, 192, 193,
195, 200, 201, 204, 205, 208, 209, 215, 216, 219, 220, 223,
224, 227, 228, 234, 236, 237, 240

Line drawings and photographs in author's collection:
pages 65, 66, 83, 85, 97, 100, 102, 113, 115, 120, 132, 136,
145, 147, 149, 153, 160, 162, 163, 168, 169, 172, 194, 196,
217, 218, 221, 233, 235

Line drawings: 36–7 Van Nostrand; 42 Scientific American;
48 Trustees of the British Museum; 84 Russell Targ/Harold
Puthoff; 117–18 Charles Hapgood; 142–3 John Steele;
148 Eliphas Levi; 150 Robert K. G. Temple; 162 Charles
Gould; National Gallery; 188 A. W. Szachnowski; 191
(see cover acknowledgement); 203 Ivan T. Sanderson;
210–11 Germanisches National Museum; 226 Cyrus Gordon

Photographs: 14 Ullstein; 18 TV Times; 20 courtesy Larry
E. Arnold, from his forthcoming book *Ablaze!* (Vol. I of
'Earth in Transition'); 23 R.B.M. Rickard; 25 M.R. Lyons;
26 NASA; 28 Novosti; 32 JPL; 36 Camera Press;
37 Illustrated London News; 38 Radio Times Hulton Picture
Library; 39 Desmond Collins; 41 French Tourist Authority;
62 National Monuments Record; 69 French Tourist
Authority; 71, 73 International Explorers Society;
72 Servicio Aerofotografico National, Peru; 86 Eric Hosking;
91 R. K. Pilsbury; 94 Australian Information Service;
98 British Tourist Authority; 99 Victoria and Albert
Museum; 100 Science Museum, London; 104 Maru; Acorn
Photographic; 105–7 Illustrated London News; 108 Radio
Times Hulton Picture Library; 109 Dr Irving Lindenblad,
US Naval Observatory; Hale Observatories; 111 Robert
K. G. Temple; Trustees of British Museum; 112 Mansell
Collection; 116 National Library, Ankara; 118–19 Charles
Hapgood; 121 Smithsonian Institute; 122 Illustrated London
News; 125 Derek de Solla Price; 126–9 Dr H. McKerrell;
130 Ashmolean Museum; 138 British Tourist Authority;
142–3 John Steele; 146 Douglas Dickins; 157 Janet Bord;
166 Mansell Collection; Sonia Halliday and Laura
Lushington; 167 Novosti; 175 Mansell Collection; 176
Trustees of British Museum; 178, 180 Screenpro Films,
producers of *The Silent Witness* and Futura Books,
publishers of the story of the making of the film;
182 Horizons West; 183, 185 Institute of Geological Sciences;
187 Novosti; 189 Project Starlight International; 198
Syndicated Features; 199 Peter Scott; 202 Royal
Geographical Society; 204 Musée de l'Homme; 206 René
Datinden; 207 Mansell Collection; Syndication
International; 209 Charles Maclean; 212–13 Bildarchiv
Preussischer Kulturkesitz; 214 Mansell Collection; 229
Bibliothèque National Paris; 230 A-M. Erlich; 231 Michael
Holford; 232 British Tourist Authority; 233 Michael
Holford; 235 Popperfoto; 236 A. G. Forment;
238 John Cleare/Mountain Camera; 239 Cliché des Musées
Nationaux; 241 Nicholas Roerich Museum